What Happened to Religious Education?

guardians shall be exonerated from the payment of the whole, or part of such expence, and the said assessors shall omit to add the amount of such books; or shall add only a part thereof, to the annual tax, of such parent, master, or guardian according to the proportion of such expence, which such parent, master, or guardian shall in their opinion be able, and can afford to pay. Provided nevertheless, that in cases where children are already supplied, with books, which shall not be considered by the Committee, as being extremely faulty, in Comparison with others, which might be obtained; and which may be possessed in such numbers, as to admit of the proper & convenient classification of the school, then, and in that case, the Committee shall not direct the purchase of new books without first obtaining the Consent of the parents, masters or guardians, of a majority of the children, so already provided for, under the term of two years, from the passing of this act, unless such books become so worn, as to be unfit for use. Provided also, that said Committee, shall never direct any school books, to be purchased or used, in any of the Schools under their superintendence which are calculated to favour any particular religious sect or tend.—

Manuscript copy of the 1827 Law of Massachusetts Forbidding the Use of Sectarian Textbooks in Public Schools (cf. *Infra*, p. 104). *Reproduced through the courtesy of the Hon. Edward J. Cronin, Secretary of the Commonwealth of Massachusetts.*

What Happened to

Religious Education?

*THE DECLINE OF
RELIGIOUS TEACHING IN
THE PUBLIC
ELEMENTARY SCHOOL*

1776-1861

by William Kailer Dunn

THE JOHNS HOPKINS PRESS
BALTIMORE, 1958

NIHIL OBSTAT:

Edward A. Cerny, S.S., S.T.D.

Censor librorum

IMPRIMATUR:

✠ Francis P. Keough, D.D.

Archbishop of Baltimore

January 23, 1958

The *Nihil obstat* and *Imprimatur* are official declarations that a book or pamphlet is free of doctrinal or moral error. No implication is contained therein that those who have granted the *Nihil obstat* and *Imprimatur* agree with the contents, opinions or statements expressed.

Distributed in Great Britain by Oxford University Press, London

Printed in the United States of America
by H. Wolff Book Manufacturing Company, Inc., New York

Library of Congress Catalog Card Number 58–10987

This book has been brought to publication with the assistance
of a grant from the Ford Foundation.

to my father and my mother

FROM WHOM I FIRST LEARNED

THE VALUE OF RELIGION

Preface

PERHAPS the most fundamental questions which any man has ever asked himself are the following three. "Where did I come from? Why am I here? and Whither do I tend?"

In the middle of the twentieth century Americans, as individuals, and as members of the community, are pondering the same fundamental queries. Material progress has brought comforts, protection against disease, and length of life. But the threat of mass extinction was never so real a menace as today. Science has advanced the means of waging war but not the methods of keeping the peace. Despite every improvement marketed for the home, the family cannot hold together. Despite the many safety devices, crime soars upward in frequency, and dips lower and lower in the age bracket. Man has almost an infinitude of diversions, yet he cannot stand to be long alone with most of them. The louder the roar of materialistic civilization, the deeper the silence in answer to the three great questions.

Today America searches for the solution which will bring order from chaos and give purpose to the striving, meaning to the jumble of modern life. "Whence, why and whither?" Man's techniques, his philosophy, his achievements are the components of something deeper and greater. What and where is the focusing point that turns the parts into a meaningful whole? To more and more Americans the answer is—Religion.

It is to a facet of so tremendous a subject that this study has addressed itself—the presence of religious instruction and the reasons for its decline in the American public elementary school in the period from 1776 to 1861. Humbly and hopefully the writer has sought to make some small contribution to an understanding of this phase of the American story.

The present volume is a condensation and a reworking, in some parts, of the writer's doctoral dissertation completed at the Johns Hopkins University in 1956. The title of the original work was *The Decline of the Teaching of Religion in the American Public Elementary School in the States Originally the Thirteen Colonies, 1776–1861.* Several significant documents dealing with the subject as treated in the dissertation have been uncovered and included in the pages which follow.

The author wishes to express his gratitude to his ecclesiastical superior, the Most Rev. Francis P. Keough, D.D., Archbishop of Baltimore, for making possible the pursuit of graduate studies in Education at the Johns Hopkins University, of which this effort is the culmination. Thanks are also due to Dr. John M. Stephens, Chairman of the Education Department, and to the other members of the Education Staff. Among them special gratitude is hereby expressed to Dr. Beulah B. Tatum and Dr. John Walton who directed the present study. Their devoted hours of guidance and patient understanding through many months of work have made the task possible to accomplish and a joy to fulfill.

Acknowledgment is made of the courteous services of officials in the various libraries in which the research was carried out. Among them are several at the Library of Congress in Washington, the Peabody Library in Baltimore and the Bar Library at the Baltimore Courthouse. Particular thanks are also due to Mrs. Jean Tomko and her assistants in the Education and Classics Library at the Hopkins, Miss Susan Futterer of the Library of the Health, Education and Welfare Department in Washington, Mrs. Julia L. Certain and her staff in the Religion and Education Department of the Enoch Pratt Library in Baltimore, the Rev. Thomas R. Leigh, S.S., Librarian of the Old St. Mary's Seminary and the Rev. William J. O'Shea, S.S., Librarian of the New St. Mary's Seminary, both in Baltimore, Miss Anna Manning of the Boston

Public Library, Miss Margaret Hackett of the Boston Athenaeum, and the following officials at the State House in Boston—Mr. Dennis A. Dooley, State Librarian; Miss Ethel M. Turner, Legislative Reference Librarian; Mr. Leo Flaherty of the Archives Division; and Miss Catherine McCarty, State Library Assistant. Thanks are also due the Rev. Joseph J. Gallagher, Archivist of the Baltimore Archdiocese.

Among other officials who gave a great amount of help are Dr. John A. Nietz of the Education Department of the University of Pittsburgh; Miss Catherine Tobin of the Massachusetts Department of Education; Mr. Stephen T. Riley and Mr. Wheeler of the Massachusetts Historical Society; Dr. Clarence S. Bingham of the American Antiquarian Society; Msgr. William E. McManus, Superintendent of Schools in the Archdiocese of Chicago; Mr. George Reed of the Legal Department of the National Catholic Welfare Conference, Washington, D.C.; and in the Research Division of the National Education Association in Washington, D.C., Drs. Madeline K. Remmlein and Hazel Davis.

In their preparatory stages, parts of the manuscript were examined by several persons whose constructive criticism was of invaluable help, but who are in no way responsible for whatever shortcomings the work may show. Appreciation for this kindly service is expressed to Dr. Carl B. Swisher and Dr. Francis E. Rourke of the Political Science Department, and Dr. Charles A. Barker of the History Department, at the Hopkins; Msgr. John Tracy Ellis of the History Department at the Catholic University of America in Washington, D.C.; Rev. John Courtney Murray, S.J., of Woodstock College, Maryland; Rev. Eugene A. Walsh, S.S., S.T.D., of Old St. Mary's Seminary, Baltimore, and Rev. Joseph M. Connolly of the Church of St. Gregory the Great, Baltimore.

Sincere gratitude is expressed to the Pastors and Clergy of the Churches in Baltimore where the writer was in residence during his years of graduate work. These include the Revs. George E. Shank of St. Martin's, John Sinnott Martin of St. Vincent de Paul, and the Rev. Paul L. Love, then Administrator of All Saints' Parish, all of Baltimore.

Indispensable services have been rendered in typing the manuscript in all its stages by Miss M. Margaret Donohue, and by Sister Mary David, SSND, Assistant Librarian at the College of Notre Dame of Maryland in Baltimore, who did the proofreading. Without their devoted and tireless efforts the work would never have come to completion.

Wm. Kailer Dunn

JANUARY 17, 1958
Baltimore, Md.

ACKNOWLEDGMENTS

The author wishes sincerely to thank the respective authors, historical society officials and publishers for permission to quote from the following works, documents under their care or books bearing their imprint: Abingdon Press (M. Phelan, *New Handbook of All Denominations* and Frank S. Mead, *Handbook of Denominations in the United States*); American Antiquarian Society (*The Samuel M. Burnside Papers*); Appleton-Century-Crofts, Inc. (Edgar W. Knight and Clifton L. Hall (eds.) *Readings in American Educational History*); Benziger Brothers (J. A. Burns and Bernard J. Kohlbrenner, *A History of Catholic Education in the United States*); The Catholic University of America Press (Burton L. Confrey, *Secularism in American Education: Its History;* Edward M. Connors, *Church-State Relationships in Education in the State of New York;* and Sister Mary Paul Mason, *Church-State Relationships in Connecticut, 1633–1953*); Coward-McCann, Inc. (Marie Kimball, *Jefferson The Road to Glory, 1743 to 1776*); Dartmouth Publications (Arthur D. Wright and George E. Gardner (eds.) *Hall's Lectures on School-Keeping*); Duell, Sloan and Pearce, Inc. (Saul K. Padover (ed.) *The Complete Jefferson*); Duke University Press (Luther L. Gobbel, *Church-State Relationships in North Carolina since 1776*); George Peabody College for Teachers (R. R. Robinson, *Two Centuries of Change in the Content of School Readers*); Houghton Mifflin Company (Elwood P. Cubberly, *Public Education in the United States* [Revised Edition], and *Readings in Public Education in the United States*); Little, Brown & Company (Louise Hall Tharp, *Until Victory—Horace Mann and Mary Peabody*); Longmans, Green & Co., Inc. (J. Moss Ives, *The Ark and the Dove*); Loyola University Press (F. X. Curran, *The Churches and the Schools*); The Macmillan Company (Edmund G. Burnett, *The Continental Congress,* and Clifton Johnson, *Old-Time Schools and School-Books*); McGraw-Hill Book Company, Inc. (John S. Brubacher, *A History of the Problems of Education*); Massachusetts Historical Society (*The Horace Mann Papers*); *History of Education Journal* (John A. Nietz, "Some Findings from Analyses of Old Textbooks"); Joy Elmer Morgan (*Horace Mann, His Ideas and Ideals*); National Education Association, Educational Policies Commission (*Moral and Spiritual Values in the Public Schools* and *Go Forth and Teach*); The Newman Press (Peter Guilday, (ed.), *The National Pastorals of the American Hierarchy*); Hugh J. Nolan (*The Most Rev. Francis Patrick Kenrick, Third Bishop of Philadelphia*); *The Review of Politics* (Will Herberg, "Religious Communities in Present Day America); Philosophical Library, Inc. (Dagobert D. Runes (ed.) *The Selected Writings of Benjamin Rush*); The University of North Carolina Press (Edgar W. Knight, *A Documentary History of Education in the South before 1860*); Sheed and Ward (Robert H. Lord, John E. Sexton and Edward T. Harrington, *A History of the Archdiocese of Boston*); Sherman M. Smith (*The Relation of the State to Religious Education in Massachusetts*); Teachers College Bureau of Publications, Columbia University (Charles B. Kinney, Jr., *Church and State, The Struggle for Separation in New Hampshire, 1630–1900;* and William W. Kemp, *The Support of Schools in Colonial New York by the Society for the Propagation of the Gospel in Foreign Parts*); E. R. Van Kleeck (*The Development of Free Common Schools in New York State*); Harold C. Warren (*Changing Conceptions in the Religious Elements in Early American School Readers*); Walter Thomas Woody (*Quaker Education in the Colony and State of New Jersey*); and Yale University Press (Raymond B. Culver, *Horace Mann and Religion in the Massachusetts Public Schools*).

Contents

CHAPTER I

The Problem

THE CONCEPT of instruction in religion confronts American educators, religious leaders and statesmen with the dilemma posed by the seeming conflict of two traditions. On the one hand there stands the tradition that Church and State are to be separated, and on the other there is the persistent concern for inculcating the religious elements traditionally underlying our morality and our institutions.

Opinion as to a resolution of the dilemma is divided. Some students of the subject feel that any sort of religious instruction has no place in the public schools.[1] Others believe that some forms of religious teaching should be introduced into these schools and that this is possible without violating the Constitution of the United States.

Aware as they are of the limitations imposed by the separation tradition, the latter group takes the position that it does not command freedom *from* religion. Such a view was brought forward

[1] John S. Brubacher (ed.), *The Public Schools and Spiritual Values* (New York: Harper & Brothers, 1944), pp. 94, 100; Vivian T. Thayer, *Religion in Public Education* (New York: The Viking Press, 1947), pp. 101–24; Conrad H. Moehlman, *School and Church, The American Way* (New York: Harper & Brothers, 1944) and *The Wall of Separation Between Church and State* (Boston: Beacon Press, 1951), p. 39; R. Freeman Butts and Lawrence A. Cremin, *A History of Education in American Culture* (New York: Henry Holt and Company, 1953), pp. 152–57; Alvin W. Johnson and Frank N. Yost, *Separation of Church and State in the United States* (Minneapolis: University of Minnesota Press, 1948), p. 260.

some years ago by F. Ernest Johnson.[2] It has been endorsed, at least as to basic theory, by the American Council on Education [3] and the National Education Association.[4] These organizations have suggested an objective, factual study *"about* religion, without advocating or teaching any religious creed." [5]

More recent thinking on the problem, in which opinions are presented both favoring and disfavoring religious instruction in the schools, may be found in the April, 1955 issue of the *Phi Delta Kappan* [6] and *Crucial Issues in Education,* edited by Henry Ehlers, Associate Professor of Philosophy, Duluth Branch of the University of Minnesota.[7] Educational journals are continuously publishing articles on the subject.[8]

[2] F. Ernest Johnson, *The Social Gospel Re-examined* (New York: Harper & Brothers, 1940), pp. 183, 190–91.

[3] Committee on Religion and Education, *The Function of the Public Schools in Dealing With Religion* (Washington, D. C.: American Council on Education, 1953), pp. 2–3.

[4] Educational Policies Commission, *Moral and Spiritual Values in the Public Schools* (Washington, D. C.: National Education Association of the United States and the American Association of School Administrators, 1951), pp. 77–78. Among others who have advanced suggestions on religious teaching, cf. Virgil Henry, *The Place of Religion in Public Schools* (New York: Harper & Brothers, 1950); James Keller, *All God's Children* (Garden City, New York: Hanover House, 1953); Sophia L. Fahs, "Religion in the Public Schools," *Religion and the Child* (Washington, D. C.: Association for Childhood Education, July, 1944), pp. 25–31; Merrill E. Bush, "The Common Denominator in Religious Values," *Educational Leadership,* January, 1954, pp. 228–32; and Paul H. Demaree, "By-Products of Attacks on Public Schools," *California Journal of Secondary Education,* xxix (Jan., 1954), 51–52.

[5] *Moral and Spiritual Values in the Public Schools,* p. 77.

[6] *Phi Delta Kappan,* xxxvi (April, 1955).

[7] Henry Ehlers (ed.), *Crucial Issues in Education, An Anthology* (New York: Henry Holt & Company, 1955).

[8] *Education Index* lists the following publications during 1957: A. E. Parker, "Consensus on Religion in the Schools," *Phi Delta Kappan,* xxxviii (Jan., 1957), 145–47. C. J. Ryan, "Democracy as a Religion," *School and Society,* 83 (June 23, 1956), 217–19 (Reply, F. C. Neff, 85 [April 13, 1957], 133–34). N. G. McCluskey, "Educators Go to Arden House," *America,* 96 (March 30, 1957), 722. H. H. Punke, "Religion in American Public Schools," *Religious Education,* 52 (March, 1957), 133–40. National Education Association Research Division, "The State and Sectarian Education," *National Ed. Assoc. Research Bulletin,* 34 (Dec., 1956), 169–215 (Excerpts, *Education Digest,* 22 [April, 1957], 9–11). R. F. Butts, "States' Rights and Education," *Teachers College Record,* 58 (Jan., 1957), 189–97. A. J. Bartky, "Theology, Science, and Philosophy in Teaching Democratic Behavior," *School and Society,* 85 (Feb. 16, 1957), 54–56. J. H. Fadenrecht, "Moral and Spiritual Values in Public

Turning from theory to practice we note two types of activity which have been undertaken to implement the thinking of those favoring religious instruction. One, of quite recent origin, is popularly known as the "Indianapolis Plan." [9] It is an attempt at the objective, factual study recommended by the American Council on Education and the National Education Association. The other type is the "Released Time" plan, long in vogue in one form or another in the United States. The constitutionality of certain aspects of this plan has been discussed and ruled upon by the Supreme Court of the United States in two famous cases of recent years, the "McCollum Case" in 1948,[10] and the "Zorach Case" in 1952.[11] As a result of these two decisions, instruction in religion may not be given in the school buildings during the regular school hours, but the children may be permitted, at the request of their parents, to leave the school building during school time and attend religious instruction in nearby church edifices.

The nub of discussion in the McCollum and Zorach Cases was an interpretation of the First Amendment to the Constitution of the United States: "Congress shall make no law respecting an establishment of religion or prohibiting the free exercise thereof." It was given by Justice Hugo L. Black in a previous decision in the "Everson Case," [12] handed down in 1947. The Justice maintained, in the majority opinion, that "the 'establishment of religion clause' . . . [the first] means at least this: Neither a state nor the federal government can set up a church. Neither can pass laws which aid one religion, aid all religions, or prefer one religion over another." [13] In the McCollum Case, the Court held that giv-

---

Education," *Educ. Adm. & Supervision*, 43 (Jan., 1957), 49–58. C. B. Smith, "American Public Schools Must Remain Secular," *Journal of Teacher Educ.*, 8 (June, 1957), 201–206. "Religion and Public Education: A Symposium," *Religious Education*, 52 (July, 1957), 247–306. G. V. Hall and T. E. Walt, "Spiritual Values Can Be Taught," *Nation's Schools*, 60 (Aug., 1957), 39–41. H. L. Davis, "Dealing With Religious Differences," *National Elementary Principal*, 37 (Sept., 1957), 83–87. C. Reed, "Democracy as a Religion; Reply to C. J. Ryan," *School & Society*, 85 (Oct. 12, 1957), 289.

[9] Cf. *The Christian Century*, LXXII (Jan. 26, 1955), 103.

[10] *McCollum v. Board of Education*, 333 U.S. 205–56.

[11] *Zorach v. Clauson*, 343 U.S. 306–25.

[12] *Everson v. Board of Education*, 330 U.S. 1–74.

[13] *Ibid.*, p. 15.

ing religious instruction in the school building during school hours was aiding religious groups, whereas in Zorach they maintained that allowing the classes in nearby church buildings did not violate the Amendment as interpreted in the two previous cases.

When the Supreme Court gave the above answers to the question "What does the First Amendment mean?" a host of commentators from the fields of law, education and religion proceeded to give their answers to the same question. In so doing, the commentators have grouped themselves into two main camps—those who support the "broad" interpretation of the Court in its "Everson" philosophy,[14] and those who support a "narrow" interpretation of the establishment clause. In the view of the latter group, the "establishment clause" was intended by its authors to forbid solely the recognition of any one religious sect or possibly a group of sects as the national religion. Consequently the Amendment does not render unlawful governmental cooperation with religious groups and aid to their endeavors, provided there is no partiality shown to any particular sect or group of sects, to the detriment of the rest.[15]

In addition to these Supreme Court decisions, there are laws on the books of each of the forty-eight states which limit the type of religious instruction which can be given in public schools. Two studies have been made dealing with these state laws. The first, *The Secularization of American Education*, was made in 1912 by

---

[14] Cf., e.g. Conrad H. Moehlman, *The Wall of Separation between Church and State* (Boston: Beacon Press, 1951); Alvin W. Johnson and Frank H. Yost, *Separation of Church and State in the United States* (Minneapolis: University of Minnesota Press, 1934 [Revised 1948]); Leo Pfeffer, *Church and State Freedom* (Boston: Beacon Press, 1953).

[15] Wilfrid Parsons, *The First Freedom* (New York: Declan X. McMullen Co., 1948); James M. O'Neill, *Religion and Education under the Constitution* (New York: Harper & Brothers, 1949); Joseph H. Brady, *Confusion Twice Confounded* (South Orange: Seton Hall University Press, 1954); the next three articles mentioned are to be found in a symposium, "Religion and the State" in *Law and Contemporary Problems*, xiv (Durham, N. C.: Duke University Law School, 1949), 1–159, viz.; Edwin S. Corwin, "The Supreme Court as National School Board" (pp. 12–22); Alexander Meiklejohn, "Educational Cooperation between Church and State" (pp. 61–72); John C. Murray, "Law or Prepossessions" pp. 23–43). Cf. also, John C. Murray, "Pluralism in America," *Thought*, xxix (Summer, 1954), pp. 165–208.

Samuel Windsor Brown.[16] The second, *Secularism in American Education: Its History*, was done by Burton Confrey in 1931.[17] The accompanying tables are found in Confrey's work and indicate when various laws and constitutional provisions were enacted concerning religion in education.[18] In explanation Confrey gives the following:

> . . . Dates represent state constitutional provisions, statutes, or legal decisions. The capital letters are used to designate the process of secularization as follows: "F" (forbidding), "D" (denying), or "P" (penalizing); "A" (authorizing) the opposite. For instance, a "C" preceding a date in Column IV means that a state constitutional provision denies public funds to denominational institutions in that state: a "D" preceding indicates that a statute or legal decision makes the same denial. A "G" preceding a date in Column IV means that public funds were granted to religious denominational institutions.[19]

For our purposes, only Columns I, II and III are apropos. "Sectarian instruction" and "Sectarian books" refer to the inculcation of religious doctrines peculiar to a specific religious group.

The present "so-far-and-no-farther" climate as to religious instruction in public education is the result of the application of the tradition of Church-State separation to schools. The application has force of law by reason of certain statutes on the books of the several states. The application has juridical standing through certain decisions of the Supreme Court which, through an interpretation of the First Amendment (made applicable to the States via the Fourteenth) has ruled unconstitutional certain plans to give religious instruction and ruled constitutional certain others. In

---

[16] Samuel Windsor Brown, *The Secularization of American Education, As Shown by State Legislation, State Constitutional Provisions and State Supreme Court Decisions* (Teachers' College, Columbia University Contributions to Education, No. 49), (New York: Teachers' College, Columbia University, 1912).

[17] Burton Confrey, *Secularism in American Education: Its History* (Educational Research Monographs, Thomas G. Foran, ed.), vi (January 15, 1931), (Washington, D. C.: The Catholic Education Press, 1931).

[18] Photostats reproduced with permission of The Catholic University of America Press, Washington, D. C., the present copyright owner.

[19] Confrey, *op. cit.*, p. 123.

	I — Forbidding sectarian instruction in public schools. Constitutional provisions forbidding it. Authorizing it.	II — Forbidding use of sectarian books. Penalizing teacher or school using them. Library denied them.	III — Forbidding the Bible. Authorizing its use. Requiring its use. Exercises, religious.	IV — Denying public funds to denominational institutions. Granting them. Constitutional provisions denying them.	V — Denying use of the school-house for religious meetings. Authorizing it.	VI — Forbidding religious test. Requiring it. Constitution forbids it.
Alabama	F1852 F1856 F1854 F1876	F1903		C1854 C1901 C1875		F1852
Arizona	F1879 C1910 F1901 F1913	FP1879 P1905 F1883L F1908L P1895L P1913	F1913E	D1879 D1895 D1883 C1910		F1901
Arkansas		F1873	R1930	C1868 C1874		F1829 R1831
California	F1855 C1879	F1855 F1924L F1870L F1883L		G1851 C1879 D1855		
Colorado	C1876		A1927	C1876 C1818 C1897 C1887	A1856 A1902 A1872	C1876
Connecticut						
Delaware						
Florida			A1869E A1889E			
Georgia		FP1895	A1895 R1922E	C1868 CG1877		F1785 F1895 F1877

Idaho	C1890	F1911	CP1890	P1911			C1890				C1890	F1905
	C1907	F1919	F1907L	F1919							F1903	F1907
Illinois	F1836				A1880	F1910E	C1870	D1887	A1872	A1909	F1835	F1837
					A1891E		D1872	D1888	A1879		F1836	F1840
Indiana	F1853		F1889	F1894	A1865	A1894	C1851	G1855	A1859	A1905	F1853	F1914
									A1894		F1894	
Iowa			F1876		A1873	A1897	C1857	D1918	A1872	A1878	F1842	F1855
					A1884E		D1872				F1843	F1858
											F1847	
Kansas	F1876		F1897	F1905	A1876		C1855	C1859	D1875	A1905		
					A1904E		C1858		A1901	A1923		
Kentucky	F1893	F1918	F1893	F1904	A1905		C1850	C1891			F1903	
	F1903		F1903L									
Louisiana	F1855	F1870			A1870	F1915	C1864	C1894			F1855	
							C1868	C1898				
							C1879					
Maine	F1916				A1854		C1820		A1817			
									A1834			
Maryland			F1872				G1818					
Massachusetts ...			F1827	F1859	R1855	A1866E	D1810	D1869			F1859	
			F1835	F1862	R1859	A1882	C1855	C1917			F1901	
			F1855		A1862	A1901						
Michigan					A1898		C1835	D1897			F1837	
							C1850	C1901			F1855	
Minnesota	F1907	F1913			A1927		C1875	C1877	A1878	A1894	F1867	F1913
									A1881		F1907	
Mississippi	F1922		F1892L	F1906	A1870	CA1890	C1868	C1890	A1840		C1890	
					A1878		D1879					

	I Forbidding sectarian instruction in public schools. *Constitutional provisions forbidding it. Authorizing it.*	II Forbidding use of sectarian books. *Penalizing teacher or school using them. Library denied them.*	III Forbidding the Bible. *Authorizing its use. Requiring its use. Exercises, religious.*	IV Denying public funds to denominational institutions. *Granting them. Constitutional provisions denying them.*	V *Denying use of the school-house for religious meetings. Authorizing it.*	VI Forbidding religious test. *Requiring it. Constitution forbids it.*
Missouri	F1835			C1875	D1878 A1899	F1825 F1835 F1840 F1841
Montana	F1872 F1895 F1893	F1872L F1895L		C1889		C1889 F1893 C1889
Nebraska	F1871 C1875 C1920		F1902	C1886	D1914	F1857 F1871 F1881 C1920
Nevada	C1864 F1880 F1885 F1900 F1912	F1885		C1864 D1885 D1900		
New Hampshire ..		F1842	A1894 A1900	C1792 C1875		
New Jersey		F1895		C1877 D1881	A1901	F1881 F1900
New Mexico	F1897	F1923	A1850	C1911		C1911
New York	F1842 F1851 F1844	F1843 F1844 F1882	A1844	G1801 G1813 C1820 D1842 D1844 G1849 D1850 G1851 G1852 D1853	D1854 D1864 D1871 C1894 D1922 A1924	F1784 F1787 F1826 F1846

8

State								
North Carolina		F1905			C1876			
North Dakota	F1887 F1831 F1881	F1899	F1891		C1889		A1899	F1883
Ohio				A1925	C1851		A1906	F1890 F1897
Oklahoma	F1890 F1895	F1901	F1908	A1895 A1903	C1907		A1925	F1921
Oregon	A1888				C1857		A1917	
Pennsylvania				A1885 A1898 R1913 Penalty	G1789 G1837 G1842 C1843	G1849 C1874	D1894 D1897	F1876 F1911 F1902 F1921
Rhode Island					C1843			
South Carolina	F1871 F1887 F1903		F1870		C1868	C1894	A1921	F1873 F1903
South Dakota		F1919	A1887 A1903		C1889	D1891		
Tennessee	F1870	F1899	A1925		C1870	C1876		F1837 F1839
Texas	F1881		A1907E		C1845			F1881 F1913
Utah	F1892				C1895			
Virginia	F1847	F1847	F1849		C1902		A1890	F1839 F1842
Vermont								
Washington	F1883	FP1883L F1890L	F1918		C1889	D1890	D1890	F1890
West Virginia			R1866		C1872	A1887	A1906	F1857 F1880
Wisconsin	C1848 F1880	F1898 F1883			C1848	D1890	A1875 D1915	F1866 F1898
Wyoming	F1883	F1891			C1889			F1886 F1890 C1889 F1891

addition to the above legal and juridical components of the picture, there is a considerable mass of public opinion supporting the application of the tradition as described.

Is the present day application of the separation tradition justified in the light of the history of religion in American life and American education? Religion was once taught in most of the schools of America. By "religion" here is meant instruction in and formation of attitudes on the doctrines, history and practices of the Christian groups which grew out of the Judaeo-Christian concept of the reciprocal relations of God and man. Was the decline of religious instruction in the American public school caused by those factors which are now alleged to impede its restoration to the curriculum?

Dr. John S. Brubacher has declared:

> The educational counterpart of the political divorce of church and state was the exclusion of religion from the public school curriculum. This secularization of public education did not occur immediately following the divorce of church and state, nor did it take the same course in each of the states. . . .[20]

"The educational counterpart of the divorce of church and state was the exclusion of religion from the public school curriculum." As Justice Black, in his Everson opinion, borrowed a metaphor from Thomas Jefferson and stated that the First Amendment erected "a wall of separation between Church and State," [21] here Dr. Brubacher borrows a metaphor from the field of matrimony and talks about the same Amendment causing "a divorce." These two metaphors imply an absolute, complete, impenetrable barrier (the wall), an absolute, complete dissolution, a wiping out of existence of a bond of union or connection (a divorce).

Are these metaphors, and the realities they imply, justifiable in the light of history? Did the Founding Fathers and the Americans of the early years of our Republic completely, absolutely and irrevocably break off all official connection with the forces of religion? Did religion as above defined disappear from the Ameri-

[20] John S. Brubacher, A History of the Problems of Education (New York: McGraw Hill Book Co., 1947), p. 334.
[21] 330 U.S. 16.

can public school and, if so, was it because of this wall-building, divorce-court procedure? Was there such a wall building, such a divorce process in the first place? And secondly, if so, was it this procedure, or was it, perhaps, something else, something allied to disestablishment, yet distinct from disestablishment, which caused religious instruction to disappear from the curriculum of the public school? These are the questions the present study will attempt to answer.

To find the answers a search will have to be made which goes *behind* the data assembled in the Supreme Court decisions and the two studies of Brown and Confrey mentioned above.[22] The gist of these two books is the *legislation* of the forty-eight states which deals with sectarian teaching, the use of sectarian textbooks (including the Bible, sectarian or not) and the appropriation of tax funds for church schools. Each of these studies has a comparatively brief analysis of the forces which worked towards the formulation of the laws.

It is here proposed to go to the "grass roots" and seek the events, the fluctuation of official and popular opinion, etc. which led to the passing of the First Amendment and the state laws. The writer senses a need of study in the area *behind the laws,* and feels that this area might be considered more vital than that of the laws themselves as a mirror of the minds of the people of that day. That data should be found in a study of:

A. The *Practices* of the various school systems in teaching religion courses in the period before and following the adoption of the Constitution and the First Amendment.

B. The *Formulation of Laws* involving religion in public life.

C. The *Controversies* in local school systems involving changes of feeling on the part of parents, church leaders and school authorities.

D. The *Writings* of the religious leaders and philosophers of education just prior to and during the 19th century.

E. *Events and Crises* which led to heightened tensions in the matter.

F. *Provisional Enactments* to adjust to given situations, which

[22] Cf. *supra*, pp. 4, 5.

amounted to temporary arrangements, the last step before the crystallization of opinion in law.

The study will limit itself to elementary education. Data involving colleges and secondary schools, if appearing, will be used only for purposes of clarification.

CHAPTER II

The Background

Colonial Schools

TO BEGIN this study in 1776, with no reference to the background of colonial education, would be to imply that the Declaration of Independence cut every cultural and religious tie with the mother country along with the political one, or that there was no educational system in existence in America before the Revolutionary War. Actually, of course, there were schools in the Colonies on the elementary as well as higher levels. And most, if not all, of these were faithful patterns of the schools of Europe, especially England.

Historians of American education are generally in agreement as to the strong religious element in the schools of the thirteen original American Colonies. As an inheritance from the Old World, the colonial elementary schools had religion as a chief aim and the main component. This religious education was not weakened essentially by a slowly increasing interest in purely secular subjects.[1]

[1] Cf. Elwood P. Cubberly, *Public Education in the United States* (revised and enlarged edition; Boston: Houghton, Mifflin Company, 1934), p. 12; Edgar W. Knight, *Education in the United States* (third revised edition; Boston: Ginn and Company, 1951), p. 73. Cf. also: John S. Brubacher, *A History of the Problems of Education* (New York: McGraw-Hill Book Company, 1947), pp. 332–33; R. Freeman Butts and Lawrence A. Cremin, *A History of Education in American Culture* (New York: Henry Holt and Company, 1953), p. 44; Evarts B. Greene, *Religion and the State, The Making and Testing of an*

Although some of the Old World educational influence came from Holland, the German states and Sweden, the predominant pattern was that of the schools of England. There is abundant evidence to indicate that religion was a basic and permeating subject in British schools both before and during the American colonial period. Indeed, in England the emphasis on doctrinal religious instruction following the Reformation formed no essential break with the Catholic past. The purpose was changed, of course, to that of enabling the students to attain salvation according to the Protestant theological system, and preparing them to cope with their Catholic opponents in the field of religious apologetics.[2] If the New World colonizers, then, remembered the schools of their youth, the institutions they erected in America would be likely to include a deep religious element.

The religious character of colonial education may also be inferred from the highly religious purpose which underlay the founding of several of the English settlements in the New World. If one concedes even a fairly high degree of economic, political and commercial influence motivating some of the colonists, it cannot be denied that they placed religion in a most prominent place among their thoughts.[3] In New England the Puritans founded a theocratic state. Dissenters from Puritanism set up their own colony in Rhode Island. The Church of England became the established religion sooner or later in the colonies of Virginia, Maryland, New York, part of what is now New Jersey, the Carolinas and Georgia. In Pennsylvania and present Dela-

---

American Tradition (New York: New York University Press, 1941), pp. 120–22; Colyer Meriwether, *Our Colonial Curriculum* (Washington, D. C.: Capital Publishing Company, 1907), Chap. I, "Elementary Course," pp. 15–40.

[2] Cf. R. Ackerman, *The History of St. Paul's School* (London: no publisher, 1816); John H. Brown, *Elizabethan School Days* (Oxford: B. Blackwell, 1933); F. J. Furnivall, *Education in Early England* (London: N. Trubner & Co., 1867); Arthur F. Leach, *English Schools at the Reformation* (Westminster: A. Constable and Co., 1896); Hastings Rashdall, *The Universities of Europe in the Middle Ages* (Oxford: The Clarendon Press, 1895); and Foster Watson, *The English Grammar Schools to 1660* (Cambridge, England: The University Press, 1908) and *The Old Grammar Schools* (Cambridge, England: The University Press, 1916).

[3] Cf. William W. Sweet, *Religion in Colonial America* (New York: Charles Scribner's Sons, 1942), Chap. I.

ware, William Penn and his fellow-Quakers were in control, although they permitted other religious groups to come to the colony. In the days before the Anglicans took over, New York had seen establishment of the Dutch Reformed Church, and Maryland, under the Lords Baltimore, was a place where people of different religious beliefs might find a New World haven for the convictions of their consciences.

The religious idealism which lay behind the founding and administering of so many of the colonies, coupled with the accepted religious emphasis in English education of those times, would lead one to expect that the colonial schools would make great efforts in religious instruction.

Massachusetts led off with the earliest known American law on education, dated April 14, 1642. It was aimed at requiring parents to see to the religious education of their children.[4] Five years later the same colony passed the famous "Old Deluder" Act.[5] The purpose of this law was to make sure that children would learn to read and know the meaning of the Scriptures. Such a religious provision is directly in line with the Calvinist doctrine that salvation is dependent upon the individual's knowing the Bible and receiving the gift of faith from this knowledge by an experience of the grace of God. In 1650 the neighboring colony of Connecticut enacted an education law which contains *verbatim* the texts of the two Massachusetts laws cited.[6] Plymouth Colony, which was not joined to the Massachusetts Bay Colony until 1692, passed a statute in 1671 requiring that parents give their children enough learning to enable them to read, among other things, the Scriptures.[7]

While one does not find such specific and strong religious education laws in the non-theocratic colonies south of New England, their leaders did make official provision for religious instruction.

[4] *The Laws and Liberties of Massachusetts* (Cambridge: Harvard University Press, 1929), p. 11.

[5] *Ibid.*, p. 47.

[6] Henry Barnard, "History of Common Schools in Connecticut," *The American Journal of Education*, IV (1857), 660.

[7] *Plymouth Colony Records*, XI, *Laws* (quoted in Elwood P. Cubberly, *Readings in Public Education in the United States* [Boston: Houghton, Mifflin Co., 1934]), p. 20. (Future references to this work will be listed as "Cubberly, *Readings*.")

Cubberly points out that when New York became an English colony, it had its own paraphrase of the Massachusetts "Old Deluder" Act in the "Duke of York's Laws of 1665." [8] Of the New Jersey effort at education, Thomas Woody writes: "Education of Colonial days existed primarily for religious ends." [9] Pennsylvania's colonial assembly passed a law in 1683 requiring that all children be taught reading, that they might be able to read the Scriptures.[10] A few Jesuit schools were opened in Maryland,[11] and Catholic historians note that there was a Jesuit school in New York City somewhere in the period from 1685 to 1690.[12]

The Church of England, being to a degree established in New York, Maryland, Virginia, the Carolinas and Georgia, became responsible to a large extent for elementary education in these parts. Though tutorial education was frequently employed in the more southern colonies, the Anglican Church sponsored charity schools there to educate the children of the poor and orphans. What was good in these schools, as well as those of the Church of England in other colonies, can be traced mainly to the efforts of the "Society for the Propagation of the Gospel in Foreign Parts." This society was organized in England in 1701 and so its efforts were felt in America in the later colonial period. It trained and licensed schoolmasters. Thus its work contributed much to the charity schools, and insured a strong religious emphasis in the curriculum.[13] Writing of the S.P.G., W. W. Kemp observes:

[8] Cubberly, *Readings,* p. 17.

[9] Thomas Woody, *Quaker Education in the Colony and State of New Jersey* (Philadelphia: Published by the author, 1923), p. 374.

[10] "Laws of the Second General Assembly of Pennsylvania Colony," Chap. CXII. From J. P. Wickersham, *History of Education in Pennsylvania* (Lancaster, 1866), p. 39. (Quoted in Cubberly, *Readings,* p. 27.) Cf. also, Thomas Woody: "Fox (Founder of Quakerism), from the first, was interested in education, particularly moral and practical. . . . He was primarily interested in (1) moral training; (2) religious instruction; and (3) education of a practical sort. . . ." *Early Quaker Education in Pennsylvania* (New York: Teachers' College, Columbia University, 1920), p. 268.

[11] J. A. Burns and Bernard J. Kohlbrenner, *A History of Catholic Education in the United States* (New York: Benziger Brothers, 1937), pp. 45, 50.

[12] *Ibid.,* p. 49.

[13] Cf. William W. Sweet, *Religion in Colonial America* (New York: Charles Scribner's Sons, 1942), pp. 57–65. Also, Edgar W. Knight, *A Documentary History of Education in the South Before 1860* (5 vols.; Chapel Hill: The University of North Carolina Press, 1949–1953), Vol. I, Chaps. II, III.

The chief motive of the Society was clearly the extension of Christianity to the virgin soil of America and keeping it alive among the Europeans pioneering in the transatlantic empire. Not only was Christianity to be fostered, but that particular form of it which was typified by the doctrine and worship of the Church of England.[14]

It seems, then, that in the vast majority of cases, the colonial leaders aimed to make religion an integral part of what the elementary school would give its pupils. In most cases the aim was to give religion the top priority. No one seems to have wanted to omit it altogether.

How completely was the religious purpose achieved? It is difficult to estimate this, since those who attended such schools are long since dead, and the records which have survived are very meager. The day of superintendents' reports, elaborate marking systems, achievement tests and the like had not yet dawned. Such memoirs of students and teachers as have been found in the course of this study will be cited, but there is not much to help one form an objective estimate.

There are, however, three sources of a documentary nature, which will give insight into the teaching of religion in colonial schools. The first is what is known of teacher requirements. The second is a study of the textbooks used. Thirdly, there do exist some records of curricular practices.

TEACHER REQUIREMENTS

While it must be admitted that the average colonial elementary schoolmaster was not highly educated and had, by modern standards, little, if any, specific training for his work, it is admirable to read of some of the efforts made to get good teachers. Among the qualifications demanded, orthodoxy in the faith of the sponsoring religious organization and probity of character ranked

[14] William W. Kemp, *The Support of Schools in Colonial New York by the Society for the Propagation of the Gospel in Foreign Parts* (New York: Teachers' College, Columbia University, 1913), p. 275. A valuable summary of Anglican efforts for colonial schools, as well as those of other religious groups, will also be found in Burton Confrey, *Secularism in American Education: Its History*, Chap. i, pp. 7–46.

highest. In New England, as Cubberly observes, "the minister usually examined the candidate thoroughly to see that he was 'sound in the faith and knew his Latin.' Little else mattered." [15]

The S.P.G. adopted, about 1711, the following regulations for schoolmasters:

> 1. That no person be admitted as Schoolmaster till he bring certificate of the following particulars: (1) his age, (2) his condition of life, whether, single or mary'd, (3) his temper, (4) his prudence, (5) his learning, (6) his sober and pious conversation, (7) his zeal for the Xtian religion and diligence in his calling, (8) his affection to the present government, and (9) his conformity to the doctrines and discipline of the Ch. of England.[16]

Brief notice must also be taken of one outstanding treatise, in which a colonial schoolmaster gave his philosophy of education. Christopher Dock, the devout Mennonite who conducted his schools in Pennsylvania in the first three-quarters of the eighteenth century, wrote the *Schul-Ordnung*, published in 1770.

Dock is justly admired for the methods of gentleness which he substituted for the usual rigorous methods of the day. But the deeply religious basis of his theory of education is, perhaps, not so widely recognized. A reading of the *Schul-Ordnung* will indicate how completely religious ideals and values permeated his teaching aims and methods.[17]

TEXTBOOKS

The textbooks of colonial times bear eloquent testimony to the preponderance of religious instruction. For the present chapter and later ones, two main sources, among others, have been examined. The first is Clifton Johnson's well-known *Old-Time Schools and School-Books*.[18] Particular reliability as to texts was

---

[15] Cubberly, *Public Education in the United States*, p. 55.

[16] *Ibid.*, p. 24, footnote.

[17] Cf. Martin G. Brumbaugh, *The Life and Works of Christopher Dock* (Philadelphia: J. B. Lippincott Co., 1908). The text of the *Schul-Ordnung* comprises pp. 91–156.

[18] Clifton Johnson, *Old-Time Schools and School-Books* (New York: The Macmillan Co., 1904).

placed in this volume because so much of Johnson's illustrative material is composed of facsimile reproductions of the originals he is describing. "The textbook equipment of the old schools was extremely meagre," he writes:

> and the average schoolboy had only a catechism or primer, a Psalter, and a Testament or Bible. For Latin students this list would have to be extended, but ordinarily it comprised all a boy ever used as long as he attended school.[19]

The second source used in the research for this study is the collection of over 7,000 old schoolbooks amassed by Dr. John A. Nietz of the Department of Education at the University of Pittsburgh.[20]

All students of colonial education are familiar with the "Hornbook," the paddle-like tablet with its alphabet, the "Sign of the Cross" and the Lord's Prayer. After mastering the Hornbook, the student turned to the catechism. This book of religious doctrine in question and answer form occupied a large part of the young pupil's time and energy. Among the most frequently used were *The Young Children's Catechism* by Isaac Watts, the Rev. John Cotton's *Spiritual Milk for American Babes, Drawn out of the Breasts of Both Testaments, for their Soul's Nourishment,* and the *Westminster Catechism* which had been drawn up in England in 1643.[21]

Condensations of Cotton's and the Westminster Catechisms were included in various editions of the most famous colonial elementary textbook of all, *The New England Primer.* Johnson observes:

> For a hundred years this book beyond any other was the school-book of American dissenters [i.e. Puritans]. Its power waned rapidly later. The cities abandoned it first, and gradually it was neglected in the villages. Still, even in Boston, it was used in the dame schools as late as 1806. Its total sales are estimated to have been not less than three million copies. Aston-

---

[19] *Ibid.,* p. 14.

[20] The writer spent some time examining these old textbooks and conferring with Doctor Nietz in the summer of 1955.

[21] Johnson, *op. cit.,* p. 13, and Butts and Cremin, *op. cit.,* p. 67.

ishingly few of these have been preserved, and early editions are among the rarest of school-books. All issues previous to 1700 have vanished, and only a few score have survived of those that were published during the next century, when it was at the zenith of its popularity.[22]

There are several nineteenth-century editions of the *Primer* in the Nietz Collection. One printed by S. A. Howland in Worcester, Massachusetts (no date given) has the following subtitle: *Containing the Assembly's Catechism; The Account of the Burning of John Rogers; a Dialogue Between Christ, A Youth, and the Devil; and Various Other Useful and Instructive Matter. Adorned with Cuts. With a Historical Introduction by Rev. H. Humphrey, D.D., President of Amberhurst [sic] College.* Humphrey was President of Amherst College in the 1830s.[23]

Besides the catechisms and the primers, there were other textbooks employed. John Coote's *The English Schoolmaster,* first published in 1596, contained, besides other material, "prayers, psalms and a short catechism." [24] *A History of Genesis,* published in 1708, contains a Preface which praised the Book of Genesis as "the Epitome of all Divinity" and advised parents to substitute it for "all fond and amorous Romances, and fabulous Histories of Giants . . . and the like; for these fill the heads of children with vain, silly and idle imaginations." [25] Spellers with religious content cited by Johnson include John Dilworth's *A New Guide to the English Tongue* and Watts' *Compleat Spelling Book.*[26]

It is not easy to say how extensively these books were used. It can be stated, however, that where they were used, the students had a great amount of religious material before them. That they were used rather fully may be surmised from the third source of information mentioned above—records of curricular practices.

22 Johnson, *op. cit.,* p. 72.

23 A somewhat extended outline of the contents of this edition and two others from the Nietz Collection will be found in Appendix "A" of the author's dissertation at The Johns Hopkins University Library.

24 Johnson, *op. cit.,* p. 22.

25 Cf. *ibid.,* pp. 46–47. Johnson does not mention the author's name nor give any other identifying data.

26 *Ibid.,* p. 61.

CURRICULAR PRACTICES

Johnson quotes an excerpt from the "Dorchester School Rules of 1645." Instead of the midday intermission on Monday it was ordered that the master

> shall call his scholars together between twelve and one of the clock to examine them what they have learned, at which time also he shall take notice of any misdemeanor or outrage that any of his scholars shall have committed on the sabbath . . .
> Every day of the week at two of the clock in the afternoon he shall catechize his scholars in the principles of the Christian religion . . .
> It is to be a chief part of the schoolmaster's religious care to commend his scholars and his labors amongst them unto God by prayer morning and evening taking care that his scholars do reverently attend during the same . . .
> The rod of correction is a rule of God sometimes to be used upon children . . .[27]

Knight, evidently summarizing this same Dorchester rule, remarks that this Monday intermission period was also used to quiz the children on the minister's sermon of the day before.[28] It must also be pointed out that the ministers themselves exercised a great deal of control over the schools. They often visited and questioned the pupils on religious doctrine.[29]

Cubberly's *Readings* contain some instructive documents on the carrying out of religious teaching. From the "Rules and Regulations . . . of the New Haven Hopkins Grammar School," drawn up in 1684:

> 5. That the Scholars being called together, the Mr. shall every morning begin his work with a short prayer for a blessing on his Laboures and their learning . . .
> 8. That if any of ye Schoole Boyes be observed to play, sleep, or behave themselves rudely, or irreverently, or be any way disorderly at meeting on ye Saboath Daye or any other tyme of ye

[27] *Ibid.*, p. 11.
[28] Knight, *Education in the United States,* p. 123.
[29] Johnson, *op. cit.*, p. 24.

Publique worships of God That . . . the Master shall give them due correction to ye degree of ye offence. . . .[30]

From the "Rules Regulating a Schoolmaster in New Amsterdam," (1661):

3. He shall teach the children and pupils the Christian prayers, Commandments, baptism, Lord's supper, and the questions with answers of the catechism, which are taught here every Sunday afternoon in the church.
4. Before school closes he shall let the children sing some verses and a psalm.[31]

From a "Contract with a Dutch Schoolmaster," Flatbush, New York, (1682):

II. When the school begins, one of the children shall read the morning prayer, as it stands in the catechism, and close with the prayer before dinner; in the afternoon it shall begin with the prayer after dinner, and end with the evening prayer. The evening school shall begin with the Lord's prayer, and close by singing a psalm.
III. He shall instruct the children on every Wednesday and Saturday in the common prayers, and the questions and answers in the catechism, to enable them to repeat them the better on Sunday before the afternoon service, or on Monday, when they shall be catechized before the congregation. . . .[32]

As to what the New York schoolmasters of the "Society for the Propagation of the Gospel" were expected to teach, the following selections from their instructions bear clear witness:

I. That they well consider the End for which they are employed by the Society, viz. The instructing and disposing Children to believe and live as Christians.
II. In order to this End, that they teach them to read truely and distinctly, that they may be capable of reading the Holy Scriptures, and other pious and useful Books, for informing their Understandings and regulating their Manners.

[30] "Transcribed from the Records of the School, by Mr. Lyman Baird. In Barnard's *American Journal of Education,* IV, 710" (Cubberly, *Readings,* pp. 63–65).

[31] "Minutes of the Orphan Masters of New Amsterdam," II, 115; trans. by B. Fernow, New York, 1907. In Cubberly, *Readings,* p. 66.

[32] Cf. Daniel J. Pratt, *Annals of Public Education in the State of New York* (Albany: The Argus Co., 1872), p. 65.

III. That they instruct them thoroughly in the Church-Catechism; teach them first to read it distinctly and exactly, then to learn it perfectly by Heart; endeavoring to make them understand the Sense and Meaning of it, by the Help of such Expositions, as the Society shall send over. . . .

VI. That they daily use, Morning and Evening, the Prayers composed for their Use in this Collection with their Scholars in the School, and teach them the Prayers and Graces composed for their Use at Home.

VII. That they oblige their Scholars to be constant at Church on the Lord's Day Morning and Afternoon, and at all other Times of Publick Worship; that they cause them to carry their Bibles and Prayer Books with them, instructing them how to use them there, and how to demean themselves in the several Parts of Worship; that they be there present with them, taking Care of their reverent and decent Behavior, and examine them afterwards as to what they have heard and learn'd.[33]

Combative Forces

Before closing this summary of the colonial period, attention must be given to several forces which arose therein to combat the intensity of the religious feeling which inspired elementary education. These combative elements may be divided into forces inside the churches themselves and forces outside the realm of strictly religious thought.

The most notable change within the religious field is what has been called the "Puritan Declension." [34] In the original set-up of the Massachusetts theocratic state the right of vote was restricted by a law of 1631 to bona-fide church members, i.e., those who had signed the covenant, having declared themselves converted by an elaborate experience of grace.

As time went on, the rigors and varied experiences of frontier colonial life caused many to face the "ordeal" of conversion less

[33] *Ibid.*, p. 109. Further information on curricular practices may be found in Christopher Dock's *Schul-Ordnung*, Sections 4 and 5. (Cf. Brumbaugh, *op. cit.*, pp. 131 ff.)

[34] For a discussion of the "declension" of Puritanism, see Perry Miller, *The New England Mind (From Colony to Province)*, (New York: The Macmillan Co., 1939–53), II, Book I, "Declension," 19–146. Cf. also, Sweet, *op. cit.*, pp. 102–09; Gaius G. Atkins and Frederick L. Fogley, *History of American Congregationalism* (Boston: The Pilgrim Press, 1942), pp. 92–94.

willingly. And so, by the law of 1662, the "Half-way Covenant" was authorized. By this decree, parents who themselves had not been "converted" could pass on to their children membership in the church and baptism rights. These children, however, had to make a declaration of loyalty to Christian principles and promise to bring up *their* children in Godly ways.

In 1664 there came another change. Hereafter, it continued to be true that one could vote in Massachusetts on condition of full church membership. Also, by the "King's mandate," if one were a half-way member or no member at all, he could still vote if he owned property and was known as a reputable character in the community.

Thus did Massachusetts decline from its original high and exclusive standards. To what extent this loss of grip affected religious teaching in the schools is hard to estimate. Whereas the political power of the church grew weaker, the evidence we have presented seems to indicate that the schools maintained their religious emphasis. It seems important to make a distinction between the legal status of the church on the one hand and the conviction of the importance of religion in the hearts of the people on the other. The former may temporarily decline without automatically affecting the latter.

The second and third generation Puritans, however, were not all satisfied to let things go down. Typical of those who would keep up the old spirit was the Rev. Cotton Mather, grandson of Richard Mather, an original Puritan, and son of Increase Mather, himself a minister, president of Harvard and a political leader. Cotton Mather strove and preached hard to stem the tide. He would restore the positive vigor and ideals of the golden age of Puritanism. But he found it a very difficult task.

While Puritanism was declining, the early eighteenth century saw a vigorous revival movement come into the colonies known as the "Great Awakening." With tracings to contemporary movements in England and on the Continent, this movement emphasized individual conversion, pietism and good works. Led by such men as Jonathan Edwards, it became, in effect, a challenge to the declining forces of orthodox Calvinism among the Puritans of

New England. The "New Lights" (Edwards' group) fought the "Old Lights" (champions of straight predestination and election) and schisms appeared in many congregations. The Great Awakening was not limited, however, to the Puritans nor to the New England scene. Other leaders mentioned by Butts and Cremin include Theodore Frelinghuysen (Dutch Reformed), William Tennent (Presbyterian), Heinrich Muhlenberg (Lutheran), Francis Asbury (Methodist) and George Whitfield (Anglican).[35] Its results in the educational world would seem naturally to have been a reemphasis on religious training of the young.

In other colonies than those of New England, as Sweet points out, the percentage of unchurched people was larger than in New England itself.[36] This seems to have been due to the restrictive nature of some groups such as the Baptists, who, like the Puritans, required conversion for church membership. Certain national groups like the Germans and Scotch Irish were either poverty stricken and scattered, or lacked religious leaders. The Anglican Church, hierarchically constituted as it is, suffered from the fact that no bishop ever visited the American Colonies. Catholics, of course, were numerically insignificant, and in most places, legislated against so tightly that they cut no impressive figure in the overall colonial religious scene.

Coupled with this not too inspiring picture of the effectiveness of church institutions were certain slowly rising secularistic forces. Out of Europe came the philosophy of the Enlightenment. The ideas of Lessing, Mendelssohn and Reimarus in Germany, of Locke and Newton in England, and of Condillac, Diderot, Rousseau and Voltaire in France made themselves felt in the minds of certain American leaders. In the religious field it produced a group of deists, among them extreme types like Ethan Allen and Thomas Paine and milder ones such as Thomas Jefferson, John Adams and Benjamin Franklin.

The "deist" differs from the "theist" not by rejecting the idea that there is a God. Both accept the existence of God. Traditionally, however, the theist emphasizes His "Providence" or contin-

[35] Butts and Cremin, *op. cit.*, p. 48.
[36] Sweet, *op. cit.*, pp. 334–36.

uous government of and care for the world. The deist admits that God is responsible for starting the world but feels that He has left it to run itself according to definable "natural laws."

Attributing to these deistic, rationalistic and scientific ideas of the Enlightenment all due success in implanting themselves in the minds of American leaders, it seems, nevertheless, that they did not penetrate deep enough vitally to affect colonial *elementary* education. The evidence we have gathered seems to indicate that the religious element remained strong and dominant, although the seeds of a secularistic trend may have been planted.

More influential were such factors as the gradually expanding Western Frontier and the rise of commerce and trade. Also, the growing number of religious sects began to cause pressure on the established groups for recognition of individual rights. Decentralization, preoccupation with material concerns, the lessening of the power of the Calvinistic and Anglican Churches—it was these things which began to weaken somewhat both the schools and the teaching of religion. Textbooks, such as Dilworth's *A New Guide to the English Tongue,* began to appear (1750 in America) which had less religious material than the *New England Primer.* Yet it would be incorrect to say that religion lost its place as the basis and primary aim of elementary education. Rather, there occurred splitting of religious organizations, and the moving of secular interests nearer the throne of religion in the colonial school room.

As the first quarter of the eighteenth century passed, two seemingly diverse currents joined in the realm of American politics. One was in the field of active politics—the growing autonomy of the colonial legislatures. The other, a philosophical trend emphasized by the "Enlightenment," was an increasing attention to the "natural rights of man." Every American school child knows the result of the meeting of the two streams—the Stamp Act Crisis of 1765, the Declaration of Independence in 1776, and the Revolutionary War by which independence was won from the British Crown.

The "doctrine" of the natural rights of man thus triumphed in the political arena. After the infant nation wrote its Constitution and Amendments, this "doctrine" of natural rights began to have a notable effect on the religious life of the nation and, eventually, on the place of religion in education.

Religion and the Law

In the decision of the colonists to cut their ties with England, did the severance of relations extend beyond the strictly political field? Was there a new policy adopted by the American people on religion and its role in the educative process? It seems accurate to summarize the colonial period and its Old World background by saying that the settlers believed that religion belonged in life and hence in education seen as a preparation for life. Did such a philosophy persevere, or was it abandoned?

A study of the legislative procedures by which the former colonists established a new sovereign state should provide a key to any changes, if such there were, made in their religious and educational convictions.[37]

RELIGIOUS SENTIMENTS IN THE CONTINENTAL CONGRESS

It has been seen that religion had been given a prominent role in the education of the American colonists. When they came to express the reasons for their revolt against the mother country, one might expect religious convictions to be included in the manifesto. Such was the case with the American Declaration of Independence. The "natural rights of man" which the colonists declared were violated by the activities of the British Crown and Parliament were represented as based on Divine authority. Their statements "That all men are created equal; that they are endowed by their Creator with certain inalienable rights," have

[37] As noted in the preceding Chapter, recent decisions of the Supreme Court of the United States on religion and public education were based on interpretations of the meaning of the First Amendment to the Constitution. Our study of religion in the Constitution and its First Amendment thus becomes the more significant in our study of the young nation's views on religion and its place in the educative process.

become household words in the nation's life. The list of grievances against the King was then outlined, noting the fruitless attempts made by the colonists to have both the Sovereign and his ministers set them right. Recognition of Divine Authority was again stressed in the conclusion.

The author was the deist, and nominal Episcopalian, Thomas Jefferson. Among the other fifty-four signers were many varieties of religious believers, from John Adams and Franklin, Jefferson's fellow deists, to the Catholic Charles Carroll of Carrollton. They left a record for posterity of their united conviction that the "natural rights of men" were rights and natural because God has so ordained.

The Continental Congress, in all its proceedings, continued to keep the religious element to the fore in its declarations and enactments. It appointed Chaplains to open and close the meetings with prayer. On July 12, 1775 a proclamation was issued for a day of national fasting and prayer. A Seal and other designs adopted expressed a belief in Divine Providence. An American edition of the Bible was endorsed and recommended to the people.[38] Of special interest were the words of the Northwest Ordinance of 1787, repeated in the Southwest Ordinance a short time later: "Religion, morality and knowledge, being necessary to good government, and the happiness of mankind, schools and the means of education shall forever be encouraged." [39]

Debate on a proposal to provide for the support of religion from profits realized from the use of public lands occurred in the Continental Congress during its meeting of April 23, 1785. The members were discussing the "Ordinance for ascertaining the mode of disposing of Lands in the Western Territory." [40] The *Journal* for April 23 states:

The following paragraph in the Ordinance being under debate: 'There shall be reserved the central Section of every

[38] Cf. Anson P. Stokes, *Church and State in the United States* (3 vols.; New York: Harper & Bros., 1950), I, 447 ff.

[39] 1 U.S. Stat. Art. III and 549, Chap. 28, Sec. 6.

[40] John C. Fitzpatrick (ed.), *Journals of the Continental Congress, 1774–1789* (Washington, D. C.: U.S. Government Printing Office, 1933), XXVIII (1785, January 11–June 30), 251, 255, 293.

Township, for the maintenance of public schools, and the Section immediately adjoining the same to the northward, for the support of religion. The profits arising therefrom in both instances, to be applied for ever according to the will of the majority of male residents of full age within the same'. A motion was made by Mr. [Charles] Pinckney, seconded by Mr. [William] Grayson, to amend the paragraph by striking out these words, 'for the support of religion'; and in their place to insert 'for religious and charitable uses'. On which it was moved by Mr. [William] Ellery, seconded by Mr. [Melancton] Smith, to amend the amendment by striking out the words 'religious and' so that it read 'for charitable uses'.[41]

When the members voted unfavorably on Ellery's Amendment to Pinckney's Amendment, the latter withdrew his original Amendment. Ellery then moved to strike out the words "and the section immediately adjoining the same to the northward, for the support of religion, the profits therefrom in both instances, to be applied for ever according to the will of the majority of male residents of full age within the same."

Rufus King asked for a division of the motion and a vote upon retaining the support-of-religion clause. When the count was taken, seventeen of the twenty-three members voted to retain the clause and six voted to strike it out. Since the vote by states shows only five affirmatives (the divided and single state votes not counting), the words were expunged. That seventeen of the twenty-three members present were in favor of such a law to support religion from public resources is a highly significant prelude to the legislative events which were to follow when the new nation drew up its Constitution and Bill of Rights. The introduction of such a phrase displeased and even shocked James Madison,[42] but it *was* introduced and seemed a good thing to a striking majority of the legislators present.

---

[41] *Ibid.*, p. 293.

[42] Edmund G. Burnett in his study, *The Continental Congress* (New York: The Macmillan Co., 1941), p. 624, cites a letter of May 29, 1785, from Madison to James Monroe (an "ay" voter): "How a regulation so unjust in itself, so foreign to the authority of Cong[res]s, so hurtful to the sale of the public land, and smelling so strongly of an antiquated Bigotry, could have received the countenance of a Com[mit]tee is truly matter of astonishment."

PROVISIONS ON RELIGION IN THE FEDERAL CONSTITUTION

The statesmen of the new republic assembled in Philadelphia in 1787 to write a constitution. There has been frequent comment in present-day writing on the fact that God's name does not appear in the short preamble nor anywhere else in the text. The omission was also the object of concern in the new states when the constitution was sent around for ratification. However, when the Preamble states that, among the purposes of the Constitution, one was to "secure the blessings of liberty to ourselves and our posterity," all that the colonists had already said in their Declaration of Independence about the divine origin of natural rights should come back to mind.

Religion receives one specific mention in the body of the Constitution. Article VI, "General Provisions," concludes with the following:

> The senators and representatives before mentioned, and the members of the several State Legislatures, and all executive and judicial officers, both of the United States and of the several States, shall be bound by oath or affirmation to support this Constitution, but no religious test shall ever be required as a qualification to any office or public trust under the United States.[43]

An oath is "a solemn attestation or imprecation in support of a declaration, promise or vow, by means of an appeal to some personage or object regarded by the person swearing as high and holy." [44] The high and holy personage invoked in American civic-inspired oaths is named in the usual phrase: "So help me God!" A solemn affirmation was allowed in place of the oath in consideration of the principles of religious groups such as the Quakers, who prefer not to use God's name to back up their statements. In all cases, however, the process under discussion witnesses that the Supreme Being is believed to be the ultimate source of right and

[43] David S. Muzzey, *History of the American People* (Boston: Ginn and Co., 1927), Appendix II, p. XVI.

[44] Funk & Wagnalls, *New Standard Dictionary* (New York: Funk & Wagnalls Co., 1943).

authority, and the officials of "this nation under God" call upon His truthfulness to witness their own integrity of purpose.

The religious test as a qualification for office or public trust is ruled out by the Constitution. In the context of the times, a religious test meant a declaration of loyalty to a particular religious group or sect.[45]

From this it would seem that, whereas the oath of office was a declaration of one's belief in the overruling supremacy of God in the affairs of men, the religious test was a declaration of allegiance to a particular sect and its religious beliefs. Here we seem to have an implication that, whereas one's conscience may demand adherence to this or that sect, (and such will not prevent a man from holding office in America), he is not free to hold such office without declaring his fundamental acknowledgement of the existence of God, and God's role as the Champion of truth. Such an interpretation seems to agree with the statements made in the state conventions now to be considered.

REACTIONS ON RELIGION AT THE RATIFYING CONVENTIONS

Elliot's classical record of several of the State Convention debates gives many an insight into the minds of early Americans on the subject of religion in the new nation.[46] The purpose of this examination has been a very specific one. Since Congress wrote the First Amendment to the Constitution in answer to demands

[45] Funk & Wagnalls *New Standard Dictionary* thus defines the "Test Act": 1. *Eng. Hist.* (1) The act of 25 Charles II., c. 2 (1672), requiring persons holding office, civil or military, or having a place of trust or receiving pay from the Crown, to take the oaths of allegiance and supremacy, subscribe a declaration against transubstantiation, and receive the sacrament of the Lord's Supper according to the usage of the Church of England. It was repealed by the Roman Catholic Relief Act, 1829. (2) Until 1871, in all English universities, a rule requiring subscription to the xxxix Articles of the Church of England as a necessary qualification for taking an academic degree. 2. *Scot. Hist.* An Act of 1681 imposing an oath on government and municipal officeholders declaring their adhesion to the true Protestant religion contained in the Confession of Faith. All tests were finally abolished by an act of 1889.

[46] Jonathan Elliot (ed.), *The Debates in the Several State Conventions on the Adoption of the Federal Constitution, as Recommended by the General Convention at Philadelphia in 1787, Together With the Journal of the Federal Convention, etc.* (5 vols.; second edition (1836), with considerable additions; Philadelphia: J. B. Lippincott & Co., 1881).

made in these conventions, it seems important to ascertain clearly what the State people wanted in the Bill of Rights concerning religion.

While paying the traditional tribute to the need and place of religion in public life, the conventions' delegates wanted two things: First, they desired that no national church be established, or, as they sometimes phrased it, that no particular sect be given a preference over others in the only field in which Congress was deemed competent—in the national field. Second, and even more fundamental, they wanted religious liberty, and they wanted Congress to refrain from that sort of participation to which they had been accustomed in colonial times—enforcement of specific beliefs by Governmental decree. This is seen in the following documents.

That religion is needed in public life was mentioned in the Massachusetts Convention in a striking speech by a "Mr. Turner." [47] "But I hope it will be considered," he declared

> by persons of all orders . . . that without the prevalence of Christian piety and morals, the best republican constitution can never save us from slavery and ruin. . . . The world of mankind have [sic] always, in general, been enslaved and miserable, and always will be, until there is a greater prevalence of Christian moral principles; nor have I any expectation of this, in any great degree, unless some superior mode of education shall be adopted.[48]

Turner then developed a plea for religious education with the following words:

> It is education which almost entirely forms the character . . . of the world. And if this Constitution shall be adopted, I hope the Continental legislature will have the singular honor, the indelible glory, of making it one of their first acts, . . . most earnestly to recommend to the several states in the Union the institution of such means of education as shall be adequate to the divine patriotic purpose of training up the children and

[47] It is not clear from Elliot who this "Mr. Turner" was. The late Richard K. Purcell, Professor of History at The Catholic University of America in Washington, in his unpublished notes on the Constitution, now in the Archives of The Catholic University of America, remarks: "Charles Turner of Scituate or [sic] Captain John Turner of Pembroke were both yes voters." Folder II, p. 7.

[48] Elliot, *op. cit.*, II, 171–72.

youth at large in that solid learning, and in those pious and moral principles, which are the support, the life and soul, of republican government and liberty, . . . May religion, with sanctity of morals, prevail and increase, that the patriotic civilian and ruler may have the sublime, parental satisfaction of eagerly embracing every opportunity of mitigating the rigors of government, in proportion to that increase of morality which may render the people more capable of being a law to themselves.[49]

In two other state conventions religion was emphasized as the bulwark of good government. "While the great body of freeholders are [sic] acquainted," said Governor Samuel Huntingdon in Connecticut, "with the duties which they owe to their God, to themselves, and to men, they will remain free." [50] In South Carolina, Charles Pinckney looked prayerfully to the founding of the Union as a "temple of our freedom." "Here we will pour out our gratitude," he declared, "to the Author of all good, for suffering us to participate in the rights of a people who govern themselves." [51]

Maryland's Attorney General, Luther Martin, gave his state convention an account of the drawing up of the proposed Constitution. He deplored the fact that whereas the colonists had revolted from England to secure "those rights to which God and nature had entitled us, . . . that we had appealed to the Supreme Being for his assistance, as the God of freedom, who could not but approve our efforts to preserve the *rights* which he had thus imparted to his creatures," [52] the American government was now proposing to insult that same God and laying itself open to His vengeful wrath by encouraging the African slave trade.

A number of state conventions heard pleas that the new Constitution be amended to rule out the possible establishment of a national religion. William Paca of Maryland proposed an Amendment "That there be no national religion established by law; but that all persons be equally entitled to protection in their religious liberty." [53] Samuel Spencer of North Carolina "was an advocate,"

[49] *Ibid.*, p. 172.
[50] *Ibid.*, p. 200.
[51] *Ibid.*, IV, 330.
[52] *Ibid.*, I, 373.
[53] *Ibid.*, II, 553.

says Elliot, "for securing every unalienable [*sic*] right, and that of worshipping God according to the dictates of conscience in particular. He therefore thought that no particular religion should be established." [54] Another North Carolina delegate, Richard D. Spaight, told the same convention:

> No power is given to the general government to interfere with it [religion] at all. Any act of Congress on this subject would be a usurpation.
> No sect is preferred to another. Every man has a right to worship the Supreme Being in the manner he thinks proper. . . . [55]

Other men in the North Carolina convention feared that there could be an establishment of some one religion, if religious tests for office-holders were ruled out. Henry Abbott, for instance, said, "Many wish to know what *religion* shall be established. . . . I am, for my part, against any exclusive establishment; but if there were any, I would prefer the Episcopal." [56]

Abbott's fears were answered by James Iredell: "I consider the clause under consideration [no religious tests]," he stated, "as one of the strongest proofs that could be adduced, that it was the intention of those who formed this system to establish a general religious liberty in America." [57] Later Iredell took up another objection that, whereas the Constitution guaranteed a republican form of government for each state, it did not offer the same insurance as to religious liberty. In answer he declared that such a guarantee would be an interference by the Federal Government in States' rights.[58] Thus, it seems clear that Iredell was concerned with the establishment of religion on a national scale.

In Virginia also, the delegates considered the danger of a national religion being established. Governor Edmund Randolph told the delegates to that convention that the impossibility of such an establishment was an adequate guarantee of the freedom of religion:

[54] *Ibid.*, IV, 200.
[55] *Ibid.*, p. 208.
[56] *Ibid.*, p. 192.
[57] *Ibid.*, p. 193.
[58] *Ibid.*, p. 195. Other interesting points were made by Iredell in this lengthy address.

. . . no power is given expressly to Congress over religion. . . .
Although officers etc. are to swear that they will support this
Constitution, yet they are not bound to support one mode of
worship, or to adhere to one particular sect. It puts all sects on
the same footing. A man of abilities and character, of any sect
whatever, may be admitted to any office or public trust under
the United States. I am a friend to a variety of sects, because
they keep one another in order. How many different sects are
we composed of throughout the United States! How many different sects will be in Congress! And there are now so many in
the United States, that they will prevent the establishment of
any one sect, in prejudice to the rest, and will forever oppose
all attempts to infringe religious liberty. If such an attempt be
made, will not the alarm be sounded throughout America? If
Congress should be so wicked as we are foretold they will be,
they would not run the risk of exciting the resentment of all,
or most, of the religious sects in America.[59]

Patrick Henry, however, was not satisfied that religious freedom would be protected. Passionately he pleaded for a Bill of
Rights. "I trust that gentlemen, on this occasion, will see the great
objects of religion, liberty of the press, trial by jury, interdiction
of cruel punishments, and every other sacred right, secured, before they agree to that paper." [60]

Henry was answered immediately by Randolph, who, when he
came again to religion, declared:

He has added religion to the objects endangered, in his conception. Is there any power given over it? Let it be pointed out.
Will he not be contented with the answer frequently given to
that objection? The variety of sects which abounds in the
United States is the best security for the freedom of religion.
No part of the Constitution, even if strictly construed, will jus-
tify a conclusion that the general government can take away or
impair the freedom of religion.[61]

Towards the end of the Virginia Convention, Zachariah Johnson took up the cudgel on Randolph's side:

We are also told that religion is not secured; that religious
tests are not required. You will find that the exclusion of tests
will strongly tend to establish religious freedom. If tests were

[59] Elliot, *op. cit.*, III, 204–05.
[60] *Ibid.*, p. 462.
[61] *Ibid.*, p. 469.

required, and if the Church of England, or any other, were established, I might be excluded from any office under the government, because my conscience might not permit me to take the test required.[62]

Johnson concludes by stating his belief that the "diversity of opinions and variety of sects" will protect religious liberty.[63]

The Virginia Convention finally did recommend adding a Bill of Rights to the Constitution. It submitted twenty provisos to be included therein. The last involved church establishment and religious liberty:

> 20th. That religion, or the duty which we owe to our Creator, and the manner of discharging it, can be directed only by reason and conviction, not by force or violence; and therefore that all men have an equal, natural, and unalienable [*sic*] right to the free exercise of religion, according to the dictates of conscience, and that no particular religious sect or society ought to be favored or established, by law, in preference to others.[64]

Elliot's accounts of the Convention debates in Pennsylvania, New Hampshire and New York contain no references to religious matters. Of the New Yorkers, Professor Purcell writes: "Never of the persecuted groups, and never victims of discrimination, the delegates from the substantial and well-bred ranks of the population were not especially worried about or interested in guarantees against religious disqualifications or the elimination of a privileged status for any ecclesiastical body." [65] Purcell's *Notes* also describe the material contained in a Master of Arts thesis at Columbia University.[66] "There were some serious debates," says Purcell, "on tests of religion for office." He adds that proponents said tests were traditional and needed. The opponents said that religion did not need the support of civil power.

In these state conventions, then, there were expressed sentiments supporting the thesis that religion belonged in public life.

[62] *Ibid.*, p. 645.
[63] *Ibid.*
[64] *Ibid.*, p. 659.
[65] Purcell *Notes*, Folder ii, p. 13.
[66] Nathaniel J. Eismann, *Ratification of the Federal Constitution by the State of New Hampshire* (unpublished Master's Thesis, New York: Columbia University, 1938). Cf. Purcell *Notes*, Folder iii, pp. 2–3.

Considerable opposition to the establishment of a national religion was heard, as well as an oft-repeated plea that men be left free to exercise religion according to the dictates of conscience. Where opposition to the government's dealing with religion was expressed, it revolved around that phase of establishment which they remembered from the heritage of England—the enforcing of belief by governmental decree. This was a form of support to religion against which their freedom-loving minds rebelled.

THE FIRST AMENDMENT

Congress answered the state conventions with what became the First Amendment to the Constitution, (and the first of the ten articles comprising the Bill of Rights):

> Congress shall make no law respecting an establishment of religion, or prohibiting the free exercise thereof; or abridging the freedom of speech, or of the press; or the right of the people peaceably to assemble, and to petition the government for a redress of grievances.[67]

The record of legislative debate and action by which the Congress arrived at the now-classic formula is fairly complicated. Details are to be found in the first volume of the *Annals of Congress,*[68] and *The Journal of the First Session of the Senate.*[69] In all, five versions of the Amendment were proposed and rejected before the sixth was adopted by the House. On September 25, 1789 the Senate voted to concur with the House, and the Amendment was ready to be given to the States for ratification.[70]

It is important to note that immediately following the record of this Senate decision comes the following:

> A Message from the House of Representatives—Mr. Beckley, their clerk, informed the Senate, that the House of Representa-

[67] Muzzey, *op. cit.,* Appendix II, p. XVII.

[68] Joseph Gales, Sr. (ed.), *The Debates and Proceedings in the Congress of the United States* (Washington: Gales and Seaton, 1834), Vol. 1.

[69] *Journal of the First Session of the Senate of the United States of America* (New York: Thomas Greenleaf, 1789).

[70] For a full discussion of the six versions of the Amendment, cf. the author's unpublished thesis at The Johns Hopkins University Library, pp. 89–94. Cf., also, Wilfrid Parsons, *The First Freedom,* pp. 30 f.

tives had passed a Resolve, appointing a Joint Committee "To wait on the President of the United States, to request that he would recommend to the people of the United States, a day of public Thanksgiving and Prayer to be observed." [71]

The Senate acted on the House resolve on September 27. Their Journal first records the *text* of the *House* document:

> Resolved, That a joint Committee of both Houses be appointed to wait on the President of the United States, to request that he would recommend to the People of the United States, a day of Public Thanksgiving and Prayer to be observed, by acknowledging with grateful hearts, the many and signal favors of ALMIGHTY GOD, especially by affording them an opportunity peaceably to establish a Constitution of Government for their safety and happiness.
> Ordered, That Mr. Boudinot, Mr. Sherman, and Mr. Sylvester be appointed of the said committee on the part of this House. [72]

The Senate then acted as follows:

> Resolved, That the Senate do concur in the above recited Resolution, and that Mr. Johnson, and Mr. Izard, be the committee on the part of the Senate. [73]

Thus, the First United States Congress ended its deliberations as its predecessor, the Continental Congress, had begun on July 4, 1776—with an acknowledgement of both the guiding hand of God in the affairs of men and of their duty as officials of a corporate society to lead its members to an expression of thanks for His goodness to the nation.

In all, twelve amendments had been offered for final discussion. Of these the one involving freedom of religion, speech, etc., was the third. The first two were ultimately rejected. Thus, Number Three became the First Amendment, and with the others formed the ten articles of the Bill of Rights. Having been ratified by the necessary number of states, they were declared a part of the Constitution by a proclamation of President Washington on December 15, 1791.

[71] *Journal of the First Session of the Senate* . . . , p. 151.
[72] *Ibid.*, p. 154.
[73] *Ibid.*

EARLY VIEWS OF THE FIRST AMENDMENT

The state conventions ratifying the Constitution had asked for an amendment prohibiting the establishment of a national religion and assuring the freedom of worship. The National Congress gave them the First Amendment. Did the people feel they had gotten what they wanted? Curiously, there seems to have been rather little writing on the subject of the Amendment in the years immediately following its becoming a part of the Constitution.

A direct reference was made to it by Thomas Jefferson in a "Letter to the Danbury Baptists" dated January 1, 1802. "Believing with you," he wrote:

> that religion is a matter which lies solely between man and his God, that he owes account to none other for his faith or his worship, that the legislative powers of government reach actions only, and not opinions, I contemplate with sovereign reverence that act of the whole American people which declared that their legislature should "make no law respecting an establishment of religion, or prohibiting the free exercise thereof," thus building a wall of separation between Church and State.[74]

This is the "wall of separation" metaphor which has been frequently quoted in current discussion of the First Amendment.[75] Actually it did not, of course, appear in either the Constitution or the First Amendment. It was written thirteen years later by a man who was not a participant in the writing of either document, as he was then serving the country in a diplomatic mission to France. Nevertheless, it is an interpretation of the meaning of the Amendment made by a great American statesman.[76]

[74] Saul K. Padover (ed.), *The Complete Jefferson* (New York: Duell, 1943), p. 518.

[75] Cf. *supra,* pp. 3, 4.

[76] It is clear that Jefferson believed the Amendment forbade the civil government to play the theologian and enforce by law the acceptance of creedal tenets. To him the phrase he used meant at least that. To that extent he may be represented as saying that a wall was erected between Church and State. When Jefferson says that a man owes account to none other than God for his faith and worship, he is emphasizing, if anything, the freedom-of-religion part of the Amendment. When he says, therefore, that the Amendment erected a wall of separation, he says he believes that neither a human being, as such, nor a collective group like the civil power, can force a man's conscience in matters of religion. This would seem to be his interpretation.

Another direct discussion on the meaning of the First Amendment is contained in Volume III of the commentary of Joseph Story, published in 1833 when this famous Associate Justice of the Supreme Court was a Professor of Law at Harvard University.[77]

The government has a right and duty to interfere in matters of religion, commenced Story, insofar as they affect the well-being of civil society. In the light of Christianity, government has a special duty to foster and encourage religion among all its citizens.[78]

The real difficulty arises, he continued, "in ascertaining the limits, to which government may rightly go in fostering and encouraging religion." [79]

He supposes three possibilities: 1—A government affords aid to a particular religion, leaving all persons free to adopt any other; 2—A government creates an ecclesiastical establishment for the propagation of the doctrines of a particular sect, and still leaves freedom to others; 3—A government creates the ecclesiastical establishment mentioned in No. 2 and rules out of all positions of public honor and trust anyone who does not belong to the established sect.[80]

Writing in favor of the first of the possibilities, Story went on to say that few would think it unreasonable for a government to encourage the Christian religion in general. Practically every American Colony down to the Revolution sustained some form of Christianity, and some states continue to do it to the present day [1833]. It is hard to see how a republic could wish to do otherwise; for Christianity is the friend of liberty. Some have thought, rightly or wrongly, he continued, that Protestantism is even more friendly to liberty than Catholicism, and so, has been carried from England to America.[81]

[77] Joseph Story, *Commentaries on the Constitution of the United States* (3 vols.; Boston: Hilliard, Gray & Co., 1833), Sections 1863–1873. Fragments of Story's commentary on the First Amendment are often quoted, but such a procedure misses the force of the whole document. Hence, it is summarized here and reproduced in full in Appendix "B" of the author's dissertation at The Johns Hopkins University Library.

[78] *Ibid.*, Sec. 1865.
[79] *Ibid.*, Sec. 1866.
[80] *Ibid.*, Sec. 1866.
[81] *Ibid.*, Sec. 1867.

Turning to the First Amendment, Story then observed:

Probably at the time of the adoption of the constitution, and of the amendment to it, now under consideration, the general, if not the universal, sentiment in America was, that Christianity ought to receive encouragement from the state, so far as was not incompatible with the private rights of conscience, and the freedom of religious worship. An attempt to level all religions, and to make it a matter of state policy to hold all in utter indifference, would have created universal disapprobation, if not universal indignation.[82]

"But the duty of supporting religion, and especially the Christian religion," the Justice continued, "is a very different thing from the right to force the consciences of other men, or to punish them for worshipping God in the manner, which, they believe their accountability to him requires."[83] The rights of conscience are beyond the reach of human power, an idea supported by the Virginia Bill of Rights, John Locke, and the precepts of both natural and revealed religion.

"The real object of the amendment," he declared

was, not to countenance, much less to advance Mahometanism, or Judaism, or infidelity, by prostrating Christianity; but to exclude all rivalry among Christian sects, and to prevent any national ecclesiastical establishment, which should give to an hierarchy the exclusive patronage of the national government.[84]

Thus, he said, the Amendment cut off the means of persecution, subversion of the rights of conscience and other allied evils.

After a digression to comment on some remarks of Blackstone, Story repeated his thesis—The dangers of ecclesiastical ambition and sectarian rivalry prompted the Amendment, which was to exclude the national government from all power to act on the subject of picking a national religion. The fact that some of the states already had establishments only heightened the danger, if the national government were "left free to create a religious establishment."[85] The prohibition against a national religion was followed by a declaration of the right of the free exercise of reli-

[82] *Ibid.*, Sec. 1868.
[83] *Ibid.*, Sec. 1870.
[84] *Ibid.*, Sec. 1871.
[85] *Ibid.*, Sec. 1873.

gion and [in the Constitution itself] a prohibition of religious tests for office. "Thus," concluded Justice Story

> the whole power over the subject of religion is left exclusively to the state governments, to be acted upon according to their own sense of justice, and the state constitutions; and the Catholic and the Protestant, the Calvinist and the Arminian, the Jew and the Infidel, may sit down at the common table of the national councils, without any inquisition into their faith, or mode of worship.[86]

The third document giving an interpretation of the First Amendment by statesmen of the nineteenth century is dated 1853. It is a Senate Committee Report answering a number of petitions made to the Thirty-Second Congress to abolish the system of appointing Chaplains for the Armed Forces and the two houses of Congress.[87] The objection was based on the First Amendment.

The Committee conceded that if the practice of appointing Chaplains did constitute "an establishment of religion" the procedure would have to be abolished immediately. So they turned to a discussion of the meaning of the term. Saying that the expression referred to what had existed in England, they declared that to be

> the connexion [sic] with the state of a particular religious society, by its endowment, at the public expense, in exclusion of, or in preference to, any other, by giving to its members exclusive political rights, and by compelling the attendance of those who rejected its communion upon its worship, or religious observances. These three particulars constituted that union of church and state of which our ancestors were so justly jealous, and against which they so wisely and carefully provided.[88]

The Committee went on to deny that any law Congress had ever passed effected such a union as described above. In the case

---

[86] *Ibid.*

[87] *Reports of Committees of the Senate,* 32nd Congress, 2nd Sess., 1852–1853; Senate Report No. 376, Jan. 19, 1853. (Washington: Robert Armstrong, 1853). This document is reproduced in full in Appendix "C" of the author's dissertation at The Johns Hopkins University Library.

[88] *Ibid.,* p. 1.

of the Chaplains of Congress no particular sect is singled out for preference. No compulsion is exercised upon a Congressman to attend. Therefore the choice of a Chaplain in no way infringes on religious liberty.

On the objection of the petitioners that the Congressmen should pay for their own religious services and not draw funds from the government to pay Chaplains, the Committee replied that if such an accommodation on the part of the government were ruled out, many other courtesies, such as messenger service, would have to be abolished. On the objection of the petitioners, "*A national Chaplaincy,* no less than a *national church* is considered by us emphatically an *establishment of religion,*" the Committee made reply:

> In no fair sense of the phrase have we a national chaplaincy; in no sense in which that phrase must be understood when connected, as it is by the petitioners, with a "national church." A national church implies a particular church selected as the church of the nation, endowed with peculiar privileges, or sustained or favored by the public in preference to other churches or religious societies. Of such a church we have no semblance, nor have we any such chaplaincy.[89]

The fact that Christians are appointed, the report continued, results from the voluntary choice of a Christian people, not from any provision of law. ". . . In a land thus universally Christian, what is to be expected, what desired, but that we shall pay a due regard to Christianity, and have a reasonable respect for its ministers and religious solemnities?" [90] Further, the petitioners were asked— Why do you not object to the universal observance of the Christian Sabbath by the closing of government offices as a national establishment of religion?

"The whole view of the petitioners," the Committee concluded, "seems founded upon mistaken conceptions of the meaning of the Constitution." [91] The fact that chaplaincies have existed from the beginning of the nation indicates that the framers of the Amend-

[89] *Ibid.,* p. 3.
[90] *Ibid.*
[91] *Ibid.,* p. 4.

ment saw no incongruity between the practice and the First Amendment. "Our fathers," they went on to say,

> were true lovers of liberty, and utterly opposed to any constraint upon the rights of conscience. They intended by this amendment to prohibit "an establishment of religion" such as the English church presented, or anything like it. But they had no fear or jealousy of religion itself, nor did they wish to see us an irreligious people. . . .[92]

The Senate Committee ended by saying that a practice (appointing chaplains) so ancient, so much approved by the founding fathers, and the entire nation, and so respected in itself should not be abolished.[93]

VIEWS ON CHURCH AND STATE IN THE
EARLY NATIONAL PERIOD

Although there seems to have been little written on the First Amendment as such in the years immediately following its enactment, there were certain things put into print on the relationship of Church and State and the importance of religious freedom.

In the *Kentucky Gazette,* published at Lexington, the issue for March 6, 1790 reproduced an article signed "A.B." from the *Virginia Independent Chronicle.*[94] It was a criticism of the paying of stipends to clergymen for opening sessions of the Virginia House of Delegates with prayer. Assuming that the article appeared in the *Chronicle* shortly before the *Gazette* reprint, it would have been written in the period between the final Congressional concurrence on the First Amendment (September 25, 1789) and its proclamation (December 15, 1791).

The writer declared he thought paying the chaplains was an unconstitutional practice. "The moment that a Minister is so fixed by law," he declared, "as to obtain a legal claim on the treasury, for religious services, that moment he becomes a Minister of State, and ceases to be a Gospel Ambassador. This is the very

[92] *Ibid.*

[93] *Ibid.* References to the Amendment in strictly educational contexts will be treated in subsequent chapters.

[94] Library of Congress, Washington, D. C., Department of Photostats, Ref. No. K 226.

principle of religious establishment, and should be exploded forever." [95]

Two small books, published in 1797, discuss the religious situation in the country at that time, without mentioning the First Amendment. The first was put out by John M'Cullogh and entitled *A Concise History of the United States from the Discovery of America Till 1795.*[96] Speaking of religion in Chapter VII, M'Cullogh described the pluralism of creeds in colonial days and the persecutions which occasionally broke out. In time it became evident that liberty of conscience was the best basis for security and happiness and guarantees of such liberty were written into the State Constitutions. One should not infer, continued the writer, that this meant any indifference towards the advancement of religion by Christian groups. The churches did not receive financial aid from the government, but all enjoyed its equal protection. "From this new state of things," he wrote, "the world will be able to determine, whether genuine Christianity is diminished by the want of civil or national establishments;—or whether these have not been a hindrance to the spreading of truth, and detrimental to morality as well as religion." [97]

The second booklet was entitled *The American Annual Register, or Historical Memoirs of the United States for the Year 1796.*[98] An anonymous article answers a piece of writing in the *New World* of November 30, 1796 signed by one "Pelham" and commenting unfavorably on the treatment of slaves in the South. The unknown writer of the *Register* article criticizes Pelham, evidently a Northerner, by attacking certain alleged ecclesiastical conditions in New England. The tyranny over the negro in the south is no worse an abuse of liberty than that of levying taxes to support the clergy in New England. This condemnation of the ecclesiastical establishment of the old Puritan states leads the writer to conclude with a generalized warning condemnatory of

[95] *Kentucky Gazette, num. cit.*

[96] John M'Cullogh (ed.), *A Concise History of the United States from the Discovery of America Till 1795 (With a Correct Map of the United States)* (2nd edition; Philadelphia: Printed & Sold by John M'Cullogh, 1797).

[97] *Ibid.*, pp. 185–86.

[98] *The American Annual Register, or Historical Memoirs of the United States for the Year 1796* (Philadelphia: Bioren & Madden, 1797).

the idea of establishment itself: "Americans ought to eye with horror everything resembling an established church." [99]

About the same time, a Catholic priest, Father John Carroll,[100] later the first American Catholic Bishop, wrote an answer to one "E.C." who had published an article favoring the establishment of Protestantism as the national religion. "E.C.'s" writing appeared in the *Gazette of the United States* published in New York City, May 9, 1789.[101]

Father Carroll's answer appeared in the *Gazette* of June 10, 1789. It was a plea for a real recognition of the rights of conscience. "Perhaps he [E.C.] is one of those who think it consistent with justice," he wrote

> to exclude certain citizens from the honors and emoluments of society merely on account of their religious opinions, provided they be not restrained by racks and forfeitures from the exercise of the religious worship which their consciences approve. If such are his views, in vain have Americans associated in one grand national union under the express condition of not being shackled by religious tests and under a firm persuasion that they were to retain, when associated, every natural right not expressly surrendered. . . . What character shall we give to a system of policy calculated for the express purpose of divesting rights legally acquired by those citizens who are not only unoffending but whose conduct has been highly meritorious? [102]

It seems impossible to read any hostility to religion as a way of life into the actions of the Founding Fathers in writing either the Constitution or the Bill of Rights. All that has been outlined so far in this study about the religious atmosphere of colonial life indicates a *social tradition* maintaining that religion belonged in the

[99] Cf. *ibid., passim* pp. 166–68. The intemperate vein of this article may be due to the *Register's* somewhat "liberal" spirit. This is suggested by the title of another of its articles, "Vindication of Paine's Rights of Man," and by a sweeping condemnation of twenty thousand printed sermons "because they do not condemn cruelty to animals." In essence, though, the article is a condemnation of the New England system which gave legal preference to one religious group over all others.

[100] John Carroll was the brother of Daniel Carroll, one of the statesmen who participated in the writing of the First Amendment.

[101] Cf. J. Moss Ives, *The Ark and the Dove, The Beginning of Civil and Religious Liberties in America* (New York: Longmans, Green & Co., 1936), pp. 387–88.

[102] Cf. *ibid.,* pp. 389–90.

world in which the Fathers had spent their days prior to the birth of the new nation. Their quarrel with the mother country had, indeed, a religio-philosophical basis. But at bottom it was not a revolt of atheists, or even of deists, against theists. Religion had been a part of their lives. They had not gone to war to eliminate religion. They did not legislate to eliminate it by their Bill of Rights.

But the former colonists, now the people of an independent state, wanted to be free. Devoted, as they were, to the doctrine of the divinely bestowed, and therefore natural, rights of man, they wanted to be free of the encroachments of the British King and his ministers. They also wanted to be free from the dictation of a national church such as England had.

When they turned to the problem of religion in their religiously pluralistic American society, their philosophy of government faced a dilemma. On the one hand, they must rule out a national, preferred status for any one sect, or any group of sects, then existing within their borders. On the other hand, they must give the members of these sects the right to worship God as their consciences dictated. A policy had to be formed. The First Amendment was a declaration of this policy. The national government was not to play the part of a theologian. It was to refrain from anything which would dictate to the sects their manner of worshiping God. The religio-philosophical basis of the policy was the desire of these liberty-loving statesmen to respect the rights of conscience, which they considered to be fundamental among the God-given natural rights of man.

This theme was observable in the debates on the ratification of the Constitution. There was a provision on the rights of conscience in each of the six versions of the First Amendment offered in the National Congress at Philadelphia. Justice Story emphasized it in the Sections from 1870 to the end of the Commentary quoted above. "The duty of supporting religion . . . is very different from the right to force the consciences of other men. . . . The real object of the Amendment was . . . to exclude all rivalry among Christian sects. . . ." [103] This seems to be the quintessence of what the Founding Fathers meant by the First Amendment.

[103] Cf. *supra*, p. 41.

But whatever may be the differences of view with regard to the historical meaning and scope of the First Amendment, it seems important to suggest here that it was not originally intended to regulate the problem of the relation between government and religion-in-education. This problem, as a constitutional problem, did not exist at the time. Our next chapter will pick up the educational thread where we left it in the story of colonial schooling. Are we to find, as of 1776 and onward, any radical changes in the religious-educational policies and practices which were designed to prepare children for life in the new republic?

CHAPTER III

Old Practices Continue

1776-1827

THE PROVISIONS for religious education—from 1776 to 1827, when Massachusetts became the first state to pass a law on the subject of sectarianism in the public schools—will be examined under four headings: State Constitutions; State Laws; Plans for New Schools Made by Private Citizens; School Practices.

State Constitutions

Around the time of the Declaration of Independence the colonies drafted new constitutions, and by 1800 all of the thirteen original states except Connecticut and Rhode Island were operating under them. The two states last mentioned continued for a time under their colonial charters, Connecticut passing a Constitution in 1818 and Rhode Island in 1842. Some of these early constitutions mentioned education and some did not. All of them had some reference to religion, and in some are to be found provisions for religion in education.

A reading of these constitutions discloses a *continuum* with the spirit of colonial times regarding the important place religion was to hold in public life. It has been seen in Chapter I that such stress on religion formed the basis of its inclusion in the scholastic curriculum. In some of the state constitutions the connection between religion and education is specifically made, although such phrases as "public instruction in morality and religion" and "public protestant teachers of piety, religion and morality" *may* have referred to clergymen as preachers in their pulpits rather than teachers in schools. Yet, some ministers exercised both functions.

Of the states which had been the thirteen English colonies, Pennsylvania, New Hampshire, Georgia and Massachusetts mentioned religious education in their Constitutions. In *Pennsylvania,* the Constitution (1776) declared, in Section 44:

> A school or schools shall be established in each county by the legislature, for the convenient instruction of youth . . .[1]

Immediately following (in Section 45) were provisos concerning religion:

> Laws for the encouragement of virtue, and prevention of vice and immorality, shall be made and constantly kept in force, and provision shall be made for their due execution: And all religious societies or bodies of men heretofore united or incorporated for the advancement of religion or learning, or for other pious and charitable purposes, shall be encouraged and protected in the enjoyment of the privileges, immunities and estates which they were accustomed to enjoy, or could of right have enjoyed, under the laws and former constitution of this state.[2]

In 1790 the Pennsylvania Legislature assembled for a review and amending of the 1776 Constitution. In Article VII, Section 3, however, they declared:

> The rights, privileges, immunities, and estates of religious societies and corporate bodies shall remain as if the constitution of this state had not been altered or amended.[3]

[1] Francis Newton Thorpe, *The Federal and State Constitutions, Colonial Charters, and Other Organic Laws of the States, Territories and Colonies Now or Heretofore Forming the United States of America* (7 vols.; Washington: Government Printing Office, 1909), I, 30.

[2] *Ibid.*

[3] *Ibid.,* p. 3099.

Thus, Pennsylvania legislated on both education and religion in its Constitution.

New Hampshire's first attempt at a Constitution was made in 1776. This document, actually started in 1775, was completed on January 5, 1776.[4] Another constitution, however, was approved in 1784 and became the governing document. Articles iv and v declared that among the inalienable rights of man was that of worshipping God according to the dictates of one's conscience, limited only in that he might not disturb the public peace or the worship of his neighbor. Article vi proceeded to discuss at some length the need of religious education:

As morality and piety, rightly grounded on evangelical principles, will give the best and greatest security to government, and will lay in the hearts of men the strongest obligations to due subjection; and as the knowledge of these, is most likely to be propagated through a society by the institution of the public worship of the DEITY, and of public instruction in morality and religion; therefore, to promote these important purposes, the people of this state have a right to empower, and do hereby fully empower the legislature to authorize from time to time, the several towns, parishes, bodies-corporate, or religious societies within this state, to make adequate provision at their own expence [sic], for the support and maintenance of public protestant teachers of piety, religion and morality:

Provided notwithstanding, That the several towns, parishes, bodies corporate, or religious societies, shall at all times have the exclusive right of electing their own public teachers, and of contracting with them for their support and maintenance. And no portion of any one particular religious sect or denomination, shall ever be compelled to pay towards the support of the teacher or teachers of another persuasion, sect or denomination.

And every denomination of christians demeaning themselves quietly, and as good subjects of this state, shall be equally under the protection of the law; and no subordination of any one sect or denomination to another, shall ever be established by law.

And nothing herein shall be understood to affect any former contracts made for the support of the ministry; but all such contracts shall remain, and be in the same state as if this constitution had not been made.[5]

4 *Ibid.,* iv, 2451, footnote "a."
5 *Ibid.,* p. 2454.

The New Hampshire Constitution, then, spoke out for "public protestant teachers." The point of greatest interest for this study is the clear desire of the legislators that religion be a part of state education.[6]

Georgia's Legislature unanimously agreed to their constitution on February 5, 1777. Article LIV read: "Schools shall be erected in each county, and supported at the general expense of the State, as the Legislature shall hereafter point out." [7] Article LVI provided that

> All persons whatever shall have the free exercise of their religion; provided it be not repugnant to the peace and safety of the State; and shall not, unless by consent, support any teacher or teachers except those of their own profession.[8]

Oaths were prescribed in connection with various functions; and only Protestants could be elected to the Assembly, though clergymen were barred from seats in this body. Interestingly, it was prescribed that on the reverse side of the State seal, amid signs of material prosperity such as "an elegant house," sheep and cattle in meadows, etc., was to be written the motto *"Deus nobis haec otia fecit."* [9]

Massachusetts passed its constitution in 1780. This document was the most elaborate of the entire original group. The Preamble acknowledged

> with grateful hearts, the goodness of the great Legislator of the universe, in affording us, in the course of His providence an opportunity . . . of entering into . . . a compact with each other.[10]

[6] *Vermont* was not one of the original colonies but was formed in 1777 of territory which had been claimed by New Hampshire and New York. In the same year a Constitution was written and was ratified by the sessions of the Legislature in 1779 and 1782 (Thorpe, *op. cit.*, VI, 3737, footnote "b"). The Constitution had a preamble and several articles on religion in general. Then in Sections 40 and 41 it repeated almost *verbatim* Sections 44 and 45 of the Pennsylvania Constitution on education (Thorpe, *op. cit.*, VI, 3748). Section 41 of the Vermont Constitution was unchanged in the revisions of 1787 and 1793 (*Thorpe, op. cit,* VI, 3760, 3770–71).

[7] Thorpe, *op. cit.*, II, 784.

[8] *Ibid.*

[9] *Ibid.*, 779–85 *passim.* The motto could be translated: "God has provided for us these good things of life."

[10] *Ibid.*, III, 1889.

Articles 2 and 3 of "Part the First" dealt with religion. Article 2 declared that "It is the right as well as the duty of all men in society, publicly, and at stated seasons, to worship the SUPREME BEING, the Great Creator and Preserver of the universe." Therefore, the Article provided, no one was to be molested "for worshipping God in the manner and season most agreeable to the dictates of his own conscience." [11]

Religious education was enjoined and cared for in Article III:

As the happiness of a people, and the good order and preservation of civil government, essentially depend upon piety, religion, and morality; and as these cannot be generally diffused through a community but by the institution of the public worship of God, and of public instructions in piety, religion, and morality: Therefore, to promote their happiness, and to secure the good order and preservation of their government, the people of this commonwealth have a right to invest their legislature with power to authorize and require, and the legislature shall, from time to time, authorize and require, the several towns, parishes, precincts, and other bodies politic; or religious societies, to make suitable provision, at their own expense, for the institution of the public worship of GOD, and for the support and maintenance of public Protestant teachers of piety, religion, and morality, in all cases where such provision shall not be made voluntarily.

And the people of this commonwealth have also a right to, and do, invest their legislature with authority to enjoin upon all the subjects an attendance upon the instructions of the public teachers aforesaid, at stated times and seasons, if there be any on whose instructions they can conscientiously and conveniently attend. . . .

And all monies paid by the subject to the support of public worship, and of the public teachers aforesaid, shall, if he require it, be uniformly applied to the support of the public teacher or teachers of his own religious sect or denomination, provided there be any on whose instruction he attends; otherwise it may be paid towards the support of the teacher or teachers of the parish or precinct in which the said monies are raised. . . .[12]

Article 18 of the Bill of Rights of the Massachusetts Constitution reads:

[11] *Ibid.*
[12] *Ibid.*, pp. 1889–90.

A frequent recurrence to the fundamental principles of the Constitution, and a constant adherence to those of piety, justice, moderation, temperance, industry, and frugality, are absolutely necessary to preserve the advantages of liberty, and to maintain a free government. The people ought, consequently, to have a particular attention to all those principles, in the choice of their officers and representatives: and they have a right to require of their lawgivers and magistrates an exact and constant observance of them, in the formation and execution of the laws necessary for the good administration of the Commonwealth.[13]

In Article 2 of Chapter II (on Executive Power) among the qualifications of a candidate for the Governorship it was noted that "he shall declare himself to be of the Christian religion." [14] The same was required of the lieutenant-governor.[15]

Article 1 of Chapter VI (on Oaths etc.) prescribe the following oath for all officers, from the Governor through both houses of the Legislature:

I, A.B., do declare, that I believe the Christian religion, and have a firm persuasion of its truth. . . .[16]

Thus did the Commonwealth of Massachusetts write provision upon provision on religion and education into its Constitution. The Massachusetts story will be followed with particularly close attention in later parts of this study because of the leadership the state exercised in American public education. Suffice it to note here how Massachusetts stressed the same point that we have seen stressed so frequently in other State Constitutions—Religion is a duty of the community as well as of the individual. Massachusetts was particularly emphatic in stating that religious practice and benefits should be extended through education.[17]

---

[13] *Ibid.*, p. 1892.
[14] *Ibid.*, p. 1900.
[15] *Ibid.*, p. 1903.
[16] *Ibid.*, p. 1908.
[17] Special attention should be drawn to the frequent use in these constitutions of the word "piety." It is defined in the dictionary as: "1. Controlling reverence toward God, indicated by loving conformity to his will; religious devoutness, godliness; 2. Religiousness in general; 3. [Archaic] Filial honor and obedience; Grateful honor as due to Superiors, benefactors or country." There is little doubt that the word is used in these early documents in the first

The Constitutions of the other nine states did not make so clear a connection between religion and education as has been found in the cases of Pennsylvania, New Hampshire, Georgia and Massachusetts. In every one of the nine documents, however, religion itself received prominent mention. If one finds statements on the necessity of acknowledging God by public worship, of the state's duty to guarantee freedom of religion and protect the rights of conscience in these documents, it indicates a conviction that religion belongs in the public as well as private life of the community. As indicated above,[18] the implied connection between religion and education will be seen in the plans and enactments in these states to be examined later in this chapter.[19]

Thus, for example, *Delaware's* constitution of 1776 enjoined all officers of the state to swear belief in the Trinity and the divine inspiration of the Old and New Testaments.[20] The state drew up a second constitution in 1792. Its preamble stated that "Through divine goodness all men have, by nature, the rights of worshipping and serving their Creator, according to the dictates of their consciences . . ."[21]

Section I, Article I began "Although it is the duty of all men frequently to assemble together for the public worship of the Author of the Universe, and piety and morality, on which the prosperity of communities depends, are thereby promoted, . . ."[22] It then went on to proclaim freedom of conscience, ruled out preferential treatment of any religious groups, and eliminated the religious test for office.

The *Maryland* Constitution of 1776 stressed religious liberty in Articles XXXIII to XXXVI. The first of these Articles declared:

---

and/or second sense, as the third meaning was current mostly in ancient Rome. With the fullness of expression characteristic of the writings of those times, it is placed *before* "religion" in the series—"piety, religion, morality." The word "piety" will be used again and again in documents to be quoted subsequently in this study. Its true meaning should not be lost. For all practical purposes, it is synonymous with "religion."

[18] Cf. *supra*, p. 50.

[19] Cf. *infra*, pp. 67–69 (New York); p. 73 (South Carolina); p. 71 (Connecticut); p. 74 (North Carolina).

[20] Thorpe, *op. cit.*, I, 566.

[21] *Ibid.*, p. 568.

[22] *Ibid.*

That, as it is the duty of every man to worship God as he thinks most acceptable to him; all persons, professing the Christian religion, are equally entitled to protection in their religious liberty. . . .[23]

In *New Jersey's* Constitution of 1776, Articles xviii and xix concerned religious liberty—Article xviii commenced "That no person shall ever, within this colony, be deprived of the inestimable privilege of worshipping Almighty God in a manner agreeable to the dictates of his own conscience. . . ." [24]

Article xix ruled out "the establishment of any one religious sect . . . in preference to another" and decreed that no Protestant was to be denied civil rights merely on account of his religious principles, and that any Protestant in good civil standing could be elected to office.[25]

The *Virginia* Constitution, written in 1776, was preceded by a Bill of Rights adopted on June 12. The constitution was adopted on June 29.[26] The last section (16) of the Bill of Rights embodied the feelings of the Virginia Legislature on religious liberty:

That religion, or the duty which we owe to our Creator, and the manner of discharging it, can be directed only by reason and conviction, not by force or violence; and therefore all men are equally entitled to the free exercise of religion, according to the dictates of conscience; and that it is the mutual duty of all to practice Christian forebearance, love, and charity towards each other.[27]

New York's Constitution, written by John Jay, was adopted April 20, 1777.[28] After prescribing oaths or affirmations for officeholders in Article 8, the text turned to religion in Articles 35, 38, and 39. In Article 35, while adopting the basic laws of England, those which "may be construed to establish or maintain any par-

[23] *Ibid.,* iii, 1689. In the phrase "most acceptable to him," it is not clear whether the pronoun refers to "every man" or to "God." Several editions of the constitution were examined and they all have the "him" with a small h. This might indicate, but does not prove, that the "him" is not "God." Yet the word "acceptable" seems to us to indicate God rather than man.

[24] *Ibid.,* v, 2597.

[25] *Ibid.*

[26] *Ibid.,* vii, 3812, footnote "a."

[27] *Ibid.,* p. 3814.

[28] *Ibid.,* v, 2624.

ticular denomination of Christians or their ministers . . ." were rejected.[29]

Article 38 established liberty of conscience with the remark that "we are required . . . to guard against that spiritual oppression and intolerance wherewith the bigotry and ambition of weak and wicked priests and princes have scourged mankind." [30]

In *South Carolina,* a Constitution was adopted on March 26, 1776.[31] Article xxxviii was a long declaration on religion: ". . . The Christian Protestant religion shall be deemed, and is hereby constituted and declared to be, the established religion of this State." [32] All Protestants were to enjoy equal religious and civil privileges. Any Protestants who formed a Church might incorporate the same under state laws, provided they had previously agreed to the following five articles:

1st—That there is one eternal God, and a future state of rewards and punishments.
2nd—That God is publicly to be worshipped.
3rd—That the Christian religion is the true religion.
4th—That the holy scriptures of the Old and New Testaments are of divine inspiration, and are the rule of faith and practice.
5th—That it is lawful and the duty of every man being thereunto called by those that govern, to bear witness to the truth.[33]

The article went on to prescribe the manner of taking oaths, gave the people the right to choose their ministers, provided the minister should promise, in addition to his acceptance of the five points already mentioned, to instruct the people in orthodox doctrine, care for the sick, conduct prayer meetings, make himself and his family Christian exemplars, and promote peace and love in the community. The rest of the article protected the rights of church groups and gave permanent title to lands held by the formerly-established Church of England.[34]

---

[29] *Ibid.,* p. 2636.
[30] *Ibid.* This remark, more vitriolic than usual in the early constitutions, is attributed by Professor Purcell's *Notes* to the implacable and life-long hatred of the Catholic Church on the part of John Jay. Cf. also, John Talbot Smith, *The Catholic Church in New York* (New York: Hall Locke Co., 1905), I, 25.
[31] Thorpe, *op. cit.,* vi, 3241, footnote "a."
[32] *Ibid.,* p. 3255.
[33] *Ibid.,* p. 3256.
[34] *Ibid.,* pp. 3256–57.

In the Constitution of *North Carolina*, drawn up in 1776, both religion and education were mentioned, but without any connection being made between the two. On the subject of religion, Article 19 briefly stated "that all men have a natural and inalienable right to worship Almighty God according to the dictates of their own consciences." [35] Article 32 eliminated the clergyman from the Legislature "while he continues in the exercise of the pastoral function." [36] Article 33 denied office or place of trust or profit in the "Civil department of the State to anyone

> who shall deny the being of God or the truth of the Protestant Religion, or the divine authority of the Old or New Testaments, or who shall hold religious principles incompatible with the freedom and safety of the State.[37]

For education, the Constitution provided in Section 41:

> That a school or schools shall be established by the Legislature, for the convenient instruction of youth, with such salaries to the masters, paid by the public, as may enable them to instruct at low prices; . . .[38]

Connecticut and *Rhode Island* used their colonial charters for some years after becoming states. In 1818 Connecticut adopted a Constitution which contained this Preamble:

> The people of Connecticut, acknowledging with gratitude the good providence of God in having permitted them to enjoy a free government, . . .[39]

Article 1 is a Declaration of Rights. Section 3 says—

> The exercise and enjoyment of religious profession and worship, without discrimination, shall be forever free to all persons in this State, provided that the right hereby declared and established shall not be so construed as to excuse acts of licentiousness, or to justify practices inconsistent with the peace and safety of the State.[40]

[35] *Ibid.*, v, 2788.
[36] *Ibid.*, p. 2793.
[37] *Ibid.*
[38] *Ibid.*, p. 2794. Note similarity to Pennsylvania (*supra*, p. 50).
[39] *Ibid.*, i, 536–37.
[40] *Ibid.*, p. 537.

Section 4 declared that "No preference shall be given by law to any Christian sect or mode of worship." [41]

Article 7 of Connecticut's Constitution was entitled "Of Religion":

> Section 1—It being the duty of all men to worship the Supreme Being, the Great Creator and Preserver of the Universe, and their right to render that worship in the mode most consistent with the dictates of their consciences, no person shall by law be compelled to support, nor be classed with, or associated to, any congregation, church, or religious association.[42]

The section went on to declare that the several denominations of Christians should enjoy the same rights to choose their ministers, build their churches, and tax their members.

The Constitution of Rhode Island was not written and adopted until 1842. To be complete in our survey of the original thirteen states, however, we note that its Preamble expressed gratitude to God for religious liberty, establishing such liberty as the law of the State, and ordained the establishment of public schools, the funds collected for them being restricted to this purpose and no other.[43]

This review of the religious and educational provisions in the Constitutions of the thirteen original states seems to indicate that the colonial acceptance of religion as a part of public life, though somewhat modified, had not been basically changed. The duty of men, both individually and as members of society, to acknowledge, thank and worship God was at the heart of colonial life, and it stayed at the root of constitutional declarations in the early national period. The modification which occurred was in the recognition of the rights of conscience guaranteed to citizens by both the Federal and State clauses on religious liberty.

One sees in these declarations the formal expression of a "social tradition." Whether completely or only partially lived up to by the people in their daily lives, this tradition, or preference for a basically religious way of life, was characteristic of the colonies and the young republic. Secularism, a philosophy that allows

[41] *Ibid.*
[42] *Ibid.*, p. 545.
[43] *Ibid.*, vi, 3222–23 and 3233–34.

little part to the claims of God and the religious duties of the people in the conduct of civic affairs, did not appear when the legislators wrote their several state constitutions.[44]

One might ask whether the many declarations in favor of religion which have been found in these State Constitutions represent more lip service behind which there lay no solid conviction. The evidence in the rest of this chapter of continued efforts at religious instruction in the schools would seem to argue that the constitutional statements were not mere formalities. Another enlightening source is found in the writings of Alexis de Tocqueville, a visitor from France, who gave his impressions after a visit to the United States in 1831.[45]

De Tocqueville told how he found religion deeply embedded in American society in his day:

> It must never be forgotten that religion gave birth to Anglo-American society. . . . In America religion has, as it were, laid down its own limits. Religious institutions have remained wholly distinct from political institutions. . . . Christianity has therefore retained a strong hold on the public mind in America; . . . In the United States Christian sects are infinitely diversified and perpetually modified; but Christianity itself is a fact so irresistibly established, that no one undertakes either to attack or to defend it. The Americans, having admitted the principal doctrines of the Christian religion without inquiry,

[44] It seems important to note how frequently in this chapter and the preceding one the religious liberty concept has been phrased according to "the *dictates* of conscience." The legislators seem to have recognized that the promptings of a man's conscience are *imperatives*. He is to be left free to worship God *as his conscience tells him he must worship God*. This is not the same idea as one gets from the modern phrase—"worship God as you please." No matter how widespread or narrowspread the latter notion of religious liberty may be in the minds of Americans today, it is *not accurate* to read it into the minds of our forefathers. To make religious freedom imply the "do-as-you-please" note is to change "dictates of conscience" to "allurements of convenience," or something of the sort. Liberty is the freedom to do what is right, as the human conscience understands what is right. Freedom to do what one pleases is not liberty, but license. It is the former notion of religious liberty which is expressed in the State Constitutions which have been examined. The impact of the notion on American education will be noted throughout the rest of this study.

[45] Alexis de Tocqueville, *The Republic of the United States of America* (Translation of *De La Democratie en Amerique*, by Henry Reeves) (New York: Edward Walker, 1849).

are obliged to accept in like manner a great number of moral truths originating in it and connected with it.[46]

The religious intensity of which De Tocqueville spoke, he attributed to the policy of Church-State separation which he found acceptable to all he met:

> . . . the religious aspect of the country was the first thing that struck my attention; and the longer I stayed there, the more did I perceive the political consequences . . . in America I found that they [spirit of religion and of freedom] were intimately united, and that they reigned in common over the same country. My desire to discover the causes of this phenomenon increased from day to day. . . . I found that they [Americans, especially clergymen] mainly attributed the peaceful dominion of religion in their country, to the separation of Church and State.[47]

Later, De Tocqueville commented upon the absence of public-office-holding among the American clergy, but made, in a footnote, an important qualification regarding education: "Unless this term ["public appointments"] be applied to the functions which many of them fill in the schools. Almost all education is intrusted [sic] to the clergy." [48]

According to the degree one allows for the safe word "almost" in the above sentence, one would agree or disagree with the writer. Yet, the impression of educational practice recorded here, and elsewhere, in De Tocqueville's book indicates that the tie-up of education and religion was still strong. Speaking in another place of education, e.g., the writer from France remarked:

> In New England, every citizen receives the elementary notions of human knowledge; he is moreover taught the doctrines and the evidences of his religion, the history of his country, and the leading features of its constitution. In the states of Connecticut and Massachusetts, it is extremely rare to find a man imperfectly acquainted with all these things, and a person wholly ignorant of them is a sort of phenomenon.[49]

---

[46] *Ibid.*, Part ii, 4–5.
[47] *Ibid.*, Part i, 337.
[48] *Ibid.*
[49] *Ibid.*, 345.

"What I have said of New England," he observed later on the same page, "must not, however, be applied indiscriminately to the whole Union: as we advance toward the west or the south, the instruction of the people diminishes."

The Forming of State Education Laws

Although all the former colonies were working to some degree on their educational systems after the Revolutionary War, more was being planned in Virginia, Massachusetts and New York than anywhere else. In the case of these three states, we shall examine both the preliminary proposals and the resulting state laws. In the other states only such laws as were found will be discussed.

In Virginia, in 1779, Thomas Jefferson presented a "Bill for the More General Diffusion of Knowledge" [50] to the Legislature. In it he proposed that each county would have its school system. For a curriculum, Jefferson proposed that in the county schools

> shall be taught reading, writing, and common arithmetick [sic], and the books which shall be used therein for instructing the children to read shall be such as will at the same time make them acquainted with Grecian, Roman, English and American history.[51]

Though this proposal of Thomas Jefferson was never passed into law, it represents, as a plan for elementary public educa-

[50] "Thomas Jefferson's Bill 'For the More General Diffusion of Knowledge,' introduced into the Legislature of Virginia, 1779" in Edgar W. Knight and Clifton L. Hall, *Readings in American Educational History* (New York: Appleton-Century-Crofts, Inc., 1951), pp. 299–306. (Future references to this collection will be listed: Knight-Hall, *Readings*.)

[51] *Ibid.*, p. 301. In his *Documentary History of Education in the South Before 1860*, II, 151, Knight reproduces a section from Jefferson's *Notes on the State of Virginia* (1782) wherein the Virginia statesman shifted his position slightly towards a deferment of religious studies until a later than elementary school age rather than a total elimination of them: "Instead, therefore, of putting the Bible and Testament into the hands of the children at an age when their judgements are not sufficiently matured for religious inquiries, their memories may here be stored with the most useful facts from Grecian, Roman, European and American history."

tion, something of a radical departure from the colonial pattern. The purpose Jefferson had in mind is described in the beginning of the Bill: "To protect individuals in the free exercise of their natural rights." [52] To do this he planned, first, by general education "to illuminate, as far as practicable, the minds of the people at large," and, second, by select education, to train leaders, "that those persons whom nature has endowed with genius and virtue should be rendered by liberal education worthy to receive and able to guard the sacred deposit of the rights and liberties of their fellow citizens." [53]

The radicality of Jefferson's proposal is nowhere more clearly shown than in the omission of any mention of religion in the curriculum. The man who, three years before, had written in the "Declaration of Independence" of the "inalienable rights" given to man by his "Creator," now proposed to begin the preparation of the people and their leaders to retain their rights without laying any basis in study of "nature's God," Who is responsible for the rights.

The explanation, if such it be, lies in a consideration of Jefferson's religious beliefs and his notion of liberty. Though nominally an Episcopalian, and actually a vestryman of that Church in Virginia,[54] he is generally accepted to have been deistic.[55]

Religion, then, for Jefferson, as for any deist, would tend to be homocentric rather than theocentric. Its emphasis will be almost exclusively on how man conceives his position with regard to God and will take little or no account of how God may wish man to act towards Himself.

The stress will be on man and on man's intellect and conscience unaided and alone. Thus, Jefferson took the idea of human liberty and exalted it for all practical purposes to the position of an idol he placed upon his altar for worship. Human liberty was a concept, for him so great, that there was little room for anything else. Consequently, in Jefferson's mind the *first* and *greatest*

---

[52] *Ibid.*, pp. 297–300.

[53] *Ibid.*, p. 300.

[54] Marie G. Kimball, *Jefferson* (3 vols.; New York: Coward McCann, Inc., 1941), I, *The Road to Glory*, 124.

[55] *Supra*, p. 25.

American ideal was the establishment and preservation of liberty. In an education program he would look to this first and concentrate on it exclusively. Hence the school plan he outlined for the State of Virginia.

This is not to call Jefferson an atheist or an irreligious man. He valued religion and admired Christianity. But it was a concept of religion and Christianity which was the fruit of his deism. He wanted, as we might expect, a man's conscience left free. "I have sworn," he once wrote, "upon the altar of God eternal hostility against every form of tyranny over the mind of man." [56]

In 1776 Jefferson had written his famous "Statute of Religious Freedom." At that time opposition to it was so violent that it failed to pass the assembly. It did become the law of the State, however, ten years later, when he was absent from America as Minister to France. He considered it the greatest achievement of his life and wished that it be included in his epitaph.[57] His tombstone reads today, in part, "Author . . . of the Statute of Virginia for religious freedom . . ." [58]

"The right of conscience," he wrote in the Bill,

> we have never submitted [to the State]; we could not submit. We are answerable only to our God. The legitimate powers of government extend to such acts only as are injurious to others, but it does me no injury for my neighbor to say there are 20 gods or no god. . . . Reason and free inquiry are the only effectual agents against error. Give a loose to them, they will support the true religion by bringing every false one to their tribunal, to the test of their investigation. They are the natural enemies of error and of error only.[59]

Thus, against all human tyranny did he truly war. Also, it must be said, in this exaltation of human reason he did oppose, consciously or unconsciously, the claims over the human mind of revealed religion to be the express will of God regarding the conduct of the human race. If such be not the case in theory, it

[56] Letter to Dr. Benjamin Rush, September 23, 1800. Cf. Marie Kimball, *Jefferson*, I, *The Road to Glory*, p. 228.
[57] Kimball, *op. cit.*, I, 225–26.
[58] Stokes, *op. cit.*, I, Illustration 26.
[59] Kimball, *op. cit.*, I, 226–27.

is difficult to see that it would work itself out otherwise in practice.

As stated above, Jefferson's plan for education was never put into effect. Nor is there a great deal of evidence to indicate that much else was done in this state towards public education for a number of years. In 1796 the General Assembly of Virginia passed an act to establish public schools. In the text of the enactment as given by Knight [60] there is no mention of any religious instruction or other religious element for the curriculum. Indeed, the only reference to any subject matter is the brief statement in Article VI: "At every one of these schools shall be taught reading, writing and common Arithmetic." [61] A later picture of the Virginia situation will be given in a subsequent chapter.[62]

The importance of religion in public life and in education received early stress in Massachusetts. In 1789, the General Court (as the Bay State Legislature is called) passed "An Act to Provide for the Instruction of Youth and for the Promotion of Good Education." [63] It enjoined upon all instructors at public institutions:

> . . . to take diligent care and exert their best endeavors, to impress on the minds of children and youth committed to their care and instruction, the principles of piety, justice and a sacred regard to truth, love to their country, humanity and universal benevolence, sobriety, industry, frugality, chastity, moderation and temperance, and those other virtues which are the ornament of human society and the basis upon which the republican Constitution is structured; . . .[64]

The law of 1789 also contained provisions that teachers should have their moral character certified by a clergyman, that the ministers (and other selectmen on the school boards) should use their influence to get children to attend school and that they themselves should visit the schools at least once every six months to see to

---

[60] Knight, *A Documentary History of Education in the South Before 1860,* II, 153–56.

[61] *Ibid.,* p. 155. The same may be said for the first statewide enactment for public schools in South Carolina, passed in 1811. Cf. Knight, *op. cit.,* pp. 156–59.

[62] Cf. *infra,* pp. 231–32.

[63] *Laws of Massachusetts,* 1788–89; Acts, 1789, Chapter 19, pp. 416–21.

[64] *Ibid.,* p. 417.

the operation of the institution and the proficiency of the scholars. The statute then reemphasized the duty of the teacher to instill in the children's minds "a sense of piety and virtue, and to teach them decent behaviour." [65]

The Massachusetts General Court was to hear more about the importance of religion in public life and in education. On June 3, 1800 the State's Governor Caleb Strong opened the legislative session with the following warning and plea:

> There is perhaps no opinion, which has more generally prevailed among civilized nations, than—that religious principles in the People, are essential to morality, and a principal support of lawful government; and that the obligation to piety, is imposed on man, by his nature— If lately opinions opposite to these are patronized, and revealed Religion in particular, is represented as unfriendly to individual or social happiness—it becomes those who believe the truth of Christianity, to endeavor to prevent the progress of those doctrines of unbelief, by every mild and prudent method—by promoting Institutions for the general diffusion of knowledge—by excluding vicious and profligate persons from the employment of instructing youth—by encouraging and supporting public teachers of Piety, Religion and Morality—and by exemplifying in their own conduct, the genuine effects of that Religion, which they regard, as the purest source of human felicity.[66]

A year later (June 4, 1801) Governor Strong again addressed the Court. His remarks on education were more extended this time and dwelt even more specifically on the place religious instruction should have therein:

> . . . Among the various subjects of State Legislation, there is none more important to the preservation of our Free Governments, or more interesting to the happiness of Society, than the Instruction of the People, and particularly the Education of Youth . . .[67]

The Governor went on to emphasize the great care given religion in the early days of Massachusetts, and expressed a hope

[65] *Ibid., passim,* pp. 418–20.
[66] *Laws and Resolves of Massachusetts,* 1800–1801, p. 568 (State House Library, Boston).
[67] *Ibid.,* p. 578.

that a like spirit would dominate the present law-making body. "As a part of this subject permit me to suggest," he continued,

> that the Institutions of the Sabbath and of publick Worship, were regarded by our Ancestors with peculiar Devotion, and that our State Constitution recommends the Support of them, while at the same time it carefully guards against a Violation of the Rights of Conscience.
>
> It will be acknowledged by everyone that publick Worship is useful as a School of good manners and of decent and orderly Deportment. But as Religion is the only sure foundation of human Virtue, the Prosperity of the State must be essentially promoted by a due Observance of the Sabbath, and by the meeting together of the Citizens to learn the duties of moral Obligation, and contemplate the wisdom and goodness with which the Almighty governs the world— In such assemblies they can hardly fail to receive useful Information in the conduct of Life, and Impressions of Reverence for the Deity which will never be totally effaced—even the Instructions that produce no apparent effect at the time may so far gain a place in the Memory, as readily to revive in it when Occasion Calls for them— It is the nature of Vice to dissolve Society; but these Institutions tend to uphold it in a Constitution favorable to Order and Virtue—by preserving them therefore we shall preserve the Virtue and secure the happiness of the People.[68]

While Virginia and Massachusetts were working at their religion and education problems, New York legislators were also planning and drafting laws. The State Assembly had passed a law in 1795 to establish common schools, but it was not successful.[69] When George Clinton was elected Governor, his opening speech to the Legislature January 26, 1802 contained this remark on schools: "The System for the encouragement of common schools having been discontinued and the advantages to morals, religion, liberty and good government arising from the general diffusion of knowledge being universally admitted, permit me to recommend this subject to your deliberate attention." [70]

[68] *Ibid.,* pp. 579–80.

[69] For a treatment of New York's early efforts, cf. Charles J. Mahoney, *The Relation of the State to Religious Education in Early New York, 1633–1825* (Washington: The Catholic University of America Press, 1941), pp. 91–103.

[70] Charles Z. Lincoln (ed.), *State of New York, Messages from the Governors (1683–1906)* (11 vols.; Albany: J. B. Lyman Co., 1909), ii, 512.

Clinton's successor, Morgan Lewis, continued the theme in his opening speech to the Legislature:

> In a government resting on public opinion, and deriving its chief support from the affections of a people, religion and morality cannot be too sedulously inculcated. To them science is a handmaid; ignorance is the worst of enemies. . . . Common schools under the guidance of respectable teachers should be established in every village, and the indigent be educated at public expense.[71]

On February 5, 1805 Lewis proposed an educational plan to the lawmakers, expressing the hope that the idea would in a few years "rear an edifice sacred to science, morals and religion, which shall exalt in dignity the American character." [72]

These early appeals for education resulted only in the legislature fostering by financial grants the then-existing church schools.[73] By 1810, however, a fund had actually been gathered for common schools (as public schools were called in those days), and on January 29, 1811 Governor Daniel D. Tompkins spoke of its use to the Assembly:

> The mode of applying the fund set apart for the encouragement of common schools, and the means of adding to the liberal patronage which has been already extended for the promotion of learning and the consequent advancement of the cause of morality and religion, will form part of the interesting matters which ought to attract your notice.[74]

The Assembly authorized the Governor to appoint a Commission to study the problem of starting common schools. On February 17, 1812, this Commission reported to the lawmakers on a school plan. Religion got a strong mention:

[71] *Ibid.,* pp. 550–51.
[72] *Ibid.,* p. 555.
[73] Cf. Mahoney, *op. cit.,* p. 92.
[74] Lincoln, *op. cit.,* pp. 675–76. These executive messages usually ended with a religious reference, e.g., Tompkins, January 28, 1812: "I offer a fervent prayer to Him who directs the passions and talents of man, and controls the destinies of nations, to inspire us with unanimity, patriotism and wisdom, in the performance of the high and responsible duties of our respective stations, and to grant that our services may redound to the lasting happiness and welfare of the state." (*Ibid.,* p. 703.)

Reading, writing, arithmetic, and the principles of morality, are essential to every person. . . . Without the first, it is impossible to receive those lessons of morality which are inculcated in the writings of the learned and pious; . . . Morality and religion are the foundation of all that is truly great and good, and are consequently of primary importance.[75]

The recommendations of the Committee formed the basis of the laws of 1812 and 1813, which established the common school system for New York. The 1812 statute made provisions for all counties in the State except the county and city of New York. There was nothing specific on religious instruction in the Act. It required that the teachers be of "good moral character" and it left a great deal of autonomy to the local township in administering the school's affairs.[76]

The following year the Legislature passed a supplementary act for New York City and County. Herein was contained an authorization that a portion of the school fund be allotted "to the trustees . . . of such incorporated religious societies in said city as now support or hereafter shall establish charity schools within the said city, who may apply for the same." [77] The officers of the religious societies were to act as inspectors in their own schools, as the inspectors of the common schools were empowered to act by the law of 1812.[78] Thus the state contributed to these religious schools, but considered them private rather than public institutions.

In the legislative addresses and enactments of five other of the original states items were found favoring religion in education. These states are North Carolina, Georgia, Connecticut, Rhode Island and New Hampshire.

[75] *Ibid.*, pp. 720–21.

[76] "An Act for the Establishment of Common Schools" (passed June 19, 1812). *New York Laws,* Thirty-fifth Session, Chap. ccxl, pp. 488–503.

[77] "An Act supplementary to the act entitled 'An Act for the Establishment of Common Schools,'" *Laws of New York,* Thirty-sixth Session, Chap. lii (Albany: Webster and Skinner, 1815), p. 39.

[78] *Ibid.*, pp. 39–40. It is interesting to find among the enactments of these two legislative sessions laws assigning lots of 250 acres apiece "for the support of the Gospel and Schools" to townships in several counties of the state. The procedure was authorized by a statute passed by the Legislature on April 11, 1808. Cf. *Laws of New York,* Thirty-fifth Session (1812), Chap. clxvii (pp. 362–66) and, Thirty-sixth Session (1813), Chap. C (pp. 107–08).

Governor Alexander Martin spoke to the Assembly of North Carolina in 1784, calling the legislators' attention to "the education of our youth." "Religion and virtue," he stated,

> claim your particular care. Legislators in all ages and nations have interwoven the Government with these essential materials; to preserve the morals of the people is to preserve the State; may men of piety and exemplary life who conduct the affairs of religion meet your countenance and receive support not incompatible with the principles of the Constitution.[79]

In Georgia, provisions on religion in education which were to apply at all levels of public education were written into the "Act of Establishment" of the State University in 1785. Thus the statute affected elementary schools as well as higher education: "It [a free government] can only be happy," the statute declared,

> where the public principles and opinions are properly directed, and their manners regulated. This is an influence beyond the sketch of laws and punishments, and can be claimed only by religion and education. It should therefore be among the first objects of those who wish well to the national prosperity, to encourage and support the principles of religion and morality, and early to place the youth under the forming hand of society, that by instruction they may be moulded to the love of virtue and good order.[80]

Among the statute's provisions, we note the following two:

> 11th. The trustees shall not exclude any person of any religious denomination whatsoever, from free and equal liberty and advantages of education, or from any of the liberties, privileges, and immunities of the university in his education, on account of his or their speculative sentiments in religion, or being of a different religious profession.
>
> 14th. All public schools, instituted or to be supported by funds or public monies in this State, shall be considered as parts

[79] Cf. Knight, *A Documentary History of Education in the South*, II, 493–94.

[80] Robert and George Watkins, *A Digest of the Laws of the State of Georgia* (Philadelphia: R. Aitken, 1800), as quoted in Knight-Hall, *Readings*, p. 193.

of members of the university, and shall be under the foregoing directions and regulations.[81]

Three years later (1795), Connecticut established a permanent public school fund. An Act of the General Court appropriated monies realized from the sale of state lands into a fund. The interest on this fund was appropriated to support schools conducted by various societies, made up, at least in part, of church groups.[82] It seems that a subsequent provision of the enactment aimed to keep the school societies as such free of sectarian domination. It denied to religious societies who shared in the interest accruing from the fund for the "support of the Christian Ministry or the public worship of God" any "Power to act on the subject of schooling." [83] Another writer has said of Connecticut education of this period:

> Between 1798 and 1818, the religious dissenters struggled against the Established [Congregational] Church's control of all educational channels. The creation of school societies along allegedly non-sectarian lines had not changed the essentially Congregational character of the common schools. . . .[84]

In 1820, a Committee was appointed in Providence, Rhode Island, to revise the rules for public schools. Among the directives they gave to the teachers was the following:

> That they endeavor to impress on the minds of the scholars a sense of the Being & Providence of God & their obligations to love & reverence Him,—their duty to their parents & preceptors, the beauty & excellency of truth, justice & mutual love, tenderness to brute creatures, the happy tendency of self government and obedience to the dictates of reason & religion; the observance of the Sabbath as a sacred institution, the duty which they owe to their country & the necessity of a strict obedience to its Laws, and that they caution them against the prevailing vices.[85]

[81] Watkins, *ibid.*, pp. 195, 196.

[82] Knight-Hall, *Readings,* p. 316 (quoting Connecticut Acts and Laws, 1795, pp. 487–89).

[83] *Ibid.,* p. 317.

[84] Sister Mary Paul Mason, *Church-State Relationships in Connecticut, 1633–1953* (Washington, D. C.: The Catholic University of America Press, 1953), p. 101.

[85] Knight-Hall, *Readings,* p. 485 (quoting *Centennial Report of the School Committee, 1899–1900,* pp. 42–43).

The legislature of New Hampshire passed a school act in 1789 which authorized the collection of funds for schools to teach the three R's. Since the selection of schoolmasters was left in the hands of the clergy, Kinney feels that the teaching of religion remained in the curriculum and retained its strict Congregational aspect until at least 1808.[86]

In this year the lawmakers passed a new statute which tended to broaden the program of studies, adding grammar and geography. Although no mention of religious instruction occurred, Kinney points out that the clergy were again given most of the responsibility for teacher selection and that the school committees were to visit their schools and "judge the progress in 'literature, morality, and religion.'" [87]

Plans for New Schools Made by Private Citizens

Dr. Benjamin Rush submitted a plan for a system of public education to the Pennsylvania Legislature in 1786. Like the Georgia Statute, it covered all levels, from the state university to free elementary schools in each township. We quote the two concluding paragraphs of this plan:

I submit these detached hints to the consideration of the legislature and of the citizens of Pennsylvania. The plan for the free schools is taken chiefly from the plans which have long been used with success in Scotland, and in the eastern states of America, where the influence of learning, in promoting religion, morals, manners and good government, has never been exceeded in any country.

The manner in which these schools should be supported and governed—the modes of determining the characters and qualifications of schoolmasters, and the arrangement of families in

---

[86] Charles B. Kinney, Jr., *Church and State, The Struggle for Separation in New Hampshire, 1630–1900* (New York: Teachers College, Columbia University Publications Bureau, 1955), pp. 152–53. Kinney cites from Lyford's *History of Concord, New Hampshire* that the textbook used for the younger pupils during this period was exclusively the *New England Primer*.

[87] *Ibid.*, p. 153 (quoting Laws of New Hampshire, VII, 771).

each district, so that children of the same religious sect and nation, may be educated as much as possible together, will form a proper part of a law for the establishment of schools, and therefore does not come within the limits of this plan.[88]

A year later, in 1787, an article in *The Columbia Magazine, or Monthly Miscellany* for April 17, laid down a plan for Agricultural and Manual Labor Schools for rural districts. Knight and Hall's footnote says the plan prompted a Dr. John de la Howe to will money in 1796 for such a school in South Carolina which is still (1951) in operation.[89] Provision 14 of the plan stated:

I hardly need mention, what ought to be an indispensable part of education in every literary institution. That the children at this rural academy would be taught the plainest and most important principles of religion and morality.[90]

The trustees of the "Society for Establishing a Free School in the City of New York" published an address in the newspapers to secure funds to erect a school building. After pointing out that several religious and benevolent societies were operating free schools for the children of their own communicants who could not afford private education, they said:

. . . There still remains a large number living in total neglect of religious and moral instruction, and unacquainted with the common rudiments of learning, essentially requisite for the due management of the ordinary business of life . . .
. . . strict attention will be bestowed on the morals of the children, and all suitable means be used to counteract the disadvantages resulting from the situation of their parents. It is proposed, also, to establish, on the first day of the week, a

[88] Knight-Hall, *Readings*, pp. 307-08 (quoting from D. D. Runes, *The Selected Writings of Benjamin Rush* [New York: Philosophical Library, Inc., 1947], pp. 98–100).
[89] Knight-Hall, *Readings*, p. 196 and footnote. (In the will by which de la Howe provided for the school he wrote, ". . . in the admittance of poor children, no manner of regard shall be paid to what Religion or sect they or their Parents profess; and that it shall be a particular charge to the master to teach and instruct them only, in the general, plain, and practical parts of religion and morality, without meddling with speculative and controverted points, or with such as constitute the particular character of any sect." Knight, *Documentary History of Education in the South*, IV, p. 71.)
[90] Knight-Hall, *Readings*, p. 199.

school, called a Sunday School, more particularly for such children as, from peculiar circumstances, are unable to attend on the other days of the week. In this, as in the Common School, it will be a primary object, without observing the peculiar forms of any religious Society, to inculcate the sublime truths of religion and morality contained in the Holy Scriptures.[91]

In 1817 we find Archibald D. Murphey offering a plan of education for the State of North Carolina.[92] In the curriculum for primary schools he proposed:

And the board should be empowered to compile and have printed for the use of primary schools, such books as they may think will best subserve the purposes of intellectual and moral instruction. In these books should be contained many of the historical parts of the old and new testament, that children may early be made acquainted with the books which contain the word of truth, and the doctrines of eternal life.[93]

Later, in the same report, Murphey mentioned religion once more, as belonging in the entire educational system:

When this or some other plan of judicious education, when light and knowledge shall be shed upon all, may we not indulge the hope, that men will be convinced that wisdom's ways are ways of pleasantness and all her paths are peace; and be induced by such conviction to regulate their conduct by the rule of christian morality, of doing unto others as they wish they would do unto them; and that they will learn to do justly, to love mercy and walk humbly before their God.[94]

The two final documents we shall cite in this section concern the educational plans of the Rev. Samuel R. Hall, a Congregational Minister. In 1823 he made a contract for services to the Congregational Church at Concord, Massachusetts. Item II of the contract read:

[91] *Ibid.,* pp. 319–20 (quoting the address, as given in W. O. Bourne, *History of the Public School Society of the City of New York* [New York: William Wood & Co., 1870]).

[92] Edgar W. Knight, *Readings in Educational Administration* (New York: Henry Holt & Co., 1953), pp. 30–46 (quoting *Senate Journal,* 1817, pp. 30–42).

[93] *Ibid.,* p. 41.

[94] *Ibid.,* p. 45.

That you allow me to establish and instruct a school such a portion of the year as I may find necessary and convenient not exceeding three-fourths of each year and that I have the provides thereof to assist in my support.[95]

A few years later, in 1829, Hall gave his ideas on the "Requisite Qualifications" for a teacher. Section Six noted that

A just *moral discernment,* is of pre-eminent importance in the character of an instructer [sic]. Unless governed by a consideration of his moral obligation, he is but poorly qualified to discharge the duties which devolve upon him, when placed at the head of a school. He is himself, a moral agent, and accountable to himself, to his employers, to his country and to his God, for the faithful discharge of duty. If he have no moral sensibility, no fear of disobeying the laws of God, no regard for the institutions of our holy religion, how can he be expected to lead his pupils in the way that they should go? The cultivation of virtuous propensities is more important to children than even their intellectual culture. The *virtuous* man, though illiterate, will be happy, while the learned, if *vicious,* must be miserable in proportion to his attainments . . . An instructor without moral feeling, not only brings ruin to the children placed under his care, but does injury to their parents, to the neighbourhood, to the town, and, doubtless, to other generations. . . . Genuine piety is highly desirable in every one entrusted with the care and instruction of the young; but morality, at least, should be *required,* in every candidate for that important trust.[96]

School Practices

Equally as important as the laws and plans so far examined will be evidence as to what actually went on in the classroom. Legislatures, educational leaders and local school boards could and did show that it was the *spirit* of the times to retain religion in an honored place. But the *teaching* itself was done by other people. What do we know of their activities?

[95] Arthur D. Wright and George E. Gardner (eds.), *Hall's Lectures on School-keeping* (Hanover: Dartmouth Press, 1929), p. 16.
[96] *Ibid.,* pp. 67–68.

Declarations of teachers such as those of the Rev. Samuel R. Hall quoted at the end of the preceding section give a clue. Not many such writings, however, have been found. The climate of the times would have favored religion in education. Since it has been indicated in Chapter II that the ideas of the Enlightenment did not penetrate too deeply into the average American mind, and since the Protestant clergy continued to exert so much influence on the schools by their teacher-certification work and school visitation, it may be *surmised* that, if anything, there was *more* teaching of religion actually done in the elementary school classroom than even the evidence given so far in this chapter would indicate.

For documentation of this point, of course, one does not have anything like the elaborate system of superintendents' reports which came into being in the middle decades of the nineteenth century. Such reporting had to await the centralization of authority worked out in the time of Horace Mann—in the middle thirties and after. There is evidence of classroom practice available, however, chiefly from three sources—first, the textbooks of the early period which have survived; second, scattered local school regulations; and, third, teacher and pupil reminiscences.

TEXTBOOKS

Material contained in the Nietz collection of old textbooks has already been drawn upon for the section on the Colonial period.[97] Doctor Nietz has stressed the value of examining these texts to learn of educational practices in former centuries. "Much of the treatment," he begins,

> in the textbooks of the history of education deals more fully with the development of educational thought than of actual

---

[97] Cf. *supra*, pp. 19 f. Several doctoral dissertations have been written on these books at the University of Pittsburgh. Among them are Earl K. Wilson, *A Historical Survey of the Religious Content of American Geography Textbooks, 1784–1895* (1951); John H. Dawson, *A Survey of the Religious Content of American World History Textbooks Written Prior to 1900* (1954); Raymond G. Hughes, *An Analysis of the Fourth, Fifth, and Sixth McGuffey Readers* (1943); and Harold C. Warren, *Changing Conceptions in the Religious Elements in Early American School Readers* (1951).

practice. It is the thesis of the writer that an analysis of the actual textbooks used in the past will reveal a truer history of what was actually taught in the schools than a study of the educational theories. This does not mean that the theories should not be studied, but failing to deal with what was actually taught results in an incomplete understanding of the history of education.[98]

Speaking of religion Dr. Nietz continues:

Several studies show that the early textbooks in several fields devoted much space to religion, with such emphasis declining after 1850 and nearly disappearing in some fields after 1900. For example, Robinson found that the readers used in the colonies prior to 1775 devoted 85% of the space to religion and 8% to morals; those between 1775 and 1825, 22% to religion and 28% to morals; those between 1825 and 1875, 7.5% to religion and 23% to morals; and those between 1875 and 1915, only 1.5% to religion and 7% to morals.

Hughes, who analyzed the contents of all of the editions of the fourth, fifth, and sixth famous McGuffey Readers, found that the lessons devoted to religion and morals even exceeded the percentages reported in the Robinson study and that the decline was not so marked in them. The first edition of the third reader in 1837 devoted 32.6% to religion and 11.2% to morals. The popular 1879 edition of the three readers devoted 8.7% to religion and 25.2% to morals. The last edition in 1901 still devoted 5.9% of the lessons to religion and 26.3% to morals.

Wilson, in his analysis of 134 geographies published in the United States before 1895, found that the 68 books before 1850 devoted an average of 5.8% of the content to religion, while the books between 1875 and 1895 devoted only 1.23%.

The two main emphases in early readers were religion, as already shown, and elocution. Even before readers appeared in graded series Caleb Bingham wrote two rather popular readers, the *American Preceptor* (1794), emphasizing religion and morals, and the *Columbian Orator* (1806), containing reading selections for developing powers of elocution.[99]

All these studies note the gradual decline, as the years went on after 1775, in the proportionate space that is devoted to religious

[98] John A. Nietz, "Some Findings from Analyses of Old Textbooks," *History of Education Journal,* iii (Spring, 1952), 79–87.
[99] *Ibid.,* p. 82.

and moral material. Among the reasons given, however, they do not mention hostility to religion *as such,* or any idea that the laws of the land forbade religious instruction. Interest in patriotism, in and after the Revolution, a growing interest in secular English literature, economic motivation because of trade and commerce, jealousies and quarrels among sectarian groups it is these things which are pin-pointed as either crowding out religious material or weakening the influence of those who might have been able to keep it in.

More significant for the present study than either geography or history books will be the *readers.* In them, during the colonial period and long after, was contained much material by which the children were indoctrinated and motivated religiously. A classic example of this has already been seen in the *New England Primer.*[100]

R. R. Robinson in *Two Centuries of Change in the Content of School Readers,*[101] gives, for the period 1775–1825, the following percentages of content in sixty-eight books examined:

> Religion—22%; Morals and Conduct—28%. Other materials include Nature Study—4%; Essay—8%; Oratory—7.5%; Geography—4%; Spelling—10%; etc.[102]

As a criterion for his distinction between "Religion" and "Morals and Conduct" Robinson says that to be considered "religious" the passage "must always have ideas pertaining to the Deity; that

---

[100] Dr. Nietz confirmed this view in a letter to the writer on July 6, 1955: "Although old geography and history textbooks contained considerable religious content, the treatment was more definitely *about* religion, rather than the teaching of religion in order to influence the lives of the pupils. However, some authors did deal with certain religions with a marked bias. On the other hand, most old readers consciously attempted to *teach religion,* so as to influence the belief and the behavior of children using these books. For example, the content of the *New England Primer* was nearly entirely religious in nature. Likewise, the content of Caleb Bingham's *American Preceptor* was mostly moral or religious."

[101] R. R. Robinson, *Two Centuries of Change in the Content of School Readers* (Nashville, Tennessee: George Peabody College for Teachers, 1930). (Cf. Nietz, *op. cit.,* p. 75.)

[102] Robinson, *op. cit.,* p. 26.

is, the word God, Lord, Savior, or some other synonymous word must be the central theme of the selection."[103] Under "Morals and Conduct" are included "Selections which are intended to tell something of truth, fairness and conduct."[104]

A second study on readers was made by Harold C. Warren, working with the collection of Dr. Nietz.[105] Noting that other investigators have attempted to determine the amount of religious material contained, Warren gives as his purpose "within the framework of this dwindling amount, . . . to establish trends in conceptions and motivations, as evidenced by omission or inclusion, substitution or repetition of ideas."[106]

Of the eighty-three readers Warren studied, seventeen were published between 1690 and 1830; fifty between 1831 and 1860; and the remaining sixteen between 1866 and 1880.

Of the period covered by the present chapter Warren observes: "The bulk of religious material decreased by 75 percent in the fifty years from 1775 to 1825 and the change in the character of the religious material employed was equally striking."[107] When giving the factors which he feels caused the decline of religious content, however, Warren's time span goes from 1775 to 1880. In listing these factors, then, we must keep in mind that he does not mean necessarily that all were at work between 1775 and 1825. Warren's list includes, as causes of decline, Nationalism, Morality (note the similarity with Robinson on this point), Secularization, Preparation for Citizenship, Foreign Influences, Adaptation to the Child, Literature and Science.[108]

It seems safe to say that the readers in the Nietz collection represent an adequate sampling of those in use in the early national period of the country. It will be noted that many of them ran into

---

[103] *Ibid.*, p. 2.

[104] *Ibid.*, p. 3. It seems that Robinson's distinction could be misleading. If the motivation for conduct was God's will, even though not mentioned in the paragraph, the passage would be better marked "religion" than "morals and conduct."

[105] Cf. footnote 97.

[106] Warren, *op. cit.*, p. 3.

[107] *Ibid.*, p. 184.

[108] *Ibid.*, pp. 173–94.

a number of editions. Also, several of them contained endorsements from clergymen and educational leaders in various parts of the eastern United States.[109] Of the books he selected from the Nietz collection Warren states on this point:

> Inasmuch as some editions of specific readers are identical, and some readers have considerable material in common, it should be possible to establish any trends which are verifiable by selecting the most representative volumes chronologically. Whereas a search through numerous collections of readers throughout the country might add to our list some rare and relevant books, the most valuable for the present purpose are clearly those which were in most common uses [sic]; and these are readily available. . . . we confine our attention to the readers of prominence and of large circulation for the sake of securing the fairest cross-section of reading material used in the primary grades throughout the country.[110]

Eighteen books from the Nietz collection whose publication dates ran from 1779 to 1826 were examined for this portion of the present study. All of them are connected with the field of reading in general, although one was a straight catechism, one was a combination catechism and primer, one was a book for teachers and one was described as a "Primer of the English Language." As their religious contents are mentioned and brief samples of the texts are given, their arrangement in the chronological order of their publication should exemplify the continued flow of religious material into the classrooms of the early national period.

An early edition of Lindley Murray's *Reader* was published in Baltimore by Armstrong and Plaskett. "1779" is written in pencil over the publisher's name on the title page and Dr. Nietz has also written 1779 on the cover. Its full title is *The English Reader: or Pieces in Poetry and Verse . . . To Inculcate the Most Important*

---

[109] On October 3, 1955, Dr. Nietz answered this writer's query on the point as follows: "In regard to the question you raise concerning the wide use of the various Readers, I would say that there is no very specific way to do this except by checking the number of editions that were published. Of course, no doubt, there were a larger number of books printed in some editions than in others. However, it seems to me to be a safe criterion concerning books printed so long ago."

[110] Warren, *op. cit.*, pp. 11–12.

Principles of Piety and Virtue. Titles in the Table of Contents include these religious pieces:

"Comforts of Religion"; "Omniscience and Omnipresence of the Deity, Source of Consolation"; "On the Immortality of the Soul"; "Creation"; "Excellence of Holy Scriptures"; "Reflections occasioned by a review of the blessings pronounced by Christ, on His disciples, in His sermon on the mount"; "Religion and death"; "Adam's Advice to Eve"; "Creator's Works Attest His Greatness"; "Address to the Deity."

In 1788, G. Douglas in "London-Derry" published *The New Catechism, Wherein The Principles of the Christian Religion are briefly set forth in a Plain, Rational and Scriptural Manner and Adapted to the Capacities of Young Persons, Chiefly Collected from the Catechisms of Dr. Watts, Dr. Mann, and the General Assembly.* A note pinned to the book reads "Westmont Ireland Came to America, 1796." A sample of its contents follows:

Qu. What is your name?
A. A or B.
Qu. How did you receive that name?
A. I received it from my parents at the time of my Baptism. . . .
Qu. What do you understand by being a member of the Church of Christ?
A. I understand that I became bound to renounce all manner of sin, by keeping God's holy commandments, and continually walking in them all the days of my life. . . .
Qu. Are all these commandments binding upon Christians?
A. They are for "*Christ* came to fulfill the law, not to destroy it. . . ."
Qu. What is meant by the word *Church*?
A. By the word *Church*, is meant the whole congregation of the Faithful; that is, all those who profess the Christian religion.
Qu. Why do we sometimes say, *The Holy Catholic Church*?
A. All Christians, by their profession, engage to lead *holy* lives; and *Catholic* signifying *universal*, the followers of Christ therefore compose the Holy Catholic (or universal) Church, as including the Christians of every country and nation in the world.[111]

Another book is Hamilton Moore's *The Young Gentleman and Lady's Monitor and English Teacher's Assistant.* In the front of

[111] Douglas, *op. cit.* in text, p. 11, *passim*, pp. 3–21.

this book is an autograph—"John S. Burnham—1823." In the back
of the book another inscription—"John S. Burnham's Book, Remember the eighth commencement, Bought in Boston, Nov. 16,
1823." From the table of contents:

> "Fortitude founded Upon Fear of God"; "On the Omniscience
> and Omnipotence of the Deity, together with the Immensity of
> his works"; "Reflections on the Third Heaven"; "The present
> life to be considered as it may conduce to the Happiness of a
> future one"; "On the Immortality of the Soul"; "Of the Scrip-
> tures as the Rule of Life"; "Commentaries on 21 Books of the
> Old Testament"; "Of the New Testament"; "Of the example set
> by Our Savior"; "A Comparative view of the Blessed and the
> Cursed at the last Day and the Inference to be drawn from it";
> "Character of St. Paul"; "Of the Epistles"; "The Epistle of
> St. James"; "Epistles of St. Peter, and the first of St. John"; "Of
> the Revelations"; "True Devotion Productive of the Truest
> Pleasure"; "Morning Prayer for a Young student at School, or
> for the Common Use of a School"; "Evening Prayer"; "Speech
> of Adam to Eve."

(*Selection*) "True Devotion Productive of the Truest Pleasure":

> You see that true devotion is not a melancholy sentiment that
> depresses the spirits and excludes the ideas of pleasure which
> youth is fond of; on the contrary, there is nothing so friendly to
> joy, so productive of true pleasure, so peculiarly suited to the
> warmth and innocence of a youthful heart. Do not therefore
> think it too soon to turn your mind to God . . .[112]

In 1794 Donald Fraser put out *The Columbian Monitor: Being
a Pleasant and Easy Guide to Useful Knowledge*.[113] The Preface
declares:

> Part Second contains a selection of Religious Dialogues, in
> which the general principles of the Christian religion are fully
> explained, in a rational and impartial manner, and may be read
> with advantage by Youth of every denomination; the frequent
> perusal of these Dialogues will, I think, have a happy tendency
> (even in this *Age of Reason and Inquiry*) in attracting the atten-
> tion of the rising generation, and powerfully impressing them,

[112] Hamilton Moore, *The Young Gentleman and Lady's Monitor and
English Teacher's Assistant* (9th ed.; Hudson: Ashbell Stoddard, 1795),
p. 271.
[113] (New York: London & Brower, 1794.)

with sentiments of *veneration, love* and *gratitude* towards the Almighty Beneficent Creator and Savior of mankind.[114]

Just after the opening of the nineteenth century Daniel Adams came out with *The Understanding Reader: or Knowledge Before*

[114] A sample of a "Dialogue between a Master and a Scholar":

Scholar: What knowledge is the most necessary?

Master: That of Religion: because nothing but Religion can make us perfectly happy, and without it we must be very miserable, in regard [sic] we are subject in this life to divers evils, both of soul and body, and at the last to death; against all which misfortunes, Religion is our only comfort and remedy, as it supports us under trouble, gives us peace of mind, secures us from sin and the fear of death, and affords a certain hope of a future eternal life of happiness. . . .

Scho.: In what does religion consist?

Ma.: In the knowledge of the one true God, and in worshipping and serving him acceptably, and we must believe that God is; that he hath given us laws and commandments to keep; that he will reward all such as observe and do what he hath commanded, and punish those who disobey him, both in this world and in the next. . . .

Scho.: Which is the true Religion? [After saying there are four religions: Christian, Jewish, Pagan and Mahometan.]

Ma.: The Christian Religion, which consists in believing in the true God and in Jesus Christ (John 17.3). This is life eternal, that they might know the only true God, and Jesus Christ, whom he sent. . . .

Scho.: How does it appear that the Christian Religion is true?

Ma.: From the very nature of it; for all that it teaches and commands men to believe and do, is perfectly agreeable to right *reason* and justice. The Christian religion requires nothing but what is reasonable, just, and worthy of God and man; it tends to make order, justice and peace reign amongst men; it sanctifies, comforts, and procures them the greatest happiness they can enjoy in this world, and in a future state. . . .

Scho.: How many parts are there in the Christian religion?

Ma.: Two; the first treat [sic] of faith, or the truth a christian ought to believe; the second of our duty, as to what we ought to do. . . .

Scho.: Of what use is the resurrection of Christ to us?

Mu.. It proves that he is the son of God, that he has made atonement for our sins, and is a pledge to us that we shall rise again at the last day. . . .

Scho.: What is meant by the Holy Catholic Church, and the Communion of Saints, mentioned in the creed?

Ma.: By the former we are to understand in general, the universal or whole Church of God, all good men from the beginning to the end of the world; and by the latter that all such good persons are the servants of the same God, all guided and sanctified by the same spirit, all live in hope of the same divine promises, of being finally made partakers of some degree of glory in the eternal kingdom of God; and consequently, that it is the duty of all persons to live together in love, and mutually assist, comfort and instruct each other; and to perform all the good offices that it becomes members of one and the same body to do for one another. *Passim,* pp. 35–48.

Oratory.[115] Its Table of Contents includes "Esther," "Paul's Defence," "Creation of the World," "On Religion," "A Sermon," and "Resurrection of Christ." From the piece "On Religion," we read, "But wherever you are, cast your eyes, you will at the same time be envisioned with the immensity of a Being who is possessed of all possible perfections, and who holdest the issues of life and death, of happiness and misery solely in his hands. . . ."[116]

In 1807 there appeared a "Third Edition With Alterations" of the Lindley Murray *Sequel to the English Reader.*[117] It contains many items similar to those quoted above,[118] and other selections, such as "Religion the foundation of content," "No life pleasing to God, that is not useful to man," "Character of the Great Founder of Christianity," "The spirit and laws of Christianity superior to those of every other religion," etc.

Also in 1807 a "New Edition" appeared of *An American Selection of Lessons in Reading and Speaking* by Noah Webster, Jr.[119] "A Morning Hymn" and "Sorrow, Piety, Devotion, Filial Obedience" are the only titles which suggest religion.

A minister of the First Church in Hingham, Joseph Richardson, produced a reader in 1810.[120] Among the many titles similar to those we have been quoting is "Free Inquiry Favorable to Religion." It reads, in part:

> Religion is equally necessary for all men, yes for all rational creatures in the universe. Religion essentially consists in love to God and fellow beings, expressed in every suitable way. Now this is equally the duty and the happiness of *all* classes of intelligent beings. . . .
> You who are in the bloom of childhood, or of youth, need this principle [of religion] to guard you against the numberless temptations to folly and sin, which constantly surround you. You need it to improve those inward accomplishments, exterior

[115] Daniel Adams, *The Understanding Reader: or Knowledge Before Oratory* (Brookfield: E. Merriam & Co., 1804.)

[116] *Ibid.*, p. 152.

[117] (Philadelphia: Alexander and Phillips, 1807.)

[118] *Supra*, pp. 80, 81.

[119] (Boston: Isaiah Thomas and Ebenezer T. Andrews, 1807.)

[120] *The American Reader . . . to improve the Scholar in Reading and Spelling while enriching the mind with Religious, Virtuous and Useful Knowledge* (Boston: Lincoln & Edmonds, 1810).

manners and innocent pleasures, which become your period of life.

You need it, as the great preparatory for a useful manhood, a comfortable old age, and a peaceful death. It is needful for persons of mature years, to moderate, to sanctify, and to prosper the worldly cares, pursuits and enjoyments of manly life.[121]

Asa Lyman published in 1811 *The American Reader . . . Particularly for the Use of Schools*.[122] Its Table of Contents includes such headings as "St. Matthew's Gospel, Chap. xii," "The Truth of Christianity proved from the conversion of St. Paul," "Love Not the World, neither the things that are in the world," "God's Address to Job," "The Messiah, A Sacred Eclogue" and "The Crucifixion."

Lessons in Elocution is the name of a book put out by William Scott in 1814.[123] Among the titles listed are "Eloquence in the pulpit," "On Truth and Integrity," "On Doing as we would be Done Unto," "On Benevolence and Charity," and "On the Death of Christ." The same year saw publication of the Tenth Edition of *The Art of Reading*, by Daniel Staniford.[124] The Preface, signed "Boston, January, 1802—First Edition" declares that "It [the book] also furnishes such lessons for reading as will naturally tend to lure the tender mind to the love of knowledge, and the practice of virtue and religion . . . and to inculcate the several duties of virtue and morality."

In 1815 John Richardson published *The American Class Book*.[125] Its titles include several of the religious pieces noted in previous works. The following is a sample of its reading matter:

"Youth the Proper Season for Forming Virtuous and Religious Habits"

"Youth is the season to form religious habits; the earliest principles are generally the most lasting; and those of a religious cast are seldom lost. Though the temptations of the world may now and then draw the well-principled youth aside, yet, his principals [sic] being continually at war with his practice,

[121] *Ibid.*, pp. 87–88.
[122] Published at Portland, Maine.
[123] (Philadelphia: John Bioren, 1814.)
[124] (Boston: West & Richardson, 1814.)
[125] John Richardson, *The American Class Book* (Philadelphia, 1815).

there is hope, that in the end the better part may overcome the worse, and bring on a reformation; whereas he who has suffered habits of vice to get possession of his youth has little prospect of being brought back to a sense of religion. . . .[126]

T. Strong published *The Common Reader* in 1818.[127] It includes "Moral Selections," "Religious Selections," "Omnipresence of God," "Death and Immortality," "The Scriptures," and "Summary of the Bible."

In 1819, "the Pastor of a Church in Beverly," Joseph Emerson, put out the tenth edition of *The Evangelical Primer, Containing a Minor Doctrinal Catechism, and A Minor Historical Catechism; To Which Is Added The Westminster's Shorter Catechism; . . . For the Use of Families and Schools.*[128] It lists letters of approbation given in 1809, by (among others) Timothy Dwight, Noah Webster, Jr., Edwin D. Griffin of Andover and W. Homshead, Pastor of the Independent Congregational Church of Charleston, South Carolina. Another letter, written in the same year, and signed by Jedidiah Morse, Joseph Lyman and others, declares, in part:

> We are clearly of the opinion, that your Evangelical Primer is the best publication of the kind, which we have seen, that it will have a great tendency to promote the knowledge of some important doctrines contained in the Bible, and to guard the rising generation against the fatal errors, which are so zealously propagated at the present day by the enemies of truth. We sincerely wish that this book may have a free and general circulation, that Families and Schools would make use of it in forming the minds of children and youth to virtue and piety, and that you may find all your labor amply rewarded in the success of your benevolent design.[129]

A book for teachers, *The Evangelical Instructor: Designed for the Use of Schools and Families,* appeared in 1821, under the

---

[126] *Ibid.,* p. 113.

[127] (Greenfield, Massachusetts: Denis & Phelps, 1818.)

[128] Joseph Emerson, *The Evangelical Primer, Containing a Minor Doctrinal Catechism, and a Minor Historical Catechism; To which Is Added the Westminster's Shorter Catechism; . . . For the Use of Families and Schools* (Boston: Samuel T. Armstrong, 1819).

[129] *Ibid.,* p. 4.

authorship of William Collier.[130] There was an earlier edition, because endorsements are reproduced from schoolmasters and clergymen in New York (1812), Boston (1813), Charleston (1813), Middleborough Academy (1811) and Baltimore (undated). In his dedication of this second edition of the book to the Massachusetts Peace Society the author expresses his hopes for his volume, if it should be used in public and private schools:

> Gentlemen: Heartily approving as I do of the design of your institution, and firmly persuaded as I am that should the Evangelical Instructor, and works of a similar character, be generally introduced, and read in our public and private schools, they would aid very essentially in promoting the benevolent and honourable object of your association, I take leave to usher the second edition of this work into the world under your protection and ask for it your patronage.

The Table of Contents is indicative of the book's scope:

> "An Essay on Reading"; "Present Neglect of Religious Education"; "Family Government"; "The Christian Philosopher"; "Of Ecclesiastical History"; "Natural History Spiritually Improved"; "The Seasons"; "Juvenile and Parental Addresses"; "Epistolary"; "Varieties", (e.g.) Character of Jonah, Particular Providence of God, Illustration of Matthew X, 6. etc.; "Select Poetry" (all religious).

In 1821 a famous book had its "Sixty-fourth (Fourth Improved) Edition." This was Caleb Bingham's *American Preceptor*,[131] one of the books mentioned by Dr. Nietz in his letter to the author of this study.[132] This edition includes "Parable Against Religious Persecution," "Sketch of Jerusalem and Palestine," "Of Queen Mary and the Martyrs," "St. Paul's Speech Before King Agrippa," and "Messiah, A Sacred Eclogue."

The following year (1822) saw another production of *Murray's English Reader*, done by Jeremiah Goodrich.[133] An autograph in the front of Dr. Nietz's copy reads "Lewis F. Massers, 1855." The volume contains sixteen religious selections, several of which ap-

---

[130] (Boston: Richardson & Lord, 1821.)
[131] (Boston: C. Bingham & Co., 1821.)
[132] Cf. *supra*, p. 78, footnote 100.
[133] Jeremiah Goodrich, *Murray's English Reader* (Philadelphia: Jos. B Smith & Co., 1822).

peared in other works cited above. Among them is a poem attributed to "Cotton," of which we give a portion:

Religion and Death

Lo! a form divinely bright
Descends and bursts upon my sight;
A seraph of illustrious birth
Religion was her name on earth.
Supremely sweet her radiant face,
And blooming with celestial grace. . . .[134]

The last example from the period under consideration in this chapter came out in 1826. It is Samuel Worcester's *A Primer of the English Language for the Use of Families and Schools.*[135] Obviously meant for very young children, it has one religious selection in its brief pages:

Some boys use bad words when they are at play. The Bible says that you must not use bad words, and you must mind what the Bible says, for it is God's book. You must not play with boys that speak bad words or tell lies.[136]

The books cited and the selections reproduced seem to give an accurate cross-section of readers used in American schools from 1775 to 1827 (and probably long thereafter).[137] It seems reasonable to say they were used in public as well as private schools. Nothing was found to indicate their restriction to such church schools as did exist. No attempt was made to weight the sample with readers containing only religious material. They were picked in chronological sequence alone. In these books, of course, there was an increasing amount of secular material which has not been specifically mentioned. Our purpose has not been to estimate the religious content percentagewise, for the other writers cited have done this already.

[134] *Ibid.,* p. 240.
[135] Samuel Worcester, *A Primer of the English Language for the Use of Families and Schools* (Boston: Hilliard, Gray & Co., 1826).
[136] *Ibid.,* p. 55.
[137] Cf. also Clifton Johnson, *Old Time Schools and School-Books* (Chap. IX, "Primary Readers"), where other titles and the religious matter contained therein are indicated and described.

An attempt has been made to show that the readers, which seem designed to teach content as well as the art of reading, continued to include religious topics with doctrinal implications, which could not have failed to raise questions and demand answers from the pupils. The selections quoted seem to show, too, that there was both *dogmatic and moral* material. Thus, not only would the mind have been enlightened on Protestant doctrine, but the child would have been prompted to action according to the motivation which Protestant teaching of the day held out to its adherents.

LOCAL SCHOOL REGULATIONS

The curricula of American elementary schools, in the early national period, gave evidence of the inclusion of the teaching of religion. Knight and Hall, in their *Readings,* include the following account of a day in a school in Middlesex County, Connecticut, in 1799:

1. *General* . . .

The Bible—in selected portions—or the New Testament, ought, in Christian schools, to be read by those classes who are capable of reading decently, at the opening of the school before the morning prayer. If this mode of reading be adopted, it will remove every objection of irreverence, and answer all the purposes of morality, devotion, and reading. Some questions may be very properly proposed and answered by the master or scholars; and five minutes, thus spent, would be very profitable exercise of moral and other instruction. . . .

2. *School Hours and Work* . . .

IN THE MORNING, the Bible may be delivered to the head of each class, and by them to the scholars capable of reading decently or looking over. This reading, with some short remarks, or questions, with the morning prayer, may occupy the *first half hour.* . . .

IN THE AFTERNOON, that the school be closed with an evening prayer, previous to which the scholars shall repeat a psalm or hymn—and also the Lord's prayer. . . .

Saturday may be wholly employed in an orderly review of the studies of the week, excepting one hour appropriated to instruction in the first principles of religion and morality; and in repeating, together, the ten commandments. That the Catechism usually taught in schools be divided, by the master, into four sections, one of which shall be repeated successively on each Saturday.[138]

As noted above,[139] the Massachusetts Law of 1789 required that the schools be supervised, and that the committee charged with this include ministers of the Gospel. "The whole delegation," says Clifton Johnson,

composed of the community's chief priests and elders—sometimes to the number of more than twenty—went in stately procession to the schools in turn. They heard the classes read in the primer, Psalter, Testament, etc. . . . "The school may be said to flourish like the palm tree" is the way one such visitation closed its commendation in the records of old Nicholas Pike's school at Newburyport.[140]

An interesting old printed handbill was found in the Harvard University Library.[141] It told of progress then being made in the primary schools of Boston:

Report Read at A Legal Meeting of the Inhabitants of the Town of Boston, Held at Faneuil Hall on Monday, 31st of May, A.D., 1819.

Attest Thomas Clark, Town Clerk

Of the children received, one half in some parts of the town, and one third in general, were ignorant of their letters, of whom many can now read in the New Testament, and several from the schools are prepared for admission of the town grammar schools who must have been, we are confident, otherwise rejected.

That religious education had a part in the "Monitorial Schools" of Joseph Lancaster was indicated in an old advertisement about

[138] *Readings,* pp. 476–77 (quoting "Visitors and Overseers of Schools, Code of Regulations, May 7, 1799"; given in *American Annals of Education,* VII [January, 1837], 17–20).
[139] *Supra,* pp. 65–66.
[140] Johnson, *Old Time Schools and School-Books,* p. 101.
[141] "Educ. 1421. 40189 (box)."

one of these institutions in North Carolina. The notice appeared in the *Western Carolinian,* of Centre, Iredell County, North Carolina, November 8, 1822:

> The object of these schools is to lessen the load of human misery; and to better the religious, moral, and social condition of society, by teaching those who attend not only to read and write, etc., but what is infinitely of more moment, the fear of the Lord, veneration of his holy word—for the ordinances of the Lord's house, and a due observance of the Lord's day. . . .[142]

The same advertisement carried a "Testimonial" signed by several people, declaring that the Lancastrian system, among other things, "in-corporates the rudiments of religion with the rudiments of language." [143]

PUPIL AND TEACHER REMINISCENCES

A book on the type of Clifton Johnson's, and edited by him, is *The District School As It Was, By One Who Went To It.*[144] The author was the Rev. Warren Burton (1800–1866). He does not say much about the religion taught in the school at Wilton, New Hampshire, which he attended from 1804 to 1818.[145] When he did mention religion, however, the recollections were not happy ones—e.g.:

> It ought not to be omitted that the Bible, particularly the New Testament, was the reading twice a day, generally, for all the classes adequate to words of more than one syllable. It was the only reading of several of the young classes under some teachers. On this practice I shall make but a single remark. As far as my own experience and observation extended, reverence for the sacred volume was not deepened by this constant but exceedingly careless use.[146]

[142] Cubberly, *Readings in Public Education,* pp. 138–39.

[143] *Ibid.,* p. 139.

[144] Warren Burton, *The District School As It Was, By One Who Went To It* (first published in 1833), Clifton Johnson (ed.) (Boston: Lee & Shepard, 1897).

[145] *Ibid.,* Introduction by Clifton Johnson, p. vii.

[146] *Ibid.,* p. 55. The Appendix to this book contains some "Pages from Old Spellers." One has a religious theme, "The Love of God and one's neighbor."

Cubberly's *Readings* contain a selection wherein a teacher in 1830 wrote of his reminiscences of the school of his childhood. When describing the visits of the Board he observed: "Formerly it was customary to examine the pupils in some approved Catechism; but this practice has been omitted for twenty years."[147] This would have made it the custom, for his school, up until 1810.

Another Cubberly selection, describing the schools of "Wyoming Valley of Northeastern Pennsylvania" in the period from 1815 to 1820, remarked that "The ministers of Gospel and the physicians were often teachers also. . . ."[148] The same writer observed also:

> Before the adoption of the Common School system each sect or Church organization had founded schools of different grades and titles for educating the children of their own creed, but they all failed in reaching the masses, those outside of their own church environments. Sectarian bigotry was then more exclusive than in later years. No doubt much of this toleration is due to the common school system.[149]

George B. Emerson wrote *Reminiscences of an Old Teacher,* a book published in 1878.[150] Although his teaching may have been done in a private school, it is interesting to note the farewell talk he was accustomed to give to his pupils. A part of it included these words:

> We have every day invited you to prostrate yourselves, with us, before the throne of mercy, and to ask of God those things which are necessary for us. . . . I believe in the efficacy of prayer. . . . Weak, frail, tempted as we are, we must pray; and however strong the temptation may be, I believe that if, in the moment of temptation, we can, in the spirit of Christ, throw ourselves in the arms of the Father and ask, Father, strengthen thy child, we shall obtain strength.[151]

In 1863 Henry Barnard published in his *American Journal of Education* some answers to letters he had sent out to several eld-

[147] Cubberly, *Readings,* p. 101 (quoting from *Annals of Education,* October, 1831, pp. 468–72).

[148] *Ibid.,* p. 103 (quoting a letter printed in the *Wilkes-Barre, Pa. Records,* in 1893, from Mrs. M. L. T. Hartman).

[149] *Ibid.,* p. 104.

[150] George B. Emerson, *Reminiscences of an Old Teacher* (Boston: Alfred Mudge & Son, 1878).

[151] *Ibid.,* p. 138.

erly men inquiring about their schoolday recollections. The article is entitled "Schools as They Were Sixty Years Ago"[152] and contains several answers, some of which mention religion.

Noah Webster's letter, dated New Haven, March 10, 1840, said: "When I was young, the books used were chiefly or wholly Dilworth's Spelling Books, the Psalter, Testament and Bible."[153] The Rev. Herman Humphrey, writing from Pittsfield, December 12, 1860, mentioned the Bible as a textbook.[154]

The Hon. Joseph T. Buckingham, writing from Cambridge, December 10, 1860, declared:

> The upper class in the school was formed entirely of females —such as could read the Bible. The lower classes read in spelling books and the New England Primer. . . .
>
> I was then four years and a half old, and had learned *by heart* nearly all the reading lessons in the Primer, and much of the Westminster Catechism, which was taught as the closing exercise every Saturday. . . .
>
> There was not, to my knowledge, any *reading book* proper, except the Bible, till Webster's Third Book, so called, came out about 1793 or 1794. A new edition of his Spelling Book furnished some new matter for reading—selections from the New Testament, a Chapter of Proverbs, and set of Tables, etc., but none of these operated to the exclusion of the Bible.

Speaking of Erastus Ripley, a teacher, Buckingham said:

> He opened the school every morning with prayer—which had not been practiced in our district.[155]

Another item in the Barnard article is the statement describing a school at Ridgefield, Connecticut, from the pen of "Peter Parley," (Samuel G. Goodrich) in his *Recollections of a Lifetime*— "According to the Catechism; which, by the way, we learned and recited on Saturday—the chief end of man was to glorify God and keep his commandments."[156]

The period examined in this chapter closes roughly with the

---

[152] Henry Barnard, "Schools as They Were Sixty Years Ago," *American Journal of Education*, XIII (1863) 123–44.

[153] *Ibid.*, p. 123.

[154] *Ibid.*, p. 127.

[155] *Ibid., passim*, pp. 129–32.

[156] *Ibid.*, p. 138.

end of the first quarter of the nineteenth century. Precisely, it closes two years later, as we shall begin the next section with the 1827 Massachusetts law on sectarian textbooks. Three speeches dating from the years 1826 and 1827 were found, of which two strongly advocated religion in education, but the third, while expressing no hostility to religion, did not include it in the realm of the educative process. The *American Journal of Education for the Year 1826* (not to be confused with Henry Barnard's later publication of the same name) carried a review of a sermon delivered in 1825 by F. W. P. Greenwood at the Boston Female Asylum.[157] The speaker declared that "the education of all youth should be strictly a religious education," and pointed out that this meant for him more than memorizing texts and included help in applying God's laws to their daily lives.[158] In commenting on this the reviewer pointed out the great importance of connecting religious training with the cultivation of the intellect, lest the new powers which education was giving to the "inferior classes" react to the detriment of society.[159]

On September 26, 1826, Charles F. Mercer delivered a "Discourse on Popular Education" at the College of New Jersey (Princeton). He paid tribute to the part religion ("the faithful conservator of the learning of the world") had played in bringing education to America. But he did not mention any place for it in the curriculum of what he conceived to be popular education.[160]

A different ideal was held up a few months later, however, by Francis Scott Key, when he spoke at St. John's College Commencement, February 22, 1827, at Annapolis, Maryland. The author of the "Star-Spangled Banner" emphasized the reciprocal importance of divine and human learning:

> We profess to be a Christian people. We have received a revelation to which everything within us and around us bears testimony of the high destiny of man, to which he is to be exalted when the ever changing scenes of this probatory state

[157] "Reviews," *American Journal of Education for the Year 1826*, I, No. 1 (Boston: Wait, Greene & Co., 1826).

[158] *Ibid.*, p. 45.

[159] *Ibid.*

[160] Cf. Knight, *A Documentary History of Education in the South*, II, 297–356.

shall have passed away, and for which he is to be fitted, by the due cultivation and employment of the faculties conferred upon him here. . . . This faith, in the triumphs it is visibly achieving before our eyes, over the moral and intellectual darkness of the world, disdains not the aid of human learning. It suffers the calm lights of philosophy and science to mingle with its purer and brighter rays, and shine upon the path of its conquests.[161]

The evidence of this chapter indicates that during the fifteen years preceding the adoption of the Constitution and Bill of Rights, and for thirty-five years beyond their adoption, there was a substantial *continuum* with the educational practice of colonial times. Religious instruction was believed to be a basic ingredient in education, and actually, it was given in the schools. Secular subjects were receiving an increasing amount of attention, but, while cutting down the *time* given to religion, seem not to have been added with the purpose of *eliminating* instruction in religion. There is no evidence that people believed that religion had no place in education, nor that the First Amendment forbade its being taught. Freedom of conscience was receiving attention, but this, in itself, expresses no hostility to religion or any urging of complete and absolute separation of Church and State in the educational field.

[161] Francis Scott Key, *On Education, A Discourse* ("After the Commencement of St. John's College, Annapolis, in St. Anne's Church, Annapolis. Published at the request of the Faculty and Alumni."). (This pamphlet is preserved in the "Maryland Room" of the Enoch Pratt Free Library, Baltimore, Maryland.) The section quoted here is from pp. 13–14.

CHAPTER IV

The Change Starts
in Massachusetts

1824-1827

IN MANY THINGS educational, America has seen the lead taken by the Colony and State of Massachusetts. Although Spanish Missionaries had established schools in the New World, including Florida and what is now New Mexico, before anything was attempted by the English,[1] it was the Puritans who first began school work in the thirteen original colonies. Previous chapters have indicated how prominent was the role played by Massachusetts statesmen and schoolmasters in developing educational practice during the colonial, revolutionary and early national periods.

A glance at the chart reproduced in Chapter I[2] will show 1827 as the earliest year in which any state legislation was passed restricting religious teaching in American schools. It is a statute concerning school books, and it was passed by the State of Massachusetts. No other state laws of this type appeared for the fol-

---

[1] Cf. Burns and Kohlbrenner, *A History of Catholic Education in the United States*, p. 23.

[2] Cf. *supra*, p. 6 f.

lowing eight years, and then it was Missouri (1835) and Illinois (1836), and not one of the original colonies, which passed them.[3] Hence the study of the decline of religious teaching in common schools, limited to the territory of the thirteen original colonies, must start with the "Bay State" Commonwealth.

Although thorough investigations have been made of the Massachusetts story in the matter of religion in education,[4] the research here has turned up some materials that throw additional light on the subject. An attempt has been made to go behind the events and concentrate on the motivation for them, an effort that has produced some new and stimulating insights into the problem.

A summary of the religious situation in Massachusetts from 1789 to 1820, as well as certain moves towards educational reform in the first quarter of the nineteenth century, will point out several designs in the pattern of things to come. The original Puritan Church-State relation was on the decline.[5] The "Great Awakening," while it accomplished a renewal of religious fervor, resulted in controversies which split congregations between the "New Lights" and "Old Lights."[6] Other factors which diminished the unanimity of Massachusetts Calvinists were the "Enlightenment" with its deistic children, awakening interest in commerce and industry, and the expansion of the western frontier.

Nevertheless, the Calvinist institution (the "Congregational Church," as it was called) was to remain the established church in Massachusetts until 1833. A certain toleration was extended to dissenting Protestant communities in the form of an exemption from tithes to the established church, provided they established a chapel of their own.[7]

In 1780, when the Massachusetts constitution was adopted, Article 3 of Part the First authorized the Legislature to require the towns and other political divisions to provide out of public

[3] *Ibid.*

[4] Cf., for example, Sherman N. Smith, *The Relation of the State to Religious Education in Massachusetts* (Syracuse: Syracuse University Book Store, 1926); and Raymond B. Culver, *Horace Mann and Religion in the Massachusetts Public Schools* (New Haven: Yale University Press, 1929).

[5] Cf. *supra*, pp. 23–24.

[6] *Ibid.*, pp. 24–25.

[7] Cf. Stokes, *op. cit.*, I, 418–21; also, Joseph F. Thorning, *Religious Liberty in Transition* (New York: Benziger Bros., 1931), p. 14.

funds for the public worship of God and the maintenance of Protestant religious instruction.[8] The money thus collected was to go to Congregational churches and schools, unless the taxpayer had designated his funds for one of the tolerated Protestant groups mentioned in the previous paragraph. Further stress was given to religious education by the Legislature's law of 1789.[9] Education in "piety and virtue" was enjoined. Teacher certification and school visitation were made legal functions of the ministers as well as the selectmen of the town.

As the life of a young nation rolled on, then, religion was ordered to be taught in the schools of Massachusetts. How well it was taught, of course, is another question. But, according to the law of 1789, backed up further by the State Constitution, it was enjoined legally that religion should be taught. Sherman Smith's study quotes some significant documentary evidence as to local school regulations. The school committee for Boston, for example, on December 14, 1789,

> Voted, That it be the indispensable duty of the several schoolmasters, daily to commence the duties of their sacred office by prayer and reading a portion of the sacred Scriptures, at the hour assigned for opening the school in the morning; and close the same in the evening with prayer.[10]

Again, a bit later, the same Committee voted:

> That the several schoolmasters instruct the children under their care, or cause them to be instructed, in the Assemblie's Catechism, every Saturday, unless the parents request that they be taught any particular catechism of the religious society to which they belong; and the masters are directed to teach such children accordingly.[11]

"Ipswich in 1792," Smith points out, "adopted an order for religious instruction of a sectarian character which continued effective until the law passed in 1827 prohibiting it. It required constant use three or four times a week of the 'Catechism of the

8 Cf. *supra*, p. 53.

9 Cf. *supra*, p. 65.

10 Smith, *op. cit.*, pp. 83–84. (Reference: "*The System of Public Education Adopted by the Town of Boston, 15th Octob. 1789,* bound in *American Antiquarian Society Pamphlets, 10.*")

11 *Ibid.*

Assembly of Divines' with Dr. Watts' explanatory notes, and the Catechism by the same author 'until they were committed to memory.' " [12] Similar decrees, involving doctrinal religious instruction, are cited by Smith for Roxbury Grammar School in 1803 and Dorchester in 1810.[13]

Smith continues with a survey of textbooks current at the time, many of which were mentioned in preceding chapters of this study. As all examinations of the textbooks disclose, there was a gradual decline, but not a complete elimination, of religious content. Evidence that at least one man noticed the change comes from the letter cited by Smith from a newspaper, the *Boston Recorder*, for January 26, 1822. A clergyman wrote "in recommendation of some new school book, because it could serve as Sabbath reading to the most advanced Christian to his edification, and the popular school books were not worthy of being the sole companions of the Bible in the family library, as was so often the case." [14]

In the early years of the nineteenth century the Congregational Church suffered a new schism. A liberal group, led by such men as William Ellery Channing and Jared Sparks, challenged traditional beliefs as to the Trinity and "total depravity." To emphasize their opposition to the traditional Trinitarians or "Orthodox" group, the Liberals called themselves Unitarians. In rejecting Calvin's doctrine of "total depravity" (man's nature, corrupted by the original sin, is unable to do anything of itself to merit salvation) the Unitarians preached that salvation comes from man's good works.[15]

Thus far, differences remained in the realm of doctrine. In 1818, however, a crisis occurred in the Congregational Church at Dedham, Massachusetts, which was to have schismatic results. The pastor resigned to accept a new post. The "Parish" of Dedham,

[12] *Ibid.*, p. 85. (Smith's reference: Felt, *History of Ipswich, Essex and Hamilton*, p. 89.)

[13] *Ibid.*

[14] *Ibid.*, pp. 92–93.

[15] Cf. Frank Mead, *Handbook of Denominations in the United States* (New York: Abingdon–Cokesbury Press, 1951), "Congregational Church," pp. 64–67; "Unitarians," pp. 178–80. Cf. also, John S. Brubacher, *A History of the Problems of Education*, p. 113.

i.e., the *juridical district* served by the Church, contained both
Liberals (Unitarians) and Orthodox (Congregationalists). The
Liberals gave a call to the pastorate to the Rev. Alvan Lawson,
a Unitarian. The Orthodox demurred. In a showdown vote, the
Liberals won, and the Rev. Mr. Lawson took over the pastorate.
At this the Orthodox withdrew from the Church, and established
themselves in a building across the street from the old Church on
the Common. When these Orthodox claimed the right over all the
Church property, the Liberals contested legally, and the case
went to the Supreme Court of Massachusetts.

In its November, 1820 term, the Court decided against the
Orthodox. It recognized the older Church as the First Church of
the Dedham Parish. Furthermore, it gave the opinion that a
Church which had existed in a parish could not withdraw from
the parish and still retain the property.[16] This decision inspired
repetition in many places. Unitarians called Liberal ministers and
Congregationalists withdrew and established new churches. As
will be seen, the divergent views of the two groups had a tremendous effect on the teaching of religion in Massachusetts public
schools.

Toward the close of the first quarter of the nineteenth century,
dissatisfaction with aspects of the public school program other
than the religious began to appear. The defects were pointed out
by a zealous young reformer, James Gordon Carter, a Harvard
graduate. From his *Essays Upon Popular Education* a selection
entitled "The Schools of Massachusetts in 1824" was reproduced
as No. 135 in the Old South Leaflets.[17]

Carter felt that reforms were needed in the areas of school construction, subject matter, methods of teaching and, above all,
teacher qualification. In the rest of the paper, however, he does
not mention specifically the content of *religious* instruction as

---

[16] Baker v. Foles 16 Mass. 492. Cf. Culver, *op. cit.*, p. 16. (Reference:
Massachusetts Reports, XVI, 487–522.) Today the visitor to Dedham sees
the schism portrayed by the two church buildings. The older one, now
called "Unitarian," stands at the head of the Common, while to the right
is the "Congregational" Church of those who went across the street.

[17] James Gordon Carter, *The Schools of Massachusetts in 1824*, from
Essays on Popular Education. (Old South Leaflets, No. 135, VI, 201–24)
(Boston: Old South Meeting House, no date [Vol. V is dated 1902]).

needing reform. The only direct mention of religion comes later when he is again speaking of *teacher qualifications* rather than subject matter:

> . . . Compare the improvement made in these little nurseries of piety and religion, of knowledge and rational liberty, not with one another,—for the progress in them is much too slow,— but with what the infant mind and heart are capable of, at this early age, under the most favorable auspices.[18]

How, then, did matters stand on the eve of the famous School Law passed by the General Court (Massachusetts Legislature) in its winter session of 1826–1827? The place of religion in education had not been challenged. The constitution of 1780 ordered the teaching of the Protestant religion, supported this by public taxation, and gave the right to select teachers to the several religious groups. The School Law of 1789 repeated the injunction to instruct in the principles of piety. A considerable amount of evidence has been produced in these pages to indicate that the law was obeyed. The textbooks, including both the Bible and denominational Catechisms which were in use, inculcated a certain amount of doctrinal as well as moral instruction. Later on, as will be seen in the next chapter, men argued as to the frequency of catechetical instruction in these earliest years of the nineteenth century. In 1844, for example, Horace Mann claimed that by 1837 the use of the catechism had disappeared in many places in the nine eastern counties. His opponent, E. A. Newton, claimed that the Assembly's Catechism was recited on Saturdays in most of the schools of the state during the entire period under discussion.[19] Assuming, at the least, some truth in each contention, it must be concluded that doctrinal religious instruction, supported by the law, went on until 1826, however sparsely or intensely, in some of the common schools of Massachusetts. To this practice James Carter did not object.

The young reformer was determined, however, that changes come in other areas of the education picture. He ended the Essay

---

[18] *Ibid.*, p. 216.

[19] Cf. *infra*, pp. 165, 166. Yet, Mann later (1848) recalled instances of strong sectarian teaching in the Massachusetts classrooms. Cf. *infra*, p. 147.

from which we have been quoting with a plea that the State Legislature take over supervision of the school program:

> If the policy of the legislature in regard to free schools for the last twenty years be not changed, the institution which has been the glory of New England will, in twenty years more, be extinct. If the State continue to relieve itself of the trouble of providing itself for the instruction of the whole people, and to shift the responsibility upon the towns, and the towns upon the districts, and the districts upon individuals, each will take care of himself and his own family as he is able, and as he appreciates the blessing of a good education.[20]

New Laws

Carter's words did not go unheeded. During the session of 1825–1826 the lawmakers passed "An Act Further To Provide for the Instruction of Youth," which began the process of centralization. It gave authority over the schools in a group of *districts* to the *Committee* of the *town* in which the districts were politically situated. The same town committee was also given authority in the selection of teachers. Further power centralization came in Section 2, on textbooks. It read, partly, as follows:

> *Be it further enacted* that the school committee of each town shall direct and determine the class books to be used in the respective classes, in the public district and town schools of the town; and the scholars sent to such schools shall be supplied with the books prescribed for their classes; . . .[21]

The law next stated that the parents were to pay for the books; that if they did not, the books were to be given to the children anyway and the cost added to the parents' next tax bill; and that if the parents were deemed unable to pay, that nothing or only a part (as the committee should decide) was to be added to the tax bill.[22]

[20] Carter, *op. cit.*, vi, 220.
[21] *Laws of Massachusetts, 1825–28*, x, Chap. clxx (Boston: Dutton & Wentworth, 1828), 300–301.
[22] *Ibid.*

As can be seen from the section cited, the law put authority over textbooks in the hands of the town committee. A town might contain one or more districts. As noted above, this was a beginning of both a centralization and an increase of power which were to be the occasion of important results in the years to come. Further action in the improvement of education was urged by Governor Levi Lincoln in his message to the General Court at the opening of the next session, January 3, 1827. The Governor spoke of the increased importance of "acquiring useful knowledge." "Education is daily assuming a practical and less abstruse character. It now connects itself with the ordinary pursuits of life, and aims, more directly, at obtaining the necessary qualifications of the business of society." [23] The rest of the "education section" of the speech points out the necessity of having better teachers and makes suggestions for establishing an institute to provide for their training.

Action upon the Governor's suggestion is recorded in a *House Journal* of January 30, 1827: "Joseph Farley of I. [Ipswich] from the Committee in Education made a Report accompanied with a bill to provide for the instruction of youth and for repealing sundry other acts on the same subject. . . ." [24] After noting the Committee's feeling that the existing educational statutes, from the law of June, 1789, to that of March, 1826, should be repealed and combined into one act, Farley stated that the Committee had prepared such a new bill, "with such few corrections and additions as appear to be demanded by the existing wants of the community." [25]

---

[23] *Resolves of the General Court of the Commonwealth of Massachusetts,* January–March, 1827 (Boston: True & Greene, 1827), p. 443. One notices here the hint of a more utilitarian philosophy of education than was heard in the speech of Governor Caleb Strong, twenty-seven years before. (Cf. *supra,* pp. 66–67.) Without overplaying the importance of such a small number of words, it might be suggested that the rise of material interests was beginning to compete with religious instruction, without directly opposing it.

[24] *House Journal,* xlvii (May 1826–March 1827), 331 (State House Library, Boston).

[25] The manuscript of Farley's Report, as well as the printed form, was examined at the State House in Boston. Ms.: *Massachusetts Archives,* Chap. 143, Acts of 1826, H. R. 29, Commonwealth of Massachusetts. Printed form:

The new bill led off with a *verbatim* repetition of the 1789 law enjoining instruction in "the principles of piety, justice, and a sacred regard to truth, love to their country etc." "The alterations in the law of the fourth of March last are few," Farley stated,

> and in the opinion of the committee, useful. The number of the school committee is not to exceed seven. Their powers and duties are rendered more definite, and the latter somewhat lessened. Without this, there is reason to believe their duties would not be performed well, and perhaps not at all. An additional provision is added to the second section and comprised in the seventh section of the reported Bill.[26]

Section 2 of the previous law,[27] then, became, *verbatim*, Section 7 of the Law of 1827, with *two* additions, or as Farley put it, *one* addition comprising two parts, as follows:

> *Provided, nevertheless,* that in cases where children are already supplied with books, which shall not be considered by the committee as being extremely faulty, in comparison with others, which might be obtained and which may be possessed in such numbers as to admit of the proper and convenient classification of the school, then, and in that case, the committee shall not direct the purchase of new books, without first obtaining the consent of the parents, masters or guardians of a majority of the children, so already provided for, under the term of two years from the passing of this act, unless such books become so worn, as to be unfit for use: *Provided, also,* that said committee shall never direct any school books to be purchased or used, in any of the schools under their superintendence, which are calculated to favor any particular religious sect or tenet.[28]

Attention is called to the latter proviso. It is the first proposal of its kind in American history.

"Report of Committee on Education to House of Representatives, January 29, 1827," pp. 8–9, *Massachusetts Legislative Documents, Senate and House, 1826 & 1827* (1st and 2nd Sessions), H. R. 29, Commonwealth of Massachusetts.

[26] Ms., Archives of Massachusetts (cf. footnote 25).

[27] *Supra,* p. 102.

[28] *Laws of Massachusetts,* x, Chap. cxliii, 562–63 (cf. footnote 25). The photostat used as the frontispiece of the present study shows this textbook law as it appears in the ms. presumably in the handwriting of a clerk of the House of Representatives. Reproduced through the courtesy of the Hon. Edward J. Cronin, Secretary of the Commonwealth of Massachusetts.

The Farley Report accompanying the proposed bill contained a significant passage in which he asked the legislators not to consider either the Law of March, 1826, or the modifications now proposed as infringements of the people's rights:

> Your Committee expect the most valuable results from the operation of the law of March last, relating to schools. They regret that the salutary provisions of that law have not been carried into effect, in every town in the Commonwealth; more especially they regret, that any portion of the community should have entertained, as they find has been the case, apprehensions of the tendency of that law to impair, or to wrest from them their rights. It is hoped that the modifications they have proposed in that law, will, at least, evince to the people their desire to protect them against any injurious tendency which the law might, otherwise, be supposed to have. If the law, as it is now reported shall not prove acceptable to all, it should be attributed to the unavoidable imperfection which attends the first essay in any new project; and the people ought to rest satisfied, that if it shall be found, after full and fair experiment, that any deficiencies, or injurious provisions, do actually exist in the law, it will undergo such modifications as to do them away. It will be truly mortifying, if,—after the earnest calls of the community for the improvement of the common schools, this earnest attempt to effect such an improvement, shall be viewed with indifference, treated with contempt, or, above all, opposed as a design to lord it over them. . . .
>
> Which is submitted—Joseph Farley, per order.[29]

From January 30, 1827, when Mr. Farley presented the Bill to the House, to March 10, 1827, when it was approved by both Senate and House and signed into law by the Governor, the Bill was given much scrutiny, and was made the subject of several amendments.[30] None of the amendments, however, touched the wording on the use of textbooks "calculated to favor any particular religious sect or tenet." The photostat of the clerk's copy of this section of the Bill, used as the frontispiece of this book, shows no corrections or changes of any sort. The blot on the word "new"

---

[29] Ms., Archives of Massachusetts (cf. footnote 25).

[30] The law is filed as a statute of 1826, since the legislative session ran from May, 1826, to March, 1827. Since it became a law on March 10, 1827, however, it will be hereafter referred to as the Law of 1827.

seems to have been an accident, and, of course, has no reference of any sort to the final proviso.

Meaning of and Reason for the 1827 Law

Intricate as the above attempt to bring out the pertinent documentation on the sectarian textbook law of 1827 may seem, the facts discovered are none too helpful in ascertaining either the *precise meaning* or the *reason for enacting* this first State statute curbing the teaching of religion in public schools. No agitation seems to have preceded its introduction. It went through the committee and general deliberations without any record of controversy. Beyond the printing of the Bill's complete text, there was little or no notice of its contents in the local press. The *Columbia Centinel* reproduced the Bill on March 21, and no further mention was made in issues examined up to that of April 11. The *New England Palladium and Commercial Advertiser* printed the text on March 23, but no further notice was taken in issues through April 13.[31] Culver says: "Newspaper comment on the whole measure is very brief." [32] He does note, however, that the Worcester *National Aegis* for February 27 carried a letter from a correspondent in which it was said: "Mr. Burnside seems to be father of the Bill and defends its provisions manfully and artfully." [33]

It was seventeen years after the passage of the law that a public controversy arose in Massachusetts over the *precise meaning* of this 1827 statute. Out of the controversy came a long letter from Mr. Samuel Burnside of Worcester, to whom specific attention was called in the documents describing the formulation and passing of the measure.[34] Horace Mann was then (1844) Secretary of

[31] These newspapers were examined in the State House Library in Boston.
[32] Culver, *op. cit.*, p. 23.
[33] *Ibid.* It is significant to note that Governor Lincoln stressed the advantages of a religious education *only three months* after he had signed the textbook law. Cf. his speech opening the Legislature's session on June 6, 1827 (*Resolves of the General Court of the Commonwealth of Massachusetts*, May–June, 1827 [Boston: Dutton & Wentworth, 1827], pp. 580–81).
[34] Cf., also, *infra*, footnote 36.

the Board of Education and he had been insisting that the 1827 law meant to exclude books which favored those doctrines or dogmatic teachings which divided the various Protestant groups in Massachusetts at that time. This position was attacked by Edward A. Newton, of Pittsfield, a former member of the State Board of Education. Newton claimed that the law meant to exclude only such books as set forth "ecclesiastical systems of Church government and discipline," and that, actually, doctrinal points such as those to which Mann objected had continued to be taught in the common schools after 1827.[35]

Newton's charge brought forth a letter from Burnside, addressed to Mann, which appeared in the Worcester *Aegis* on June 4, 1844. It gives a clear explanation of the meaning which was attached to the law by one whose claims to have been its originator seem fairly well substantiated.[36]

Burnside states that he had read the letter signed E.A.N. and that he wished to refute one of the many errors that it contained, on one of which he could speak from personal recollection. It was the Newton statement that the prohibition of the 1827 textbook law extended only to descriptions of church polity and not to doctrine.

"Now, sir," writes Burnside, "it happened to me to take some part in the passage of that Act. . . . I drew the bill almost in the very words in which the law stands expressed . . . if the construction Mr. Newton puts on the 23d section [the textbook proviso] did not originate with him, I am quite sure that no individual of the Legislature would then have claimed the honor of its invention." [37]

[35] *The Common School Controversy; Consisting of Three Letters of the Secretary of the Board of Education, of the State of Massachusetts, In Reply to Charges Preferred Against the Board, by the Editor of the Christian Witness and by Edward A. Newton, Esq., of Pittsfield, Once a Member of the Board; to Which Are Added Extracts from the Daily Press, in regard to the Controversy* (Boston: J. N. Bradley & Co., 1844), p. 22.

[36] Burnside stated in the letter that he attended meetings of the Education Committee and was asked to aid the Education Committee as they drafted the bill. The *House Journal* records that on March 6 (1827) "Messrs. Burnside and Hubbard were placed on the [Education] Com'ee." (P. 496.)

[37] *The Common School Controversy*, pp. 48–49.

Burnside then gives his recollection of what the law was supposed to mean:

The committee did not understand that any doctrines of the
dogmatic theology had been taught in our schools for many
years—they were all of opinion that such doctrines ought to be
excluded—that our schools could not otherwise be sustained—
that the school room should never become the battle ground of
polemic combatants—they considered the 18th article of our
Bill of Rights as limiting the extent of the religious instruction
to be given in our schools—and the 7th section of the bill was
intended to conform to it.

Then the 23rd section of the bill was deemed necessary, and
was introduced only to limit, or rather to accommodate, the
books to be used in their moral and religious character, in the
topics of instruction required by the 7th section:—for upon
the ground presented by the section it was believed all sects of
christians might walk harmoniously together—and that children and youth would be well fitted, by such instruction, to
judge for themselves, in after life, what system of disputed doctrines was best entitled to belief. The idea of Mr. Newton that
the 23d section was "intended to mean the exclusion of ecclesiastical systems of church government and discipline," is without
foundation—such a notion, I am sure, never once entered the
mind of any individual of the committee, or of either branch of
the Legislature. I know the bill was universally understood as
excluding doctrinal subjects of dogmatic theology, and that no
other portion of it met with so much favor as this. Not a word
was uttered against it. It was not considered as altering the system of popular instruction, but as legalizing it, as it was understood to exist; for, as I before said, it was not believed that
controverted doctrines were then taught, certainly not, where
they were objected to.[38]

The writer next recalled that Emory Washburn, a fellow-towns-
man, had also been in the 1826–1827 Legislature. Burnside states
that he checked his recollection of the textbook law with Washburn and was authorized to say that Washburn agreed with him.

The remainder of the Burnside letter describes the teaching of
religion in the public schools in and around Worcester at the time
of his writing (1844). Members of the town committee "have
required teachers to give religious instruction, within the meaning of the constitution and the statutes—but have enjoined them,

[38] *Ibid.*, p. 49.

on the other hand, to abstain from doctrines, which occasion strife." [39]

Samuel Burnside states that he himself had done some teaching in the public schools of New Hampshire, Vermont and Massachusetts. "In every place," he states, "I was in an orthodox society. Now I never taught such [orthodox] doctrines, though I then embraced them—nor was I required or even permitted to teach them." [40] At one school, he recalls, he introduced the Westminster Catechism in his classes, but, because of parental objection, later discontinued its use.[41]

Burnside and Washburn, then, maintained that the law meant to exclude books favoring the *doctrines* on which there was a difference among Protestant sects. They felt it did not mean either of two alternate extremes—the banning of religion altogether or (Newton's position) the banning only of the descriptions of ecclesiastical polity. Burnside makes a reference to the 18th Article of the Bill of Rights as considered normative for religious instruction in the schools. This article, reproduced on page 54 *Supra,* merely says that piety and other virtues are necessary for good government and that the people should demand such traits in their rulers. It is not clear just how this statement can be regarded as defining what type of religious instruction might be permitted or should be enforced in a public school.

So much for the *meaning* of the law. Now—what was the *reason* for its passage? James Carter, who is credited with having inspired the entire agitation for school reform, seems not to have been worried about the religious instruction being given.[42] The only "worrying" which has been noticed was that of a "portion of the Community" which had expressed concern about what the *March 1826* law had done or might do to their "rights." [43] Powers formerly held by *district* committees were given to *town* committees. Did the district committees fear that a sectarian group might gain control of a town committee and effect the inculcation of their particular beliefs upon all the schools of the several dis-

[39] *Ibid.,* p. 50.
[40] *Ibid.*
[41] *Ibid.*
[42] Cf. *supra,* pp. 100–101.
[43] *Supra,* p. 105 (Farley's *Report*).

tricts under that town, to the prejudice of the rights of conscience of those who belonged to another or several other sects? Or, did the districts fear that the bitter battles then actually being waged, especially between the Orthodox and the Unitarians, would be carried into the schools?

If the legislature passed a law prohibiting books favoring a particular sect, because apprehension had been expressed that peoples' *rights* were in danger, what right could be involved but the right of conscience in regard to freedom of religion? The Constitution of 1780 granted freedom of worship, and commanded the teaching of the Protestant religion.[44] Perhaps there was a felt need to reconcile the two notions—freedom of worship and necessity of protestant teaching. A man might wonder how free he was if the teaching was of another sect. What else, then, could the lawmakers have been trying to protect, if not the rights of conscience?

In the letter described above, Samuel Burnside cited Emory Washburn as a member of the 1826–1827 Legislature who had agreed with his (Burnside's) interpretation of the *meaning* of the 1827 law. The writings of Burnside and Washburn may offer a clue to the *reason* they may have had for supporting the sectarian textbook law.

Samuel Macgregor Burnside was a graduate of Dartmouth (1805) and later studied law with Judge Artemas Ward of Boston. A resident of Worcester after 1810, he took a deep interest in public education throughout his life.[45]

Burnside emphasized his belief in the basic importance of a religious education in an undated address, given at the opening of larger quarters for the Female School in Worcester:

> A leading object of the education we here propose to give you, to make you acquainted with the essential thruths [sic] of Christianity, and to form the habits of your lives under the influence of the Spirit of its devine [sic] author. If we do not succeed in this, we consider ourselves as failing altogether. We do

---

44 Cf. *supra,* p. 53.
45 Archives of American Antiquarian Society, Worcester, Massachusetts. We are indebted to Mr. Clarence S. Bingham, Director of the Society, for the material here reproduced from its files. While there are some Burnside Diaries in the Antiquarian Society's material, unfortunately there is a gap between 1822 and 1828, when the sectarian textbook law was in the making.

not flatter ourselves, that we shall benefit either you or our country, by sending you into her service with minds stored with knowledge, if you carry with you hearts dead to Christian virtue. Our country needs the influence of well educated females to uphold her institutions; but if their talents, their learning and accomplishments be not directed by Religion, they impart no moral strength to Society; they breathe no moral life into the body politic, and yield no support to the cause of civil liberty and human improvement. Woman, without religion, is no help to man. You see, then, what we hope you will be hereafter.[46]

In 1832, Burnside delivered a lecture on education before the American Institute of Instruction.[47] "Man comes into existence with physical, moral, and intellectual faculties, perfectly suited to the condition," he stated,

in which his Maker has placed him, and in every respect sufficient to secure the ultimate end of his being. These are to be unfolded, strengthened, exercised and applied to their appropriate uses. . . .[48]

"But it is my purpose," he said later in this speech,

to contend earnestly that the moral or religious nature of man, (and in whatever I say, I make no distinction between them, for I know of none) is a proper subject of school education; that the kind of instruction and discipline this nature requires, should form a part, and the most considerable part too, of the system, and that the classification of our schools, to which your attention is to be invited, should be made in view of creating the greatest facilities for imparting religious knowledge, and forming religious habits. If it be true, according to one of the theories I have stated, that piety is the natural fruit of religious instruction, and is seldom, perhaps never produced by extraordinary, supernatural influences, then this education assumes an interest, as vast as the eternal destinies of our race; and even if we suppose its interest limited to a preparation only of the heart for the operation of divine agency, its importance is incalculably great.[49]

[46] Archives, American Antiquarian Society, p. 12 of ms.

[47] Samuel M. Burnside, *On the Classification of Schools*, in *The Introductory Course and the Lectures Delivered Before the American Institute of Instruction in Boston, August, 1833* (Boston: Carter, Hendee & Company, 1834), pp. 73–93. (An editor's note states: "This lecture was delivered in 1832, but the publication of it was omitted through mistake.")

[48] *Ibid.*, p. 73.

[49] *Ibid.*, pp. 75–76.

Burnside then turned to the common school and its possibilities for religious instruction:

> I consider its advantages for moral education as forming its highest ground of preference . . . The only objection I know to exist, arises from the discordant opinion of the religious sects, which abound in the community. To this objection a satisfactory answer was furnished by the eloquent gentleman who immediately preceded me in this course of lectures;— "There is common ground enough for imparting to youth all necessary religious instruction, without disturbing the peculiar doctrines of any sect of Christians." To this just sentiment, I may be pardoned, I trust, for adding my own belief, that this ground is also spacious enough for sincere Christians of all denominations to walk together to that future world, where the distracting controversies of this will never enter.
>
> But our desire is only to train children to the practice of Christian virtues from Christian motives; that is, from reverence of God, an habitual sense of his perfections, his presence, and of personal accountability, and from a love also of country, and the whole human family. To make them theologians or metaphysicians in these seminaries, is neither necessary nor practicable. This is all I mean by a religious education, or a religious character, and whatever more is attached to these terms by others, it will not be denied, that such a character is wanted for the concerns of this life, and I would humbly trust, that it is some preparation for a better.[50]

Burnside was surely a devotee of religion in education. When he pinned himself down to specifics, he declared that he meant by this "to train children in the practice of christian motives." This is something less than full Christian theology and something more than natural religion or pure ethics. But it is clear that he was as firm in 1832 against sectarian instruction for all the children in the schools as he claims he was in 1827. In this speech he declared that he wanted religious education. He did not want sectarian instruction. He was less clear as to the reason for the latter restriction.

With the confusion caused by the error of printing Burnside's discourse in a later group of lectures,[51] we should not be able

---

[50] *Ibid.*, pp. 93–94.
[51] Cf. footnote 47.

to do much on the identity of "the eloquent gentleman who immediately preceded me in this course of lectures," were it not for
the quotation Burnside gives us. It seems to identify the talk as
one given by "R. Park," entitled "Religious Education." [52] It is
included in the Lecture Series for 1835, but whether it was given
then or earlier, cannot be established for certain. In any case, it
is an interesting parallel with Burnside's ideas.

Park stated that he was not a Minister.[53] That he believed in
a religious education was soon made clear: "It is then of vital
importance to our country, that all the rising generation should
be instructed in the principles and practices of true religion as
the sum total of virtue and morality." [54] After declaring that both
parents and ministers should give religious instruction, Park
addressed the teacher:

> . . . Your employment is the noble one of instruction. And
> what instruction can be more important, than that which is
> necessary to make men Christians in heart as well as in name?
> Teach them to love their parents, their brethren and con-
> nexions [sic]; teach them to love their neighbor as themselves;
> but especially teach them to love the Lord their God with all
> their heart, and soul, and strength; for this includes all moral
> virtue. . . . Teach them that in the performance of their daily
> labors, the discharge of their social relations, the government of
> their hearts and lives—in all this, if done in the right spirit, they
> are proving themselves Christians, inasmuch as they follow the
> example of the Saviour. . . .
> Let me add, all this you may accomplish without proscribing
> the tenets, or offending the prejudices, of any sect of professed
> Christians. There is common ground, on which they all meet,
> enough for you to occupy, without disturbing the separate folds
> and enclosures which are their places of retirement [cf. the
> Burnside quote on page 112 of this book]. It will perhaps be a
> duty to point out the extremes of Christian doctrine; but still
> you may derive practical instruction from them all. [He follows
> with examples of differences in doctrine]. On these and other
> points Christians may differ in opinion; but all their creeds pro-

[52] R. Park, *Religious Education, Lectures Delivered Before the American
Institute of Instruction in Boston, August, 1835* (Boston: Charles J. Hendee,
1836), pp. 102–10.
[53] *Ibid.*, p. 102.
[54] *Ibid.*, p. 104.

fess the same object, and should produce the same result. . . . Not that it is a matter of indifference what doctrines we embrace; for some of them must be wrong, and this must weaken the vital strength of religion. But what I deem of far greater importance, the ground on which all should meet, is Christian practice. This seems to me the best test of all doctrines; the one which Our Saviour propounds when he says, "by their fruits ye shall know them." And on this ground would I base the religious instruction of youth. Their doctrinal views will ripen with time, and may undergo changes; their practical principles should be fixed at once, and remain ever after immutable as the laws of nature.[55]

Park here allowed more latitude in making the children aware of doctrinal differences than did Burnside. His language was also somewhat stronger in describing how much of the vital content of Christianity should be imparted. Yet he did not want the doctrinal differences stressed, but rather left for the consideration of more mature years. Unfortunately for our present purpose, Park did not state clearly *why* he opposed sectarian teaching.

We now turn to Emory Washburn, the man from whom Burnside got a confirmation of his recollections of the meaning of the 1827 law. He was, indeed, a member of the Legislature in the 1826–1827 session. He served on the Board of Education and interested himself in the Normal Schools. He has been described as a "moderate Calvinist" and of a "reverent and devout spirit." [56] Two of his addresses contain some material giving an insight into his ideas on religion in his day and its place in education.

On March 31, 1831 he addressed the Worcester Lyceum on the "Classes of Society." [57] "The public journals have told us," he declared,

of the efforts of self-styled reformers who are laboring in some of our cities to create jealousies among different classes of citizens, and are striking at the very foundations of civil society. They sieze [sic] upon known and necessary evils to effect an

[55] *Ibid., passim,* pp. 107–109.

[56] Cf. A. P. Peabody, "Memoir of Hon. Emory Washburn," *Proceedings, Massachusetts Historical Society,* xvii (1879–80), 23–32.

[57] Emory Washburn, *A Lecture Read Before the Worcester Lyceum, March 30, 1831* (Worcester: Dorr & Howland, 1831) (Boston Athenaeum, *Miscellaneous Tracts,* Series B, 2089, Vol. 31).

entire revolution, and in a feigned devotion to the cause of the people, advocate a system of universal education as something novel, in order, as they pretend, to create what has in fact ever existed here, and from the same cause too, an equality amongst the citizens of our country.

They thus delude the public by a promise to give them what they in fact already have the means of enjoying, and make their zeal for education a covert for their attack upon the Christian religion, which has done more for the diffusion and support of true republican principles in the world, than all other causes combined.[58]

This censure of certain "self-styled reformers" is significant in that it links an advocacy of "universal education" with an attack on the Christian religion.[59] He felt that the promised advantages of education for all had been and continued to be at the disposal of the people, through the medium of Christianity. It seems impossible, however, to deduce categorically from these words anything more definite on just how the education issue was thought to have been used to injure the Christian religion. Yet, against the background of the times, the speaker's words suggest dissatisfaction with such theories as those of Burnside and Park.

On December 7, 1848 (the late date should be noted) Washburn spoke at the dedication of the State Reform School at Westborough, Massachusetts: "It [the reform school] aims by discipline," he said,

> to fit its inmates for the honorable duties of life, and to restore them back to society, to merit, and to share its rewards. Here religion, with its precepts and its promises, will reach the intellects, and may we not hope, touch the hearts of those who may be gathered here. Here the instructions of the schoolroom will open, to the minds of the ignorant, the blessings and delights of knowledge.[60]

This examination of some writings of the period gives insight into the minds of the men of Massachusetts during the time following the enactment of the 1827 law forbidding the committees

[58] *Ibid.*, p. 20.
[59] Does Washburn refer here to the Unitarians?
[60] Emory Washburn, *An Address at the Dedication of the Massachusetts State Reform School in Westborough, Mass., Dec. 7, 1848* (Boston: Dutton & Wentworth, 1849) (Boston Athenaeum, *Tracts*, Series B, 1587, pp. 17–18).

to authorize sectarian textbooks. It points out that the earnest and deep-seated conviction of earlier days that religion belonged in public education had not been lost. Faced with the fragmentation of the once-unified Calvinist group in Massachusetts, however, these men seemed to grope for a way to keep religion in the curriculum. Were they trying to preserve the rights of conscience, and prevent the current theological battles from invading the common schools? Perhaps they considered the elimination of sectarian differences the only solution. Yet they did not want the elimination of sectarian doctrines to mean, and did not think it would mean, that Christianity would be excluded from the school and a system of ethics or natural theology remain. They thought they saw the possibility of *retaining Christian principles and Christian living* in the body of material which would be left after sectarian differences had been taken out of the picture. Up to this point *we are sure* they wanted what *they felt to be religion* kept in education. We *infer* that their fight against sectarianism was based on a desire to protect freedom of conscience.

If the above inference is correct, if the purpose of the 1827 law was to protect the rights of conscience, then this statute marks the beginning in state educational law of what might be called a legal tradition looking to the freedom of religion. As can be seen from the Confrey tables in Chapter I, other states gradually passed similar enactments on the subject of sectarian books and teachings. The 1827 law in Massachusetts seems to reflect the philosophy of the "freedom of religion" clause in the First Amendment. In this sense the Massachusetts law was a continuation rather than a beginning of the tradition. It was the first in a series of such laws on the level of the states. It did not set itself in opposition to the American social tradition that "religion belonged." It said, rather, "The rights of conscience must be respected."

CHAPTER V

The Fate of Religion

under Horace Mann

1834-1848

IN THE YEARS which immediately followed the passage of the law of 1827 there was little change in the school situation. People like James G. Carter continued to agitate for better teacher training, but no formal action was taken by the Legislature. In 1834 a law was passed which created a school fund. The money was to be realized from the sale of lands belonging to Massachusetts and located in Maine. Distribution of the fund depended, first, upon the town's raising by taxation at least a dollar for each child from four to sixteen years of age and, second, upon its making an annual report on conditions in its schools to the Secretary of State.[1]

In 1835 the Legislature revised the 1827 education law. In the provision regarding textbooks favoring sectarianism discussed in the last chapter, the changes were so slight that they could in no real sense alter the meaning of the law.

[1] *Laws of Massachusetts,* March 31, 1834, Chap. 169, pp. 241–42. The reader will also understand why Samuel Burnside in his letter to the Worcester *Aegis* spoke of the "23rd Section." Cf. *supra,* p. 108. Burnside wrote in 1844, after the 1834 revision.

After the revision this section read as follows:

The school committee shall never direct to be purchased or used in any of the town schools, any books which are calculated to favor the tenets of any particular sect of Christians.[2]

In contrast to the comparative inactivity in the realm of school reform, there was much ado in the legislative halls after 1827 about the state Church. It culminated in 1833 in a revision of the Constitution of 1780, which effected a complete disestablishment of the Congregational Church. The original paragraphs had stated that the legislature should require the "towns, parishes, precincts and other bodies politic; and religious societies, to make suitable provision, at their own expense, for the institution of the public worship of GOD etc." [3] This, in practice, had meant public tax money for the Congregational Church. Dissenters had been allowed to divert their tax to their own denomination, provided there were such institutions to which the dissenters went for worship.[4]

Although in a constitutional convention held in 1820 attempts were made to substitute a voluntary system of support for religious worship, only certain modifications on oaths and abjurations, and the dropping of the law requiring belief in the Christian religion were passed. The essential provisions for financial support remained the same.[5] In 1830 the agitation to change the Constitution was renewed. In the 1832–1833 legislative session the Constitution was amended. Article xi supplanted Article iii of the original Constitution,[6] with the following provisos:

As the public worship of God, and instructions in piety, religion and morality, promote the happiness and prosperity of a

[2] *Revised Statutes of the Commonwealth of Massachusetts* (Under the Supervision of Theron Metcalf and Horace Mann), 1835, (Boston: Dutton & Wentworth, 1836), Chap. 23, Sec. 23, p. 22. (Cf. *supra*, p. 104.) Hence, one finds in the documents of the period that the law is sometimes referred to as the "1826–1827" law and sometimes as the "1834" law.

[3] Cf. *supra*, p. 53.

[4] *Ibid.*

[5] Thorning, *op. cit.*, p. 77 (quoting the *Journal of Debates and Proceedings in the Convention of Delegates, 1820–1821*, Boston, 1853, pp. 633–35).

[6] Cf. *supra*, p. 53.

people, and the security of a republican government; therefore, the several religious societies of this commonwealth, whether corporate or unincorporate, at any meeting legally warned and holden for that purpose shall ever have the right to elect their pastors or religious teachers, to contract with them for their support, to raise money for erecting and repairing houses for public worship, for the maintenance of religious instruction, and for the payment of necessary expenses. . . . And all religious sects and denominations demeaning themselves peaceably, and as good citizens of the Commonwealth, shall be equally under the protection of the law; and no subordination of any one sect or denomination to another shall ever be established by law.[7]

The new law freed the civil governmental agencies from the obligation to support the Congregational Church. It recognized the right of the individual denominations to tax their own members for church activities, including religious education. It also declared that the law would recognize membership in religious groups as legally existing unless proper steps were taken by a dissenter to notify the church authorities of his departure.

Although the establishment which existed in Massachusetts up to 1883 was not so absolute that the civil arm was given power over the definition of doctrine or the right to force acceptance of doctrine, it did keep the Congregational group in a highly favored position through the financial support furnished by public taxation. Massachusetts, then, became the last State to end that type of establishment which afforded a single religious group a status of preference over all the others.[8]

It is a matter of speculation whether or not this act of disestablishment significantly affected the history of religious instruction in Massachusetts public schools. Burnside's letter on the framing of the textbook statute in 1827 stated his recollection that the majority of the education *committeemen* were Orthodox, (i.e., Congregationalist). This proposed section of the education bill was never the subject of amendments or controversy of which we have found record. Among the great number of votes cast in

---

[7] Thorning, *op. cit.*, pp. 90–91 (quoting *Proceedings of Convention of 1820*, p. 667). The new law was ratified by the people on November 11, 1833 (Thorning, *op. cit.*, p. 90).

[8] Cf. Stokes, *op. cit.*, I, 426, 721.

its favor in both houses of the Legislature, many were doubtless those of Congregationalists. Thus the Established Church, as such, seems not to have fought, and in some ways its members seem to have supported the effort to eliminate sectarian indoctrination in the schools. In the decade and a half following disestablishment, as will be pointed out, certain acrimonious controversies arose over the interpretation and application of the 1827 law. Whether the activities of the Congregational Church would have been different than they were in the textbook agitation, if it had remained the legally preferred group, and whether such a different attitude on the part of this Church would have made the controversies come out other than they did, are problems on which it seems very hazardous to be definite. This much can be said, however,—the 1833 disestablishment act, eliminating in a religiously pluralistic society the preferential status of a single sect, was a move in favor of freedom of conscience. As such, it falls in line with the series of events and pronouncements which started in the Federal Congress. That body emphasized the principle of the rights of conscience in the First Amendment by ruling out on the national level the establishing of any one group as the national religion in preference to all others, and guaranteeing that the Congress would not infringe the freedom of worship. Another link in the chain is surely the Declaration of Religious Rights in the Massachusetts Constitution of 1780. Disestablishment of the Congregational Church in 1833 continued the pattern. There is no indication, however, that men were weakening in the conviction that religion belonged in public life. There was, rather, a growing emphasis on the principle of freedom of worship and belief. Did they foresee that the two convictions would come into conflict in public education?

So matters stood when in 1837, the General Court of Massachusetts decided to strengthen its policy of centralization and create a State Board of Education. In his January address opening the session that year, Governor Edward Everett said:

> I submit to the Legislature, whether the creation of a board of Commissioners of schools, to serve without salary, with authority to appoint a secretary, at a reasonable compensation, to be paid from the school fund would not be of great utility.

. . . The wealth of Massachusetts has always been and always will be, the mind of her children; and good schools are a treasure, a thousand fold more precious, than all the gold and silver of Mexico and Peru.[9]

Pleading for the enactment of legislation to support the Governor's recommendation of a Board of Education was the ardent enthusiast, James G. Carter, whose influence was noted in the 1824–1827 period.[10]

The Legislature responded by passing an act creating the Board. It was to consist of eight persons, who, with the Governor and Lieutenant-Governor as members *ex officio,* were to serve eight years. The first person named was to retire and be replaced after the first year, the second after the second year, and so on. The Board was required to lay before the Legislature annually an abstract of the school returns, (i.e., the report from the towns on the schools' condition). It was also authorized to appoint a Secretary:

> who shall under the direction of the board collect information of the actual condition and efficiency of the common schools and other means of popular education; and diffuse as widely as possible throughout every part of the Commonwealth information of the most approved and successful methods of arranging the studies and conducting the education of the young, to the end that all children in this Commonwealth, who depend upon common schools for instruction, may have the best education which those schools can be made to impart.[11]

Finally, it was ordered that "The board of education shall make a detailed report to the legislature of all its doings, with such

[9] *Resolves of the General Court of the Commonwealth of Massachusetts, January–April, 1837* (Boston: Dutton & Wentworth, 1837), pp. 465–66. In the closing words of the Governor's address is found a reiteration of the principle that religion is an asset to public life (cf. pp. 467–68).

[10] James G. Carter, *Speech of Mr. Carter of Lancaster Delivered in the House of Representatives of Massachusetts, Feb. 2, 1837* (Boston: Light & Starns, 1837). (Pamphlet in the Harvard University Library, Educ. 1421.3.837.box.) Still strong for teacher training, Carter repeated his previous theme, in which the religious element was taken for granted. "The character of the schools," he declared, "and of course their moral, intellectual and religious influence upon the community depend almost solely on the character of the teachers."

[11] *Laws of Massachusetts, 1837* (Boston: Dutton & Wentworth, 1837), Chap. 241, pp. 277–78.

observations, as their experience and reflection may suggest upon the condition and efficiency of our system of popular education, and the most practicable means of improving and extending it." [12]

Culver lists the names and affiliations, both political and religious, of the first board chosen: Governor Everett, Whig and Unitarian; Lieutenant-Governor George Hull, Whig and Unitarian; James G. Carter, Whig and Unitarian; Rev. Emerson Davis, Whig and Trinitarian [Orthodox]; Edmund Dwight, Whig and Unitarian; Horace Mann, Whig and Unitarian; [At Mann's resignation to become the Board's Secretary, his place was filled by Rev. George Putnam, Whig and Unitarian]; Edward A. Newton, Whig and Episcopalian; Robert Rantoul, Jr., Democrat and Unitarian; Rev. Thomas Robbins, Whig and Trinitarian; and Rev. Jared Sparks, Whig and Unitarian. [13] Denominationally speaking, then, the first board was highly weighted in favor of the Unitarians. In addition to their Secretary, Horace Mann, there were seven of them to two Trinitarians (or Orthodox) and one Episcopalian.

The choice of Horace Mann as the first Secretary of the Board of Education brought into the machinery of the Massachusetts school system a man whose work was to have tremendous influence on the public schools not only of his own state but of the entire American nation. A study of the man and his activities thus becomes exceedingly important.

Born May 4, 1796, into a strict Calvinistic family, [14] Mann had been graduated from Brown University, and studied and practiced law at Dedham, Massachusetts, before his election to the Bay State Legislature in 1827. [15] Chosen for the Senate in 1833, he was serving as its President in 1837 when appointed Secretary to the newly created Board of Education.

[12] *Ibid.*, p. 278.

[13] Culver, *op. cit.*, pp. 31–32 (quoting "Minutes of the Board," State House, Boston).

[14] For biographical data, cf. Mary P. Mann, *Life of Horace Mann, By His Wife* (Boston: Walker, Fuller & Co., 1865; from the series, *The Life and Works of Horace Mann* [5 vols.; Boston: Walker, Fuller & Co., 1865–68]) and Louise Hall Tharp, *Until Victory—Horace Mann and Mary Peabody* (Boston: Little, Brown & Co., 1953).

[15] Mann did not take his seat, however, until two months after the passage of the 1827 textbook law. Cf. Tharp, *op. cit.*, p. 57.

Mann's Diary records some of the emotions with which he accepted the appointment.[16] His heart was torn between thoughts of the bitterness and opposition he was sure to meet in his work and the bright opportunities to enhance the future of the people which lay in the work of the Secretary. Forebodings of possible failure and the calamitous results for the common weal haunted him.[17] Yet he placed his confidence in prayer, as the Diary shows for June 29, the day the position of Secretary was actually offered to him:

> God grant me an annihilation of selfishness, a mind of wisdom, a heart of benevolence! How many men I shall meet who are accessible only through a single motive, or who are incased in prejudice and jealousy, and need, not to be subdued, but to be remodelled! . . . There is but one spirit in which these impediments can be met with success: it is the spirit of self-abandonment, the spirit of martyrdom. . . . In all this, there must be a higher object than to win personal esteem, or favor, or worldly applause. A new fountain may now be opened. Let me strive to direct its current in such a manner, that if, when I have departed from life, I may still be permitted to witness its course, I may behold it broadening and deepening in an everlasting progression of virtue and happiness.

Because of the prominent part which Mann took in reshaping the policy of religious education in Massachusetts, consideration must be given to his personal religious convictions. Since the efforts he made to implement his policy in this field resulted in some acrimonious controversies, it will be helpful also to consider briefly the way he reacted to opposition.

As to the first, there seems to be little doubt that Horace Mann was a deeply religious person. His was a religion, however, peculiarly his own, and its formation had roots in a violent reaction against orthodox Calvinism which started in his boyhood. When Horace was fourteen, his older brother Stephen was drowned on

[16] Horace Mann, *Diary*. This manuscript is preserved among the Mann papers at the Massachusetts Historical Society in Boston.

[17] Cf. entries for June 14, 28, and 29, 1837. Other items in the *Diary* show his continuing spirit of devotion to duty in the ensuing years. Cf., e.g., the entry for November 17, 1839: ". . . I seem to myself to know that the time will come when Education will be reverenced as the highest of earthly employments. That time I am never to see, except with the eye of faith. . . ."

a Sunday, having avoided the service in the local Congregational Church.[18] Mrs. Tharp, who states that the story was related to her by members of the Mann family, tells how the local minister, the Rev. Nathanael Emmons, spoke at the funeral service:

> The young people were all in church this time. Dr. Emmons described "the terrible Last Judgement" and "the lake which burneth with fire and brimstone." He left no doubt as to the future eternal fate of Stephen Mann. In the stunned silence which followed the minister's final words, Horace heard his mother groan.[19]

Experiences such as this turned the mind of the youthful Horace Mann against the strict Calvinist doctrine. Many years later, he described his boyhood feelings in a letter to a Mr. Craig:

> I feel constantly, and more and more deeply, what an unspeakable calamity a Calvinistic education is. What a dreadful thing it was to me! If it did not succeed in making that horrible thing, a Calvinist, it did succeed in depriving me of that filial love for God, that tenderness, that sweetness, that intimacy, that desiring, nestling love, which I say it is natural the child should feel towards a Father who combines all excellence. . . . I am as a frightened child, whose eye, knowledge, experience, belief even, are not sufficient to obliterate the image which an early fright burnt in upon his soul. I have to reason the old image away, and replace it with the loveliness and beauty of another; and in that process, the zeal, the alacrity, the fervor, the spontaneousness, are, partially at least, lost.[20]

While a student at Brown University, Mann wrote an essay on the union of Church and State which gives an insight into his aversion for this aspect of religion, as he understood it. Grossly inaccurate as his examples from Catholicism are, the essay reveals the trend of a mind which in more mature years was to take an immovable stand against anything which he considered to be an approach to Church-State union in this country.[21] To the young

---

[18] Tharp, *op. cit.*, p. 26.

[19] *Ibid.* (Cf. also Tharp's Chap. Note 4 for Chap. iii, p. 323).

[20] Mann to Craig, Boston, (probably) January, 1856, Mary P. Mann, *op. cit.*, pp. 479–80.

[21] The text of this essay, which is preserved in the "Mann Papers" at the Massachusetts Historical Society, is reproduced in full in Appendix "E" of the writer's dissertation in The Johns Hopkins Library.

essay writer it was an "atrocious deed" to unite "the high destinies of religion with the fluctuating caprices of governmental power." Where such a union has occurred it has "given to the most enormous vices and basest crimes the dignity, the sanctity, the impunity of religion, and to spotless religion the foulest stains of depravity, blending the sacred character of the one with the shocking impurities of the other."

Thus, Mann felt, at this early age, that religion suffers from an official connection with the state. As examples, he referred to "that government which boasts of being the most enlightened and liberal on earth" [22] and to "that Vice-gerent of Hell the Pope of Rome." [23] This anti-Catholic bias, based as it was on certain errors of fact,[24] obviously influenced him in his vigorous opposition to any union of Church and State.

That Horace Mann thought almost constantly in a religious vein is patent to anyone who reads his Diary, his letters and his school reports. The reports, especially, are filled with religious references, not only when he is writing directly on the subject of religious education but in many other connections. A sample of the latter type is:

> As the progenitor of the human race, after being perfectly fashioned in every limb and organ and feature, might have lain till this time, a motionless body in the beautiful garden of Eden, had not the Creator breathed into him a living soul, so children, without some favoring influences to woo out and cheer their faculties, may remain mere inanimate forms, while surrounded by the Paradise of knowledge.[25]

[22] France? England?

[23] It should be remembered that in 1817 the Pope was the civil ruler of the Papal State, as well as the spiritual leader of the Catholic Church.

[24] Mann writes, e.g., that the Pope forgives sins in return for the payment of money and grants permission for further sin if more money is forthcoming.

[25] Horace Mann, *First Annual Report of the Board of Education, together with the First Annual Report of the Secretary of the Board* (Boston: Dutton & Wentworth, 1838), p. 47. (Quotations from these reports are taken from the Facsimile Edition of the twelve reports published by the Horace Mann League, commencing June, 1947. Each volume, starting with the year 1837, contains the reports of both the Board and its Secretary. Hereafter the Reports will be designated by their number [one to twelve] and the year which they cover.) For other examples of indirect religious references, cf. *Sixth Report*, p. 109; *Seventh Report*, p. 110; *Ninth Report*, pp. 96–97.

Horace Mann's deep devotion, however, was to a religion which might be described as his own brand of Unitarianism. Having broken with orthodox Calvinism, he attended the services of the Unitarian group throughout most of his life. The Diary contains many references to sermons he heard at Unitarian services.[26]

Mann, of course, believed in the existence of God and in the spirituality and immortality of the soul, as his many references to a future life attest. He seems to have believed in future rewards and also in future punishments, although his biography suggests an evolution in his attitude on the duration of the punishments. "If I believed in total depravity, I must, of course, believe in everlasting punishment," his wife quotes him as saying, "but I consider both unworthy of God." [27] Yet in a letter reproduced a few pages later, Mann states, "I have come round again to a belief in the eternity of rewards and punishments, as a fact necessarily resulting from the constitution of our nature." [28]

We have already seen in the Craig letter that what Mann found most revolting in Calvinism was his (Mann's) feeling that the system left nothing of the kindness and love of a father in the idea of God. In his approach to God as a Father, however, we shall see a mixture of natural theology [God discoverable by human reason alone] and a certain reliance on the Bible "speaking for itself." Any notion of a Church, divinely commissioned as a living teacher and interpreter of the Scriptures, divinely commissioned to teach in God's name, the while divinely protected from falling into doctrinal error, is completely scorned. Jesus Christ is deeply admired by Horace Mann and the Christian system of morality is thought by him to contain the answer to many of the world's ills. As a Unitarian, Mann would not have believed that Jesus Christ is God. There seems to be no evidence that he departed from this Unitarian position. Thus, though Mann

---

[26] Cf., e.g., entries for July 2, 1837 (Rev. Mr. Taylor's sermon); April 1, 1838 (Rev. Taylor again); September 1, 1839 (Why Ministers' Sermons are not effective). Towards the end of his life, while President of Antioch College (Ohio), Horace Mann joined a sect called the "Christian Church" which was active in that region. Cf. Mary P. Mann, *op. cit.*, p. 434.

[27] Mary P. Mann, *op. cit.*, pp. 6–7.

[28] *Ibid.*, p. 15.

wanted the Bible to be read by all, and especially in the schools, his confidence that it would "speak for itself," [29] seems little more than his accepting it as a lofty, indeed the loftiest, code of natural ethics, i.e., morality coinciding with the unaided dictates of reason.

Mann was stunned by the untimely death of Charlotte Messer, his first wife. When he visited her grave he recorded in his Diary his sense of total and irrevocable loss. "Her spirit—where is it? Shall I see & know it again?" [30] The unhappiness caused by his loss lasted through years of brooding. He suffered from bad health. He suffered from the attacks of his enemies. In all these trials there seems to be no evidence that he turned to God in prayer. He was doubtless devoted to the cause of humanity. He admired sermons, if they treated of tolerance and forebearance. Yet the supernatural, while accepted in theory by Horace Mann, seems never to have become *vital* to him.

Judged from his writings and actions, Horace Mann comes out a theist; he comes out a Unitarian in his overt rejection of the Orthodox teachings; and he comes out something of a deist, (despite his talk of God as a Father) in his belief in a God Who made the world and then left it pretty much to itself until it should turn at least its human inhabitants back to Him for judgement.

Thus, his religious beliefs add up to a sectarian position somewhat unique in itself. As Secretary of the Board he will be seen striving according to his understanding of the 1827 textbook law, to keep out of the common school curriculum the sectarian teachings of the Orthodox and other Protestant groups. To supply the vacuum left thereby, will he be found substituting his own brand of religion? Will this result in a *sectarianism* heretofore unknown in the Massachusetts system of education?

As will be seen, there was to be considerable and bitter opposition to Mann's views. This brings up the *second* facet of his character suggested for examination on page 123. How did he react towards his opponents? Anyone as passionately devoted as he to

[29] Cf. *infra,* p. 148.
[30] Cf. *Diary,* entry for March 23, 1839, and Tharp, *op. cit.,* p. 187.

what he believed to be best for the public schools would face the danger of trampling on the honest convictions of others. It appears that Mann was not immune. At times he seemed to question the intelligence of his opponents and doubt the sincerity of their motives.[31]

When his *Seventh Report* was attacked, for example, Mann wrote to his friend, George Combe:

> The Episcopalians here have always borne me a grudge because I have condemned the spirit of the English Church in denying all education to the people, which they could not pervert to the purposes of proselytism. . . . Of course, they had too much craft to avow the real grounds of their hostility, but fabricated charges, in regard to which they excited the sympathy of others. Hence, they were in the false position of a man who acts from one set of motives, while he avows another.[32]

Later the same year Mann again wrote to Combe, this time about the Orthodox:

> The orthodox have hunted me this winter as though they were bloodhounds, and I a poor rabbit. . . .
> There are two classes,—the one who are orthodox only by association, education or personal condition. These may be good people, though they always suffer under that limitation of the faculties which orthodoxy imposes. The second class are those who are born orthodox, who are naturally or indigenously so; who, if they had had wit enough, would have invented orthodoxy, if Calvin had not. I never saw one of this class of men whom I could trust so long as a man can hold his breath. These are the men who are assailing me.[33]

Combe once more heard from Mann about an opponent. This time it was the Rev. Matthew Hale Smith.

> . . . I sent you a mighty great Abstract of School Returns which I had got out, and also copies of a controversy, which, in the way of by-play, I had had with one of the wild beasts of Ephesus; and a more untameable hyena I do not believe St. Paul

[31] The controversies with these opponents will be examined later in this Chapter. Cf. *infra*, p. 150 ff.

[32] Mann to Combe, Wrentham, April, 1844. Mary P. Mann, *op. cit.*, p. 225.

[33] Mann to Combe, Boston, Dec. 1, 1844. Mary P. Mann, *op. cit.*, pp. 230–31.

ever had to encounter,—once a preacher of the annihilation of the wicked, then a Universalist, and now a Calvinist of the Old Testament stamp.[34]

Having completed our sketch of some characteristics of Horace Mann himself, we shall now turn to the work of the Education Board and its Secretary in the field of religious education in public schools. It will be recalled that they were guided by two legal provisions. The law of 1827, revised in 1834, enforced instruction in "the principles of piety" [35] and forbade the purchase or use of sectarian textbooks.[36] Although the Board members mentioned some viewpoints of their own in the annual reports, their statements are more frequently an endorsement of the reports of their Secretary. It is on Horace Mann, then, valiant and sincere champion of the cause of public education, that we must concentrate the greater attention. Far from leaving his rugged nature at home when he worked at his tasks, he took both it and his religious convictions into the fray, as he fought for what he believed to be the correct role of religious instruction in the common schools of Massachusetts. In tracing the course pursued on religion in public schools after the appointment of the Board we shall examine: the Reports of the Board itself; the Reports of their Secretary; a presentation of the viewpoints of their opponents in the controversies which arose during Mann's tenure of office; an analysis of motives on each side; evidence as to how Mann's work was viewed in the years immediately following his Secretaryship.

Reports of the Board

It will be recalled that the law of 1827, having enjoined instruction in the "principles of piety," made no restriction on the way this was to be done except to forbid the use of *books* of a sectarian

---

[34] Mann to Combe, West Newton, April 25, 1847. Mary P. Mann, *op. cit.*, p. 255. Other examples of the same are found in Mrs. Mann's book, e.g., pp. 514, 519. Mann's anti-Catholic bias, though not important to this study, is exemplified in the same book on pp. 177, 180, 207, 211.

[35] Cf. *supra*, p. 104.

[36] Cf. *supra*, pp. 104, 118.

character.[37] As they started their work, then, the Board addressed themselves to the question of textbooks. After stating that "the multiplicity of school books and the imperfection of many of them is one of the greatest evils at present felt in our Common schools," [38] the Board decided to remedy the situation by the "selection of the best of each class now in use, and a formal recommendation of them by the Board of Education." [39] The recommendation, of course, would be made to the town Committees, which had final choice.

In their *Second Report,* the Board members called attention to a law enacted April 12, 1837 authorizing the school districts to spend money to start a library.[40] To help the local committee make a wise choice, the Board arranged with Marsh, Capen and Lyon, a Boston publishing house, to put out two series of books, one for younger and one for more mature students, which the Board would recommend.[41] "Each book in the series," they declared,

> is to be submitted to the inspection of every member of the Board, and no work to be recommended, but on their unanimous approval. Such a recommendation, it was believed, would furnish a sufficient assurance to the public that a sacred adherence would be had to the principle which is embodied in the Legislation of the Commonwealth, on the subject of school books, and which provides that "school committees shall never direct to be purchased, or used in any of the town schools, any books, which are calculated to favor the tenets of any particular sect of Christians." [42]

In their *Third Report,* a year later, the Board annexed an advertisement prepared by Marsh, Capen, Lyon and Webb, publishers, giving a list of books which the Board had recommended.[43] Some were ready for sale and others were still in process of preparation.

[37] Presumably, therefore, there was nothing to prohibit religious instruction of any sort (including doctrinal instruction of a sectarian nature) by oral and visual methods.

[38] Board, *First Report* (covering 1837), p. 14.

[39] *Ibid.,* pp. 14–15.

[40] Board, *Second Report* (covering 1838), p. 18.

[41] *Ibid.,* p. 20.

[42] *Ibid.*

[43] Board, *Third Report* (covering 1839), pp. 24–32.

In the series for more mature students the volumes which were ready for circulation included two titles treating the idea of God as discoverable by reason: Paley's *Natural Theology* (two volumes) and Rev. Henry Duncan's *The Sacred Philosophy of the Seasons, illustrating the Perfections of God in the Phenomena of the Year*. (Adapted for American readers by the Rev. F. W. P. Greenwood, D.D. of Boston).[44] Among the titles still in preparation for the maturer students, subject to the Board's approval, were *Christianity and Knowledge* by Rev. Royal Robbins; *Moral Effects of Internal Improvements*, by Robert Rantoul, Jr., Esq.; Rev. Romeo Elton's *Lives of the Reformers;* and *Do Right and Have Right* by Mrs. Almira H. Lincoln Phelps.[45] In the "Juvenile Series" (all in preparation) none of the titles listed suggests religious or ethical content of any sort or level.[46]

There is a section, commenting on this book list, which seems to indicate that the Board thought religion had no place at all in the common school curriculum. After stating their hope that the books offered would cause no fear of a "sinister effect" on "religious instruction," the Board members said:

> . . . The subject of religious instruction has been placed by the Legislature of the Commonwealth, where public sentiment and the necessity of the case would place it and keep it, even without legislation. In a community, where the utmost liberty of religious profession exists,—where it is the dearest birthright of every man, that he may worship God according to the dictates of his conscience, any attempt to make the public schools, (supported as they are by the common expense for the common benefit) an instrument for advancing or depressing the opinions of any sect of christians, would meet what it would merit, the prompt rebuke of every considerate citizen. Although it may not be easy theoretically, to draw the line between those views of religious truth and of christian faith, which are common to all, and may, therefore, with propriety be inculcated in school, and those which, being peculiar to individual sects, are there-

---

[44] *Ibid.*, pp. 26, 27. The Rev. Dr. Greenwood was noted in the present study to have declared in 1825 that the "education of all youth should be strictly a religious education." Cf. *supra*, p. 94.

[45] *Ibid.*, pp. 28, 29, 30. This advertisement says of the Robbins book, "The design of this work is to show what Christianity has done for the human intellect, and what that has done for Christianity." (P. 28.)

[46] *Ibid.*, pp. 30, 31.

fore by law excluded; still it is believed, that no practical difficulty occurs in the conduct of our schools in this respect. It is
the general sentiment of the people of all denominations, that
religious instruction shall be left to parents at the fire-side and
to the religious teachers, to whose ministrations parents and
guardians may choose to confide their own spiritual guidance
and that of those dependent on them./The Legislature therefore
has but acted in accordance with the sense of the community,
in prescribing that no books shall be directed by school committees, to be purchased or used in any of the town schools,
"which are calculated to favor the tenets of any particular set
of christians." [47]

It seems, though, that by "religious instruction" the Board
means "religious instruction of a sectarian character." They mention the "utmost liberty of religious profession." This would indicate the general purpose of the Legislature's enactment to keep
sectarian textbooks out of the schools. The Board members of
1844 (*Eighth Report*) restated the idea that religion belongs in the
curriculum. The *Eighth Report* stressed "the importance of cultivating, as well the moral and religious, as the intellectual faculties
of our children by the frequent and careful perusal of the Sacred
Scriptures, in our schools." [48]

In this *Eighth Report* the Board then took note of the steady increase of the use of the Bible in the common schools. "It now
appears," they stated (referring to the current report of Horace
Mann, their Secretary)

> that, of the 308 cities and towns of the Commonwealth, it [the
> Bible] is used in the schools of 258 towns, as a regular reading
> book, prescribed by the school committees; and that, in the
> schools of 38 towns, it is used, either as a reading book, or, in
> the exercises of devotion. From nine of the remaining towns,
> no answers were received,—and, in the schools of three towns
> only, it is found not to be used at all. [49]

Three years later, in 1847, the Board's *Eleventh Report* claimed
that every one of its members advocated for the public schools a

[47] *Ibid.*, pp. 14–15.
[48] Board, *Eighth Report*, p. 15.
[49] *Ibid.*

program of "daily Bible reading, devotional exercises, and the constant inculcation of the precepts of Christian morality," with the following reservation as to sectarianism:

> The law, as revised in 1826,—eleven years before the establishment of the Board—rests upon grounds of popular support, which cannot be relinquished, except with the relinquishment of religious liberty;—and there is probably no one sect which would consent that any other should exercise the authority which the law withholds from all. . . . and so far as the members [of the Board] or the Secretary are charged with any errors of omission or commission, in relation to religious instruction in the schools, they have only to refer to the design of the law, and the limitation of their powers and duties, and will be content to abide a strict and impartial judgement.[50]

Reports of the Secretary

As has been claimed, the guiding spirit of the Board was Horace Mann. His ideals and efforts in the field of religious education must be carefully studied to see what happened in the schools of Massachusetts. The subject will be treated in three parts: A—Mann wanted religion, as he conceived it, in the curriculum; B—He wanted sectarianism kept out of the curriculum; C—The Secretary summarized his whole position on the subject at the end of his twelfth and last report.

MANN WANTED RELIGION IN THE CURRICULUM

In his *First Report*, Mann wrote on the fitness of the available textbooks affording instruction in religion. After quoting the "non-sectarian" proviso of the 1827 law, the Secretary declared:

> Probably, no one would desire a repeal of this law, while the danger impends it was designed to repel. The consequence of the enactment, however, has been, that among the vast libraries

[50] Board, *Eleventh Report*, pp. 9–10. Actually, as has been seen, the law was revised in the early months of 1827. Cf. *supra*, pp. 104 f.

of books, expository of the doctrines of revealed religion, none have been found, free from that advocacy of particular "tenets" or "sects," which includes them within the scope of the legal prohibition; or, at least, no such books have been approved by committees and introduced into the schools.[51]

Mann saw clearly the dilemma which the existing situation presented. The law enjoined religious instruction. It also forbade sectarian textbooks. The more general provision was being negated by the special proviso. What was to be the solution? The *First Report* continues:

> Independently, therefore, of the immeasurable importance of moral teaching, in itself considered, this entire exclusion of religious teaching, though justifiable under the circumstances, enhances and magnifies, a thousand fold, the indispensableness of moral instruction and training. Entirely to discard the inculcation of the great doctrines of morality and of natural theology has a vehement tendency to drive mankind into opposite extremes; to make them devotees on one side or profligates on the other; each about equally regardless of the true constituents of human welfare. Against a tendency to these fatal extremes, the beautiful and sublime truths of ethics and of natural religion have a poising power. Hence it will be learnt with sorrow, that of the multiplicity of books used in our schools, only three have this object in view; and these three are used in only *six* of the two thousand nine hundred and eighteen schools, from which returns have been received.[52]

The Secretary of the Board was proposing the insertion of ethics and natural theology in the place of the sectarian doctrines of the current Protestant groups in Massachusetts. From his statement it seems incorrect to deduce that Mann was proposing a *religious* curriculum based on the "ground . . . spacious enough for sincere Christians of all denominations to walk together . . ."[53] or the "Common ground, on which they all ["Professed Christians"] meet" of Park.[54] To the extent that Mann's system could be called religious, it was a system based on natural and not re-

---

[51] Mann, *First Report*, p. 62.
[52] *Ibid.*
[53] Cf. *supra*, p. 112.
[54] Cf. *supra*, p. 114.

vealed theology.[55] To dwell merely on this one statement of Horace Mann, however, and to deduce from it that *he wanted no religion* in the curriculum would be basing too much upon a small foundation. Could it be that despite his words "this entire exclusion of religious teaching" he really meant "this entire exclusion of sectarian teaching"? If this be so, then Horace Mann meant that natural theology and ethics were, for him at least, the religion to be taught. It is this which he offers for the common school curriculum in his *First Report.* As the years went on, however, Mann seems to have expanded his ideas to include more than the above in his concept of a common-school curriculum of religion.

To begin with, there are many things in the later writings of Horace Mann which indicate a continuing conviction that religion of some sort must form a part of true education and should therefore find a place in the common school curriculum.

In a lecture delivered in 1838, "The Necessity of Education in a Republican Government," [56] Mann defined education, saying, in conclusion, "And, finally, by the term education I mean such a culture of our moral affections and religious sensibilities, as in the course of nature and Providence shall lead to a subjection or conformity of all our appetites, propensities, and sentiments to the will of Heaven." [57] Later in the same lecture he declared:

> The same Almighty Power which implants in our nature the germs of those terrible propensities, has endowed us also with reason and conscience and a sense of responsibility to Him, and in his providence, he has opened a way by which these noble faculties can be elevated into dominion and supremacy over the appetites and passions. But if this is ever done, it must be

[55] Natural theology is commonly taken to mean knowledge of God derived from the workings of the human reason alone and unaided by any supernatural revelation. In itself it cannot be called distinctively Christian. Christians, of course, may and do use it as the basis on which they rest their motives of acceptance of supernatural revelation through the Old Testament writers and Jesus Christ.

[56] Horace Mann, *Lectures and Annual Reports.* This is Vol. II of the series, *Life and Works of Horace Mann,* Mrs. Mary P. Mann (ed.), (Cambridge: Published for the editor, 1867), Lecture III, pp. 143–88.

[57] *Ibid.,* p. 144.

mainly done during the docile and teachable years of child-hood. . . .

If this dread responsibility for the fate of our children be disregarded, how, when called upon in the great eventful day, to give an account of the manner in which our earthy duties have been discharged, can we expect to escape the condemnation: "Inasmuch as ye have not done it to one of the least of these, ye have not done it unto me"? [58]

In a Diary entry for January 20, 1839 (which will be examined again for the condemnation it carries of sectarianism in education) [59] Mann wrote: "The fundamental principles of Christianity may and should be inculcated [in the public schools]." Later still, in the *Eleventh Report* (covering 1847) he will be found advocating Bible reading as a substitute for the sectarian teachings he violently opposed. [60]

A lecture given in 1840 and reproduced in the same volume as that in 1838 was called "What God Does and What He Leaves for Man to Do in the Work of Education." [61] Mann speaks as follows of the "sublimest form of parent love": [62]

So the voice of another sentiment, . . . I mean the religious sentiment, the sense of duty to God. . . . This sense of duty to God compels the parent to contemplate the child in his moral and religious relations. . . . "If, then, God is Truth,—if God is love,—teach the child above all things to seek for Truth, and to abound in Love." [63]

Horace Mann concludes this lecture with a plea for action by teachers. It is clear that he does not wish sectarian doctrines taught (a point we shall take up later) but there is included in his plan an appeal to Christ and His example which goes beyond what is ordinarily considered mere "natural theology":

As educators, as friends and sustainers of the Common School system our great duty is to . . . keep them unspotted from the world, that is, uncontaminated by its vices; to train them up to the love of God and the love of man; to make the

[58] *Ibid.*, pp. 187, 188.
[59] Cf. *infra,* p. 139.
[60] Cf. *infra,* p. 141.
[61] Mann, *Lectures,* Lecture iv, pp. 191–237.
[62] *Ibid.*, p. 209.
[63] *Ibid.*, pp. 209–10.

perfect example of Jesus Christ lovely in their eyes; and to give to all so much religious instruction as is compatible with the rights of others and with the genius of our government—leaving to parents and guardians the direction, during their school days, of all special and peculiar instruction respecting politics and theology, and at last, when the children arrive at years of maturity, to commend them to that inviolable prerogative of private judgement and of self direction, which, in a Protestant and a Republican country, is the acknowledged birthright of every human being.[64]

Is Horace Mann here expanding his idea of the religion to be taught in the schools? To natural theology and ethics he has added "the fundamental principles of Christianity," "the example of Jesus Christ" and Bible reading. Note should also be taken of his stress on "private judgement." This is Protestant dogma, not natural theology.

In the Fourth of July oration he delivered at Boston in 1842, Mann stressed virtue, as well as knowledge, as school aims:

I have said that schools should have been established for the education of the whole people. . . . In them the principles of morality should have been copiously intermingled with the principles of science. Cases of conscience should have alternated with lessons in the rudiments. The multiplication table should not have been more familiar, nor more frequently applied, than the rule to do to others as we would that they should do unto us. The lives of great and good men should have been held up for admiration and example; and especially the life and character of Jesus Christ, as the sublimest pattern of benevolence, of purity, of self sacrifice, ever exhibited to mortals. In every course of studies, all the practical and preceptive parts of the Gospel should have been sacredly included; and all dogmatical theology and sectarianism sacredly excluded. In no school should the Bible have been opened to reveal the sword of the polemic, but to unloose the dove of peace.[65]

A believer in the immortality of the soul, Horace Mann felt that education should prepare for the life to come. Less expansive, but no less clear, is his statement in a letter to the school children of

[64] *Ibid.*, pp. 289–90.

[65] Horace Mann, *Go Forth and Teach, An Oration Delivered Before the Authorities of the City of Boston, July 4, 1842* (Centennial Edition; Washington, D. C.: National Education Association, 1937), pp. 44–45.

Chautauqua County, New York, dated Boston, July 27, 1846: (Mann refers to the children in the Massachusetts schools:)

> I wish them all to know and feel how good their Creator is; how wise and benevolent in all he has created for their use, and what glorious provision he has made for their well-being, not for today only, or tomorrow, or the next year, or their lifetime, but for a never-ending existence,—for this would make them supremely happy.[66]

There is a lengthy section of the above-cited letter to the school children of Chautauqua County in which Mann extolled the wonders of the Godhead and urged his readers to learn of Him as much as they could:

> . . . *You must be religious;* that is, you must be grateful to God, obey his laws, love and imitate his infinite excellences. The works of God are full of wonders and beauties. . . . But God himself is greater than his works. If you were delighted and charmed with a curious instrument, or with a piece of exquisitely wrought machinery, would you not like to know its contriver and builder . . . especially if his ingenious mind and skillful hand could form a thousand such pieces in a day? . . . Such, and more than this, and more than the tongue of a man or of angel can describe, is your Maker; and he who does not know him, though he may know everything else, is ignorant of the greatest and best part of all knowledge. There is no conceivable privation to be compared with an ignorance of our Creator. If a man be blind, he but loses the outward light. . . . But if he is "without God", he is a wanderer and a solitary in the universe, . . . with no home or sanctuary to flee to, though all the spirits of darkness should have made him their victim.[67]

MANN WANTED SECTARIANISM KEPT OUT OF THE CURRICULUM

Positive as was Horace Mann's wish that religion, as he defined it, should be in the common school curriculum, just as determined

[66] Horace Mann, "Letter to the School Children [of Chautauqua County, New York]," Boston, July 27, 1846, in Joy Elmer Morgan, *Horace Mann, His Ideas and Ideals* (Washington, D. C.: National Home Library Foundation, 1936), p. 107. At the end of his *Tenth Report,* also, Mann makes a striking plea for education that may prepare the human soul for eternity (pp. 238–39).

[67] From Morgan, *op. cit.,* pp. 119–20.

was he that sectarianism must stay out. In his *First Report* (covering 1837), as his eyes fastened themselves upon his goal of common school education for all, he lashed out at the private schools then operating in Massachusetts. It was his belief that the inculcation of sectarian doctrines in the private schools fostered among children the hostility that characterized the warring Protestant groups in New England at that time:

> Amongst any people, sufficiently advanced in intelligence, to perceive, that hereditary opinions on religious subjects are not always coincident with truth, it cannot be overlooked, that the tendency of the private school system is to assimilate our modes of education to those of England, where churchmen and dissenters,—each sect according to its own creed,—maintain separate schools, in which children are taught, from their tenderest years to wield the sword of polemics with fatal dexterity; and where the gospel, instead of being a temple of peace, is converted into an armory of deadly weapons for social, interminable warfare. Of such disastrous consequences, there is but one remedy and one preventive. It is the elevation of the common schools.[68]

Under date of January 20, 1839, Mann's Diary records his determination that sectarian doctrines shall not be taught in the common schools. It is worthy of note that, whereas the law itself forbade only the use of sectarian textbooks, Mann is extending his opposition to any form of its inculcation:

> Sunday. Both Reports in [School and Hospital]. Some efforts making by disappointed orthodoxy to disaffect the public with the Board. They want, at least some of them, their doctrines introduced. This cannot be, either theirs or those of any others, considered as sects merely, [*sic*] The fundamental principles of Christianity may and should be inculcated. This should be done thro' the medium of a proper text-book to prevent abuses. After this, each denomination must be left to its own resources, for inculcating its own faith or creed.

A very severe condemnation of sectarianism in education is found in the *Seventh Report*. In the spring of 1843 Mann had gone to Europe and travelled extensively in England, Ireland, Scotland, Prussia, and other German states, and passed through

[68] Mann, *First Report*, pp. 56–57.

Holland and Belgium to Paris.[69] During this trip he made many visits to Old World Schools, especially in the first four countries named. The religious instruction he found there drew alternately his praise and condemnation.

In summarizing his reaction against the sectarian doctrines he found being taught in the schools of Europe, Mann indicated that his basic objection was his belief that the various doctrines were all man-made interpretations of religion devised to capture the allegiance of helpless peoples. "Religion," he stated, "is the first necessity of the soul";

> but because every human being . . . must still be a wanderer and an outcast, until he can find a Supreme Father and God, in whom to confide, . . . crafty and cruel men have come in, and have set up . . . false gods for its [the soul's] worship and then, claiming to be the favorites and ministers of Omnipotence, have dispensed the awful retributions of eternity against all questioners of their authority, . . . Hence throughout wide regions of country, man is no longer man. . . . The heavenly spark of intelligence is trodden out from his bosom.[70]

Still warring against sectarianism in his *Eleventh Report,* Mann outlined the requisites for operating the Massachusetts Schools, if they were to stay "the desolating torrent of practical iniquity by drying up its fountain-head in the bosoms of the young." [71] The first requisite was the observance of *"the cardinal principles of the present New England systems."* [72] Among these principles was the inculcation of "Principles of piety," as enjoined by the law. "But lest any individual or body of individuals," he continued,

[69] Mann, *Seventh Report* (covering 1843), pp. 19–20.

[70] *Ibid.,* pp. 186–87. Mann had prefaced his remarks on the teaching of religion in European schools with a comment on the Massachusetts system. After quoting the law of 1789 and its insistence on the inculcation of "principles of piety etc.," he observed: "The aim of our law obviously is, to secure as much of religious instruction as is compatible with religious freedom." (*Ibid.,* p. 17.) It is difficult to say whether his strictures on the Old World system are completely the voice of a man who respects the rights of conscience, or, to some extent at least, the voice of a Unitarian who despised all other denominational teaching but that of his own sect. Nevertheless, we are merely establishing here Horace Mann's uncompromising opposition to the teaching of what he calls "sectarian religion" in public education. We shall continue to find in his writings the same idea.

[71] Mann, *Eleventh Report* (covering 1847), p. 88.

[72] *Ibid.*

. . . should seize upon the statutory injunction, or upon some part of it, as pretext for turning the schools into proselytizing institutions, the law rears a barrier against all sectarian encroachments. That which is "calculated to favor the tenets of any particular sect of Christians," is excluded from the schools.[73]

As a substitute for sectarianism, Mann then spoke up for Bible reading. Thus, it seems clear that as the years went on, he advocated more than the "ethics and natural religion" suggested in his *First Report*.[74] Mann here brings out an interesting point which he will be found stressing again and again. If the various sects all believe in the Bible, he says in effect, all they believe in will enter the school through the medium of Bible reading:

The use of the Bible in schools is not expressly enjoined by law, but both its letter and its spirit are in consonance with that use. . . . Whoever, therefore, believes in the Sacred Scriptures, has his belief, in form and in spirit, in the schools; and his children read and hear *the words themselves* which contain it. . . . By introducing the Bible, they [the school authorities] introduce what all its believers hold to be the rule of faith and practice; and, although, by excluding the theological systems of human origin, they may exclude a peculiarity which one denomination believes to be true, they do but exclude what other denominations believe to be erroneous. Such is the present policy of our law for including what all Christians hold to be right, and for excluding what all, excepting some one party, hold to be wrong.

. . . thus, through the medium of our schools, that song which ushered in the Christian era,—"Peace on earth and good-will to men"—may be taken up and continued through the ages.[75]

The above selection indicates anew how Mann, evidently with the Board's support, extended the textbook law to a prohibition of any and every form of sectarian teaching.[76] His *Fourth Report* (covering 1840) makes the claim that during 1840, at least, his

[73] *Ibid.*, p. 90.

[74] Cf. *supra*, p. 134.

[75] Mann, *Eleventh Report*, pp. 90–91. Mann seems to suggest that he was really saving Christianity from obliteration in the schools. Just what was to be left of the *content* and *meaning* of the Christian message, after *everything* that *any one party* objected to was passed over or eliminated from discussion, seems not to have worried the Secretary at this point.

[76] Note the phrase, "the law rears a barrier against all sectarian encroachments."

policy was endorsed by clergymen as well. In the reports from the School Committees, mostly prepared by clergymen, Mann thought "there was not one, which advocated the introduction of sectarian instruction" and all "demand, that the great axioms of a Christian morality shall be sedulously taught,—and that the teachers . . . be patterns of the virtues they . . . inculcate." [77]

The *Fifth Report* (covering 1841) and the *Eighth* (covering 1844) each record isolated cases where sectarian doctrine was alleged to have been taught, despite the law and/or the Secretary's interpretation thereof. The 1841 case involved two communities, Shirley and Harvard, made up entirely of members of the religious sect called "Shakers." [78] They refused to allow their teachers to be examined or the schools to be visited by the town committee. [79] The *Eighth Report* states that in the school year of 1842–43, a school was broken up "because the teacher persisted in inculcating sectarian doctrines upon his pupils, after having been remonstrated with, both by the inhabitants of the district, and by the superintending committee. . . ." [80] In commenting upon the Shaker case of 1841, Mann dwelt on the danger of individual communities defying the general state law. In this instance, he observed, the harm within the community was lessened by the fact that all belonged to one sect. The possibility that these people might have resisted examination of their school because they felt that a resulting prohibition of their religious teaching would violate their conscientious convictions was not considered by the Secretary. [81]

So far, then, it appears that Horace Mann faced the dilemma of the times (religion must have a place in the public school curriculum—yet the rights of conscience must be kept intact) by *substituting* for complete doctrinal instruction in one or several

[77] Mann, *Fourth Report*, p. 59.

[78] " 'The Shakers' were at first a set of English Quakers. . . . Ann Lee became the leader of the Shakers. . . . She came to America in 1774 with a small band of followers and established a Church at Watervliet, New York." M. Phelan, *New Handbook of All Denominations* (Nashville, Tennessee: Cokesbury Press, 1937), p. 89.

[79] Mann, *Fifth Report*, p. 66.

[80] Mann, *Eighth Report*, p. 67. Mann gives a reference in this case to "Abstract Mass. School Returns, 1843–44," p. 121.

[81] Mann, *Fifth Report*, pp. 66–69.

of the existing Protestant faiths, instruction in ethics, natural theology, "the example of Jesus Christ and the basic principles of Christianity." The last named components were to be taught through the then-general practice of reading the Bible in the schools. In his *Eighth Report* Mann had supplied figures (already given in a quotation from the Board's *Report* of the same year) [82] to indicate the prevalence of Bible reading by 1844.[83] His concluding comment expressed his satisfaction with the results his religious curriculum was effecting:

> Acknowledging, then, before heaven and earth, and with humility and contrition of spirit, that we fall greatly short of what we should be; yet I believe all attempts will prove unavailing to disparage the religious character of Massachusetts, as compared with the rest of Christendom, or to show that its institutions and its people are not as deeply imbued with the divine spirit of Christianity as those of any other community upon the face of the earth.[84]

MANN SUMMARIZED HIS POSITION IN THE TWELFTH REPORT

It was in his last report (covering 1848) that Horace Mann wrote a lengthy defense of his position on religion in public education.[85] Because it is something of a valedictory to his career as a public educator, and is so thorough an analysis of his stand, it is here given a separate presentation.

• The Secretary commenced with a well-reasoned and exalted declaration of his belief in the necessity of religion in human life. Morality, he conceded, is unattainable without religion, and no community will ever be religious without religious education. Devoid of religious principles, the race can sink to great depths; enlightened by them, it can rise higher and higher. Yet, in this area, as in others, it must be educated.[86]

". . . If man be not a religious being," he continued, "he is among the most deformed and monstrous of all possible exist-

---

[82] *Supra,* p. 132.
[83] Mann, *Eighth Report,* p. 75.
[84] *Ibid.,* p. 76.
[85] Mann, *Twelfth Report,* pp. 98–144.
[86] *Ibid.,* p. 98.

ences." [87] His passions need a fear of God; his sentiments need the love of God; without the capability of knowing God, "his whole nature is a contradiction and a solecism . . . as . . . a circle without a circumference is a mathematical absurdity. The man . . . who believes that the human race . . . can attain to happiness, or avoid misery, without religious principle and religious affections, must be ignorant of the capacities of the human soul, and of the highest attributes in the nature of man." [88]

To prove this point, Mann dwells on the impossibility that a human be completely satisfied with either sensual or intellectual delights. ". . . Without some Being," he declared:

> all-glorious in his perfections, whom the spirit [of man] could commune with and adore, it would be a mourner and a wanderer amid all the splendors of the universe. . . . There is not a faculty nor a susceptibility in the nature of man . . . that will ever be governed by its proper law, or enjoy a full measure of the gratification it was adapted to feel, without a knowledge of the true God. . . .[89]

All other knowledge, the Secretary continued, would be meagre, if we should fail to learn of the Author of knowledge itself. It would be less painful for an artist to be presented with a truncated statue when he expected to see the entire figure, "than [to have] a system of human culture from which religious culture should be omitted." [90]

The same would be true, Mann went on, for all the higher affections and capabilities of the human soul. "If, in surveying the highest states of perfection which the character of man has ever yet reached upon earth, we select, from among the whole circle of our personal or historical acquaintances,—those who are adorned with the purest quality and the greatest number of excellencies, . . . why should not the soul be lifted into sublimer extasies [sic] . . . if it could be raised to the contemplation of Him, whose 'name alone is excellent'?" [91]

[87] *Ibid.*, p. 99.
[88] *Ibid.*
[89] *Ibid.*, pp. 100–101.
[90] *Ibid.*, p. 102.
[91] *Ibid.*

". . . Such is the force of the conviction to which my own mind is brought by these general considerations," he concluded,

> that I could not avoid regarding the man, who should oppose the religious education of the young, as an insane man; and were it proposed to debate the question between us, I should desire to restore him to his reason, before entering upon the discussion. If, suddenly summoned to eternity, I were able to give but one parting word of advice to my own children, or to the children of others;—if I were sinking beneath the wave, and had time to utter but one articulate breath, or were wasting away upon the death-bed, and had strength to make but one exhortation more,—that dying legacy should be, "Remember thy Creator in the days of thy youth." [92]

After this lofty discourse Mann asked the question: "How shall so momentous an object be pursued? . . . Shall we ourselves abide by the dictates of religion . . . or . . . shall we seek to educate the community religiously through the use of the most irreligious means?" [93] The "irreligious means" Mann conceived to be those used in regions where there existed a union of Church and State.[94] He turned, however, to relate to this Church-State system (which was non-existent in America at the time of the *Twelfth Report*) those who, in America, advocate "'Parochial' or 'Sectarian Schools'." [95] It is against their charge that the public schools are irreligious that he wishes to defend himself and the Board. "I know, full well," he declared, "that it [the Massachusetts system] is unlike the systems which prevail in Great Britain, and in many of the continental nations of Europe, where the Established Church controls the education of the young, in order to keep itself established." [96]

All attempts at religious education, Mann continued, can be reduced to two systems:—The first "holds the regulation and con-

---

[92] *Ibid.*, p. 103. (Mann's wife records that among his last words was an exhortation addressed to the man he hoped would succeed him as President of Antioch College: "Preach God's laws, Mr. Fay; *preach them*, PREACH THEM!" *Life*, p. 552.)
[93] *Ibid.*
[94] *Ibid.*
[95] *Ibid.*, p. 104.
[96] *Ibid.*, p. 105.

trol of the religious belief of the people to be one of the functions of government. . . ." According to the other system,

> . . . religious belief is a matter of individual and parental concern; and, while the government furnishes all practicable facilities for the independent formation of that belief, it exercises no authority to prescribe, or coercion to enforce it.[97]

Admitting that the first mentioned system is not without its plausibility, Mann stated that trouble would arise because it would be necessary for the government to define what religion is as well as what it is not.[98] Mann further stated by way of theory that if what the government was enforcing were infallibly the truth, then the government would be justified in enforcing it, and punishing, for the sake of the common good, those who maintain error.[99]

Trouble, however, arises from the fact, he continued, that each religious group thinks itself the infallible possessor of the truth. In the face of this, "after seeking all possible light from within; from without, and from above, each man's belief is his own standard of truth; *but it is not*," he immediately added, "*the standard for any other man. . . .* [The other man] must have his own standard, which to him must be supreme." [100]

Approaching the point he was trying to make, Mann said that the actual result of the "infinite errors and enormities, resulting from systems of religion devised by man" [101] had resulted in the abjuration of religion and lapse into atheism by many. The medium between the two extremes of "ecclesiastical tyranny" and

[97] *Ibid.*

[98] *Ibid.*, pp. 105–106.

[99] *Ibid.*, p. 107. This is a singular position for a man professedly dedicated to the sacredness of the rights of conscience. It is in the logic of the Church-State-Union concept that the government should cooperate in preventing the spread of erroneous doctrine by forbidding those it considered erroneous publicly to preach their beliefs; but it is not in the logic which recognizes the rights of conscience to force the individual to alter his conscience regarding the position he himself *as an individual* holds to be the correct one.

[100] *Ibid.*, p. 108. Mann followed this section with an opinion that it is inconceivable that any religious groups could validly claim to be the mouthpiece of God speaking to men (pp. 108–09).

[101] *Ibid.*, p. 110.

the "greater evils of atheism" was the Massachusetts system, which Mann summarized as follows:

> It [the medium] is promulgated in the great principle, that government should do all it can to facilitate the acquisition of religious truth; but shall leave the decision of the question, what religious truth is, to the arbitrament, without human appeal, of each man's reason and conscience;—in other words, that government shall never, by the infliction of pains and penalties, or by the privation of rights or immunities, call such decision either into pre-judgment or into review. The formula in which the Constitution of Massachusetts expresses it, is in these words: "All religious sects and denominations, demeaning themselves peaceably and as good citizens, shall be equally under the protection of law; and no subordination of one sect or denomination to another shall ever be established by law." [102]

Mann then recounted some of the history of the changes in policy on teaching religion in Massachusetts schools. When he came into office he found sectarian textbooks in use, he heard oral instruction as "*doctrinal,* as any ever heard from the pulpit. . . ." [103] and directions by committeemen to teachers ordering the use of sectarian catechisms. He conceived it his duty to oppose *both* the textbooks *and* the oral instruction. ". . . I endeavored," he said, "to set forth what was supposed to be the true meaning and intent of the [1827] law." [104] Expressing his grief at the opposition his efforts had encountered, Mann emphatically declared:

> . . . I avail myself of this, the last opportunity which I may ever have, to say, in regard to all affirmations or intimations, that I have ever attempted to exclude religious instruction from school, or to exclude the Bible from school, or to impair the force of that volume, arising out of itself, are now, and always have been, without substance or semblance of truth. [105]

Turning back to the schools themselves, Mann next declared that they were not theological seminaries. He pointed out that they were forbidden to teach sectarian doctrine and also prohibited "from ever teaching that what they do teach, is the whole of

[102] *Ibid.,* p. 111.
[103] *Ibid.,* p. 113.
[104] *Ibid.,* p. 114.
[105] *Ibid.,* p. 116.

religion, or all that is essential to salvation." "But our system," he continued,

> earnestly inculcates all Christian morals; it founds its morals on the basis of religion; it welcomes the religion of the Bible; and, in receiving the Bible, it allows it to do what it is allowed to do in no other system,—*to speak for itself.* But here it stops, not because it claims to have compassed all truth; but because it disclaims to act as an umpire between the hostile religious opinions.[106]

In the final part of his treatise, Mann presents four arguments against any change in his policy. In the first place, since the schools are public schools, they are for all and all are taxed to support them. The citizen, however, is not taxed to support the schools as religious institutions, but as institutions founded to prepare the children to be good citizens and not a menace to the state.

". . . The religious education which a child receives at school, is not imparted to him, for the purpose of making him join this or that denomination, when he arrives at years of discretion, but for the purpose of enabling him to judge for himself, according to the dictates of his own reason and conscience, what his religious obligations are, and whither they lead."[107]

If a man were taxed to support a school which taught the students a religion he did not believe in, Mann continued, "He is excluded from the school by the Divine law, at the same time that he is compelled to support it by the human law. This is a double wrong."[108] The double wrong is, first, political—that he must send his children elsewhere and pay double; and second, religious— that he is constrained against the divine law as he sees it.

The writer's next argument for the Massachusetts system was based on the notion of "jurisdiction." Religion lies outside the jurisdiction of human government and within the jurisdiction of divine government.

> And, hence it is, that religious rights are inalienable rights. Hence, also, it is, that it is an infinitely greater offence to invade

[106] *Ibid.*, pp. 116–17.
[107] *Ibid.*, pp. 117–18.
[108] *Ibid.*, p. 118.

the special and exclusive jurisdiction which the Creator claims over the consciences and hearts of men, than it would be to invade the jurisdiction which any foreign nation rightfully possesses over its own subjects or citizens. . . . Hence I infer that our system is not an irreligious one, but is in the strictest accordance with religion and its obligations.[109]

For his third argument, the Secretary attempted to prove that the Massachusetts system was not anti-Christian or un-Christian because it used the Bible in the classroom. This line of reasoning, noted before in the *Eleventh Report,*[110] is now given fuller development:

> The Bible is the acknowledged expositor of Christianity. In strictness, Christianity has no other authoritative expounder. This Bible is in our Common Schools, by common consent. . . .
> If the Bible, then, is the exponent of Christianity . . . how can it be said that Christianity is excluded from the schools. . . .
> Is it not, indeed, too plain, to require the formality of a syllogism, that if any man's creed is to be found in the Bible, and the Bible is in the schools, then that man's creed is in the schools? . . . If a vase of purest alabaster, filled with myrrh and frankincense, and precious ointments, were in the school, would not their perfumes be there also? And would the beautiful vase, and the sweet aroma of spice and unguent be any more truly there, if some concocter of odors, such as nature never made, should insist upon saturating the air with the products of his own distillations, which, though pleasant to *his* idiosyncrasy, would be nauseous to every body else? [111]

Mann's final argument was the presentation and rejection of what he conceived to be the four other possible ways of handling the problem:

> 1. Establish schools and exclude all religion— No one in Massachusetts would want this.[112]
> 2. Prescribe a system of religious instruction and enforce it by State authority—This would be Establishment of religion.[113]

[109] *Ibid.,* pp. 120, 121.

[110] Cf. *supra,* pp. 140–41.

[111] Mann, *Twelfth Report,* pp. 121–23. Mann's argument suggests the story about the biology supply house which received an order: "Send me one amoeba." The company shipped back a gallon container of water with the note "Your amoeba enclosed. You find it."

[112] *Ibid.,* p. 124.

[113] *Ibid.,* p. 125.

3. Establish schools and let the sect which could get a majority control the religious instruction— Each sect would strive to get the mastery and chaos would result. The Bible would decrease and the catechism would become dominant.[114]

4. Government drop all education and leave it to private enterprise— Education, fragmented, would decline; teachers would not be attracted to the work; some sects, not now able even to support their ministers, would not have an educated ministry, if they tried to run schools too.[115]

This philosophy of Horace Mann seems to have gained widespread acceptance by the end of the 1840's. However, there were people in Massachusetts who still believed that doctrinal religion belonged in the common schools. Their strenuous opposition must now be reviewed.

The Controversies

Five major controversies, either directly or indirectly involving religious instruction, marked Mann's career as Secretary of the Board. They involved Mann with: 1) Frederick A. Packard (1838); 2) A Move to Abolish the Board of Education (1840); 3) Edward A. Newton (1844); 4) The Boston Schoolmasters (1844); and 5) Rev. Matthew H. Smith (1846). It is important to examine both their ideas and the defense of his policies made by the Secretary.

THE CONTROVERSY WITH FREDERICK A. PACKARD

Frederick Adolphus Packard, born in Massachusetts in 1794, was the son of a minister who held charges in Marlborough and Lancaster. In 1829 he became the Recording Secretary and Editor of Publications for the "American Sunday School Union," with headquarters in Philadelphia. Packard was a member of the Congregational Church, but also attended Presbyterian and Episcopal churches in Philadelphia.[116]

---

[114] *Ibid.*, pp. 127–31.
[115] *Ibid.*, pp. 131–37.
[116] Cf. "Frederick Adolphus Packard," *Princeton Review, Index Volume* covering 1825–1868 (Philadelphia: Peter Walker, 1871), 265–71.

In 1838 he proposed a ready-rack library for common schools and in March wrote a letter to Horace Mann with a view to interesting the Secretary in endorsing the library. A suggestion was made in the letter that Mann give his opinion as to whether a book called *The Child at Home* by [Rev. John S. C.] Abbot, would be acceptable in the Massachusetts District School Libraries. Mann's reply was negative. Thus began a series of communications between the two men which boiled into an acrimonious controversy.[117]

The gist of the argument was this: Packard wanted his library in the Massachusetts schools and felt the laws of Massachusetts not only did not forbid but implied acceptance of such volumes in the religious instruction course. Mann maintained that the laws forbade their acceptance and objected to them further because of certain propositions which he felt should not be taught to children.

In his first letter to Packard, Mann told of having read *The Child at Home*, as per suggestion.[118] Bluntly he gave his opinion that "it would not be tolerated in this State, as a District School Library book. . . . The book would be in the highest degree offensive to the Universalists. . . .[119] The whole scope and tenor of the book would ill accord with the views of the Unitarians, whether clergymen or laymen. . . ." Mann then listed as his reasons: 1) that the book makes no discrimination between serious and slight sins, threatening eternal perdition as punishment for trivial acts of neglect and disobedience; 2) obedience is made a

[117] Culver, *op. cit.*, p. 57. All the letters, except Packard's first, are preserved in the *Mann Papers* at the Massachusetts Historical Society and are reproduced in full in "Appendix A" of Culver's work (pp. 241–84).

[118] Mann to Packard, Boston, March 18, 1838 (Culver, *op. cit.*, pp. 241–43).

[119] The Universalists comprise a sect somewhat like the Unitarians (yet considering themselves distinct from them) which was organized at a 1790 convention in Philadelphia from scattered groups which had been formed in America by three men, George de Senneville, John Murray, and Hosea Ballou. In 1899 they summed up their belief as follows: "We believe in: the Universal Fatherhood of God; the spiritual authority and leadership of His Son, Jesus Christ; the trustworthiness of the Bible as containing a revelation from God; the certainty of just retribution for sin; the final harmony of all souls with God." Frank S. Mead, *op. cit.* (*Handbook of Denominations in the United States*), "Universalists," pp. 181–83.

higher virtue than love of God; 3) the book dwells too much on long-term rather than immediate retribution for bad conduct; 4) God is not presented in an amiable aspect; 5) whereas the book is based on the assumption that children naturally are disinclined to love what is good, the conclusion takes an opposite point of view, namely that virtue is attractive to children. Mann closed by apologizing for the hasty composition of the letter, saying, "I hope however, that I have given you some *hints*, why the book would be offensive here."

Packard's answer [120] admitted that the Universalists *would* take offense at the book, but then queried how the basic law on teaching religion could be obeyed "without reference to the character and government of God. Nor can I conceive how the character and government of God," he wrote,

> can be introduced for the purpose of illustrating and enforcing these principles of piety, without "*favoring some particular religious tenet*" which is expressly forbidden by the statute of 1826, at least so far as school-books are concerned. The very definition of piety is "*discharge of duty to God*" and how can the principles of piety be taught intelligibly without constant reference to the character of God and to the provisions and sanctions of His law as revealed in the Holy Scriptures? My own impression is that all which it is intended to keep out of public schools, may be kept out and yet a vast number of religious books strictly speaking may be admitted.

Thus, Packard maintained that the two provisions of the law are in contradiction one to the other unless an interpretation is made. Mann's retort to this letter was: "Is it possible, my dear Sir, you can mean to say; that no person who does not adopt those views [Abbot's as explained by Packard] can be pious! Is no Universalist *pious*? And who is he that understands the character and attributes of God?" [121]

A further statement of Mann's position, familiar to us by now, occurred in the Secretary's last letter in the series.[122] After ex-

[120] Packard to Mann, Philadelphia, March 28, 1838 (Culver, *op. cit.*, pp. 243–45).

[121] Here we find Mann taking refuge behind the supposition that to fulfill adequately a given relationship with God, one must encompass in his finite mind all knowledge of the Infinite.

[122] Mann to Packard, Boston, July 22, 1838 (Culver, *op. cit.*, pp. 256–69).

pressing a distaste for controversy, he quotes the 1827 law against sectarian textbooks, reviews the history of its enactment and its subsequent popularity both with legislators and the public. "The great idea [of the law] is," he wrote,

> that those points of doctrine, or faith, upon which good, and great men differ, shall not be intruded into this mutual ground of "The Schools." The Children of Men of all Denominations, attend the school together. If one man claimed to have his peculiar doctrines taught, why not another? Why not all? Until you would have a Babel of Creeds in the same school, which a Heathen would be ashamed of. All therefore, or almost all amongst us acceded to the essential justice, as well as the practical expediency of this Course. . . . The tendency of all this, is most happy. It brings opponents to act in concert together for the attainment of a great good—and thereby restores the lost feelings of Brotherhood which Controversy tends to obliterate—Besides, suppose there were attempts to teach peculiar tenets in the Schools, and the Schools were thereby broken up, as they undoubtedly would be, each advocate for the Course would be as far from his object as he was before. . . .[123]

Later in the same letter, Mann replied to a charge of Packard's that during a conversation they had held together Mann had opposed teaching religion to children:

> I never advanced to you, nor to any mortal, the opinion, that the mind of a Child, should not be influenced on Religious Subjects until its judgement is sufficiently matured to weigh the evidence, and Arguments for itself. Such a notion conflicts with my whole theory of the nature, and character of a Child's Soul. What I said was, that "Creeds, obstruse points, which divide one set of Christians from another ought not to be taught to children." [124]

Mann then explained the illustration from the Natural Sciences he had used, and continued:

> Such was my illustration, and my conclusion was that the Religion of Heaven should be taught to children, while the creeds of men should be postponed until their minds were sufficiently matured to weigh Evidence and Arguments. Your next

123 *Ibid.*, pp. 256–57.
124 *Ibid.*, p. 266.

assertion, that I said generally and without exception, that "the doctrines of revealed Religion could not be safely connected with a course of Public Instruction," is too erroneous to be credited a moment by anyone." [125]

The answer to this letter was Packard's last to Mann and thus closed the series.[126] In one part he stated again his belief that Mann misconstrued the 1827 statute to make it exclude teaching revealed religion:

> The monstrous construction you put upon the statute prohibiting "the purchase or use, in any of the town schools, of any *school books* which are calculated to favor the tenets of any particular sect of Christians," whereby you think authority is given to *exclude all religious teaching*—would soon be exploded;—Your avowed theory which makes religion and ethics the basis of the system would be set aside before it had gained a foothold, and the people of the Puritan state would drive you back upon the Bible and the precepts and principles of *revealed religion,* as the true and only basis of such a system —The *law itself* is wise, wholesome, necessary; but *your interpretation of it* would be pronounced forced,—mischievous,— absurd.[127]

Packard repeated in this letter the charge that Mann did avow in their conversation that religious instruction should be postponed beyond the period of childhood:

> You did say to me in substance, if not in *totidem verbis,* that the mind should be left to judge of religious doctrines for itself and that no influence should be used to bias it on religious subjects, until the judgement is sufficiently matured to weigh the evidence and arguments for itself. You admit that you said that "creeds and obstruse points which divide one sect of Christians from another" ought not to be taught to children—and when you enumerate these creeds and points it will be found (as I found it) that they embrace any and all points of faith on which any person in Christendom differs from any other person in Christendom.[128]

[125] *Ibid.,* pp. 266–67.
[126] Packard to Mann, Philadelphia, September 19, 1838 (Culver, *op. cit.,* pp. 270–84).
[127] Culver, *op. cit.,* p. 270.
[128] *Ibid.,* p. 277.

Towards the end of the letter Packard stated his opinion that Mann obviously did not want Christianity to be the basis of the Massachusetts system of instruction—"so far as your influence is concerned—the Christian religion will not be recognized as the basis of the system of public instruction in Massachusetts." [129] To Packard this appeared as a major change in the State's educational policy:

> Your official connexion [*sic*] with the Board of Education, seemed to me to make the entertainment of these views by you a matter of momentous interest, which none but an infinite mind can comprehend. If they should become incorporated with the system of instruction about to be established, *under your auspices*, on a firm and durable basis, I cannot doubt that the most sacred institutions and usages of my native State would be uprooted and abolished. [130]

The selections here made from the many pages of the Mann-Packard correspondence are an attempt to give only the basic points of the involved series of charges, refutations and counter-charges which went on between the two men for many weeks. The important questions for this study are— 1) Did Packard argue for doctrinal religion in the schools because he felt it *belonged* in education if the term "religious" was to be applied to the school system as developed in America? 2) Did Mann argue against the inclusion of doctrinal religion because he felt it did *not belong* in the American educational picture, or because he thought including it an *impossible achievement*, given the necessity of preserving the system from chaos and/or guaranteeing the rights of conscience?

From the material already gathered on Horace Mann, plus his letters to Packard, an answer to the second question will be essayed later. [131] As to the question on Packard, it seems well first to probe a bit more by referring to some other of his writings. Some months after the last of the Mann-Packard letters, a pamphlet appeared giving four letters addressed to the Rev. Dr.

[129] *Ibid.*, p. 280.
[130] *Ibid.*, p. 282.
[131] *Cf. infra,* p. 184.

Humphrey, President of Amherst College.[132] Although no author is given, it is quite clear from a number of sources that they were written by Packard.[133] The letters include a substantial repetition of the charges made by Packard in the correspondence with Mann—education must include religion; the history of Massachusetts shows religion to have been the law of education; Horace Mann's interpretation of the law of 1827 has resulted in a substitution of ethics and natural religion for what was previously taught.[134]

Packard repeated the thesis that the national religion must be in the nation's schools in an article written for the July, 1841 issue of *Princeton Review.*[135] This time he made *"Christianity"* coterminous with *"Protestantism,"* and what he wanted taught was "scriptural truth as received by the great body of Protestant Christians in the United States." [136] Three reasons were given by Packard— 1) Government institutions must bear a Protestant character and so the schools must be made Protestant; 2) Protestantism itself must be propagated, therefore the state must not be allowed to put aside all claims for religion in education; 3) The Scriptures must be diffused, mainly through the agency of public school children.[137] He then called for unrestricted use of the Bible in the schools; protested government interference with religious instruction; and, for Massachusetts, wanted the authority over such instruction put in the hands of the school districts or individual teachers. Finally, he appealed to all Christians to reject every connection with any school system which did not make the

[132] *The Question, Will the Christian Religion Be Recognized as the Basis of the System of Public Instruction in Massachusetts? Discussed in Four Letters to the Rev. Dr. Humphrey, President of Amherst College* (Boston: Whipple & Damrell, 1839).

[133] Cf. Culver, *op. cit.,* pp. 94–95.

[134] Cf., e.g., *The Question* . . . , Letter ii, p. 9; Letter iv, pp. 20, 24–25.

[135] "Religious Instruction in Common Schools," *Biblical Repertory and Princeton Review,* xiii (July, 1841), 315–68. Authorship is attributed to Packard by the *Index Volume* (1871), p. 271. Interestingly, he observes that the views of the non-religious party in education may be found explained in the "Letters to President Humphrey." He also includes a long quotation from the Humphrey letters, pp. 322–26.

[136] *Ibid.,* p. 355.

[137] *Ibid.,* pp. 360–64.

true religion of Jesus Christ the groundwork of education.[138]

One of the reasons Packard gave for developing public schools as propagators of Protestant influence was that they might serve as a bulwark against Catholicism. "And it is well," he wrote, "that Protestants should have fully and distinctly before their eyes this truth, that just in proportion to the advancement of Roman Catholics in influence, (that is in numbers, wealth and intelligence) Protestant institutions are brought into danger." [139] Packard felt that his plan, however, was not anti-Catholic. It would merely pass them by, for he stated: "We think that schools might be maintained, without interfering with Roman Catholics, or seeking their cooperation, where Protestant children might be instructed in the branches of useful learning, and, at the same time, in the great doctrines and duties of the Christian religion, without giving offence to any candid and sober-minded parent." [140]

Therefore, the question posed above,[141]— Did Packard think doctrinal religion belonged in education?—must receive an affirma-

[138] *Ibid.*, pp. 364–68. Packard repeated his castigation of Mann years later when he reviewed the *Life* of the Secretary written by Mrs. Mann. Once more he charges him with being false to the traditions of Mass., and offers as an inscription for Mann's monument: "He did what he could to obliterate from the youthful mind the notion of the Providential government of the world, and to bring into exercise the noble but neglected faculty of causality." Cf. "Horace Mann," *Biblical Repertory and Princeton Review*, xxxviii (Jan., 1866), 94. The review is attributed to Packard by the *Index Volume* (1871), p. 271. The date is here given as 1865. There is no article entitled "Horace Mann" in the 1865 volume (xxxvii).

[139] Packard, "Religious Instruction in Common Schools," pp. 359–60.

[140] *Ibid.*, p. 363. The rights and claims of Catholics in the matter of education do not loom very large in that part of the Massachusetts story under consideration in this study. Although Irish immigration started around 1830, it did not immediately assume large proportions. In 1835 an arrangement unique for the times was made in Lowell, where a considerable group of Irish-Catholic immigrants had settled. Catholic teachers were assigned to the public schools and care was taken that the books used had no material offensive to Catholics. The plan lasted for about a decade and then fell into decline. Cf. Sherman Smith, *op. cit.*, pp. 191–97. By 1848, though, the Irish-Catholic population had grown greatly. In his *Twelfth Report*, Horace Mann mentioned that if sectarianism should be brought into the Boston Primary Schools, 5,154 children "of foreign parentage" (almost half the primary school population) "would be immediately withdrawn from the schools" (p. 135).

[141] *Supra*, p. 155.

tive answer. As far as Massachusetts is concerned, he thought doctrinal religious education belonged in the tradition from Pilgrim days and that it was enjoined by the law of 1789. Moreover, the religion was to be Christianity as determined by Protestants. The basis of his whole structure was, in his mind, that in reality Christianity (as defined) was the religion of the American people. In 1838, and thirty years after, (cf. footnote 138) Packard regarded Horace Mann as the avowed destroyer of the Christian religion in the public school.

Among the events stirred up by the appearance of the "Letters to Dr. Humphrey," was an exchange between Horace Mann and the Rev. Dr. Richard S. Storrs. It is brought in here as another instance of the policies of the Secretary being challenged, this time by a clergyman. Storrs declared his appreciation of Mann's sincere efforts but stated:

> Will you allow me to say, my dear Sir, that I have no confidence in the ultimate success of any project for the intellectual and moral improvement of our youth, which is not based on the religion of the Bible? And will you allow me to say further, that by the religion of the Bible, I mean the kernel, not the shell—the substance not the shadow? Those there are as you are well aware, who profess great veneration for the Bible, and talk much of piety, and of its dignity and even innocency of human nature, while they treat with great contumely every doctrine regarded by others as essential to the Christian system. . . .[142]

Later in the letter Storrs commented unfavorably, first, on the mere reading of the Scriptures without comment, as practiced in the Normal Schools, and, second, the fact that at the time of his writing (1839) all but three members of the Board were Unitarian.

On the other hand supporters of Mann's position did not remain silent. Culver notes (1) two anonymous letters in the Boston papers favoring the Board and the Secretary; (2) the resolution favorable to Mann offered by the Rev. Warren Fay, and supported by the Rev. O. H. Dodge, at a meeting of the Middlesex County Association for the Improvement of Common Schools;

---

[142] Storrs to Mann, Braintree, February 20, 1839. (Reproduced in Culver, op. cit., pp. 98–101. The section here quoted is on page 99.)

and (3) an editorial reversal on the part of the *Trumpet and Universalist Magazine*. The *Trumpet* first attacked Mann and the Board for what it called an effort "to introduce religion into the Common Schools of Massachusetts." Then it switched over to support of the Board when it viewed the appearance of the "Letters to Dr. Humphrey" as an attempt to put sectarianism in the curriculum.[143]

The Mann-Packard controversy and the various declarations it prompted on the part of others indicate that many leaders in Massachusetts life had not changed their conviction that religion belonged in public life and in public education. True, they fought among themselves, often quite bitterly, as to *how, how much* and *what kind* of religious instruction was to be given to children. Yet, they agreed that public education should include religion of some sort. Here, Mann and the Board came through the controversy without serious damage to their policy. However, the earnestness with which it was challenged is not without significance.

THE MOVE TO ABOLISH THE BOARD

In January, 1840, Governor Marcus Morton's opening speech to the Legislature set in motion a move to take power from the Board of Education and place it with the towns. The House of Representatives directed its Committee on Education to look into the matter. As a result the Committee reported a bill to abolish the Board and the Normal Schools.[144] The bill failed in the House, the vote being 245 *against* and 182 *for* its passage. By and large, this move to abolish the Board was a political affair, yet it was not without its religious implications. This is shown by the texts of the Majority and Minority reports from the Committee on Education which accompanied the proposed bill. They were reproduced by Mann in the *Common School Journal* the following summer.[145]

---

[143] Cf. Culver, *op. cit.*, pp. 100–109, *passim*.

[144] *Ibid.*, pp. 134–36.

[145] *Common School Journal*, ii (August 1, 1840), 225–34. One of the agitators against the Board was Orestes Brownson, at that time an agnostic and later a convert to Catholicism. For some interesting light on Brownson's

Among its reasons for abolishing the Board, the Majority Report stated:

> . . . In a country like this, where such diversity of sentiments exists, especially upon theological subjects, and where morality is considered a part of religion, and is, to some extent modified by sectarian views, the difficulty and danger of attempting to introduce these subjects into our schools, according to one fixed or settled plan, to be devised by a central Board, must be obvious. The right to mould the political, moral, and religious, opinions of his children is a right exclusively and jealously reserved by our laws to every parent; and for the government to attempt, directly or indirectly as to these matters, to stand in the parent's place, is an undertaking of very questionable policy. Such an attempt cannot fail to excite a feeling of jealousy with respect to our public schools, the results of which could not but be disastrous.[146]

Later the Majority Report again mentioned religion, this time in connection with the school libraries. The Report admitted that the Board would try to keep the library free from sectarian objections, but touched the same theme developed by Packard— Can a library stripped of books with sectarian views present anything but a viscerated religion? [147]

The Majority Statement concluded with a declaration that state control of education, as exemplified in the powers given the Board "seems to your Committee a great departure from the uniform spirit of our institutions,—a dangerous precedent, and an interference with a matter more properly belonging to those hands, to which our ancestors wisely intrusted [sic] it." [148]

The Minority Report, which (as Culver points out from a study

---

poor opinion of Horace Mann and his theories of religious pedagogy, cf. Arthur E. Bestor, Jr., "Horace Mann, Elizabeth Peabody and Orestes A. Brownson, An Unpublished Letter With Commentary," reprinted from *Proceedings of the Middle States Association of History and Social Science Teachers, 1940–41* (New York: Teachers College, Columbia University, 1941).

[146] *Common School Journal*, II (August 1, 1840), p. 227.

[147] *Ibid.*, pp. 227–28.

[148] *Ibid.*, p. 229.

of Mann's Diary) [149] the Secretary helped to prepare, defended the Board against the charge of infringing the right of towns as districts, but remained silent on parental rights. On the question of the charge that library books could be of no value unless they were to some extent of a partisan and sectarian character, the Minority Report cited Paley's *Natural Theology* as "one of the soundest treatises ever written" yet "no one could tell whether its author were orthodox or heterodox."

The Minority Report then asked what would become of the Law of 1826 [150] which ordered the teaching of piety and yet forbade the use of any books inculcating sectarian tenets. "In this connection," said the Minority,

> we will quote a sentence or two from Professor Stowe: "I pity the poor bigot," says he, "or the narrow-souled unbeliever, who can form no idea of religious principle, except as a sectarian thing; who is himself so unsusceptible of ennobling emotions, that he cannot conceive it possible that any man should have a principle of virtue or piety superior to all external forms, and untrammelled by metaphysical systems. From the aid of such men we have nothing to hope, in the cause of sound education; . . ." [151]

The arguments of the Minority, at least as to religion, seem to be weaker and more emotionally formed than those of the Majority. Yet the vote went against the Bill and the Board continued to function. It is important to note that the procedure of teaching "piety," yet eliminating sectarianism, still seemed to pose a problem to Massachusetts leaders. Even more important was the declaration on parental rights made in the Majority Report. There seems to have been scant attention paid to this concept in the writings we have been examining.

THE CONTROVERSY WITH EDWARD A. NEWTON

The third major dispute which involved Horace Mann and his religious policy occurred in 1844 with a former member of the

[149] Culver, *op. cit.*, p. 138.
[150] Cf. *supra*, p. 105, footnote 30.
[151] *Common School Journal, num. cit.*, p. 233.

Board, Edward A. Newton, an Episcopalian, of Pittsfield. It was this controversy which called forth the Burnside letter on the 1827 law which was examined in Chapter IV.[152] The story of the controversy is told in the twenty-one extracts from letters and newspaper articles which make up a well-known pamphlet, *The Common School Controversy*.[153] The extracts will here be called "Items."

Item 1 was a communication, later identified as the work of Newton, addressed to M. A. De Wolfe Howe, editor of *The Christian Witness*, an Episcopalian organ, and printed in its issue of February 23, 1844. Entitled "Christian Education," it compared the current Massachusetts system of religious instruction to that mentioned in the will of Stephen Girard providing for the college near Philadelphia which bears his name. Quoting Daniel Webster's speech in a United States Supreme Court case contesting the Girard will, Newton declared that the Massachusetts system laid the axe to the root of Christianity by excluding the teaching of the Christian religion.[154]

Item 2 is an editorial comment by Howe. It is called "The System of Public Education in Massachusetts," and appeared on March 8. The editor said that what Newton had assailed was *"the separation of religious and moral culture from religious teaching."* [155] The *third item*, appearing in *The Witness* on March 15, was further editorial comment on an extract from the *Christian Reflector*, a Baptist paper. (The latter saw a parallel between the Girard will and the current Massachusetts procedure and declared that such was not the will of the Pilgrim Fathers.) [156]

This brought forth a letter from Horace Mann addressed to the *Witness* editor. It was published in the Episcopalian paper on March 29. (*Item 4*). Mann reviewed the articles of February 23 and March 8 and declared his resentment of the parallel between the Girard will and his (Mann's) and the Board's policies. He made among others, the following points:

152 Cf. *supra,* pp. 107 f.
153 *The Common School Controversy* (Boston: J. N. Bradley, 1844). The full title of the pamphlet is given in Chap. iv, footnote 35, p. 107.
154 *Ibid.,* p. 3.
155 *Ibid.,* p. 4.
156 *Ibid.,* pp. 6, 7.

1. The Massachusetts system is not the Board's creation but that of state law.

2. The only objection to Girard's system is its prohibition that clergymen hold positions at the college or even visit the institution. Yet, in Massachusetts, clergymen serve on the school committees and visit the schools frequently.

3. Only the Normal Schools are under the Board directly, and in them the Bible is read every day.

4. In Girard's boarding college the students would get no religion, whereas in Massachusetts the children would get it at home, in Church and in Sunday School.

5. Five of the eight Board members are Orthodox clergymen and they all approve the current procedure.

6. He (Mann) advocates Bible reading in the schools.

7. Instilling virtues is a part of Christianity.

8. The law outlawing sectarian books does not prohibit, and necessarily implies, that Christian books may be introduced and instruction in Christian truth given. All Christian books and Christian instruction are not necessarily sectarian.[157] On this point he further said:

> Under these provisions of the constitution and laws, may not children be taught to love the Lord their God with all their heart, and their neighbor as themselves; may they not be taught to do to others as they would be done by; may they not be taught to do justly, to love mercy and to walk humbly with God; may they not be taught to visit the fatherless and widows in their affliction, and to keep themselves unspotted from the world; may they not be taught to honor father and mother; to keep the Sabbath holy; not to steal; not to kill; not to bear false witness against neighbors; not to covet? . . .[158]

9. More than 1000 reports sent to him (Mann), probably a majority from clergymen, discovered how far religious instruction might be given "without trenching upon the rights of individuals."[159]

10. He (Mann) fears that "if the day ever arrives when the school room shall become a cauldron for the fermentation of all

[157] *Ibid.*, pp. 8–12.
[158] *Ibid.*, p. 12.
[159] *Ibid.*, p. 13.

the hot and virulent opinions, in politics and religion, that now agitate our community, that day the fate of our glorious public school system will be sealed, and speedy ruin will overwhelm it." [160]

Item 5—In the same issue (March 29) the editor of the *Witness* published his comments on the Mann letter. The nonsectarian materials advanced by the Secretary were all right as far as they went, said the editor, "but they leave untouched what we, and all orthodox Christians esteem the essentials of Christianity,—the way of salvation by Jesus Christ." [161] He further inquired if the Pilgrim Fathers would have considered "the doctrines of grace" sectarian? Must liberality be allowed to unbridled heresies such as Universalism, Millerism,[162] Mormonism, Papism? What particular sect does it favor to say that God was in Christ? This is common ground to all Christians except the above named heretics, and to teach anything less in the schools is sectarian in itself.[163]

Item 6—This called forth a second letter from Mann, which the *Witness* would not publish. The *Boston Courrier*, however, ran it on April 9. It was called "Common Schools and the Christian Witness." (*Item 7*). Here Mann declared that what he called "unsectarian religion" *was* unsectarian. As to the doctrines of grace, Mann said that, if they were in the Bible and the Bible was read to children, then they were in the school.[164] Beyond this, Mann supposed, the religious groups would have to get their own catechisms. To do this the religious groups would have to train teachers and pass laws as to what they must teach, and this would be establishment of religion.[165]

---

[160] *Ibid.*, p. 14.

[161] *Ibid.*, p. 15.

[162] Millerites, a group of Adventists. "As a religious movement it [Adventism] began with an awakening on the advent [second coming of Christ] question . . . in the early years of the nineteenth century. It became strongest and most clearly defined in the United States under the leadership of William Miller (1782–1849), a farmer of Low Hampton, New York." Mead, *op. cit.*, p. 15.

[163] *Ibid.*, pp. 15–16.

[164] Cf. *supra*, p. 149. As we have seen, this argument was to be repeated in Mann's *Twelfth Report*.

[165] *Common School Controversy*, pp. 18–21.

Item 8—It was now Newton's turn to write and the *Witness* published an article,—"Our Common Schools" on May 17 to which were signed the initials, "E.A.N." Newton declared he was not against the Massachusetts system, but against the way the Board had changed it. For two centuries the Massachusetts schools had taught doctrinal religion and it was a doctrine agreed on by Orthodox Congregationalists, Baptists, Episcopalians, Methodists and Presbyterians, "without any reserve whatever in the laws, or prohibition as to the teaching of *sectarian* religion." [166]

In the early part of the present century, Newton went on to say, a new sect arose [167] and in 1827 a new law on textbooks appeared. No one thought much of it until ten years later. However, says Newton, (in 1827)

it was not construed to mean the excluding of religious teaching, in the great *doctrines* of the gospel; this had given no offence for two hundred years to the religious denominations making together the great body of the people; it was interpreted to mean, if to be operative, the exclusion of ecclesiastical systems of *church government* and discipline, but as these had never been obtruded so as to disturb the public repose, no danger was apprehended from them, and *religious teaching*, as here understood, continued to be practised in our schools.[168]

Ten years later, continued Newton, the Board of Education, with eight out of eleven belonging to the new sect, gave a rigorous interpretation to the 1827 law. They ruled out what they considered sectarian and what others considered vital. The Board ruled out the Assembly's *Catechism* and allowed only Scripture reading. A religion on which all are agreed is a mockery, unless one means what is termed natural religion.[169]

On May 29 appeared *Item 9*—Mann's reply to Newton. It was printed in the *Boston Courrier* under the title, "Our Common Schools." It made, among others, the following points:

[166] *Ibid.*, p. 22.
[167] The Unitarians?
[168] *Common School Controversy*, pp. 22–23. This was directly challenged by Samuel Burnside. Cf. *supra*, pp. 106 f.
[169] *Ibid.*, pp. 23–24.

1—As to the teaching of doctrinal religion: In the nine eastern counties of the State, containing more than five eighths of its population, the teaching of the Assembly's Catechism and of Orthodox doctrines, had been, not entirely, but mainly discontinued, long before the existence of the Board. The Catechism had been objected to by the Orthodox Baptists themselves. In many places, the discontinuance dates back, at least, to the beginning of the present century. I have met with many persons, educated in our schools, who never saw the Assembly's Catechism. So convinced was public sentiment of the equity and justice of the law of 1827, against sectarian teaching in the schools, that in all the common school conventions I have ever attended, in almost all of which the subject of moral and religious instruction has been introduced, there has been but one instance where such teaching was advocated; and there it was resisted on the spot, by an Orthodox clergyman.[170]

2—School committee reports, since the establishment of the Board, are all on file, and all but two support Mann's position.

3—Newton's interpretation of the 1827 law (ecclesiastical polity, not doctrine, forbidden) is new to Mann.

4—Newton's statement that the 1827 law was inoperative until 1835 is challenged.[171]

7—The Board does nothing to advance or repress any Christian sect, because religious liberty exists in Massachusetts. The Board's policy aroused the hostility of those who wanted to proselytize in the schools.

9—As to Newton's demand to teach orthodox doctrines, there are anti-Orthodox in every Massachusetts town and district, who would rebel. Chaos would result and religious liberty would be violated.

10—He has not used his position to force his religious views. Neither has anyone on the Board, but only Mr. Newton himself.[172]

This letter ended the exchange among Mann, Newton and the *Witness* editor. *Items 10 to 21 in the Pamphlet are press reactions to the controversy, including the long letter from Samuel Burn-*

---

[170] *Ibid.*, p. 26.

[171] Yet, in his *Twelfth Report,* as has been noted (cf. *supra,* p. 147), Mann was to declare that when he took the Secretary's position in 1837, he found sectarian textbooks in use and sectarian doctrine taught orally.

[172] *Ibid.*, pp. 26–32.

side. All of the newspaper stories reproduced in the *Common School Controversy* side with Mann and the Board. The pamphlet closes with the statement that, as it was going to press, it noticed an article in the *Christian Reflector* on the controversy. The *Witness* had said of the *Reflector*—"it agrees with us." [173] The *Reflector* denied this. The pamphlet compiler said the *Reflector* was the only paper in the state which was known to have given even the slightest countenance to the *Witness* attack on the Board of Education.[174]

So ended the third controversy. Again, Mann weathered the storm and seems to have had the support of a goodly segment of the press. The opposition brought up many points which had been argued before. The chief of these was the claim that Mann's system did not merit the title of Christian instruction, as it was in reality a new brand of sectarianism. The 1827 law was labeled by Newton as a direct machination of the Unitarians. (Burnside's letter seems to contradict this). Newton's claim that the law was meant to exclude only descriptions of church polity does not seem to be supported elsewhere.

In contrast to Mann's other statements (e.g., in the *Twelfth Report*) the Secretary seems to have laid a special emphasis on the possibility of Christian instruction from books and other methods which would not be sectarian. (Cf. *Item* 4, No. 8). He challenged Newton's contention that doctrinal religion continued to be taught in the decade after 1827, but his figures covered only the eastern part of the state. His statement on the "hands-off" policy of the Board on the matter of Bible study (*Item* 9, No. 6) might suggest that there was room for doctrinal teaching, at least of an oral or visual nature. He was clear and strong in pointing out the difficulties of getting the Catechism taught (*Item* 7) even if such would not be opposed by the anti-Orthodox (*Item* 9, No. 9).

[173] Cf. *supra*, p. 162.

[174] *Common School Controversy*, p. 55. There is no doubt that this pamphlet was prepared to uphold Mann's position in the controversy. Note the title, *The Common School Controversy, Consisting of Three Letters of the Secretary of the Board of Education . . . In Reply to Charges Made Against the Board etc.* In the research for the present study, however, no other material was found supporting Newton's side.

THE CONTROVERSY WITH THE BOSTON SCHOOLMASTERS

When Horace Mann's *Seventh Report* [175] was circulated, it stirred opposition among the members of the "Principals' Association," an organization of the masters of the grammar schools in Boston.[176] A committee of the Association issued a pamphlet—*Remarks on the Seventh Annual Report of the Hon. Horace Mann, Secretary of the Massachusetts Board of Education.*[177] It was signed by thirty-one of the masters.[178]

Of the four sections of the *Remarks,* only the last had a connection [179] with religion, and this an indirect one. The fourth section, entitled "School Discipline," dealt with Mann's treatment of punishments. In the *Seventh Report* Mann had written a section entitled "Corporal Punishment." [180] There he records the punitive practices he had found in the various European countries he had visited. In Germany, corporal punishment was allowed but rarely used. In Holland it was obsolete. In Scotland and England it was frequently used. In Paris, surveillance was so thorough that corporal punishment was deemed unnecessary. Mann himself took the position that such punishment might be used as a last resort, but insisted on the teacher cultivating friendly relations with the pupil and trying to stir obedience from motives of love, loyalty and the intrinsic attraction of virtue. It was his reporting of the European systems in a manner favorable to his own views that seems to have aroused the Boston schoolmasters who, themselves, used corporal punishment regularly.

In their *Remarks* the schoolmasters' committee emphasized that

[175] Cf. *supra,* pp. 139 f.

[176] "Grammar Schools," it will be remembered, were secondary schools which were generally run under private auspices.

[177] *Remarks on the Seventh Annual Report of the Hon. Horace Mann, Secretary of the Massachusetts Board of Education. Prepared by a committee of the "Association of Masters of Boston Public Schools"* and published by that body (Boston: Charles C. Little & J. Brown, 1844).

[178] Culver, *op. cit.,* p. 189.

[179] *Remarks,* pp. 103–44.

[180] *Seventh Report,* pp. 160–65.

obedience must be based on the absolute authority of the teacher:

> . . . As the fear of the Lord is the beginning of divine wisdom, so is the fear of the law, the beginning of political wisdom. He who would command even, must first learn to obey. . . .
>
> Obedience recognizes the existence of abstract authority; and all authority originates in the highest source! As St. Paul writes to the Romans, "Let every soul be subject unto the higher powers. For there is no power but of God; the powers that be are ordained of God. Whosoever therefore resisteth the power resisteth the ordinance of God." [181]

To this Horace Mann issued a *Reply*.[182] He reviewed his stand on the means by which he believed obedience could best be gotten from children. Then, towards the end of the *Reply,* Mann indicated his suspicion that religious bigotry was behind the attack of the schoolmasters. He then reiterated his position that sectarianism could not be allowed in the schools under the current laws of Massachusetts.[183]

The document called forth a *Rejoinder* from the schoolmasters, "Part Four" of which, signed by one Joseph Hale, dealt with the question of punishment.[184] It placed the subject directly on a religious basis, and the point on which the discussion was made to turn was the doctrine of total depravity. If the child is innately evil then he must obey implicitly: "If then all authority is of God," declares Hale,

> and must be obeyed, it becomes indispensable, in order to settle the question whether compulsion may ever be absolutely necessary or not, that we decide whether there is in the nature of man an innate element of evil, prompting him to rebellion. If there is, then compulsion results from resistance; if not, then the impulses are all that is necessary to secure duty; tempta-

---

[181] *Remarks,* pp. 127, 129 (quoting Epistle to the Romans, 13.1–2).

[182] Horace Mann, *Reply to the Remarks of Thirty-one Boston Schoolmasters on the Seventh Annual Report of the Hon. Horace Mann; Secretary of the Massachusetts Board of Education* (Boston: W. B. Fowle & N. Capen, 1844).

[183] *Ibid.,* pp. 171–72.

[184] Joseph Hale, Part Four of *Rejoinder to the "Reply" of the Hon. Horace Mann; Secretary of the Massachusetts Board of Education, to the "Remarks" of the Association of Boston Masters, upon his Seventh Annual Report* (Boston: C. C. Little & J. Brown, 1845).

tion is at an end; virtue is a negation; vice a nonentity; repentance a work of supererogation.[185]

To this *Rejoinder* Mann published an *Answer*.[186] The Secretary made it clear that he felt the whole controversy was an attempt to force sectarianism into the schools. "One of the Masters said in my hearing," Mann wrote,

and has been known to say the same thing repeatedly to others; —that the plan now was to convert this *whole* controversy into a *sectarian* movement against the Board, in order, by combining religious opposition with the opposition of malcontents from all other causes, to overthrow the Board of Education! [187]

Whether or not there was such a plot is not important here, for nothing came of the controversy as far as unseating the Board was concerned. As the texts of the controversial pamphlets stand, the schoolmasters based their opposition to Mann's views of punishment on the Calvinist doctrine of total depravity. Mann countered with statements based on his view of the innate goodness and improvability of human nature from its own inherent efforts. It is important to see in this controversy that in 1845 the Orthodox (at least some of them) were still dissatisfied with the way the traditions of Massachusetts education were being handled. Right or wrong in their stand, they took it and fought for what they believed. The controversy was but another evidence of essential agreement between opponents as to the importance of religion and the specific end to be achieved in child training, but violent disagreement, based on opposite theological views, as to the correct means to be chosen to attain it.

THE CONTROVERSY WITH THE REV. MATTHEW H. SMITH

The final dispute to be considered in this study occurred in 1846. It started when an Orthodox minister, who had been a

---

[185] *Ibid.*, p. 57. For an analysis of the "orthodox" view on total depravity and the position of the "liberals," cf. H. Shelton Smith, *Changing Conceptions of Original Sin* (New York: Charles Scribner's Sons, 1955).

[186] Horace Mann, *Answer to the "Rejoinder" of Twenty-nine Schoolmasters, part of the "Thirty-one" who published "Remarks" on the Seventh Annual Report of the Secretary of Massachusetts Board of Education* (Boston: W. B. Fowle & N. Capen, 1845).

[187] *Ibid.*, p. 16.

Universalist, the Rev. Matthew Hale Smith, preached a sermon to a group of Sunday School workers in Boston. The title of his discourse was "The Ark of God on a New Cart." Paralleling an Old Testament reference about the punishment of Oza, who was struck dead for having touched the Ark of Covenant,[188] the Rev. Mr. Smith charged that society was being punished for having tampered with religious instruction in the schools. Specifically he declared:

> Modern reformers have taken the education of youth under their special care. Men, wise above that which is written, have made common schools the theatre of their experiments and labors. . . .
>
> An effort has been made, and that too with some success, to do three things with our common schools. 1. To get out of them the Bible and all religious instruction. 2. To abolish the use of the rod, and all correction, but a little talk. 3. To make common schools a counterpoise to religious instruction at home and in Sabbath schools. The Board of Education in Massachusetts has aided in this work in two ways. 1. By allowing an individual, under the sanction of its authority, to disseminate through the land crude and destructive principles, principles believed to be at war with the Bible and with the best interests of the young for time and eternity. 2. By a library which excludes books as sectarian that inculcate truths, which *nine-tenths of professed Christians of all names believe,* while it accepts others that inculcate the most deadly heresy—even universal salvation. We ask not that religion shall be sustained by law; but we do ask that impiety and irreligion shall not be supported by the state. When religious and intellectual culture are divorced, is it strange that we have a harvest of crime?[189]

Mann answered the charges of Smith, saying, first of all, that the efforts of the School Board had been aimed "to promote and encourage, and whenever they have had any power, as in the case of the Normal Schools, to *direct* the daily use of the Bible in

[188] Second Book of Samuel, vi, 1–10 (King James Version); Second Book of Kings, vi, 1–10 (Douay Version).

[189] Matthew Hale Smith, *The Bible, The Rod, and Religion in Common Schools* (Boston: Redding & Co., 1847). This pamphlet contains the text of the "Ark" sermon as well as other materials related to the controversy, including the correspondence which passed between Mann and Smith. The section of the sermon quoted here is found on pp. 10–11.

school." [190] When Smith again accused Mann of trying to get religious instruction out of the schools, the Secretary made reply as follows:

> Everyone who has availed himself of the means of arriving at the truth, on this point, knows that I am in favor of religious instruction in our schools, to the extremest verge to which it can be carried without invading those rights of conscience which are established by the laws of God, and guaranteed to us by the Constitution of the State.[191]

As Smith had thus brought the controversy into greater prominence by publishing the sermon and his correspondence with the Secretary in his pamphlet *The Bible, The Rod, and Religion in Common Schools,* Horace Mann published his *Sequel to the So-called Correspondence.*[192] Once again he denied any opposition to teaching religion in school:

> . . . You accuse me before the world, of being opposed to religion in our schools. I regard hostility to religion in our schools, as the greatest crime which I could commit against man or against God. Had I the power, I would sooner repeat the massacre of Herod, than I would keep back religion from the young. My own consciousness acquits me of your accusation. I call the All-searching Eye to witness that it is as false as anything ever engendered in the heart of man or fiend.[193]

Later in the pamphlet [194] Mann sarcastically developed a picture of what he thought would result if sectarian doctrines were taught in the common schools with the local town or district officials deciding the materials. Not only would a half-dozen creeds be taught in the different schools of a given town, but, as the religious majorities fluctuated, so would the doctrines taught. "This year there will be three Persons in the Godhead; next year, but One; . . . This year, the everlasting fires of hell will burn,

190 *Ibid.,* p. 24.
191 *Ibid.,* p. 33.
192 Horace Mann, *Sequel to the So-called Correspondence between the Rev. M. H. Smith and Horace Mann. Surreptitiously published by Mr. Smith, containing a Letter from Mr. Mann, suppressed by Mr. Smith, with the Reply therein Promised* (Boston: William B. Fowle, 1847).
193 *Ibid.,* p. 31.
194 Cf. *ibid.,* pp. 40–41.

to terrify the impenitent; next year, and without any repentance, its eternal flames will be extinguished, . . . This year, the ordinance of baptism is inefficacious without immersion; next year one drop of water will be as good as forty fathoms; etc."

Mann then described the political involvements he thought would follow.[195] If the districts and towns were to decide what theology was to be taught in the school, the religious faith of the committeemen would become a factor in their choice as well as in the choice of the teachers. Some court would be appointed to select them, and if it were the Governor of the State who would appoint the court, then he himself would have to be chosen on the basis of his religious beliefs. This would amount to the establishment of a state religion and Massachusetts would return to the "inquisition, the fagot and the rack."

"Let me ask here, too," he continued, "where is the consistency of those, who advocate the right of a *town* or a *district* to determine, by a majority, what theology shall be taught in the schools, but deny the same right to the *State?*" "This would be true," he went on to say, "even if the State had written out the theology it would enforce. But ours has not. It has only said that no one sect obtain any advantage over other sects by means of the school system, which for purposes of self-preservation, it has established." [196]

Smith answered with another pamphlet, *Reply to the Sequel.*[197] After picking at a number of small points in Mann's *Sequel,* Smith took up the three main subjects once again: The "Bible in Schools," the "Rod in Schools" and "Religion in Schools." On the first he declared that Mann, if honest, would oppose the Bible in schools because he [Mann] did not believe the Scriptures are the word of God.[198]

On the third point (Religion in Schools) Smith commenced as follows: "I have not accused Mr. Mann with being opposed to what *he calls* religion in schools. On the contrary, I charge him

[195] Cf. *ibid.,* pp. 41–42.

[196] *Ibid.*

[197] Matthew Hale Smith, *Reply to the Sequel of Hon. Horace Mann, being a Supplement to the Bible, The Rod and Religion, in Common Schools* (Boston: J. M. Whittemore, 1847).

[198] *Ibid.,* p. 13.

with being a dogmatist—a sectarian, zealous and confident, as all sectarians are. I have accused him, and do accuse him, of deciding what those 'principles of piety' are, which the Constitution demands to be taught in schools, and of deciding what may be taught in schools, and what shall not." [199]

"I charge him," Smith wrote later in the same section,

> with standing at the entrance to the common schools and making his own notions the standard of the character and quantity of the religion that may be introduced into schools. I charge him with beating down, insulting, and treating with marked contempt, all who dissent from his views—all who ask for those common sanctions which are as essential to this life as the next. I charge him with denouncing those who dissent from his opinion—who ask for something better, something more scriptural—as "dogmatic," "persistent," working with a resolution to force sectarianism into common schools, or to scatter them to the wind. I charge him with accusing those who ask that our common school system be kept where it has rested for 200 years, of *thrusting forward* private opinion." [200]

Smith made also the following thrust:

> If the Christian religion is removed from the common schools, we know not what may take its place—it may be the mythology of the Brahmins. In that religion, men deified those who scourged them, no less than those who did them good. In the Parthenon, shrines were erected, not only to the "benignant deities of light and plenty, but also to those who preside over the small-pox and murder." [201]

Two results seem to have come from this Smith-Mann controversy. First, it brought out some very forceful statements from Mann about his position. Second, Smith charged the Secretary more clearly, perhaps, than any other opponents, with introducing into the schools a new brand of religion, the sectarian position of Horace Mann himself. Though Smith's cause did not triumph any more than those of his predecessors, it was another protest—the protest of a man who felt that the heart had been cut out of traditional religious education, that something very undesirable had been put in its place, and that Massachusetts was

199 *Ibid.,* p. 24.
200 *Ibid.,* pp. 28–29.
201 *Ibid.,* p. 31.

worse off as a result. His voice should not be lost in the roar of acclaim for Mann, as we try to evaluate the over-all picture of religious instruction in the Bay State.

Reaction to Mann's Work in Massachusetts in the Immediately Following Years

Evidence indicating both that the social tradition on religion in public education continued in Massachusetts after Mann's resignation and that there was satisfaction with the actual method of imparting it according to the Secretary's method is found in a pamphlet published, in a second edition, in 1854 by an Englishman, the Hon. Edward Twistleton.[202]

In the Preface, the author tells how on a visit to New England in 1851 he circulated a questionnaire among several prominent New Englanders "to elicit information as to the effects, in a *religious* point of view, of the New England system of free schools." [203] Actually most, if not all, of the twelve men questioned seemed to be in some way connected with Massachusetts, and so their opinions are apropos in this chapter.[204] Five questions were asked:

1. Have you reason to believe that the system of instruction adopted in the common schools of New England interferes with the special religious tenets of any particular denomination of Christians?

[202] Edward Twistleton, *Evidence as to the Religious Working of the Common Schools in the State of Massachusetts, with a Preface by the Hon. Edward Twistleton, Late Chief Commissioner of Poor Laws in Ireland* (London: James Ridgeway, 1854).

[203] *Ibid.*, p. 5.

[204] Hon. Daniel Webster; Hon. Edward Everett; Hon. George Bancroft; The Right Rev. Dr. Eastburn, Protestant [Episcopal] Bishop of Massachusetts; Hon. William Appleton, late Representative of Massachusetts in Congress; Hon. R. C. Winthrop, late Representative of Massachusetts in Congress; Hon. F. C. Gray, late Senator of Massachusetts, and author of a work on Prison Discipline; Hon. G. C. Hillard, late Senator of Massachusetts, and author of a work called "Six Months in Italy"; William H. Prescott, Esq., the Historian; J. Sparks; George Ticknor, Esq., author of "History of Spanish Literature"; and Henry W. Longfellow. Cf. Twistleton, *op. cit.*, pp. 6–7.

2. Is it within your knowledge that, apart from the common schools, the children educated in them do practically receive instruction in the tenets of the religious denomination to which they respectively belong?

3. If they do receive such instruction, what are the agencies by which it is communicated to them?

4. In your opinion, is the system of instruction pursued in the common schools of New England indirectly favourable to the cultivation of the religious sentiments and to the promotion of morality?

5. Generally, do you approve or do you disapprove of that system; and what are the main grounds on which your approbation or disapprobation of it is founded? [205]

The answers of all twelve men were laudatory of the Massachusetts school system. Question 1 received a clearly negative answer from all of them. Questions 2 and 3 do not concern us here, although it can be noted in passing that their answers indicate a high degree of confidence in the Sunday Schools of the period.

Questions 4 and 5 are pertinent to this study. When asked if the system of instruction was favorable to the cultivation of religion and morality (Question 4), each of the twelve men answered in the affirmative and with varying degrees of emphatic agreement.[206] On the last question, eleven of the twelve stated that

---

[205] *Ibid.*, pp. 36–38.

[206] Samples of their replies are:

Webster—The system "promotes religious sentiments, encourages a reverence for the Scriptures, and tends, always indirectly, and sometimes directly, to the formation of a religious character in the pupils. The morals of the children are always carefully watched by their teachers."

Everett—"I answer this question decidedly in the affirmative."

Bancroft—"The common school system of instruction in New England has been of incalculable service to the promotion of morality, and makes the whole population susceptible of a higher degree of knowledge on subjects connected with religion. . . ."

Eastburn—"I think so. A general respect for religion and its institutions would be promoted by that system. . . ."

Appleton—"No teachers would be approved or continued unless of a moral and religious character. Their example would be followed to some extent by their pupils. . . ."

Winthrop—"In the highest degree." [Makes reference to the law on inculcating "principles of piety" and the rule that normal school students are

they approved of the Massachusetts school system's way of inculcating religion and morality. Bancroft did not answer the question.[207]

---

educated "in the principles of piety and morality common to all sects of Christians."]

Gray—"It is so, by affording special securities that the teachers shall be exemplary as moral and religious men. . . ."

Hillard—". . . I could not believe otherwise, without believing ignorance to be the natural ally of religion and morality. . . ."

Prescott—"I should say directly favorable to both. The morning exercises are usually preceded by the reading of a portion of the Scriptures, and thus a reverence is inculcated in the child for the sacred volume, and the teachings it contains, as the guide of his life. . . ."

Sparks—"I cannot but think so. The books . . . [although non-sectarian] are nevertheless of a moral and religious tendency. . . ."

Ticknor—"I have no doubt that the system . . . tends greatly to the preservation of social order, to the diffusion of a spirit of enquiry for the truth, and to the cultivation of religious sentiments, and of a sense of duty to man and to God; . . ."

Longfellow—"I give an affirmative answer to this question, and have no doubt that such is the result. Were it otherwise, the common schools must long ago have been abandoned as worse than useless." Twistleton, *op. cit.*, *passim*, pp. 37–73.

[207] Phrases from their replies are:

Webster—". . . In my own recollection of these schools there exists . . . a fresh feeling of the sobriety of the teachers . . . reverence with which the Scriptures were read. . . ."

Everett—"I think our school system, in theory, perfect; in practice it varies . . . with local circumstances. . . ."

Eastburn—". . . Individually should prefer arrangements under which the tenets of my own Church were directly taught . . . yet, . . . I approve . . . because it ensures the means of providing a more efficient system of instruction than could permanently be maintained for all . . . in any other way."

Appleton—". . . Approve . . . believing . . . [the system] to be better than any other within my knowledge; . . ."

Winthrop—". . . Unqualified approbation . . ." [like the common blessings of Providence] "I cannot conceive of our getting along without them, under a political system like ours. . . ."

Gray—". . . Because . . . highly important . . . that the children . . . be . . . associated in similar pursuits . . . religion . . . is best taught in a school devoted to that single object [religion]; . . . if thus taught in the church . . . children will be likely to regard this study as . . . more sacred . . . etc."

Hillard—". . . In a country like ours, with no established religion, . . . it is quite impossible that the system itself should provide for distinct religious training. . . ."

Prescott—". . . On the present plan, all . . . may receive an education

Twistleton's pamphlet also contains evidence offered by the Rev. Dr. Barnas Sears, Mann's successor in the Secretaryship.[208] In answer to the question, "Will you be so good as to explain the precise form and extent of the religious instruction which is given in the common schools?" Sears answered, in part, as follows:

> . . . A great diversity exists in regard to the form in which religious instruction is given in the schools. Religion is not taught as a matter of theology, according to the forms of the Catechism, but is generally inculcated as a matter of devotion and of Christian morals. The Scriptures are almost universally used in some way in the public schools.[209]

The final question, and Dr. Sears' answer, follow:

> Do you think that the System of instruction pursued in the common schools of New England is indirectly favourable to the cultivation of the religious sentiments?
> I have no doubt of it, whatever; and I will add further, that I believe that it is directly so, and in a very high degree. It is a general sentiment among committees and teachers that moral education founded on the religious sentiment is indispensable to the highest success of the schools; that all the other ends both of discipline and instruction, are better answered where there is a high moral and religious tone of feeling. At the teachers' conventions, associations, and institutes, both in public lectures and discussions, the importance of religious instruction is generally made very prominent. Everybody that writes

---

fitting them for the duties of this life; . . . all are taught that reverence for religion which is a good basis for those particular tenets which may be inculcated elsewhere."

Sparks—"A system may be fairly judged by its results. . . . I am not aware that the people of any country . . . have exhibited the fruits of moral and religious culture in a more eminent degree, than the inhabitants of New England."

Ticknor—". . . I believe this New England system to be more effectual than any system of teaching has yet been made elsewhere to secure the well-being of a State. . . ."

Longfellow—". . . However poor a man may be, he feels that the education of his children, to a certain point, is secured to them, and that good morals will be taught them, and their religious sentiments cherished and cultivated." Twistleton, *op. cit., passim*, pp. 38–73.

208 *Ibid.*, p. 74–85.
209 *Ibid.*, pp. 74–75.

on the subject or speaks on the subject, no matter to what party or sect he may belong, presents it in the same light.[210]

While it might be objected that the men of Massachusetts were not going to give any unfavorable answers to the gentleman from across the sea, the pamphlet, as it stands, reflects satisfaction with the religious teaching carried out as a result of Horace Mann's work. The Social Tradition still held that religion "belonged." The elimination of traditional Protestant doctrine was agreeable, as was the substitution which had been made. That the men questioned do not necessarily represent a complete sample of public opinion may be conceded. But what these men said has a definite value.

The Ideals and Motivation of Horace Mann and His Opponents

Though we have seen the enactment of the 1827 textbook law as the first legal step in the elimination of doctrinal religion from the American public school, it was a step that was brought to completion only in the régime of Horace Mann. Since this movement in Massachusetts was the occasion and, to a notable extent, we think, the cause of a profound change in the history of American education, an attempt will now be made to point out the motives behind the activities of both the Secretary and his opponents.

Our review of the development of public education in Massachusetts from 1827 until the retirement of Horace Mann as Secretary of the Board in 1848 has shown the leaders of that state confronted with and attempting to resolve a great dilemma. One of its horns was the avowed spirit of the times, to which we have found not a single exception, supporting the view that religion belongs in public life and religious instruction belongs in public education. The other horn was the felt need to protect the rights of conscience in religious matters, with the accompanying need to keep religious strife out of the public school system. That

[210] *Ibid.*, p. 81.

which remained constant in this period and formed a *continuum* from earlier years was the social tradition that religion "belonged." That which changed was the dominance of the Congregational Church, as new Protestant sects arose to prominence, to power, and finally, to complete legal equality with the old Calvinist Church.

As the temper of the times became ripe for equality of religions among Protestants, and the rights of conscience came in for more and more recognition, the figure of Horace Mann entered the scene. Although it would be inaccurate to call him a religious or educational dictator, he was without doubt the most influential leader of his day in the realm of religious education. What Mann stood for became the accepted practice, although not without many controversies and long years of effort. To epitomize the picture then, it is necessary to epitomize the ideals and the motivation of Horace Mann. His place in the history of religious education in America will only be set in higher relief as the ideals and motivation of his opponents are also given in summary form.

Horace Mann was a religious person. Horace Mann wanted religion in public education. Fervent declarations of this, and violent protests when he was contrarily accused, rolled from his lips and his pen all through his career as Secretary of the Board. This study indicates that any characterization of Mann as a conscious, deliberate destroyer of religion in education is without foundation in fact.[211]

When faced by the alternate horn of the dilemma, posed by the doctrinal instruction which still played a large part in the scheme of public education, Horace Mann took an uncompromising and unchangeable stand against continuing any semblance of the traditional Protestant indoctrination. The divergent views of the various sects he wanted kept out of the school curriculum. The child could choose later which type he felt he should embrace. If the sects wished to present their claims to the youthful mind, they could do so at home, from the pulpit or in the Sunday

---

[211] In his last years, when President of Antioch College, a private institution at Yellow Springs, Ohio, Mann constantly encouraged religious instruction and practice in the lives of the students. Cf. Mary P. Mann, *Life*, pp. 435, 464, 467, 468.

school. To achieve this elimination of sectarian doctrine, Mann went beyond the letter of the 1827 law and fought for what he believed to be its spirit—elimination of any sort of sectarian teaching by any method whatsoever.[212]

It was clear to Mann that if he was not to abandon his basic conviction that religion belonged in education, something must remain after sectarianism was taken out. Or, if the excision of sectarianism left no religion at all, something would have to be substituted in its place. At first Mann seems to have worked for the replacement of Protestant Christianity by ethics and natural theology. Over the years, however, he made clear that what he wanted in addition was the basic principles of Christianity to be garnered by the children from listening to the reading of the Bible.

When accused by his opponents of thus having cut the heart out of Christian instruction, Horace Mann countered with two rebuttals. First, he declared he laid no restriction on the explanation of the Scriptures, short of getting into sectarian tenets. Second, he tried to turn the argument back on his opponents by saying that if their creeds were in the Bible and the Bible was in the school, then their creeds were in the school, and, presumably, the children would be able to find them.

Out of the years of struggle came the following result: The teachers were influenced towards inculcating a system of religion which amounted to an acceptance of the existence of God, His Providence and His preparation of a life beyond the grave. Mankind is to relate itself to God in this life by trying to practice the virtues extolled in the Bible, in emulation of the maxims and good deeds of Christ. Such good works will contribute to the preservation and enrichment of the democracy that is America and help the soul to a place in the life to come.

Such a system of religion (and it should never be forgotten that such Mann conceived it to be and wanted it, *as religion*, in the common schools) comes close to being a summation of Unitarian theology. It is easy to see, then, how the traditional Protestants of his day regarded the Secretary's plan as a new brand of

[212] Cf. *supra*, pp. 140–42.

sectarianism; and it is hard to say that they were wrong. It is difficult to see it as a "Common denominator of Christianity" plan. It is not accurate to call it un-Christian or anti-Christian in every aspect. Hence it amounts to a new interpretation of Christianity by a born and bred Protestant who followed his principle of private judgement with perfect logic but with consequences that set him off clearly from his brother descendants of Luther, Calvin and the other leaders of the Reformation.

Mann stated in his *Twelfth Report* that the government "should do all it can to facilitate the acquisition of religious truth." [213] When accused of using his government position to advance his personal religious beliefs in the Massachusetts schools, he issued a vigorous denial. [214] While it would seem unfair to say that he used his position to strike more effectively at his enemies, who had to fight as private citizens, yet Horace Mann did take every advantage which his official position offered to advance the type of religious education he believed most likely to teach to the children the truth.

The result was that his system was accepted and received in his lifetime great popular support. Some years later a questionnaire directed to several leading citizens of Massachusetts was answered in a way that indicated the support had not been withdrawn.[215] His system appears to have set the pattern for public school systems in other parts of the nation, and, thus, as will be indicated later, formed the kernel of the religious elements of public school curricula which have lasted even to our own day. What motivation, then, inspired Horace Mann to work for the goal which has been described?

Horace Mann was animated with a love of religious liberty. He was sincere in his desire to keep the children and their parents from being imposed on by teachers who might inculcate doctrines against their conscientious convictions. To him the danger of proselytism in the Massachusetts schools of his day was a real one. In the religiously pluralistic society which Massachusetts had become, he thought he saw no other way to defend the rights of

[213] *Supra*, p. 147.
[214] *Supra*, p. 166.
[215] Cf. *supra*, pp. 175 ff.

conscience than by eliminating traditional Protestant sectarianism from the schools. If he thought his substitution was a sectarianism all its own, he never gave evidence of any compunction of heart. The kindest and fairest interpretation of Horace Mann's policy would be to regard it as a valiant and tireless campaign to secure the American blessing of freedom of religion. The unkindest view would be that which would see him deliberately destroying all opportunity for the sectarianism of traditional Protestants, that he might ruthlessly force his own upon the American people. It is the conclusion of this study that the truth lies at a point some seventy-five percent *in favor* of the former interpretation.

Coupled with Mann's love of religious liberty was a not unrealistic fear on his part that chaos would result in the Massachusetts public schools, if the Protestant theological wars then raging in the Commonwealth should be allowed to penetrate the classrooms. One cannot forget that the Orthodox-Unitarian battles had been splitting parishes and causing financial as well as spiritual havoc. The *theory* that religious instruction carried out with due regard for the rights of conscience should raise no objection from a people devoted to the importance of the spiritual is completely and unquestionably valid. But in the actual situation of early nineteenth century Massachusetts, the theory's application was fraught with real danger. As Mann dreamed, then, of the blessings of universal education, it was only prudence on his part that made him ponder the outcome of sectarian strife in the given situation of his day.

A third motive, which cannot be overlooked, was Horace Mann's hatred and contempt not only for Orthodox Calvinism but for all that the much-abused term "dogmatic religion" held for him. Right or wrong in his hatred, he also *hated* the concept of Church-State union. That religion in education, given to a degree beyond what he wanted, need not imply or remotely lead to a legal union of Church and State was a thought which seems never to have entered his mind. That more doctrinal content in a religious curriculum might be productive of better results than his "love mercy and walk humbly with God" [216] concept could hardly have gained an audience in his soul. What he conceived to be man-made reli-

[216] Cf. *supra,* p. 163.

gious systems coming between Creator and creature, thrust upon helpless people by unprincipled and vicious ecclesiastics (and this included every traditional Christian group) were an abomination which he loathed and opposed throughout his life. That his own system could only with difficulty withstand the very charge he heaped upon others seems not to have been given much consideration.

Culver acknowledges a part of this motivation when he says that "Horace Mann had a definite anti-orthodox complex." [217] Volatile as were his emotions, deep as were the scars left upon his character by his early Calvinistic experiences, heir as he was to a detestation of what was encompassed by the words "England and her Established Church," contemptuous, and even somewhat fearful of all that was implied in the term "Papism," Horace Mann thought it his duty to stave off from Massachusetts all that suggested the approach or the retention of such sources of "evil."

An answer to the question proposed on page 155 of this study can be given at this point: "Did Mann argue against the inclusion of doctrinal religion because he felt it did *not belong* in the American educational picture, or because he thought including it an *impossible achievement,* given the necessity of preserving the system from chaos and/or guaranteeing the rights of conscience?" Mann argued against the inclusion of doctrinal religion in the public school, *perhaps* because he felt it did not belong there, but certainly because he thought including doctrinal religion would violate the rights of conscience, theoretically and practically, and because, speaking practically, its presence would hurt the school system and the welfare of the community. Whether the substitute he offered was a desirable or undesirable protection *for* religious liberty, and a protection *against* the evils Mann feared is a question to be answered at the conclusion of this study.

What of the activities of Mann's opponents? They too wanted religion in education. Their constant appeal was to the tradition in Massachusetts history. The system inherited from Pilgrim days was in their eyes meaningless without a religious foundation. Hence there was no question with them of anything but a con-

[217] Culver, *op. cit.,* p. 224.

tinuance of the customs of their youth and the instruction in doctrinal religion to which they and their fathers were accustomed.

The essential point in their attacks on Mann and the Board was that the heart had been cut out of religious instruction when the doctrinal elements were removed. Without the teaching of that which God had revealed as to grace, the fall, redemption, salvation and the like, the inculcation only of maxims of conduct, however lofty in themselves, could not be called the teaching of Christianity. Christianity was a way of life based on more than exhortations to virtue. It had a compelling force beyond any and all mere ethical desirability, in that it was the direct manifestation of the will of God in man's regard. What Mann and the Board were introducing was a new sectarian doctrine, a system lacking the necessary components of Christianity. Hence they felt bound to resist it in every way they could.

As these men faced the great dilemma, they chose to concentrate on the first alternative. If the law enjoined teaching "Piety," and "Piety" included an awareness of the doctrinal content of revealed religion, then doctrinal religion had to be taught. To the problems presented by the other horn of the dilemma they seemed to have paid comparatively little attention or dismissed them as unimportant.

The rights of conscience are not mentioned in their declarations. The law of 1827, they conceded, was meant to avert the danger of direct proselytism, but no more. Packard felt that the scriptural truths accepted by Protestants could be taken in by all with no harmful results. Newton maintained that only the inculcation of the various Church polities would present a danger. Those who signed the *Majority Report* on the 1840 bill to abolish the Board felt that an injustice would be done the pupils and their parents, if books which challenged thinking on divergent views were eliminated. The Boston Schoolmasters thought an incorrect notion of God's delegated authority was creeping into the school system. Smith felt an angry God was punishing society for the crimes of those who had eliminated the true religion from Massachusetts classrooms.

None of these men seemed to worry about the reactions of

divergent groups within the Commonwealth. If they considered the possibility of strife within the school system, it found no mention in their writings. The majority of Protestants would go along with the program, as they had in the past. The developing pluralism within Protestant ranks seems not to have weighed heavily in their thoughts. As for minority groups, they could be bypassed and left to shift for themselves.

The motivation of Mann's opponents is not easy to analyze. It seems accurate to say that all of them were outraged at a spectacle which to them was a butchering of true Christianity. Due credit ought to be allowed for a sincere and conscientious reaction. They felt it their duty to protest, to try and arrest the harm they believed was being done. On the other hand, the *possibility* of less worthy motives cannot be totally ignored. Packard seems to have been concentrating a great deal on his job of selling books.[218] Newton was thought by Mann to have been stung by the Secretary's censures of the Church of England in his *Seventh Report*.[219] Political motives are considered as having had much to do with the effort to abolish the Board in 1840.[220] The Boston Schoolmasters were said by Mann to have been embarrassed when the public realized the extent to which they were using corporal punishment.[221] Smith did not escape the suspicion of seeking publicity by hitching his cart to the brilliant star of Horace Mann.[222] If such factors were operative, they are balanced by what has been noticed of the part played in Horace Mann's activities by his "anti-orthodox complex." The historian must tread carefully and respectfully among the evidence of motivation on the part of men who have been dead for a hundred years. The impression garnered from this study would place the mark for Mann's opponents *about where it was put* in the case of the Secretary himself— seventy-five percent in favor of pure motivation.

[218] Cf. Packard Letter to Mann, March 28, 1838 (Culver, *op. cit.*, p. 245).
[219] Cf. Mann Letter to Combe, April, 1844, *supra*, p. 128.
[220] Cf. Culver, *op. cit.*, pp. 127 ff.
[221] Cf. Letter of Mann to Combe, Dec. 1, 1845 (Culver, *op. cit.*, pp. 193-94).
[222] Letter of George Emerson to Mann, Jan. 19, 1847 (Culver, *op. cit.*, p. 206, footnote).

The Picture at Mann's Resignation

The resulting Massachusetts picture, at the time of Horace Mann's resignation in 1848, may be summarized as follows:

1. While the legal separation of Church and State ended in Massachusetts (and the nation) with the disestablishment of the Congregational Church in 1833, the Social Tradition of the union of religion and public life and the essential place of religion in public education remained.

2. The teaching of doctrinal religion, which had been an accepted part of public education, was legally restricted and, in practice, gone or almost completely gone.

3. The religious teaching which remained, speaking only of that which enjoyed official sanction, was composed of ethics, natural theology and what was gotten from the reading of the Bible.

4. The rights of conscience were protected for those who objected to traditional Protestant indoctrination (with the exception of those who considered straight Bible reading without the authoritative interpretation of their Church as a sectarian tenet in itself).

5. The rights of conscience were not protected for those who considered Mann's ideas on religion a sectarian system.

In conclusion—it seems incorrect to say that Horace Mann set out to make the public schools Godless. His plan, however, did make the schools teach less of what Christianity claims God has said and more of what Horace Mann felt. In eliminating traditional Protestant doctrine, Mann did give a goodly measure of protection to the rights of conscience. Strangely, neither Mann nor any of his contemporaries seemed to have given much thought to a method which might have conserved both alternatives presented by the great dilemma. In imparting religious instruction by public school teachers, they always took it for granted that whatever would be taught would be taught to all children indiscriminately. A system of "to each his own" never got into the picture. Mann saw it at work on his European trip, but brushed it aside with short shrift.

To Horace Mann must be credited help toward a continuance

of the social tradition of religion in American life. To his credit he fought for the rights of conscience. He eliminated the threat of religious strife in the schools. He also effected the removal of doctrinal religion with the substitution of a much weaker, even if more generally acceptable, system of religion.

CHAPTER VI

The Two Traditions

in the Other States

1825 - 1861

THE EXAMINATION of the fate of doctrinal religious instruction in Massachusetts brought out four main points: from the opening of the nineteenth century until well into the 1850's, the idea that religion belonged in education was not lost; as the years passed, however, the conviction that sectarian indoctrination must be eliminated from the public school grew and triumphed; the educational and church leaders, as well as many statesmen, groped for a way to keep religion in and keep sectarianism out; the result was a reduction of the earlier doctrinal content of the curriculum to a system of ethics and reading the Bible.

With regard to the other states which had constituted the thirteen original colonies, answers will be sought in this chapter to two questions— Did the leaders in those states also feel that religion belonged in public education? What was their conviction as to sectarianism in public instruction? The following chapter will look for the results which followed their attempts to implement these convictions.

In keeping with the policy to which the study set itself, an effort will be made to probe behind the declarations, the controversies and the practices of educators to seek the motivation which prompted their thoughts and activities. No claim is made that the developments in each of the twelve states have been exhaustively treated. Rather, the material which has been assembled will be analyzed, in the hope that trends in the areas of the two questions asked in the preceding paragraph may be discovered.

Convictions about the Place of Religion in Public Education

Chapter III presented data drawn from all of the thirteen original states, showing that the thirty-five years following the birth of the American republic saw a continuation of the colonial conviction that religion belonged in public life and public education. The present query, then, should commence around 1825. The evidence will be presented in the following three categories—statements of Protestant leaders, Catholic leaders, and lay leaders who wrote or spoke as statesmen or educators rather than as representatives of religious groups. Most of the last named, of course, were probably affiliated with some Christian body. No pronouncements from members of the Jewish communities in the 1825–1861 period were found in the present research. Some of the writers to be quoted answered both of our questions in the same declaration. Thus, it will at times be difficult to separate the material in precisely the way which has been planned.

PROTESTANT OPINION

In presenting the declarations of Protestant clergymen and lay officials such as Frederick A. Packard, on the subject of religion in education, it is necessary to bear in mind not only the great diversity of sects included under the term Protestant, but also the divisions of doctrinal belief among groups within a given sect. When studying Protestant opinion in the early nineteenth century, one must also remember that then there existed no councils of churches, such as those of the present century, where certain views held in common by divergent sects are expressed. For these reasons the opinions of an individual minister are not necessarily the reflection of his fellow Protestant clergymen either within or without his own denomination. Thus the quotations to be given here may or may not have reflected the minds of all American Protestant leaders of the day. For this very reason the virtual unanimity expressed in favor of religion in education becomes the more striking.[1]

One of the most prolific writers on religious instruction in the schools was the Rev. Charles Hodge, a Presbyterian on the faculty of Princeton University. Articles written by him in the *Biblical Repertory*, later known as the *Biblical Repertory and Princeton Review*, between 1828 and 1861, show a continued concern with what he considered the serious defects of the American public school curriculum in this field. All of them will be examined, that the development of the man's thought during the period of steady decline in religious teaching may be observed.

In the early articles he stated his alarm over the practice of leaving religion out of the public schools and entrusting it entirely to the Sunday school classes. "Unless some plan can be adopted," he declared in 1828,

> of introducing religious instruction into the common schools, we must consent to see a large portion of our population growing up in ignorance of the first principles of moral and religious truth. . . .[2]

Four years later, while reviewing a book[3] in the *Biblical Repertory*,[4] Hodge declared his uneasiness about entrusting religious instruction to the Sunday school exclusively:

[1] There was no selectivity employed in gathering this material. Everything bearing on the subject which was found is to be reported. A rich source of material is a collection of tracts and pamphlets in the Library of the Department of Health, Education and Welfare, Washington, D. C.

[2] Charles Hodge, "Introductory Lecture Delivered in the Theological Seminary, Princeton, New Jersey, November 7, 1828," *Biblical Repertory and Princeton Review*, I (new series) (Princeton: Hugh Madden, 1829), 86.

[3] William B. Sprague, D.D., *Lectures to Young People* (New York: John P. Haven, 1831).

[4] Charles Hodge, review in *Biblical Repertory and Theological Review*, III (new series) (Philadelphia: Russell & Mastren, 1831), 295–306. The second part of the title, *Theological Review*, seems to have been only a temporary change from *Princeton Review*. Although unsigned in the 1831 volume, the article is credited to Hodge in the *Index Volume* published in 1871 (p. 209).

We believe there are few institutions of the present age, more extensively useful than the American Sabbath School Union. Still this system does not and cannot embrace all our rising population. . . . We think, therefore, that it should be a constant object with the friends of religion, to try to secure a religious character to the instructions of the common school. Here everything depends upon the teacher and upon the system. . . .[5]

The writer continued with an explanation of his idea that a system of religious instruction based upon the Bible, as was carried out in the Sunday schools, would be acceptable in the schools of the state.[6]

Hodge repeated his theme that religion belonged in public schools in a strong article written in 1846.[7] In the conclusion, he summed up the causes which had led to the decline of religious instruction in the common school. He then stated his conviction that the decision to abandon such teaching was an unwarranted assumption of power on the part of state officials.[8] The necessity of including all classes of people in the common school, he declared, brought into being a "standard of doctrine" with which even the "lowest and loosest sects" would be satisfied. "An immediate outcry is made about religious liberty, and the union of Church and State," he continued, "if in a public school any religious instruction is given to which any of these parties object."

The result, according to Hodge, was the confining of school instruction to secular branches, with religious instruction being left to the parent or pastor. "The whole [school] system is in the hands of men of the world, in many of our states, and is avowedly secular." Pointing out that education without religion is irreligious, he claimed that such a system "cannot be neutral, and in fact is not neutral."

Hodge then reminded his readers, first, that the common school was the only educational means for large masses of the people, who had no means of supplying the religious deficiency. Secondly,

[5] *Ibid.*, p. 303.
[6] *Ibid.*
[7] Charles Hodge, "The General Assembly, Parochial Schools," *Princeton Review*, xviii (1846), 433–41. The article is attributed to Hodge in the *Index Volume*, p. 210.
[8] *Ibid.*, pp. 438–39.

he said, large groups of Americans had shown their repugnance to education without religion by refusing to send their sons to colleges where Christianity was not doctrinally inculcated. He then made his indictment of the existing common-school system as tyrannical: "What right has the state," he asked,

> a majority of the people, or a mere clique, which in fact commonly control such matters, to say what shall be taught in schools which the people sustain? What right have they to say that no religion shall be taught, than they have to say that popery shall be taught? Or what right have the people in one part to control the wishes and convictions of those of another part of a state as to the education of their own children? If the people of a particular district choose to have a school in which the Westminster or the Heidleberg Catechism is taught, we cannot see on what principle of religious liberty, the state has a right to interfere and say it shall not be done; if you teach your religion, you shall not draw your own money from the public fund? . . . We regard this whole theory of a mere secular education in the common schools, enforced by the penalty of exclusion from the public funds, and state patronage, as unjust and tyrannical, as well as infidel in its whole tendency. The people of each district have the right to make their schools as religious as they please; and if they cannot agree, they have the right severally of drawing their proper portion of the public stock.

Again in 1854, in an extended article entitled "The Education Question," Hodge came out strongly with the thesis that religion belonged in public education because the state has an obligation to teach the true religion.[9]

After repeating, in substance, his 1846 statement of the reasons given for abandoning religious instruction, Hodge first pointed out how many types of leaders had gone along with the new plan:

> This is the ground publicly assumed by the majority of our public men; it has received, directly or indirectly, the sanction of several State legislatures; it is avowed and acted upon by superintendents and commissioners; it is advocated by some of our most influential religious journals, and by many of our prominent religious men.[10]

[9] Charles Hodge, "The Education Question," *Princeton Review*, xxvi (July, 1854), 504–44. The article is attributed to Hodge in the *Index Volume*, p. 210.

[10] *Ibid.*, p. 507.

As an example of this opposition, Hodge gave an extended quotation from a speech made in August, 1853 by E. C. Benedict, President of the Board of Education of New York.[11] Hodge's rebuttal to the ideas of Benedict includes both instances which he cited to prove the existence of religious instruction and arguments against his opponent's position. He gave an example from the schools for the deaf and dumb, where, "by common consent not only Christianity but Protestant Christianity, is inculcated."[12] Moreover, he felt, the enactments which the various states had made were being honored more in the breach than in the observance:

> The reason why so little resistance has been manifested to the edicts of legislatures and superintendents, [forbidding religion in public education], is that the people utterly disregard them. . . . We know of public schools, both in New Jersey and Pennsylvania, in which the Westminster Catechism is taught every day; and we believe that, in very many cases, the children in our own common schools are taught just what their parents see fit to have them learn. . . . The people will never submit with their eyes open to a merely secular, which is only another name for an irreligious, godless education.[13]

Turning to the theory that separation of Church and State forbids religious instruction, Hodge countered that the State has the duty of educating its citizens. "If, therefore," he continued,

> the work of education is, by the providence and word of God, thrown upon the State, it must be an education in religion. The State is bound to see that the true religion is taught in all the schools under its control. . . . All the early advocates of popular education, the authors of the common school system, as adopted in our several States, have insisted on the vital importance of training the young in the principles of piety and morality.[14]

[11] *Ibid.*, pp. 508–509. Hodge states that the Benedict quotation is reproduced from a book he reviews in this article, *The Bible and Our Public Schools,* by Dr. George B. Cheever, pp. 2, 37–38. A section of Benedict's speech, taken from another source, will be found *infra*, pp. 233–35.

[12] *Ibid.*, p. 513.

[13] *Ibid.*, pp. 514–15.

[14] *Ibid.*, p. 519.

Hodge then devoted several pages to his claim that Protestant Christianity is the religion of the United States.[15] The conclusion he draws is reminiscent of the position taken by Frederick A. Packard in the articles referred to in Chapter V of this study.[16] Hodge declared:

> Thus if a number of Christians and Protestants organize themselves as a State or political community, they are obviously bound to regulate their legislative, judicial and executive action by the principles of their religion. No law in this country which does violence to Christianity, can be rightfully enacted by Congress, or by any State Legislature; nor would such a law, if enacted, bind the consciences of the people. . . .[17]

In 1861 Hodge wrote lamenting a divorce between religion and education in American public schools.[18] After declaring that such a phenomenon had arisen only in the nineteenth century, he attributed the rupture directly to sectarianism: "The germinal principle or cause of this change was the existence, rapid multiplication, and controlling influence of different sects or denominations in our American Christianity." [19]

Continuing his thesis that pluralism lay at the basis of American religious problems, Hodge gave an opinion on the reasons for Church and State separation which is difficult to interpret: "This [sectarianism] was the reason," he declared:

> perhaps to a certain extent, unconsciously operative, why the framers of our national and state constitutions acted upon the principle that civil government among us could have no distinct religious character or aims. Such governmental indifferency with respect to all forms of religion, was indispensable to exact equality of the citizens before the government, whatever might be their differences or conflicts of religious belief. Whence it followed, that when the States came to organize their vast and all-moulding system of governmental education, in order that these might be universal by the votes of a population with

---

[15] *Ibid.*, pp. 520–24.
[16] Cf. *supra*, p. 156.
[17] Hodge, "The Education Question," p. 522.
[18] Charles Hodge, "Covenant Education," *Princeton Review*, xxxiii (1861), 238–61.
[19] *Ibid.*, p. 246.

endless diversities of religious belief, might be equally for the benefit of all, and might be in harmony with the principles of the governments, all distinctive religious character and aims had to be excluded from them. But in as much as the department of morals is inseparable from religion, and must follow its fate, the next step, inevitable in logic, was to exclude from the governmental schools all moral instruction, and to reduce the idea of education to that of mere intellectual culture.[20]

When Hodge said "civil government . . . could have no distinct religious character or aims" and talked about "governmental indifferency with respect to all forms of religion," did he mean that the government could favor no one sect over another, or did he mean the government could have nothing to do with religion in any way whatsoever? The former interpretation would seem to come nearer his earlier articles cited above. If he meant the latter, it is hard to see how he could have censured so repeatedly the position of the secularist Commissioner of New York, Erastus Benedict.[21]

To return to the decade starting with 1830, only two other articles from Protestant pens were found besides what has been cited from the writings of Dr. Hodge. The first is entitled "Moral Education."[22] Though the writer did not specifically mention religion as the basis of moral education, the implication of his words seems to be that religion is involved:

> Who has a finished education? He has it who, though he may have only learned to read and write, has learned beside the difference, the immense difference, between the holy and profane; has cultivated his moral capacities; has acquired sound opinions, and firm principles, and good habits; has preferred and chosen the paths and the rewards of virtue.[23]

Among the things the writer said would be helped by moral education are temperance and observance of the Lord's Day, and he concluded:

[20] *Ibid.*
[21] Cf. *supra,* p. 194.
[22] "Moral Education," *The Christian Examiner,* X (March, 1831), 1–14. The author of this article is listed in the catalogue of the Peabody Library in Baltimore simply as "Greenwood." This same name is written in pencil at the top of the article in the Peabody's copy itself.
[23] *Ibid.,* p. 3.

Why should we say more— The simple fact that the course and the fate of this country depend, under Providence, on the character of the mass of its inhabitants, is proof sufficient to my mind, that the moral education of all classes, and all ages, but more particularly of the poor and the young, is the one thing needful.[24]

The other pamphlet, done in 1837, maintained that the importance of religion in education was felt by a great majority of Americans. It was written by the Rev. B. P. Aydelot, M.D., and is entitled *Report on the Study of the Bible in Common Schools*.[25] "If there is any one point," Dr. Aydelot said:

on which the public mind is united, it is, that education to be useful, or even safe, must be Christian. And as the Bible is the only common standard of Christianity, so it can be the only universal text book. Hence, we may account for the fact, . . . that at nearly all the meetings of the friends of education for some years past in various parts of our country, there have been resolutions unanimously adopted, recommending in the strongest terms, the general introduction of the Bible into our schools.[26]

Packard's article, "Religious Instruction in Common Schools," which has already been discussed,[27] appeared in the *Princeton Review* in 1841. The years immediately following saw several other publications wherein Protestant leaders declared their belief in the importance of religious training in the schools. Among them was an address by Calvin E. Stowe, D.D., Professor of Biblical Literature at Lane Seminary, Cincinnati. Its title was *The Religious Element in Education, An Address Delivered Before the American Institute of Instruction, Portland, Me., Aug. 30, 1844*.[28] "Religion," he declared,

must be the basis of all right education, and an education without religion is an education for perdition. . . . It is my object in this lecture (I) to exhibit some of the reasons why instruction

[24] *Ibid.*, pp. 9–10.
[25] B. P. Aydelot, *Report on the Study of the Bible in Common Schools* (Cincinnati: N. S. Johnson, 1837).
[26] *Ibid.*, p. 3.
[27] *Supra*, p. 156.
[28] Calvin E. Stowe, *The Religious Element in Education* (Boston: William D. Ticknor & Co., 1844). (If inclusion of this pamphlet must be justified, Maine once was a part of Massachusetts.)

in the Christian religion should make an essential part of every system of education . . . (II) To answer some of the more plausible objections which are usually urged against such instruction and (III) to show how much instruction can be given faithfully and efficiently in our common schools and other public institutions without violating any of the rights of conscience.[29]

Another pamphlet appeared in 1844 from the pen of George Washington Burnap.[30] The writer's thesis was that in a democracy the voice of the people should resound the voice of God. "And this leads me," he declared,

> to speak of our duties. If the voice of the people is *not* the voice of God, we must endeavor, since we are to be governed by it, to *make* it the voice of God by educating intellectually, morally, and religiously those who utter it. If we cannot trust to humanity in the aggregate, to what portion of it can we trust? We have chosen our sovereign, and as we must obey him, so it is most fortunate that we can educate him.[31]

To those who were objecting to a doctrinal content in the religious education of young people, John B. Kerfoot, Rector of St. James (Episcopal) College in Maryland, had this to say in 1846:

> We have had to deal with those who adopt the fancy that it is a wrong and an injustice to the young to mould their hearts and shape their creed after any very definite model; that though Christianity is very valuable as an element of good in the individual and in the community, yet it is quite possible to communicate it without giving it any very marked character, leaving it to be to each one what he would have it to be; and in fact, that to do otherwise—to aim at a decided influence over the young conscience, and to stamp deeply, and, *if we can*, indelibly upon the heart and mind the definite lineaments of religious doctrine and principle, is a gross and unpardonable violation of the rights of conscience as ascertained in our favored age.
> This is the false theory I would reject. Nor is it presented as a

[29] *Ibid.*, pp. 7–8.

[30] G. W. Burnap, *Church and State, or the Privileges and Duties of an American Citizen, A Discourse* (Baltimore: John D. Toy, 1844).

[31] *Ibid.*, p. 17. Burnap, however, seems not to have advocated that the religious instruction be given in the common school. "And when the Sabbath spreads its stillness over the land, let him [the citizen] consider how many millions of the future arbiters of his country's destiny, are gathered into the house of God, and sitting at the feet of Jesus, there learning to choose the thing that is good, as well as to know the thing that is true and right."

man of straw, to be set up and beaten down for our amusement. It is and has been to us here a painful reality.[32]

In the *Eleventh Report* of Horace Mann there is an interesting set of letters which came to the Secretary in answer to a circular letter of his sent out in 1847. Mann's letter, written to eight experienced teachers in several of the original states, asked a question which we have summarized as follows: Supposing all public school teachers were of high intellectual and moral character, and all normal children of the community were in school ten months a year from the ages of four to sixteen, what percentage of those you have taught could be so educated as to be a benefit, and not a detriment to society? [33]

Of those to whom he wrote, Mann stated: "All of them without exception are well known believers in a theological creed, one of whose fundamental articles is, the depravity of the human heart." [34] This would seem to indicate the "Orthodox," i.e., the Congregationalists.

Seven of the eight letters point to religion as essential in true education: [35]

> *John Griscom* (Burlington, N. J.): . . . I have long regarded this root [of moral conduct] to be . . . *Faith in Christ.* . . . This faith in the Lord Jesus Christ, I believe, *must be made the subject of careful instruction.* . . . I cannot but think that the time will come when *Christian morality,* as taught in the Bible, notwithstanding the collision of sectarian opinions in the adult population, will be regarded by most parents, quite as important a matter of *learning,* as rules of syntax or algebraic equations. . . .

> *D. P. Page* (Albany, N. Y.): . . . I am firmly of the opinion that the right of expectation of a religious character would be increased very much in proportion to the excellence of the training given, since God never ordains means which He does not intend to bless. . . .

---

[32] John B. Kerfoot, "First Baccalaureate Address," July 30, 1846, in *Three Addresses Delivered at the Commencements of St. James, Washington County, Maryland* (Fountain Rock, Washington Co., Maryland: 1848), p. 22.
[33] Cf. Mann, *Eleventh Report* (covering 1847), pp. 56–57.
[34] *Ibid.,* p. 86.
[35] *Ibid., passim,* pp. 62–85.

Solomon Adams (Boston, Mass.): . . . It is his [the teacher's] province to bring all those moral appliances to bear upon the soul, which are suited to lead it into harmony and truth and with God,—to train it to the perception and love of truth and goodness. . . .

F. A. Adams (Orange, N. J.): . . . I might speak of the various opportunities for making a deep moral impression, that arise in school, from the reading of the Scriptures, from the truths of nature brought to view in the studies of the school, from the sickness or death of companions, or from cases of moral delinquency. . . .

E. A. Andrews (New Britain, Conn.): . . . I would be far from attributing so important results [removing evils from society] to any system of merely intellectual training, or even to the most perfect combination of intellectual, physical, and moral discipline, to the exclusion of that which is strictly religious. . . .

Roger S. Howard (Thetford, Vt.): . . . The power of a truly enlightened and Christian System of Common School education is but little understood and appreciated. . . .

Catherine E. Beecher (Brattleboro, Vt.): . . . I have ever considered *intellectual* culture as subordinate to the main end of education, which is, the formation of that character which Jesus Christ teaches to be indispensable to the eternal well-being of our race. . . .

Curiously, the one letter which does not lay stress on religion in education came from the Rev. Jacob Abbott of New York City. This clergyman laid his main emphasis on the character and example of the teacher. Among the conditions he gave, however, for the teacher being "prepared for his work" was "if he is governed honestly and really by religious principle in all his conduct and character." [36]

In 1856 an article appeared in the *Bibliotheca Sacra and American Biblical Repository* entitled "The Bible in Schools." It was the work of Rev. J. H. Seeyle, Pastor of the First Reformed Church of Schenectady, New York.[37] "We start by affirming the position,"

[36] *Ibid.*, p. 74.
[37] J. H. Seeyle, "The Bible in Schools," *Bibliotheca Sacra and American Biblical Repository,* XIII (Oct., 1856), 725–41 (Andover, Massachusetts: Warren F. Draper, 1856).

he wrote, "that the state can only exist on the basis of some form of religion. . . . We can no more separate in the present condition of man, religion and the state and consider the one independent of the other, than we can any two faculties of the human soul." [38]

Seeyle's reasoning, however, makes religion the handmaid of the state. The state must teach religion to its subjects not for the sake of religion but for the sake of the state. "The very fact that the state must have some religion as a support for its own authority," he continued,

> demands that some means for teaching this religion be employed. It would be suicidal for the state to neglect this. Better for it to give up all other instruction than that its religion should be disregarded in its schools. The state itself has a more vital interest in the continued influence of its religion over its citizens, than in their culture in any other respect. [39]

Seeyle's article was in a sense another link in the tradition that religion belongs in public life. On the other hand, he would have the state regard religion as valuable only insofar as it helps the state, and not as the owed expression by society of dependence on a higher Power. In this sense, Seeyle was not in the tradition, but furnishes a preview of the pragmatic religionists of the end of the nineteenth century. [40]

Two undated pamphlets, each from the pen of a Protestant clergyman, were found in the research for this study. Their condition indicated great age, but no evidence could be found as to the year of their publication. The first is entitled *The Bible in the*

[38] *Ibid.*, p. 727.

[39] *Ibid.*, p. 732. This pragmatic view of religion, so different from the majority of writings of the period, is not carried to its logical limit by Seeyle. He does admit the role of the individual conscience in refusing to accept a religion from the state even at the cost of being punished. But he sees no wrong in the state going ahead with its religious program of whatever nature, in disregard of the individual conscience. "The authority of the state," he said, "may never be subordinated to the individual conscience." (P. 740.)

[40] Cf., e.g., Wm. Kailer Dunn, *James H. Leuba's Theory of Religion* (unpublished Master's dissertation, Catholic University of America, Washington, D. C., 1935).

Public Schools, by Andrew P. Peabody, D.D.[41] Its theme is a link in the social tradition which has now become familiar:

> But I am not prepared to admit that religious instruction and influence should be excluded from our schools. We are by profession a Christian people. We recognize the great principles of religion, of Christianity, in the devotional services in our legislatures and our courts of justice, and in the use of oaths in every department of public administration. Shall our children be trained as citizens, without the inculcation of those fundamental religious ideas, which will impress upon them the significance of prayer, and the dread solemnity of an oath?
>
> Sectarian teaching should, indeed, be carefully excluded. But I know of only two ways of excluding it. You must either choose none but irreligious or non religious teachers, or you must give your teacher a manual of religion that is non-sectarian.[42]

The other undated item is a pair of little pamphlets, "Publications No. 479 and 480" of the "Tract Society" of New York. Their author is the Rev. R. S. Rust.[43] In the first pamphlet, *Religion in the Common Schools,* Rust gave three reasons why religion should be inculcated:

> 1. [Because of] the similarity of aim existing between education and religion. . . . A proper education seeks to eradicate the evil propensities of the heart, beautify the soul with light and love, and make men pure, useful, and happy. The object of religion is almost identical, embracing merely a wider range of effort and a more comprehensive culture, . . .[44]

---

[41] No place, publisher, or date appears on the title page. On the back of the pamphlet appears an advertisement of the Massachusetts Bible Society, 15 Cornhill, Boston. On the front cover of the copy used is pencilled "R. B. Warter, 7/10/1874." Whether this is the original purchaser's name or not could not be determined.

[42] *Ibid.,* p. 6.

[43] R. S. Rust, *Religion in Common Schools* (479) and *The Method of Introducing Religion into Common Schools* (480) (New York: Tract Society, 200 Mulberry St., no date). The tracts were found in the bound collection of pamphlets entitled "Religion in State Schools" in the Library of the Department of Health, Education and Welfare in Washington, D. C. Across the top is written "Regards of the Author. Are they worthy of an insertion in your Journal? R.S.R." Could this be Henry Barnard's *Journal?* Other pamphlets in the collection have Barnard's autograph on the covers.

[44] *Ibid.,* p. 2.

2. The nature of the being to be educated imperatively demands the recognition of religion.[45]

3. Religious influence is demanded in the school, in view of the child's natural proclivity to evil. . . .[46]

For the accomplishment of this exalted mission, I know of no instrumentality combining so many excellences, so universal in design, and so early in effort, as the common school, thoroughly imbued with the spirit of the Christian religion.[47]

A rich supply of further documentation on the Protestant attitude towards religion in public education will be found in F. X. Curran's *The Churches and the Schools.*[48] The author's primary sources are mainly nineteenth-century church periodicals and the proceedings of Protestant synods and conventions. In the pages covering the years 1825–1861, the reader finds many affirmations that religion belongs in education. At the Episcopalian General Convention of 1838, for instance, concern was expressed about the separation of learning from religion in the common schools. The delegates asked themselves if the situation did not call for the erection of parochial schools. Influential Episcopal journals such as the *Churchman,* the *Journal of Christian Education* and the *Church Review* echoed these sentiments in succeeding years.[49] Among the Reformed Churches, the Dutch Reformed Synod of 1846 showed a tendency to ignore complaints about books in the common school libraries, because it considered such matters as "the business of the state."[50] The *Mercersburg Review,* organ of the German Reformed, however, took a different stand, editorializing on both the need of religion in public education and the fact that it was actually not to be found there.[51]

The Methodists and Baptists, as groups, seem to have been less vocative on the question of religion in the schools. Methodism was content with the public school system and hoped to improve it by

[45] *Ibid.,* p. 5.
[46] *Ibid.,* p. 10.
[47] *Ibid.,* p. 12.
[48] Francis X. Curran, S.J., *The Churches and the Schools, American Protestantism and Popular Education* (Chicago: Loyola University Press, 1954).
[49] *Ibid.,* pp. 17, 19, 20, 25, 27.
[50] *Ibid.,* p. 61.
[51] *Ibid., passim,* pp. 61–64.

preparing young Methodists to be teachers.[52] Its paper, the *Christian Advocate,* though, did run one series of articles in 1838 in which it emphasized the duty of the public schools to educate in religion.[53] The same theme was developed in a Baptist organ, the *Christian Review* in 1841.[54]

The quotations given here from Protestant leaders indicate a continuance of the tradition that public education should be religious. More declarations of the same sort will be encountered below when the efforts to work out methods of religious instruction and the controversies are reviewed. It is not here claimed that the tradition was maintaining all its earlier vigor among Protestant clergymen and laymen. By no means, however, was it extinct by the end of the 1840 decade.

CATHOLIC OPINION

Before the Revolution the Catholics in America were few in number, and with the exception of Maryland, widely scattered. Moreover, the spirit of the colonial period did not permit them to rise prominently in public life. From 1790 on, however, the Catholic Church was increasingly heard from in national affairs. The Diocese of Baltimore was erected by the Holy See in 1789 with Father John Carroll of Maryland as the first American Catholic Bishop.

Given the close-knit organization of the Catholic Church under the leadership of its Bishops, it seems that a satisfactory overall view of the trend of Catholic opinion may be gathered from the correspondence, meetings and proclamations of these leaders. The problem of tracing the development of their thinking is somewhat simplified in the present case by the fact that for the period under consideration (1776–1861), and for many years thereafter, Baltimore was the deliberative center of American Catholic

---

[52] *Ibid.,* pp. 82, 89.

[53] *Ibid.,* pp. 82–83.

[54] *Ibid.,* p. 100. Curran does not treat specifically of the Lutherans or Presbyterians because of studies already in print on these two groups: Walter H. Beck, *Lutheran Elementary Schools in the United States* (St. Louis: Concordia Publishing House, 1939); Louis J. Sherrill, *Presbyterian Parochial Schools* (New Haven: Yale University Press, 1932).

activity. Baltimore's Bishop Carroll had under his spiritual jurisdiction in 1789 all the Catholics in the United States east of the
Mississippi River with the exception of Florida and the territories
around New Orleans and Detroit. As the Church developed, new
dioceses were carved from this immense territory and were
assigned new Bishops. Meanwhile, Baltimore was raised, in 1808,
to the rank of an Archdiocese and Carroll to the rank of Archbishop. Later further subdivisions were made and new arch-
dioceses, with groups of "suffragan" dioceses around them, were
created, *e.g.*, in New York, Boston, St. Louis, etc.

In the early national period, then, Baltimore was the honored
center of Catholicism, and its Archbishops were, for all practical
purposes, the leaders of the American hierarchy. In 1791 Bishop
Carroll held a Synod [55] there, to which he invited the priests of
his geographically mammoth charge. Between 1829 and 1849
Baltimore saw the convening of seven Provincial Councils, to
which the Bishops came for deliberation. In 1852 the First Plenary
Council of Baltimore was held.

For the period of the present study, the Archives of the Archdiocese of Baltimore contain a rich source of material. Included
are letters from many American Bishops to the Baltimore Archbishops, copies of some of the letters the Baltimore prelates
themselves wrote, and many documents pertaining to the seven
Provincial Councils and the First Plenary Council. From this
material [56] and from the published decrees of the Councils,[57] plus
the Pastoral Letters [58] addressed by the Council Bishops to the
Catholics of America, the examination of Catholic thought will

[55] A Synod is a meeting of the Bishop and the priests of a single diocese.
A Provincial Council is the meeting of an Archbishop and the suffragan
Bishops of his province. A Plenary Council is the meeting of the Arch-
bishops and Bishops of a nation.

[56] Archives of the Archdiocese of Baltimore, Chancery Office, Baltimore,
Maryland. Hereafter, the material quoted from this source will be designated
"AAB."

[57] *Concilia Provincialia Baltimori Habita ab anno 1829 usque ad annum
1849* (2d ed.; Baltimore: John Murphy & Co., 1851), hereafter referred to as
Provincial Councils.

[58] Peter Guilday (ed.), *The National Pastorals of the American Hierarchy*
(1st ed., 1923; reprinted, Westminster, Maryland: The Newman Press, 1954),
hereafter referred to as Guilday, *Pastorals*.

be made. Our method will be to list the opinions and recommendations in this chapter, and reserve the decisions for the next.

When Bishop Carroll held his Synod in 1791 there were hopes, but little of achievement in the way of actual schooling of any sort in America beyond what was left of colonial education. Yet the Pastoral Letter issued in connection with the Synod, though not published until May 28, 1792, opened with the subject of Christian education:

> Knowing, therefore, that the principles instilled in the course of a Christian education, are generally preserved through life, and that *a young man according to his way, even when he is old, he will not depart from it,* (Prov. xxii. 6) I have considered the virtuous and Christian instruction of youth as a principal object of pastoral solicitude. Now who can contribute so much to lighten this burthen, which weighs so heavy on the shoulders of the pastors of souls and who can have so great an interest and special duty in the forming of youthful minds to habits of virtue and religion, as their parents themselves? . . .[59]

Carroll went on to express confidence that a child who might fall into sin would be brought back to repentance by the efficacy of the religious training he had received. Appealing to parents to be zealous in educating their children in their faith, the Bishop represented the work as an acceptable service to God, a discharge of parental duty, an aid to the Church, a benefit to the nation and a source of parental happiness both here and hereafter. The children would "remember with gratitude," he concluded, "and repay with religious duty, your solicitude for them in their infancy and youth." [60]

In Carroll's mind, how was this instruction to be carried out? "It appears that in the early years of the republic," state Burns and Kohlbrenner, [Carroll] "entertained the hope that Catholics would be able to unite with members of other denominations in the establishment of schools that would be acceptable to all. No doubt, the new conditions led to the expectation of the appear-

[59] Guilday, *Pastorals*, p. 3.
[60] *Ibid.*, p. 4.

ance of a spirit of complete equality for all denominations." [61]
Meanwhile, instruction at home and by the priest and his assistants would have to do.[62]

The story of the slow, painful efforts to develop Catholic
schools during the first quarter of the nineteenth century has been
written elsewhere.[63] It is sufficient to note here that the effort *was*
made, on all levels from elementary to college, indicating that the
traditional Catholic emphasis on an education entirely under
Catholic auspices was not abandoned in America.

The Massachusetts anti-sectarian textbook law was passed in
1827. Taking this date, two years before the First Provincial Council of Baltimore, as a starting point, the systematic search of the
Baltimore Archives was begun to look for evidence on the opinions of Catholic leaders regarding religion in the common schools,
and the participation therein by Catholic children.[64]

In 1828 two Bishops wrote to Baltimore's Archbishop James
Whitfield regarding items for discussion in the First Provincial
Council. Benedict Joseph Fenwick, S.J., of Boston, urged the
forming of a plan for printing Catholic schoolbooks. "As matters
stand," he wrote,

> all the children educated in the common schools of the country
> are obliged to use books compiled by Protestants by which
> their minds are poisoned as it were from their infancy. . . .[65]

---

[61] *A History of Catholic Education in the United States*, p. 63; Theodore
Maynard, *The Story of American Catholicism* (New York: The Macmillan
Co., 1941), p. 464; Annabelle M. Melville, *John Carroll of Baltimore* (New
York: Charles Scribner's Sons, 1955), pp. 151 f.

[62] Father Stephen T. Badin, the first priest to be ordained in the territory
of the thirteen original States, wrote to Carroll in 1798 from his mission in
Kentucky: ". . . The youth need much attention; I have 2 catechists, who
perform well the important work they are charged with; . . . I catechize
myself once a month; but it is too seldom, & the difference [?] or penury of
catechism books make [sic] the progress of children very slow." (AAB,
Box 1-E-9.)

[63] Cf. Burns and Kohlbrenner, *op. cit.*, pp. 59 ff.

[64] It is not maintained that the entire story is to be found in the Baltimore
Archives. The most notable lack is that of copies of letters *from* the Baltimore
Archbishops to their fellow leaders. To round out the complete picture a
search would have to be made in the archives of all diocesan offices east of
the Mississippi.

[65] AAB, 23-H-4a, Fenwick to Whitfield, Boston, Sept. 10, 1828.

The other letter came from John England of Charleston, South Carolina, who proposed to discuss:

> . . . The best mode of counteracting the pernicious influence of our adversaries, in their publications, schools and societies all directed against us.
>
> The best mode of regulating the instruction of our own youth, & determining how we could best procure for them the most extended [?] course of solid religious instruction.[66]

The Council issued two decrees relating to education. The thirty-fourth decree, noting that many children were in danger of losing their faith or having their moral life corrupted because of the lack of adequate teachers to whom their training could safely be entrusted, declared the necessity of opening schools which would teach faith and morals along with the other subjects.[67] The thirty-fifth decree spoke of current textbooks which attacked the principles and doctrines, and distorted the history of the Catholic Church. It decreed that books freed of these errors and approved by the Bishops be published as soon as possible.[68]

Out of the Council came two Pastorals, one addressed to the laity and the other to the clergy. They were signed by Archbishop Whitfield and six Bishops.[69] In the Pastoral to the laity,[70] parents were exhorted to give moral training at home, and warned to be careful of the type of school to which they sent their children,

[66] AAB, 23-G-4, England to Whitfield, Charleston, S. C., December 26, 1828.

[67] "Quoniam quamplurimos adolescentes ex Catholicis parentibus, praesertim pauperibus, ortos, in multis Provinciae hujus locis expositos esse, et adhuc exponi constat magno fidei amittendae periculo, vel morum corruptelae, ob inopium talium magistrorum quibus tantum munus tuto committi possit; necessarium omnino censemus ut Scholae instituantur, in quibus juvenes edoceantur fidei morumque principia, dum litteris imbuuntur." *Provincial Councils*, p. 84.

[68] "Cum non raro plura reperiantur in libris qui in scholis plerumque adhibentur, quibus principia fidei nostrae impugnantur, dogmata nostra perperam exponuntur, et ipsa historia pervertitur, . . . ea de causa statuimus quamprimum edendos in scholarum usum, erroribus omnino expurgatos, atque judicio Episcoporum approbatos libros, quibus nihil contineatur quod Catholicae fidei odium vel invidium parere possit." *Provincial Councils*, p. 84.

[69] Bardstown (Kentucky), Charleston, Cincinnati, St. Louis, Boston and Philadelphia.

[70] Guilday notes that both Pastorals were written by Bishop England. *Op. cit.*, pp. 19, 39.

lest the ground gained by home training be lost.[71] The Bishops called attention to the dangers they saw in many textbooks currently used in the common schools and noted the plan they had formulated to offset the menace to Catholic children's faith:

> . . . The school-boy can scarcely find a book in which some one or more of our institutions or practices is not exhibited far otherwise than it really is, and greatly to our disadvantage: the entire system of education is thus tinged throughout its whole course; and history itself has been distorted to our serious injury. . . . We have therefore associated ourselves and some others, whom we deem well qualified for that object, to encourage the publication of elementary books free from any of those false colorings, and in which whilst our own feelings are protected, those of our fellow-citizens of other religious denominations shall be respected.[72]

In the companion Pastoral, addressed to the clergy, the Bishops pointed out that the priests must consider it their duty to instruct the young, lest the whole system of Catholic life become meaningless to the rising generation:

> . . . If the great truths of religion be not deeply inculcated upon the youthful mind, your discourses will be scarcely intelligible to those who will have been left untaught; . . . Unless you watch over them when they are first exposed to temptation, they will be robbed of their innocence, they will lose their horror for vice, they will be familiarised [sic] with crime, and when their habits are thus formed in early life, what prospect can you have of successfully engrafting virtue upon this stock of evil which has been deeply rooted in a soil of sin? . . .[73]

The Second Provincial Council was held in 1833. Its ninth decree legislated further on textbooks, appointing as a committee the Presidents of Georgetown University in Washington, St. Mary's University in Baltimore and Mt. St. Mary's College in Emmitsburg, Maryland, and directing this committee to work on the problem.[74]

That the textbook problem continued to occupy the Bishops' minds is indicated by a letter which Bishop Fenwick of Boston

[71] Guilday, *op. cit.*, pp. 24–27.
[72] *Ibid.*, p. 28.
[73] *Ibid.*, p. 57.
[74] *Provincial Councils*, p. 105.

wrote to Archbishop Samuel Eccleston, Whitfield's successor, in 1834. Fenwick sent Eccleston a geography which he thought suitable for Catholic schools, saying:

> You will perceive that I have not lost sight of the Catholic school-book question—neither ought it to be lost sight of; for I deem it one of the greatest importance in the days in which we live.[75]

Continuing on the subject of textbooks, it is to be noted that the plans formulated seem not to have borne much fruit. In 1842, Bishop John Hughes of New York wrote to Archbishop Eccleston regarding the agenda for the Fifth Provincial Council:

> I think also it would be well if the Bishops could agree in the support of some establishment for the publishing of Books, especially elementary books for children in schools. Otherwise it will be attempted here & there, and but [sic] in so obscure a way, that no good will result to religion . . .[76]

The situation grew better, however, as we learn from a letter of Archbishop Eccleston to Bishop Francis P. Kenrick of Philadelphia, written the following year:

> I am happy to be able now to inform you that arrangements have already been made, materials collected, and presses purchased to carry into effect the wishes of the [Second] Council, and place in the hands of Catholic children books prepared in a proper spirit, and duly approved by competent judges.[77]

But whatever the Bishops might think of the quality of books they might use in their own existing schools, they were more deeply concerned with what was happening in those conducted by the state. Writing to Eccleston regarding the questions to be discussed in the Third Provincial Council, (1837) Bishop John B. Purcell of Cincinnati suggested:

> 1. Should we allow Catholic youth to frequent schools wherein protestant bibles are the text-books . . .
> 6. . . . Provisions for Male & female Schools of our own—

[75] AAB, 24-V-5, Fenwick to Eccleston, Boston, Nov. 21, 1834.

[76] AAB, 25-E-7, Hughes to Eccleston, New York, Dec. 5, 1842.

[77] AAB, 27A-M-9, Eccleston to Kenrick, no place, "Feast of the Seven Dolors, 1843." Letters received by Kenrick in Philadelphia were brought by him to Baltimore when he became Archbishop of Baltimore on Aug. 3, 1851.

and books . . . free from vile slanders and calumnies against the Catholics . . .[78]

Again before the Fourth Council (1840) Archbishop Eccleston received suggestions from Bishops Kenrick of Philadelphia and Matthias Loras of Dubuque. Kenrick mentioned the dangers in the existing public school education and asked whether it was to be favored or condemned.[79] Loras wondered how they might go about getting competent Catholic teachers whose zeal would match that of those who labor "that they might receive a corruptible crown, but we an incorruptible one." [80]

The sixth decree of the Council, stating that the purpose of public education in many parts of the country was to serve the interests of heresy, warned pastors to look to the Christian and Catholic education of youth. It bade them prevent Catholic children from reading the Protestant version of the Bible and from participating in Protestant hymns and prayers. The decree further urged resistance to these practices and constant but moderate effort to get those in authority to remedy the situation.[81]

The Pastoral letter which came from the Fourth Council devoted considerably more space to education than had any of the previous ones. When commenting upon the reception being

[78] AAB, 25-Q-6, Purcell to Eccleston, Cincinnati, Oct. 8 [?], 1836.

[79] "Quid faciendum ut puerorum prospiciatur Christianae educationi, et quomodo cavendum est ne publico systemate scholarum pueris catholicis noceatur, vel fidei inferatur praejudicium? Utrum publico systemati favendum sit vel repugnandum?" (AAB, 25-F-10.) F. P. Kenrick to Eccleston (no place), Feb. 8, 1840.

[80] ". . . Nihil majoris momenti proponi posse opium media ad suppeditandas ac etiam informandas Catholicos et competentes scholae magistros. . . . Zelum Protestantium in ista materia omni nostra aemulatione dignum est, *et illi quidam ut corruptibilem coronam accipiant, nos autem incorruptam.*" (AAB, 25-J-3.) Loras to Eccleston, Dubuque, Feb. 10, 1840.

[81] "Cum constet publicae educationis rationem plerisque in his Provinciis ita iniri, ut haeresibus inserviat, puerorum catholicorum mentibus sensim sine sensu falsis sectarum principiis imbutis, monemus pastores ut omni quo valent studio catholicorum puerorum Christianae et Catholicae educationi prospiciant, et diligenter invigilent ne versione protestantica bibliorum utantur vel sectarum cantica aut preces recitent. Ideo invigilandum erit, ne in publicas scholas libri vel exercitia hujusmodi introducantur, cum fidei pietatisque discrimine. Constanter autem et moderate hisce sectarum conatibus ubique resistendum est, eorum qui auctoritate valent opportunum adhibere remedium implorato auxilio." (*Provincial Councils*, pp. 171–72.)

accorded the Catholic schools, the Bishops pointed out two mistakes which they had observed. Some parents were keeping their children out of school and giving them the money which would otherwise have been spent on tuition. Others were sending their children to less costly schools and then putting them in better ones only for a short final period. "The great evil in both cases," the letter continued,

> is the danger to which they are exposed, of having their faith undermined, the imperfect instruction which they receive, if they get any, upon the most important subject of religion, the nearly total abandonment of their religious practices and their exposure in their tender youth to the fatal influence of that false shame which generally arises from the mockery or the superciliousness of those who under-value their creed. . . .[82]

Continuing the topic of education, the Pastoral letter then devoted several pages to a vindication of the Church's right to teach in the name of God. Turning to the subject of the Bible, the Bishops explained their objections to the practice in the common schools of reading to Catholic children versions of the Scripture not approved by the Catholic Church.[83] Another objection to current practice in the common schools involved the use of textbooks inimical to Catholics. In this connection the Church leaders explained their views on the public school system in its religious endeavors:

> We can scarcely point out a book in general use in the ordinary schools, or even in higher seminaries, wherein covert and insidious efforts are not made to misrepresent our principles, to distort our tenets, to vilify our practices and to bring contempt upon our Church and its members. . . . It is not then because of any unkind feeling to our fellow-citizens, it is not through any reluctance on our part, to contribute whatever little we can to the prosperity of what are called the common institutions of the country, that we are always better pleased to have a separate system of education for the children of our communion, but because we have found by a painful experience, that in any common effort it was always expected that our dis-

[82] Guilday, *Pastorals*, p. 125.
[83] Cf. *infra*, pp. 267 ff.

tinctive principles of religious belief and practice should be yielded to the demands of those who thought proper to charge us with error; and because we saw with great pain the differences which an attempt to combine and to conciliate principles, which we have never been able to reconcile, has produced in a distant Church which has always been found faithful. . . .[84]

Three years later, the Fifth Provincial Council met at Baltimore, but issued no decrees on education, even though Eccleston had heard from Bishop Michael O'Connor of Pittsburgh urging that Catholic schools be erected in every parish.[85] Yet the Pastoral letter which followed, after emphasizing the duty of parents to see that their children received religious training and were shielded from erroneous teachings, spoke as follows in condemnation of sectarianism in public education:

. . . We have seen with serious alarm, efforts made to poison the fountains of public education, by giving it a sectarian hue, and accustoming children to the use of a version of the Bible made under sectarian bias, and placing in their hands books of various kinds replete with offensive and dangerous matter. This is plainly opposed to the free genius of our civil institutions. . . .

Let them, [the parents] therefore, avail themselves of their natural rights, guaranteed by the laws, and see that no interference with the faith of their children be used in the public schools, and no attempt made to induce conformity in any thing contrary to the laws of the Catholic Church.[86]

During the next six years, two more Provincial Councils were held, the Sixth in 1846 and the Seventh in 1849. Although there is no mention of educational matters in the decrees or Pastoral letters of either meeting, the papers for the Sixth Council furnish some valuable data as to the continuing anxiety of the Church leaders.

---

[84] Guilday, *op. cit.*, p. 134.

[85] AAB, 24-O-7, O'Connor to Eccleston, Pittsburgh, Dec. 2, 1842.

[86] Guilday, *op. cit.*, pp. 152–53. Dioceses represented for the first time by the signatures to this letter included Louisville, New York, Natchez, Richmond, and the Vicariate-Apostolic of Texas. Seventeen names in all are appended to the document.

A committee of priests had been assigned the question—"How to provide for the Christian education of children, especially those of parents who are poor?" [87] Their report stated, in part:

> They [the committee] regard this question of paramount necessity, and would therefore most earnestly recommend the establishment of schools in every congregation thru [sic] the province and that where means are not sufficient for the support of a school, a charitable education society should be organised, and subscriptions and collections for this purpose taken up by the Pastor. And if it would not be too officious, they would humbly suggest the idea, that the Bishops on the occasion of their usual visitations would vouchsafe to visit these schools, hold examinations etc. and impress on the Public the vital importance of such institutions in which Christian education together with morality and religion is happily imparted and urge the necessity of sustaining them.
>
> This energy, zeal, and active cooperation on the part of the clergy would infuse themselves into the Laity, and would, in the opinion of your congregation, produce a vast amount of good. [88]

By 1852, the Province of Baltimore had been divided into several provinces, each with its own Archbishop and suffragan dioceses. Hence the meeting of that year was denominated the First Plenary Council of Baltimore. Archbishop Francis P. Kenrick, formerly of Philadelphia, now headed the See of Baltimore, and was named Apostolic Delegate to the Council, representing Pope Pius IX.

A Committee of prelates, headed by Archbishop John B. Purcell of Cincinnati, was put in charge of the education question. [89] At the ninth Private Session of the Council the Bishops voted on a resolution to inaugurate societies to render [financial?] support

[87] AAB, 27A-R-3 (enclosure) "Tractanda . . . in Sexto Concilio Baltimori Habendo, die 10 Maii 1846."

[88] AAB, 27A-R-8. The report concluded with words of praise for the Brothers of the Christian Schools who had recently opened a school in Baltimore, and expressed a hope that the Bishops would try to get more of them to come to the States. The committee members signing the report were the Revs. John Barry (Charleston), Charles C. Pise (Detroit), Edmund T. Collins (Cincinnati) and Charles J. Carter (Nashville). At the end of the report is a pencilled note: "Laid on the table."

[89] AAB, 32B-F-1.

for Catholic schools, and the motion was defeated by a vote of 16 to 15.[90]

Two questions were submitted for reports from Committees of priests: "How to provide for the education of youth?" and "What remedy must be offered for the abuse of the Public School?" [91]

The answer to the first question was written up by a Committee Chairman, the Rev. Dr. Charles I. White, of the Archdiocese of Baltimore.[92] After dividing the topic into what system should be adopted and by what means a fund was to be raised, the report made the following points on the problem of the system itself:

1. The establishment of a parochial school system is indispensable, in view of the evils which follow from frequentation of schools "in which no impressions of true religion are made upon the mind of youth." Parochial schools were defined as those to which only Catholic children were admitted, which were staffed by teachers approved by the pastor and in which catechism instructions were frequently given.

2. The school must be considered as an "auxiliary to the pastor and others who are charged with the proper education of young persons." Hence the pastor must give it constant care, select "teachers whose piety and other qualifications render them competent to such an office," supervise the catechetical instruction, and urge parents and others to cooperate with him in the work, by sending them to school and church and by "confirming by word and example the salutary influence which he exercises over them."

3. Since those who devote themselves to teaching "for the glory of God and their own personal sanctification are manifestly the best qualified for this important task" the pastor should endeavor to assure such [sisters and brothers] for the school.

On the problem of fund raising, the second half of this Committee's report, Father White's document had three suggestions: (1)—Funds raised by the Church and not needed for the support of the pastor should be appropriated for the school; (2)—Tuition

[90] AAB, 32B-F-1, p. 20.
[91] "Qua ratione juventutis educationi providendum est?"; "Quod remedium publicarum scholarum abusui offerendum?" (AAB, 32B-E-1.)
[92] AAB, 32B-E-16.

would have to be asked from those who could afford it; (3)—"That although the system of public taxation for schools, as it exists in this country, is loudly to be condemned, it is advisable that an effort should be made, so far as prudence will suggest, to secure a portion of the public fund for the support of our parochial schools."

It is not clear from the documents in the Baltimore Archives who prepared the second report on the "Remedy for the Abuse of the Public Schools." It appears to have been written in another hand than that of Father Charles I. White who penned the document just quoted. It is possible that it was done by one of the priests listed on the committee for the general question for the fourth session, "On the Institutions for Youth and Allied Matters." [93]

The report [94] commences by observing that the question, as asked, "implies the existence of an abuse and the necessity of applying the proper remedy, if any can be found."

As to the "abuse," the Committee stated that "the radical disease of the public school system throughout this country is the exclusion of all religion therefrom, in other words, its Godlessness,—." As cause for this the Committee saw the principle of the system's foundation—"that the State, setting aside the parent & the pastor, has the right & is bound to educate the children of the Community."

In addition, the report observed, the State Constitutions, by forbidding the civil government to "establish or teach any religion" made the schools "essentially *infidel* & even *atheistical;* for to teach the existence of God & the duty of worshipping him, is to teach religion, what the State is in theory debarred from doing." Nor did any Catholic need to be told how trying to teach "such religious truths . . . as all are agreed on" is "false & vicious in principle & fatal in its results."

As to how the public school system was working out in practice, the Committee stated their feeling that it was being used to

[93] "De juv. Instit. et promisc. Rebus." The committee included the Revs. John McElroy (Chairman), James Dolan, Josue M. Young, L. Obermeyer and C. I. White. (AAB, 32B-D-21.)

[94] AAB, 32B-E-17.

corrupt religiously "the rising generation & particularly the children of Catholic parents." Probably having in mind the activities of the Native American Party which had been at work in the United States for some years, and of the "Know Nothing" group which was formed the very year the Plenary Council met, the report spoke of a "vast conspiracy to stop the spread of the Catholic faith, and, if possible, to crush the Catholic Church." The Committee stated their conviction that the conspiracy "has at its command no engine of such gigantic force, no weapon so formidable as our public school education."

Next the report spoke of a specific problem which will be developed later in this chapter—participation by Catholic public school children in the reading of the Protestant Bible, and the reciting of Protestant hymns and prayers. "And when Catholics object to these things," they stated,

> they are immediately held up to public execration as enemies of the Bible & of free institutions. . . . Melancholy experience has shown the consequences of all this. Catholic children exposed to insidious, if not open attacks on their religious principles and practices, *become ashamed* of *their faith*. . . . it is morally impossible, [that] their faith should not be weakened & their feelings warped.

Three more points were made in this first section of the report—(1) Catholic children who went to public school were being withdrawn from the instructions and pastoral care needed at the time of their first Communion and Confirmation; (2) mingling with those of other beliefs and lacking the vigilant care of Catholic teachers, Catholic children faced the danger of commencing sinful habits; (3) the development of Catholic schools was being hampered because members of the Church had to pay taxes for institutions, from which they derived no benefits.

The second half of the report discussed the subject of "remedies." An archivist has labelled it with a new number,[95] but it is obviously a continuation of the preceding, and is written in the same hand.

The Committee commenced by stating they did not want to

[95] AAB, 32B-E-18.

suggest any out-and-out attack on the public schools as a system well received by a majority of the people. However, they wished to point out in passing that other groups besides the Catholics [Episcopalians and Presbyterians were mentioned by name] were not satisfied with the schools as they existed. Furthermore, the Committee felt, the main enthusiasm for the system was to be found in the cities rather than in the country districts where "in many places [it] is positively unpopular & condemned as a failure."

Citing the authority of the Fourth Provincial Council of Baltimore, which had urged constant and moderate resistance to those who were misusing the public schools, the committeemen then recommended four lines of activity:

1. That Catholics, as soon as deemed expedient, ask the Legislatures so to modify the laws that "their proportional share of the public money" be given to "free schools, asylums & academies furnishing education gratuitously or as cheap as the public schools."

2. That the Bishops and pastors "immediately make united & powerful efforts to establish free schools . . . when it is practicable to do so . . . & . . . encourage & aid the institution of pay schools under the direction of Catholic teachers approved by the Bp. & pastors."

3. That where Catholic schools exist, the parents be urged to send their children to them and (if the Bishop should approve) "be even required to do so on pain of being denied the Sacraments."

4. That Catholics refrain from any public appeal at that time which might "have the effect of exciting the Protestant Community" but rather "employ such instructions [?] and influences as may arouse the Catholic Community to a sense of their rights & duties in this matter, & secure at the proper time the necessary legislative action."

Seeming to follow these suggestions, the Bishops of the Plenary Council did not include in their official decrees any direct statement on the "abuse of the public schools." Instead, in their twelfth and thirteenth decrees they took the positive side by reemphasizing the importance of catechism classes for children and the dire need of more Catholic schools and capable teachers to staff them.[96]

In their Pastoral letter, the Bishops of the Council reminded parents of their duty to give their children an "education based on religious principles, accompanied by religious practices and always subordinate to religious influence." [97] It warned them not to be deceived into providing an education without religion, which would leave their children bereft of means to control their passions and insure future happiness. If religious instruction is separated from the secular, the student's mind is filled with error, his heart with vice and the secular learning itself will contribute to "destroying the happiness of the child,

> embittering still more the chalice of parental disappointment, and weakening the foundations of social order. . . . Encourage the establishment and support of Catholic schools; make every sacrifice which may be necessary for this object; spare our hearts the pain of beholding the youth whom, after the example of our Master, we so much love, involved in all the evils of an uncatholic education, evils too multiplied and too obvious to require that we should do more than raise our voices in solemn protest against the system from which they spring. . . .[98]

The Catholic Church, then, maintained throughout the first sixty years of the American nation her traditional position not only that religion belongs in education, but that no school program can be considered adequate without instruction in religious doctrine being the basic and most important part. Gravely concerned with the situation they found in America, the Catholic

---

[96] The twelfth decree: "Moneant episcopi sacerdotes curam animarum exercentes, ut institutioni juventutis in doctrina christiana per se operam dent, nec putent ipsis licere quae sui muneris sunt negligere, rejecto omnino in alios onere juvenes, aliosque rudes, fidei morumque principia edocendi." *Concilium Plenarium Totius Americae Septentrionalis Foederatae, Baltimori Habitum, Anno 1852* (Baltimore: John Murphy & Co., 1853), pp. 46–47. The thirteenth decree: "Hortamur episcopos, et attentis gravissimis malis quae ex juventute haud rite instituta sequi solent, per viscera misericordiae Dei obsecramus, ut scholas unicuique ecclesiae in eorum diocesibus annexas, instituendas curent; et si opus fuerit, et rerum adjuncta sinant, provideant ut ex redditibus ecclesiae cui schola annexa sit, idonei magistri in ea habeantur." (*Ibid.*, p. 47.)

[97] Guilday, *op. cit.*, p. 190.

[98] *Ibid.*, pp. 190–91.

leaders did not oppose the common school as a public institution, but they did oppose the religious phase of the common school curriculum as it existed in those days, because they felt it was inimical to the common good, and, especially, to the faith of Catholics. Unwilling to leave the resulting religious training of their children a vacuum, they set themselves to the task of raising another educational system which would match the secular program of the public school and supply the necessary training in religious truth.[99] ,

OPINIONS AND PRACTICES OF LAY LEADERS

Did lay people, including the teachers themselves, think that religion belonged in education? Before attempting to answer this question, two qualifications are to be noted. First, some of the people quoted in this section may have been Protestant clergymen without the fact appearing either from the title "Reverend" or a Doctorate in Divinity attached to their names in the writings examined. Second, the enormity of the lay field, including statesmen, educators, politicians, newspapermen, makes even an attempt at a survey seem an overwhelming task. It is surely one in which generalizations are hazardous procedures. However, such material as was found, by a systematic search in Baltimore libraries and that of the Department of Health, Education and Welfare in Washington, will be presented. Trends, at least, may be observed.

Connecticut is selected as a starting point not only because of the similarity of its laws to those of Massachusetts, but because of the prominence of its first Secretary of the Board of Education, Henry Barnard. This man accepted the secretary's position in

---

[99] For further reading in Catholic educational philosophy of the period, cf. Rt. Rev. M. J. Spalding, *An Address to the Impartial Public, Being the Introduction to the Miscellanea* (Louisville: Webb & Levering, 1854); Orestes Brownson, "Paganism in Education," A Review of Abbé J. Gaume's *Le Ver Rongeur des Sociétés Modernes, ou le Paganisme dans l'Education, Brownson's Quarterly Review,* VI (New Series) (April, 1852) (Boston: B. H. Green, 1852), pp. 227–47.

1838 and in August of that year there came out under his editorship the first issue of *The Connecticut Common School Journal*.[100] The following month, two articles appeared, both unsigned, on the subject of the Bible in the schools. The first contained comment on an extract from "Travels on the Continent of Europe" by "President Fisk." [101] Fisk narrated a conversation with Fellenberg, a Swiss educator, who had expressed surprise at the paucity of religious education in the American public school. "The great principles of our religion," Fellenberg was quoted as saying, in part:

> would come into collision with no man's views who believed in Christianity; and that, at any rate, party views were nothing in comparison with the importance of religious training; and therefore every good man ought to be willing to make some sacrifices of party views for the great benefits of an early religious education.[102]

The editor of the *Journal* commented as follows:

> It will gratify many of our readers, we have no doubt, to hear so decided an expression in favor of that great fundamental feature in the school system of our ancestors, viz., the use of the Scriptures in schools, from the excellent Mr. Fellenberg, the founder of the noble institution of Hofwyl, in Switzerland. It is gratifying to hear it approved by our much respected countryman, President Fisk. We are happy to say, however, that the Bible is becoming used more and more every year in our schools, and that although too extensively neglected, it is probably less so than Mr. Fellenberg supposed.[103]

In the same issue the second editorial was entitled "The Daily Use of the Bible in Schools." Here the writer noted that religious training was the chief purpose of Connecticut schools in colonial

100 Henry Barnard (ed.), *The Connecticut Common School Journal*, I-III (1838–1842) (Hartford: Case, Tiffany & Co.), IV (1842) (Hartford: W. S. Williams).

101 Very likely, Wilbur Fisk (1792–1839) Methodist clergyman and first President of Wesleyan University, Middletown, Connecticut. Cf. Allan Johnson and Dumas Malone (eds.), *Dictionary of American Biography* (New York: Charles Scribner's Sons, 1931), VI, 415–16.

102 *Ibid.*, I, No. 2 (September, 1838), 13.

103 *Ibid.*, p. 14.

times. The law enjoined the reading of the Scriptures as the best means towards the goal. After noting a revival of the use of the Bible and methods of teaching it at the time of his writing, Barnard (or his writer) concluded:

> It [the subject of Bible teaching] is one which will probably be ever esteemed a vital one in Connecticut; and if Monsieur Cousin so warmly urged upon the government of France to make religious instruction the corner stone of their national system of education, and urged with success the example of Prussia, we may with greater confidence invite the people of our state to supply their schools with the Scriptures, and point to the laws passed by their fathers for this very end, nearly two centuries ago, and (so far as we have the ability to comprehend so vast a subject), to the noble effects produced even by their imperfect observance.[104]

On October 16, 1839 the "Second School Society" of Norwich, Connecticut, heard a report from a school-visiting committee. Among the recommendations the visitors stated:

> We think that every school should have *moral* as well as *intellectual* instruction; and great care should be exercised in the selection of teachers with reference to this. We also deem it highly important to have a religious influence brought to bear on our children in the schools—that the leading principles of the Christian religion should be inculcated on the mind; that the existence of God may not be forgotten, but constantly recognized—because we believe that knowledge without religion, only qualifies the possessor to do the more of evil to his fellow-men.[105]

In his 1850 Report Barnard devoted a paragraph to religion in the curriculum of the state normal schools:

> To cultivate a truly religious feeling—to lay the foundation and implant the motives for a truly religious life, . . . will be one of the cardinal objects of the Normal School. Every suitable effort, consistent with perfect religious toleration, will be made, to give a deep moral and religious tone to all the exercises, and to the whole character of the institution, from a deep conviction that a sense of responsibility to God, and of love to man, must

[104] *Ibid.*, p. 15. Other articles favoring religion in education may be found in the *Common School Journal*, II, 78; III, 37, 70.

[105] *Common School Journal*, III, No. 2 (Nov. 15, 1840), 25.

form the mainspring of a teacher's activity, while it is the surest pledge of success.[106]

It seems that Barnard and his associates were one with the social tradition that God belonged in education. Attention was also paid by the Connecticut superintendent to the dangers of sectarianism. Yet, like Horace Mann, Barnard wanted religion to be taught, wanted Christianity to be taught, mainly through Bible reading and study.[107] No evidence was found to indicate that Barnard changed his views on religious education, when he went to Rhode Island as head of the public schools (1845–1849).[108]

In Maryland, we find that the school commissioners of Baltimore were asked by the City Council early in 1839 whether or not the Bible was used in the public schools. Curiously, the commissioners did not seem to know. They replied, however, "that it was their intention to give the subject an early and respectful attention." [109] The *Annual Report* for 1839 records that on March 4:

> . . . A resolution was passed by a majority of the Board, allowing the use of the Bible in all the schools, as a reading book. It may be proper here to remark, that the teachers are instructed, in all cases, to allow the Doway [sic] Bible to be used by those children whose parents prefer the same to the common translation.
> . . . The chief object in adopting the use of the sacred volume was, to endeavor, by every available means, to imbue the minds of the scholars with that moral influence which its inspired pages are so well calculated to impart. And in doing this it was never intended, in the smallest degree, to interfere with the conscientious scruples, or religious opinions of any

[106] Henry Barnard, *Fifth Annual Report of the Superintendent of Common Schools of Connecticut to the General Assembly, May Session, 1850* (New Haven: Osburn & Baldwin, 1850), p. 19.

[107] For an extended treatment of the Connecticut picture, cf. Sister Mary Paul Mason, *Church-State Relationships in Education in Connecticut, 1633–1953* (Washington: The Catholic University of America Press, 1953).

[108] During this period, Barnard edited the *Journal of the Rhode Island Institute of Instruction.* The index to volumes I-III (1845–1848) did not indicate any articles on religious instruction or Bible reading. There are, however, several articles on "Moral Instruction."

[109] Board of School Commissioners of Baltimore City, *Eleventh Annual Report,* December 31, 1839 (no printer listed), p. 4. (The first sixteen annual reports of this group (1820–1844) are to be found in the "Maryland Room" at the Enoch Pratt Library in Baltimore.)

individual or sect, under any name. With these the Board have nothing to do; and any attempt to introduce sectarian principles, by any means whatever, into the Public Schools, would merit, as doubtless it would meet, the public indignation. The Commissioners claim no merit for the performance of what they deem their duty; but believing as they do, that the Holy Scriptures have provided an invaluable blessing to the Christian world, they therefore indulge the hope that a salutary influence will be diffused in the schools from that pure and sacred source.[110]

The same report in listing the year's expenditures, contains the following entry for August 7, 1839—"$144.25 to Maryland State Bible Society, for Bibles and Tests [Testaments] for all the Schools." [111]

The instruction of the Board to allow the Douay Version (the official Catholic translation of the Scriptures into English) to be read to Catholic children seems to have been an enactment unique in those times. In 1842, the Catholic Bishop of Philadelphia, Francis P. Kenrick,[112] made a request that the same thing be done in the public schools of that city. But as will be seen later, what followed the Bishop's plea was anything but satisfactory to him.[113]

In 1851 an address of J. F. Monmonier given at the cornerstone laying for the Eastern (Girls') High School in Baltimore indicated religion as one of the goals of education:

> We desire to instruct the whole mass of the community thoroughly in morality, and increase their intellectual ability. We design to produce a respect for the laws, a love of morality and a reverence for religion. . . . And our designs will be accomplished and our reward received, by making him [the citizen] an intellectual and social being, prepared to fulfill his destiny on earth, and assisting him in fitting his immortal mind for the blissful possession and the enjoyment of eternity.[114]

The following year Martin J. Kerney, Chairman of the Committee on Education in the Maryland House of Delegates, published

[110] *Ibid.*, p. 4.
[111] *Ibid.*, p. 14.
[112] Later, Archbishop of Baltimore.
[113] Cf. *infra*, pp. 271 f.
[114] John F. Monmonier, M. D., *Address Delivered at the Laying of the Cornerstone of the Eastern Female High School, September 21, 1851* (Baltimore: James Lucas, 1851), p. 14.

a pamphlet advocating a share in public funds for non-public institutions of learning. This highly-controversial subject is not properly in the field of this study.[115] In presenting his case, however, Kerney spoke out for religion in education:

> . . . It is well known that there are thousands of individuals belonging to the various denominations which compose the Christian family, who regard the education of their children as a solemn duty: who are deeply impressed with the importance of giving them a *religious education*. . . . Education without religion, is the most fearful instrument that can be placed in the hands of man. Like a ship without a helm, it drives its possessor headlong to every excess, to crime without a blush; to violation of order without restraint; to anarchy and bloodshed; to the destruction of society; to the ruin of the state, and finally, to the regions of never-ending woe. We have only to turn to the records of the past to read the truthfulness of the picture here drawn. Every step we take in this investigation, demonstrate [sic] the truth, that the surest safeguard of society lies in the moral education of the people; that mere literary teaching is not sufficient to hold together the elements of society.[116]

Kerney's pamphlet was answered on October 1, 1852 by an anonymous writer who signed himself "Publicola." [117] He stated his agreement with Kerney "that every child should receive not only a secular, but a religious education." [118] Immediately, however, "Publicola" made a distinction between *"practical"* and *"sectarian"* religion. "The former," he continued,

> (exemplified in the precepts—Love thy neighbor—Do unto others as ye would that they should do unto you) may be taught by the schoolmaster—the latter (including the *peculiar* and distinguishing doctrines of every denomination) should be taught by the parents or the clergy.[119]

[115] On this question, cf. Richard J. Gabel, *Public Funds for Church and Private Schools* (Washington, D. C.: The Catholic University of America Press, 1937).

[116] Martin J. Kerney, *Public Education, Or the School Question Examined* (Baltimore: no pub., 1852), pp. 10, 12.

[117] "Publicola" (pseud.), *Reply to Mr. M. J. Kerney's Letter on the Public School Question*, October 1, 1852. (No printer's name or place or publication date. Cover missing from copy in Rare Book Section of Education Library, The Johns Hopkins University.)

[118] *Ibid.*, p. 4.

[119] *Ibid.*

Thus, "Publicola" seems to have agreed with the spirit of the times in ruling out sectarianism from public instruction. His definition of "practical religion" is reminiscent of that in the *First Report* of Horace Mann.[120]

About the same time that Kerney and "Publicola" were having their controversy, Baltimoreans heard an address by S. F. Streeter entitled "The Teacher's Calling." [121] It emphasized the dignity of the teaching profession on several points, and, when the speaker came to religion, he declared:

> But, elevated as is the preacher's calling, the teacher stands, or should stand on common ground. He, too, is bringing up laborers for the field of Life;—and education for life involves the deepest principles of morality and religion. . . . The teacher, then, whose duty it is to develope [sic] harmoniously all the powers of the young, and to prepare them most efficiently for the labors of life, becomes of necessity, to a certain extent, the co-laborer of the divine. . . .[122]

The following March, the President of the Female Seminary in Frederick, Maryland, H. Winchester, spoke in the House of Delegates at the state capital, Annapolis.[123] On the subject of religious education, he declared himself in favor of the public schools' inculcating "the great general principles of Christianity, as set forth by the founder of our religion, and a high standard of morality." [124] But he is fiercely against bringing in any of the "mooted, sectarian dogmas which for hundreds of years have engendered discord, and strife, and bitterness, and contention." [125]

Later in his speech Winchester made an interesting reference to sectarianism having been excluded from the Federal Constitution and so from public education. The remark came after a sec-

[120] Cf. *supra*, pp. 133–35.

[121] S. F. Streeter, *The Teacher's Calling, An Address Delivered Before the Maryland Institute of Education, September 24, 1852* (Baltimore: John Murphy Company, no date).

[122] *Ibid.*, pp. 7–8.

[123] H. Winchester, *A Lecture on Popular Education Delivered in the Hall of the House of Delegates, Annapolis, March 2, 1853* (Frederick, Maryland: Schley & Haller, 1853).

[124] *Ibid.*, p. 10.

[125] *Ibid.*

tion on the undesirability of providing public funds for religious schools:

> As the glorious fathers of our republic excluded sectarianism from the constitution of the United States, they concluded that it would be perfectly safe to exclude it from the public schools, and rigidly to enforce the law to disburse no public money that did not unequivocally comply with all the requisites of the public code.[126]

No proof is offered by Winchester for his claim that the men who wrote the Federal Constitution made a decision to exclude sectarian religion from the public schools.

A different note was sounded a year later in Baltimore when Brantz Mayer spoke to the graduates of the Central High School. Though not opposed to religion, nor minimizing its value in human life, Mayer denied it any place in the curriculum of the public school:

> I deny that civil education to be perfect *must* of necessity be accompanied by theological. There are many persons who contend that theology and religion are not synonymous, but that while religion comprises the liberal Christianity of all sects, theology limits its professors to their peculiar dogmas. The culture, therefore that has been deemed appropriately *public,* is an exclusively CIVIL education, in which all branches of literature, language, art, science, and accomplishment, may be taught without infringing individual faith, or, *even naming creeds.* In other words, the pupil is left to the teacher, in school, and to the pastor in the pulpit.
>
> There can be no danger of religion's decay as long as education is vigorous, for it is impossible that the educated mind can be infidel. There is clerical vigilance enough in the land to inform our youths without converting the civil teacher into a temporary ecclesiastic. Let us keep the Church and State apart in every manner. The soul and mind are so near akin that their marriage would be incestuous.[127]

Mayer's talk was followed by some informal remarks by Gov-

[126] *Ibid.,* p. 14.

[127] Brantz Mayer, *Address at the Third Annual Commencement of the Central High School of Baltimore, August 1, 1853* (Baltimore: James Lucas, 1853), pp. 17–18. Mayer's central idea, that religion was not to be taught in

ernor Louis Lowe.[128] A religious outlook on life formed a chief part of Lowe's talk:

> They [the graduates] must remember that the life upon which they were, so to speak, about to enter, was but the threshold of the temple of Eternity . . . that, therefore, the duties of life must be measured and appreciated by the relation which they bear to that future state in which we all believe. And, consequently, that every good citizen must also be a good Christian, aiming at that perfection of the heart which chasteneth all things, and without which the fires of unkindled intellect would consume and destroy, rather than illumine and fructify this Earthly habitation of ours.[129]

Public schools in Washington, D. C. were authorized by an Act of Congress, May 15, 1820.[130] Only two were in operation, however, up until 1844. On December 23 of that year a Board of Trustees met for the first time and their work resulted in more schools in the following months.[131] A statement implying that the place for religious instruction was the home and not the school is included in the *Second Report* of the Trustees:

> We commend the [public] schools to the public encouragement, support and patronage. Let ample means be provided to afford to all the children of the city a sound public school education, improved by a course of good reading and parental instruction at home, in morality, virtue and religion. Then, with the blessings of Providence, will they do honor to the city that bears the name of Washington, and grow up to be such men

---

public schools, was beginning to be heard with more frequency after 1850. The arguments he gives, however, are in something of a unique class. To call "religion" the common denominator and to call religious disputes "theology" is certainly peculiar. And to refer to mental and spiritual interactivities (products as they are of the one personality) as an "incestuous union" is altogether bizarre.

[128] They are given in summary form in the same booklet.

[129] Mayer, *op. cit.*, p. 20.

[130] The District of Columbia was, territorially speaking, a part of the thirteen colonies. Hence a presentation of data found on its schools has been included.

[131] *Reports of the Board of Trustees of the Public Schools*—Washington, D. C., *First Annual Report—1844* (for year ending June 30, 1845) (No place, printer, or date given). (Reports examined at Library of Health, Education and Welfare Department, Washington, D. C.)

and women as we would wish, when we retire from the stage of life, to leave behind us, and entrust with the interests and destinies of the future.[132]

Yet, in praising the actual work of the teachers, the same Report mentioned religion, if somewhat vaguely. "Without noise or show you are engaged in diffusing knowledge, in implanting broad, generous and noble principles, giving to the young high aspirations for excellence, inspiring a reverence for truth, justice, goodness and the laws of God." [133]

In a letter included in the *Third Annual Report,* J. L. Henshaw, Principal of the Washington First District School, implied that directives were given to the teachers which limited religious instruction. Still, he felt that he could and did bring in some of the content of natural theology:

> While I have felt it to be my duty to keep within the sphere of instruction prescribed by those rules [of the School Board], I have not felt myself precluded from discoursing occasionally, upon other and higher branches of knowledge; upon astronomy, that so powerfully tends to lead the mind "to look through Nature up to Nature's God." [134]

Subsequent reports indicate the use of the Bible in schools, public prayers, talks by clergymen, etc., in the public schools of the District of Columbia.[135]

The separatist point of view was represented by a declaration of the School Board of Philadelphia quoted by Frederick A. Packard in his *Princeton Review* article, "Religious Instruction in the Common Schools": [136]

> That as all the sects contribute in the payment of taxes to the support of public schools, the introduction of any religious or sectarian forms as part of the discipline of the schools must have a tendency to impair the rights of some; and that whilst

[132] *Second Annual Report* (1846), p. 22.

[133] *Ibid.*, pp. 22–23.

[134] *Third Annual Report* (1847), p. 15.

[135] E.g., *Tenth Annual Report* (1854): "By direction of the Trustees, selections from the Bible are read in all public schools as an opening exercise." (P. 23.)

[136] Cf. *supra,* p. 156.

this Board is convinced of the utter impossibility of adopting a system of religious instruction that should meet the approbation of all religious societies, they are equally satisfied that no injury need result to the pupils from confining the instruction in our schools to the ordinary branches of elementary education, inasmuch as ample facilities for religious improvement are presented for the choice of parents and guardians in Sabbath Schools and other establishments for that purpose, which are organized and supported by various religious communities.[137]

Later in his article, though, Packard quoted from the *Annual Reports* of this same group (*passim* from 1824 to 1835) in which they say, e.g., "the children . . . are instructed in the great principles and solemn obligations of Christianity, as set forth in the Holy Scriptures." [138]

Public education south of the Potomac was slower to develop than in the states we have examined thus far. Knight's *Documentary History of Education in the South* cites the 1837 decree which provided for public schools in Georgia and another for North Carolina which came out two years later.[139] There is little mention of curriculum and nothing on religion in these laws. Regarding North Carolina, however, additional information is provided in a study by Luther L. Gobbel.[140]

The first North Carolina primary schools were started in 1840, but complete administrative machinery was not functioning until a decade later.[141] In 1852 Calvin H. Wiley, a Presbyterian, became first State Superintendent, and emphasized the need of religious instruction. "The object of all education, therefore," he wrote,

[137] Packard, "Religious Instruction in Common Schools," pp. 6–7. The full set of "Resolutions" by the Board, of which the section quoted by Packard is a part, is found in Hugh J. Nolan, *The Most Reverend Francis Patrick Kenrick, Third Bishop of Philadelphia, 1830–1851* (Philadelphia: American Catholic Historical Society of Philadelphia, 1948), pp. 289–90. Nolan gives the date of the resolves as December 9, 1834.

[138] *Ibid.*, p. 18.

[139] Knight, *op. cit.*, II, 168–77.

[140] Luther L. Gobbel, *Church-State Relationships in Education in North Carolina Since 1776* (Durham, North Carolina: Duke University Press, 1938), pp. 172–204.

[141] *Ibid.*, p. 176.

should be not to learn to dispense with the agency of God, in our affairs, but to lead us more directly to Him. . . .[142]

Wiley endeavored to implement his ideal by approving the use of the Bible in the schools, and by insisting that "school committees appointed to examine and pass on the qualifications of those wishing to teach in the common schools should construe strictly the constitutional provision which made it impossible for those 'who deny the Being of God, or the divine authority of the Old or New Testament' to hold any civil trust." [143]

Gobbel states that the various (Protestant) sects in North Carolina were happy with the common school religious program and quotes from the inaugural address of Governor Ellis in 1859 as follows:

> Our educational system is but an index to the state of religion and morals among our people . . . instead of jarring of conflicting sects, we have the harmonious action of all denominations of Christians, in teaching the great truths of practical religion, and introducing that moral training among the people, which is an essential preparation to their exercising properly the functions of self-government.[144]

In the State of Virginia plans for a school system were offered by Henry Ruffner in 1841.[145] Although nothing came of his proposals, at least until after the Civil War,[146] it is worthy of note that Ruffner stressed religious qualifications for schoolmasters:

> . . . an unblemished moral character and sound principles of Christian piety. If not in full communion with a Christian church, he should at least be free from religious infidelity and profaneness of language or sentiment and be well acquainted with the Holy Scriptures.[147]

---

[142] *Ibid.*, p. 182 (quoting *Annual Report, Superintendent of Common Schools, 1858–1859*, p. 42).

[143] *Ibid.*, p. 183.

[144] *Ibid.*, p. 185 (quoting *Executive and Legislative Documents, 1860–1861*, p. 17).

[145] Knight, *op. cit.*, v, 92–103.

[146] *Ibid.*, p. 103.

[147] *Ibid.*, p. 100.

In the normal schools Ruffner would have included in the curriculum "natural theology, the evidences of Christianity, [and] the Bible." [148]

Virginia, meanwhile, did have some "charity schools" for the children of the poor. Some interesting data on these institutions is found in an article, "Common School Education in Virginia" in the August, 1844 issue of the *Common School Journal of the State of Pennsylvania:* [149]

> This title ["Common School Education"] is rather a misnomer, as there is not in Virginia, strictly, any system of education by Common Schools, such as exist in Pennsylvania, and the states north and east of us. There is, however, an extended and somewhat successful plan, similar to that formerly existing among us, having for its object the education of *indigent children at the public expense.*[150]

Later in the article some quotations are given from the "Remarks of the County Commissioners of Virginia":

> The children patronized by the [school] fund make a reasonable progress in learning, and the *teachers generally possess a good moral character.* . . .
> The Schools are visited carefully and general observation made of the manner in which they are conducted, and rigid regard is paid to the morals of the teachers—some of them stand high, and in many instances the children are rapidly advancing . . . the teachers are men of good moral character, and most, if not all of them professors of religion, and are well qualified to teach all the branches of a common English education, etc.[151]

Knight's *Documentary History* gives three more items indicating a belief in religious education among leaders in the South. In 1832 Joseph Caldwell, President of the University of North Carolina, wrote a series of letters on the condition of public schools in his state. Letter IX [152] includes a striking description of the plight

[148] *Ibid.*, p. 103.
[149] *Common School Journal of the State of Pennsylvania*, I, No. 8, 225–32.
[150] *Ibid.*, p. 225.
[151] *Ibid.*, p. 229.
[152] Knight, *op. cit.*, II, 397–402.

of poor children whose "training" is bereft of religious values.[153] In 1839, the Rev. Benjamin M. Smith gave Governor David Campbell of Virginia a report on education in Prussia which contains a highly laudatory section on religion in the schools of that country.[154] Finally, an estimate of public schools in Charleston, S. C., given in 1858 by the Hon. C. G. Memminger, spoke of the deep religious value of the education given to girls to fit them to be the future mothers of families.[155]

Up to this point, no data have been produced from the State of New York. Between the years 1825 and 1842, a series of controversies with far-reaching legal effects occurred in the Empire State, which will be examined below when state laws are considered. Since this part of the chapter is dealing with expressions of lay opinion, the views of Erastus C. Benedict, the New York State superintendent attacked by Hodge,[156] will be set forth. It is to be noted that this speech came some years after the above-mentioned controversies.

Benedict favored religious education for the young, but he wanted such instruction given at home or in church, and was, perhaps, the most avid proponent of a completely secularized education in the public schools to appear on the American scene up to his day. In a speech given in Pittsburgh in August, 1853, he set out his ideas at great length.[157] After some introductory remarks on the need of a religious education and the spirit of liberty in America, Benedict declared:

> But in nothing are our institutions more peculiar than in their relations to religion. . . . No law can be made by the National

[153] *Ibid.*, pp. 400–401.
[154] *Ibid.*, pp. 441–43.
[155] *Ibid.*, V, 197–98.
[156] Cf. *supra*, p. 194.
[157] Erastus C. Benedict, *Religion in Public Schools, A Paper Read Before the American Association for the Advancement of Education at Their Third Session, Held at Pittsburgh, Pennsylvania, August, 1853* (Newark, New Jersey: A. Stephen Holbrook, 1854). Cf., also, E.C.B., *Remarks of Erastus C. Benedict, Esq. on his re-election as President of the Board of Education, at its organization, January 14, 1852* [No place, printer, or date]. (Ordered that a copy be requested, and that it be located on the minutes and printed— Albert Gilbert, Clerk.)

Government respecting an establishment of religion, and the free exercise and enjoyment of religious profession and worship, without discrimination or preference, are here by our organic laws, secured to all mankind within our jurisdiction. This liberty of religion, while it was founded in the true nature of religion, and was from its own nature a necessity, was even more so for us when we threw open our gates of welcome to all that chose to come and take part in our great American Association, and assume the allegiance of freedom and mutuality. It could not fail to be foreseen that the inflowing streams from other nations must always be of various religious faith and worship. . . . This diversity must always continue; the people of all sects would take up arms to prevent the establishment of a Government religion. Every step toward it, and every tendency to it, must surely fail.[158]

This direct reference to the First Amendment is so far couched in terms that indicate the "narrow interpretation," that is, that its purpose was to rule out a national religion and protect religious liberty. In his explanation of liberty, however, Benedict swung directly over to the "broad interpretation" that government should have nothing to do with religion at all:

But the character of this liberty is often misunderstood. It is not a right to demand from the government an equal support for all religions, as some seem to think, but the right to be entirely free from government regulation. It is the law of liberty only— not the law of equality; not that the Government is bound to patronize all alike, but that it has no right to patronize any. . . . We cannot compel, or control, or prohibit, or direct it [religion], and it is our conscientious duty to resist all attempts to compel one to observe or to propagate a system of religion which he believes to be false, and the highest oppression is that which compels us to support every form of religion. The state has no means of ascertaining the true religion, . . . and is guilty of as great a usurpation and does as great a violence to religious liberty by supporting all, as it would by prohibiting all sects of religion.[159]

When he turned to the subject of religion in the public school

[158] *Ibid.*, pp. 10–11.

[159] *Ibid.*, p. 11. The reader will not miss the distinction between the government's obligation to support all religion, which is criticized by Benedict, and the government's freedom to do so, if it chooses, which is not mentioned at all.

curriculum, Benedict poured out his sarcasm. It was the following passage that brought out the protest of Dr. Hodge: [160]

> So with the schools—whenever we can find a few children together shall we compel them to lay aside their occupation for the time, and read the Bible, or say their prayers, or perform some other religious duty? Will it be sure to make them better? Is it the best mode of giving religious instruction? Shall we require it at the dancing school, the riding school, the music school, the visiting party, and the play-ground—shall studies, and sports, and plays, and prayers, and Bible, and creed, and catechism, be all placed on the same level? Shall we insist that secular learning cannot be well taught unless it is mixed with sacred forms? Shall Algebra and Geometry be always interspersed with religion? Instead of *quod erat demonstrandum* shall we say *selah* and *amen*? Shall we bow at the sign *plus*? Can we not learn the multiplication table without saying grace over it?— So of religious instruction, will it be improved by a mixture of profane learning? Shall the child be taught to mix his spelling lessons with his prayers, and his table-book with his catechism?— If there were any necessary relation between religious and secular instruction, which required that they should be kept together, the subject would have another aspect.[161]

To conclude this section on the opinions of professional educators and other thinkers, we shall summarize the deliberations of two conventions of educational associations. From October 17 to 19, 1849 the "National Convention of the Friends of Common School Instruction" was held in Philadelphia. The President of the Convention was Horace Mann. The Vice-Presidents included Joseph Henry of Washington City, John Griscom of New Jersey, Rev. Samuel Lewis of Ohio, Rt. Rev. Alonzo Potter of Pennsylvania and Greer B. Duncan of Louisiana.

The School Commissioners of Baltimore sent Dr. John F. Monmonier, Rev. J. N. M'Jilton and Thomas M. Abbett as delegates. In their published *Report* to their local Board, the following impressions were given of the session on Moral and Religious Instruction:

[160] In "Appendix B" to Benedict's *Religion in Public Schools* notice is taken of another ministerial attack on his ideas, a book by the Rev. George B. Cheever, *The Right of the Bible in our Public Schools* (Benedict, *op. cit.*, pp. 25–26).

[161] Benedict, *Religion in Public Schools*, p. 16.

Not less important than the proper training of the mental and physical faculties, was regarded the education of the heart. . . . A large number of the gentlemen . . . declared that in the training of the child a course of moral and religious instruction is indispensable. Upon the propriety and necessity of such training all were agreed, but in the way it was to be accomplished an almost insuperable difficulty was presented. The exceptionable feature was traced to the instructor and appeared in the impropriety of his imparting his own religious views to his charge. From every portion of the country represented, we heard that efforts had been made to instill virtuous sentiments into the young mind, by the reading of the Scriptures in the schools and the study of appropriate moral lessons; but no systematic attempt in our country was known to have been successful in giving instruction of a religious character. It was stated by the delegate from Canada that in the Normal School at Toronto, of which he was principal, religious instruction was given privately at the school by the ministers of the different denominations to which the pupils belonged. The creed of each was taught by their own religious instructors.[162]

The delegates went on to report that the example of teachers was considered a powerful moral stimulus. As to the Scriptures, all agreed that a portion should be read each day, "but no particular religious exercises were suggested." [163] Then the Baltimoreans gave their own reactions:

With us it must be admitted, that there has not been sufficient effort to educate the moral nature of youth. The fear of sectarian bias has deterred us from our duty in this important relation. The subject is one of the most interesting and important character, involving the highest duties of mankind in their relation to God and to each other, and it should be well examined, and if possible a plan digested upon which the moral and religious training of our pupils may be effected.[164]

Following this the delegates expressed a confidence that something might be done:

[162] John F. Monmonier, J. N. M'Jilton and Thomas M. Abbett, *Report of the Delegation Appointed by the Commissioners of the Public Schools of Baltimore to Represent the Board in the National Convention of the Friends of Common School Instruction* (Baltimore: The Publication Rooms, 1849), pp. 16–17.

[163] *Ibid.*, p. 17.

[164] *Ibid.*

It is doubtless possible for a teacher to instruct the children under his care in the practice of virtue and morality without giving his instructions a sectarian bias. The greatest difficulty in the case is to secure the right sort of teachers, and it is not a little strange that it should be so. It is that wonderful a person entrusted with the education of the youthful mind can engage in the constant duty of scholastic instruction without feeling as it were the divinity striving within him, and impelling him to the discharge of an obligation so full of interest and of such high consideration. Legislation upon this subject by our Board, if dispassionately, thoughtfully and seriously conducted, would certainly result in good.[165]

The second convention was that of the "American Association for the Advancement of Education" held in New York City in 1855.[166] A Professor Charles Davies offered the following resolution:

> *Resolved,* That the sentiments expressed by our late President, Prof. Bache, in his recent address, that moral and religious instruction should form a prominent element in all our systems of public education, is in accordance with the firm belief and earnest convictions of this Association.[167]

Among the first speakers was the Rev. Dr. Talmadge of Georgia. The Report gives his remarks in the indirect discourse form:

> . . . That as he was the only delegate from the several Southern Atlantic States he felt called upon to say that in that section the great question of religious education was becoming an absorbing topic. They were beginning to feel that intellectual education was a curse, unless moral and religious education go with it, and he therefore desired an expression of opinion on the subject, by the Association.[168]

Bishop Potter then arose to urge caution as to the resolution, warning against the danger that its adoption might imply an approval of sectarianism in public education. This drew applause.

[165] *Ibid.,* pp. 17–18.
[166] Cf. "Moral and Religious Instruction in Public Schools, Report of a Discussion before the American Association for the Advancement of Education, at New York, in 1855," *American Journal of Education,* II (July, 1856), 153–72.
[167] *Ibid.,* p. 153.
[168] *Ibid.,* p. 154.

After further discussion it was moved to change the statement to read:

> *Resolved,* That the recognition by our late President, Prof. Bache, in his retiring address, of the preeminent importance of moral and religious culture in the training of youth, meets upon the part of this Association with the profoundest sympathy and approbation.[169]

A Mr. Randall then spoke in favor of returning to the original statement, saying that in view of the way religion was taught (Bible reading, the Lord's prayer and hymn singing) "Gentlemen need entertain no apprehension of sectarian danger." [170] Randall then observed that, apropos of the change from the first resolution, saying "public education," to the second, substituting "the training of youth," at a recent meeting of the New York State Teachers' Convention at Utica, it was advocated "that the religious and the moral element ought not to enter into our systems of public instruction; that religious teaching and moral teaching should be left to the family and to the Church." [171] Randall declared himself opposed to the Utica statement, saying that "the idea is very prevalent throughout the country, that intellectual teaching alone . . . is not the sort of teaching which should be given in our seminaries of learning." [172]

A Dr. McElligott then moved to amend the amendment as follows:

> *Resolved,* That appropriate portions of the Holy Scripture ought daily to be read in all schools and other institutions devoted to secular education, as a public recognition of the Divine Authority of the Bible, as a confirmation of the religious teachings which the pupils are always presumed elsewhere to receive, and as a means of diffusing directly from their source the wholesome influences of sound morality.[173]

Later a Mr. Clark from New Orleans stated that it would be impossible to get even Dr. McElligott's resolution approved in

[169] *Ibid.,* p. 156.
[170] *Ibid.*
[171] *Ibid.,* p. 159.
[172] *Ibid.*
[173] *Ibid.,* p. 160.

all parts of the country, because some would say that the reading of the Bible, especially the King James Version, was sectarian. After this "President Tappan" offered a set of substitute resolutions:

> *Resolved,* That the sentiments expressed in the remarks of Prof. Bache . . . that religion and morality constitute the foundation and best part of education—is worthy alike of the Christian and the man of science.
>
> *Resolved,* That this Association, on endorsing this sentiment mean to indicate thereby their full belief that the most perfect harmony exists between the Word and the works of God; that the scientific and erudite theologian who expounds the first, and the devout and reverent philosopher who investigates the history and laws of the second, cannot essentially differ, but must move toward the same end, for the good of man and the glory of God.[174]

Bishop Potter then rose to say that he regretted the division of opinion among the members and doubted that it was proper for them to pass any resolutions at all. He thought they should do no more than exchange views in meetings of the Association and that they should not fall to wrangling.

A Professor Agnew then moved that consideration of the whole subject be indefinitely postponed. This was rejected and "On motion of Mr. Scott, the resolution (with amendments) was laid upon the table." [175]

One sees in the progress of this meeting a mirroring of the entire fate of religion in American public education. Strong at the beginning, it gradually weakens and becomes more vague, until there is little or nothing tangible left. The reader will not miss the cause—fear of sectarianism.

Convictions on Sectarianism in Public Education

It has become evident already that the clergymen, educators and other American leaders quoted in this chapter were opposed

[174] *Ibid.,* pp. 168–69.
[175] *Ibid.,* p. 172.

to sectarian teaching in public education. While giving their declarations that religion belongs in public life and that it should (or should not) be found in public schools, it would have been impossible to filter out their pronouncements on sectarianism without hopelessly confusing a picture already difficult to present. In some of the thirteen original states this feeling on sectarianism crystallized, as happened in Massachusetts, by the passing of laws which prohibited its inculcation in the common schools.

Before considering these laws, however, brief notice will be taken of one clergyman's views which favored, rather than opposed, such sectarian teaching. Late in 1852 an exchange of letters, later published in pamphlet form, appeared in the *Presbyterian Banner* of Philadelphia. The correspondents were A. B. Brown and Rev. John Maclean, D.D.[176] In a postscript to the second letter, Maclean addressed the editor of the *Banner,* offering thoughts on the relation of Church and State to schools:

> For the common school in any given district, let the people resident in that district select a sufficient number of suitable persons to act for them, and let the persons so chosen prescribe the course of instruction in the common school; and direct what religious exercises and teaching shall take place in the school. As the condition of its aid in maintaining the school, the State should merely require, that the teachers be competent, and that no children be excluded from the privileges of the school, on account of their own religious sentiments, or those of their parents. If the several Churches are satisfied with the extent and character of the religious teaching, let them give their countenance to the school; and in this way, without interference with the rights of conscience, and without any direct joint action both the State and the Church may aid in that all important work of training the youth of our land.[177]

Admitting that cases might arise, where a majority might force its convictions to the detriment of religious minorities, Maclean would stick to his plan as preferable to the greater evil, "the mischief that must inevitably result from the entire neglect of reli-

[176] A. B. Brown and Rev. John Maclean, D.D., *Letters on the True Relations of Church and State to Schools and Colleges* (Princeton: John T. Robinson, 1853).
[177] *Ibid.,* p. 17.

gious instruction in our common schools." [178] If cases of real violation of conscience should result, he suggested that the parents could decide whether or not to remove the children from the school. "To our apprehension," he continued,

> it would be better in some cases, for the children to be kept from the common school, than to subject them, on the one hand, to the danger of unsound religious teaching; or to expose them, on the other, to the evil of being practically taught, that religion has nothing to do with the practical affairs of life. It is the interest of the State as well as the interest of the Church, that the youth should be taught to believe and feel, that the highest of all duties, is to love and fear God: yet, in laying down principles to guide a community in matters of education, it would be impossible for any man, or set of men, to devise a scheme that would be free from all objection. Our aim, therefore, must be to adopt a system that shall combine in itself the greatest amount of good to the entire community, with the least degree of interference with individual rights. [179]

Attention will now be given to the laws which were passed against sectarianism in the common schools. Two studies, noted earlier, [180] have been made on this subject. The schema on p. 242 has been adapted from the table of Burton Confrey's study reproduced in Chapter I. [181] Here the legislation of the thirteen original colonies is indicated in the three categories of sectarian instruction, sectarian textbooks and use of the Bible.

Thus legislation was passed on sectarianism (Columns I and II), during the period under study, in four of the original thirteen states: Massachusetts, New Hampshire, New York and Virginia. The Massachusetts legislation has already been considered. [182] The New Hampshire law is almost identical with the Massachusetts proviso:

No book shall be directed to be used as a school book which is

[178] *Ibid.*, pp. 17–18.
[179] *Ibid.*, pp. 18–19.
[180] Cf. *supra*, pp. 4–5.
[181] Permission has been granted by The Catholic University of America Press in Washington, D. C., to use this material.
[182] Cf. *supra*, Chaps. iv, v.

Schema of Legislation on Religious Instruction in the Thirteen Original States (Adapted from Confrey)

	I	II	III
	Forbidding Sectarian Instruction in Public Schools	Forbidding Use of Sectarian Books. Penalizing Teacher or School Using Them	Forbidding, Authorizing or Requiring Bible Use
Connecticut			
Delaware			
Georgia		FP-1895	A-1895
			R-1922
Maryland		F-1872	
Massachusetts ..		F-*1827** F-*1855**	R-*1855** A-1862
		F-*1835** F-1859	R-1859 A-1866
		F-1862	A-1882 A-1901
New Hampshire .		F-*1842** F-1895	
New Jersey			A-1894
			A-1900
New York	F-*1842** F-*1851**	F-*1843** F-1882	A-*1844**
	F-*1844**	F-*1844**	A-*1850**
North Carolina ..		F-1873 F-1905	
		F-1881	
Pennsylvania ...			A-1885
			A-1898
			R-1913–Penalty
Rhode Island ...			
South Carolina...	F-1871	F-1870	
Virginia	F-*1847**	F-*1847**	
		F-*1849**	

* The dates italicized fall within the compass of the present study.

calculated to favor any particular religious or political sect or tenet.[183]

The Virginia statutes appear not to have been state laws but provisions for individual counties. Under the heading "No sectarian instruction in public schools," Confrey gives the following:

[183] *Revised Statutes,* 1842, Chap. 73, Sec. 12, as quoted by Confrey, *op. cit.,* p. 88. Confrey notes (*ibid.*) that the law was repeated in the *Compiled Statutes* of 1853, Chap. 77, Sec. 13.

THE TWO TRADITIONS IN THE OTHER STATES   243

Amending an Act of Feb. 25, 1846, for the counties of Loudon, Fairfax, and Kanawah, an act of the following year prohibits the giving of any instruction in the public schools which shall favor the tenets of any religious sect or denomination. *Session Laws of* 1846–7, Ch. 33, Sec. 5, Act March 10, 1847.[184]

Under the heading "No sectarian texts permitted," Confrey writes:

The Act referred to in the preceding paragraph [Sectarian Instruction Proviso given above] included: "No books shall be used nor instruction in the public schools calculated to favor the doctrinal tenets of any religious sect or denomination."

Amending an Act of Feb. 25, 1846, establishing Free Schools in the Counties of Frederick and Jefferson, we find the provision: "No books of an immoral or irreligious tendency, and none of a strictly sectarian character shall be used therein." *Session Laws* 1846–7, Ch. 32, Sec. 9, Act March 20, 1847.

"The board may prescribe the methods of instruction and the books to be used, provided, That they shall not be immoral or irreligious in their tendency or of a sectarian character." *Ibid.* 1848–9, Ch. 110, Sec. 9, Act March 14, 1849, establishing free schools in the County of Albemarle.

"No books of an immoral tendency and none of a strictly sectarian or partisan character shall be used therein." *Ibid.* Ch. 110, Sec. 8, Act March 8, 1849, establishing a Free School System in King George County.[185]

Note should be taken of the language used in these county laws of Virginia. Sectarian *instruction,* as well as textbooks, was forbidden. Also, *irreligious instruction and books* were prohibited. There was a breadth to these local laws which was not found in the more famous statute of Massachusetts.

The State of New York enacted laws forbidding sectarian instruction five years earlier than Virginia. Her statutes on sectarian textbooks also antedated Virginia's by four years.[186] The significance of the events leading up to this New York legislation ranks second only to the Massachusetts story in the history of American education. As in the case of the "Bay State," New York's history of religion in public education is filled with controversy over sec-

---

184 Confrey, *op. cit.,* p. 116.
185 *Ibid.* These Virginia laws are also reproduced by Brown, *op. cit.,* p. 75.
186 Cf. Chart, *supra,* p. 242.

tarianism. It has been the object of study in a number of works.[187] Since the heart of the New York affair was a dispute over the use of public funds for religious education, we shall summarize it only, and look for the implications it contains for religion and sectarianism in public education.

As already noted, schooling in New York, both in colonial and early national days, was carried on largely by private societies of a religious nature.[188] From 1795 until 1825 these denominational schools received a certain amount of financial assistance from the State. It was found, however, that these schools, possibly from lack of space and funds, did not take in the children of many New York City parents who were without religious affiliation. Hence, in 1805, a private organization, the "Free School Society," was incorporated for New York City and also shared in state funds. In 1825, as the result of a dispute between the Bethel Baptist Church and the Free School Society, the Common Council of New York enacted an ordinance which deprived all religious schools of state aid. Public money continued to be given to the Free School Society and two or three other minor non-religious groups.[189]

From 1825 to 1840 the Free School Society (which in 1826 legally changed its name to the "Public School Society of New York") continued to receive state aid, and its power and the number of children it taught grew steadily. As incorporated, however, it remained a private organization, "unlike the free common

[187] Cf., e.g., John R. G. Hassard, *Life of The Most Reverend John Hughes, D.D., First Archbishop of New York With Extracts From His Private Correspondence* (New York, D. Appleton and Co., 1866); W. O. Bourne, *History of the Public School Society of the City of New York* (New York: Wm. Wood & Company, 1870); Edwin R. Van Kleek, *The Development of Free Common Schools in New York State—The Campaigns to Eliminate the Rate Bill and to Divert Public Funds from Sectarian Schools* (unpublished Ph.D. thesis; New Haven: Yale University, 1937); Edward M. Connors, *Church-State Relationships in Education in the State of New York* (Washington: The Catholic University of America Press, 1951). The present summary of the controversy of 1840–42 will draw upon Hassard, Van Kleek and Connors and use certain documents published by the participants in the dispute.

[188] Cf. *supra*, pp. 16, 22–23, 67–69, 73–74.

[189] Connors, *op. cit.*, pp. xvii–xviii, 1.

schools in the rest of the state which came under direct state supervision."[190] Quoting from various *Reports* of the Public School Society, Connors shows that they gradually developed a non-denominational type of religious instruction which included reading from the Scriptures.[191]

During the 1830's, as immigration swelled the number of Catholics in New York City, their church leaders began to feel alarm at seeing the number of Catholic children participating in the religious program of the Public School Society. In 1834 Bishop John Dubois of New York made several requests of the Public School Society regarding one of its schools on Mott Street, near his Cathedral. Among other things, he asked for the appointment of a Catholic teacher, the use of the building for after-hours religious instruction, the elimination of certain passages in the textbooks which he considered objectionable, and that he be permitted to visit the school occasionally to make suggestions for improvements to the trustees. The Bishop's petitions were denied by the trustees, although they did promise to remove objectionable passages from the texts. When the Bishop did not press this point further, the matter was dropped without any action.[192]

On January 7, 1840 Governor William H. Seward of New York addressed the Legislature at Albany on the subject of the growing number of children of the immigrants who were pouring into the State. Part of his speech included the following:

> The children of foreigners, found in great numbers in our cities and towns, and in the vicinity of our public works, are too often deprived of the advantages of our system of public education in consequence of prejudices arising from differences of language or religion. It ought never to be forgotten that the public welfare is as deeply concerned in their education as in that of our own children. I do not hesitate, therefore, to recommend the establishment of schools, in which they may be instructed by teachers speaking the same language with them and professing the same faith. . . . Since we have opened our country and all its fullness to the oppressed of every nation,

[190] *Ibid.*, p. 3.
[191] *Ibid.*, pp. 3–5.
[192] *Ibid.*, pp. 12–13.

we should evince wisdom equal to such generosity by qualifying their children for the high responsibilities of citizenship.[193]

The Catholic Church in New York City was by this time under the leadership of Bishop John Hughes. He was in Europe at the time of Seward's speech, but the trustees of the seven Catholic schools in the city, under the leadership of Father John Power, Bishop Hughes' Vicar General, petitioned the Common Council for a share in the school fund.[194] This was protested by the Public School Society and the Commissioners of School Money of New York City. Shortly afterwards, a Presbyterian Church and two Hebrew Congregations also petitioned for school funds. Several Protestant and independent groups in the city entered protests against any such distribution.[195]

The various parties made known their views, and on April 27 the Committee on Arts and Sciences and Schools of the Board of Assistant Aldermen made public their findings in a pamphlet known as "Document 80." [196] The Catholic side was described as follows:

> Objection was made, on the part of the Catholic petitioners, to the public schools now existing and supported from the school fund, on the ground that no religious instruction was communicated there, or if any was given, it was of a character which reflected upon the doctrines of the Catholic Church. The latter branch of this objection was denied on the part of the Public School Society.
> The petitioners, who appeared, also contended that they contributed in common with all other citizens who were taxed for the purpose, to the accumulation of the Common School Fund, and that they were therefore entitled to participate in

[193] William H. Seward, *The Works of William H. Seward,* George E. Baker (ed.) (New York: Redfield, 1853), II, 215–16. The following editor's note is appended to the paragraph quoted: "This portion of the Governor's speech was widely and severely criticized at the time, but the wisdom and justice of its suggestions are now generally acknowledged.—Ed." P. 216.

[194] Hassard notes that "the Common Council were members *ex officiis*" of the Public School Society. (*Op. cit.,* p. 225.)

[195] Connors, *op. cit.,* pp. 17–18.

[196] Board of Assistant Aldermen of New York City, *Report of the Committee on Arts & Sciences & Schools of the Board of Assistants on the Subject of Appropriating a Portion of the School Money to Religious Societies, For the Support of the Schools, (Document 80)* (New York: no pub., 1840).

its advantages; that now they received no benefit from the fund, inasmuch as the members of the Catholic Churches could not conscientiously send their children to schools in which the religious doctrines of their fathers were exposed to ridicule or censure. The truth and justice of the first branch of this proposition cannot be questioned. The correctness of the latter part of the argument, so far as the same relates to books or exercises of any kind in the Public Schools, reflecting on the Catholic Church, was, as is herein before stated, denied by the School Society.[197]

The Committee then presented the point of view of the Public School Society:

On the part of the Public School Society it was contended that any appropriation of the School money, to any religious denomination for the purpose of educating the children of that denomination was foreign to the design of the Common School system, as organized by law, hostile to the spirit of the Constitution, and at variance with the nature of our free institutions.[198]

Commencing their answer, the Aldermen's Committee asked two questions which they considered the basis of a solution:

First—Have the Common Council of this city, under the existing Laws relative to Common Schools in the city of New York, a legal right to appropriate any portion of the School Fund to Religious Corporations?

Second—Would the exercise of such power be in accordance with the spirit of the Constitution and the nature of our government? [199]

On the first point the Committee reviewed the history of the granting of funds to private organizations, such as the religious groups and the Free School Society and the withdrawal of the practice regarding the former in 1824, as a result of the Bethel

[197] *Ibid.*, pp. 337–38.

[198] *Ibid.*, p. 338. It is not clear whether the "Constitution" was meant to signify the state or the national one. (Cf. *infra*, p. 248, Committee's answer.) It is quite clear that the logic of the Society in decrying aid given to non-public institutions such as those of the Catholics, the Presbyterians and the Jews, actually was cutting the ground out from under the basis on which they themselves were receiving aid.

[199] *Ibid.*, pp. 338–39.

Baptist Church controversy. They also noted that power was given to the Common Council in the 1824 Act and asked if any limitation was put on their discretion as to what "Institutions" and "Schools" might in the future be designated as recipients. They concluded that a church is not an "Institution" or "School" and hence they deduced that the 1824 law was meant to exclude churches.[200]

As to the second question, the Committee entered into a ten-page discussion of the propriety of giving public funds to religious societies in the light of the State Constitution. This document, they observed, said that "the free exercise and enjoyment of religious profession and worship, without discrimination or preference, shall be forever allowed, in this State, to all mankind." [201]

The Committee asked whether giving the money as requested by the petitioners would violate this constitutional provision. Recalling the religious controversies of history, they stated that both the Federal Constitution and the State Constitutions had tried to prevent the recurring of this in America by declaring,

> in some form or other, that there should be no establishment of religion by laws; that the affairs of the State should be kept entirely distinct from, and unconnected with, those of the Church; that every human being should worship God, according to the dictates of his own conscience; that all churches and religions should be supported by voluntary contribution; and that no tax should ever be imposed for the benefit of any denomination of religion, for any cause, or under any pretence, whatever. These principles are either expressly declared in the several Constitutions, or arise by necessary implication from the nature of our Governments, and the character of our republican institutions.[202]

Giving money to the petitioners, the Committee then stated, would violate these principles, inasmuch as it would be establishing a preference on the part of the civil authority for one or a small number of religious groups. If the money were made available to all groups, a plan to which they knew the Catholics

200 *Ibid.*, pp. 343–44.
201 *Ibid.*, p. 346. Ref. "Art. 7, Sec. 3d."
202 *Ibid.*, p. 347.

would not object, it would be "repugnant to the principles of our government." If the doctrines

> of all the religious denominations of the state, were taught, in the slightest degree, at the expense of the people, under the authority of law, there would still be a legal religious establishment, not confined to one or a few sects, it is true, but covering many.[203]

It is significant that in the nine remonstrances, (five of them from Protestant Church groups) which were appended to the Committee report, no mention was made of the equal-distribution plan being objectionable. The "single preference" plan was condemned several times. The remonstrance of the Methodist Episcopal Church admitted that several years before it had sought such aid for its own church school and then abandoned the plea in favor of "having the entire system of Common School instruction in the city carried out in one general plan." [204] The Methodists added, however, that if the petition of the Catholics, [Presbyterians and Jews] was granted,

> then we, your memorialists, representing the Methodist Episcopal Church, . . . ask and claim that an equitable proportion of said Public School Fund be appropriated to the Methodist Eipscopal [sic] Church, to enable them to resuscitate their former school, and erect others, to be managed and conducted by them as they, in their discretion, may judge proper.[205]

Bishop Hughes, on returning to New York, took up the contest, and, as a result of a number of meetings with his priests and the trustees of the Catholic Schools, a document was issued under the title, *Address of the Roman Catholics to Their Fellow Citizens of the City and State of New York.*[206] The first point made was that the disregard for religion in the schools of the Public School Society was the encouragement of a special kind of sectarianism. The purpose of the Legislature in appropriating funds to schools

---

[203] *Ibid.,* p. 351.
[204] *Ibid.,* pp. 379–80.
[205] *Ibid.,* p. 380.
[206] *Address of the Roman Catholics to Their Fellow Citizens of the City and State of New York* (New York: Hugh Cassidy, 1840).

must have been (whatever construction the lawyers of the Common Council put upon it) to diffuse the blessings of education among the people, without encroachment on the civil and religious rights of the citizens. . . . This was certainly their general intention, and no other would have justified their bountiful appropriation of the public funds. By carrying out the measure, this patriotic and wise intention has been lost sight of —and in the city of New York at least, under the late arbitrary determination of the present Common Council, such intention of the Legislature is not only disregarded, but the high public ends to which it was directed, are manifestly being defeated.[207]

"Is then, we would ask you, fellow citizens," the *Address* continued, "practical rejection of the Christian religion in all its forms, and without the substitution of any other, the basis on which you would form the principles and character of the future citizens of this great commonwealth?" [208] The statement next emphasized that this

new sectarianism, antagonist [sic] to all *Christian* sects, has been generated in, not the Common schools, as the State originally understood the term, but in the *public* schools of the public school society . . . and is supported, *to the exclusion of all others* at the public expense. Have the conscientious Methodists, Episcopalians, Baptists, Lutherans and others, no scruples of conscience at seeing their children, and the children of their poor, brought up under this new sectarianism? It is not for us to say; but for ourselves we can speak: and we cannot be parties to such a system except by legal compulsion and against conscience.[209]

Later the *Address* turned to list the specific grievances of the Catholics against the curriculum of the schools maintained by the Public School Society:

Besides the introduction of the Holy Scriptures without note or comment, with the prevailing theory that from these even children are to get their notions of religion, contrary to our principles, there were in the class book of those schools, false (as we believe) historical statements respecting the men and things of the past times, calculated to fill the minds of our children with errors of fact, and at the same time to excite in them

207 *Ibid.*, p. 4.
208 *Ibid.*
209 *Ibid.*, p. 6.

prejudice against the religion of their parents and guardians. These passages were not considered as sectarian, inasmuch as they had been selected as mere reading lessons, and were not in *favor* of any particular sect, but merely against the Catholics. We feel it is unjust that such passages should be taught at all, in schools to the support of which we are contributors, as well as others. But that such books should be put into the hands of our own children, and that in part at our own expense, was in our opinion, unjust, unnatural, and at all events, to us intolerable.[210]

The Catholics concluded by explaining that, in view of the above, they had been forced to open their own schools and for the support of these they wanted a share in the public funds. Pointing out that they were contending for "liberty of conscience and freedom of education," they held that "the laws of nature, of religion, of the very Constitution of the country, secure to parents the right of superintending the education of their own children." [211] The document was signed by Bishop Hughes and eight laymen.

After the *Address* was circulated the Public School Society offered to alter the textbooks in such a way as to remove passages objectionable to Catholics. Bishop Hughes, however, showed little willingness to cooperate, as he seemed to feel that any such effort would be fruitless and would not solve the basic problem involved—the carrying on of schools which fostered a spirit of sectarian indifference. "As if we have nothing to do," the Bishop declared,

> but to mark out a passage, and it will disappear! Are we to take the odium of erasing passages which you hold to be true? And have you any right to make such an offer? If we spend the necessary time in reviewing the books to discover offensive passages, you give us no pledge that you will even then remove the objectionable matter. . . . And even if you should remove it, another board of officers may succeed you tomorrow and restore every thing that you have marked out.[212]

Protestant reaction, both to the *Address* and to the report that the Public School Society had submitted its texts to Bishop

210 *Ibid.*, p. 10.
211 *Ibid.*, p. 13.
212 Hassard, *op. cit.*, p. 238.

Hughes for revision, was violent. Although it seems clear that Hughes actually did not accept the plan, Rev. Charles Hodge, writing fourteen years later, in the article, "The Education Question" [213] lamented the supposed fact:

> To what an abyss of degradation was the Empire State led down by her puny politicians, when she submitted all her school books to be expurgated by Bishop Hughes! . . . May this infamy remain ever without a parallel, and may those blackened books be soon committed to the flames, and replaced by others luminous with Protestant Christianity! Nothing short of this can ever efface the stigma which mars the lofty brow of that great state.[214]

Meanwhile, Bishop Hughes continued his campaign and demanded a hearing before the Common Council. His request was granted and all parties, *pro* and *con,* were invited to appear on October 29, 1840. Lawyers represented the Public School Society, ministers represented the Protestant Churches and Hughes himself spoke on the other side for the Catholic cause. For two days the speeches went on and often left the question of education for incursions into theology and church history. The Common Council then asked that the interested parties submit written opinions. Their final decision, rendered January 11, 1841, rejected the Catholic petition for state funds.[215]

Undaunted, Bishop Hughes prepared to appeal to the Legislature at Albany. When the members of the Legislature received the Catholic petition they referred it to John C. Spencer, the Secretary of State and, *ex officio,* Superintendent of Common Schools. The Secretary recommended to the Legislature that the Public School Society not receive so much of the public funds as they were getting, and that a system of local option be allowed in public schools on the question of religious instruction. According to this the local school district could work out a system suitable to the parents whose children attended the schools.[216]

As elections were due, the Legislature postponed considera-

---

[213] Cf. *supra,* p. 193, footnote 9.
[214] Hodge, *op. cit.,* p. 536.
[215] Connors, *op. cit.,* pp. 24–28.
[216] *Ibid.,* pp. 31–32.

tion of the problem until after November. Meanwhile both sides continued to agitate the school question and to try to get members elected to the Legislature who would favor their particular view. When the lawmakers reconvened in January, 1842, Governor Seward's opening address indicated the heart of the education problem to be:

> . . . Whether it is wiser and more human to educate the offspring of the poor, than to leave them to grow up in ignorance and vice; whether juvenile vice is more easily eradicated by the court of sessions than by the common schools; whether parents have a right to be heard concerning the instruction and instructors of their children, and taxpayers in relation to the expenditure of public funds; whether in a republican government it is necessary to interpose an independent corporation between the people and the school-master, and whether it is wise and just to disfranchise an entire community of all control over public education, rather than suffer a part to be represented in proportion to its numbers and contributions. Since such considerations are now involved, what has hitherto been discussed as a question of benevolence and of universal education, has become one of equal civil rights, religious tolerance, and liberty of conscience.[217]

William B. Maclay, an assemblyman from New York City, then drew up a bill which aimed to solve the school problem by applying Spencer's philosophy of local educational control. The Public School Society was to lose its power over the school fund and local ward commissioners were to be elected and given power over the educational institutions in their territory. The bill passed the House, but in the Senate it was approved only after a section had been inserted which provided that:

> No school above mentioned, or which shall be organized under this act, in which any religious, sectarian doctrine shall be taught, inculcated or practiced, shall receive any portion of the school moneys to be distributed as hereinafter provided; and it shall be the duty of the trustees, inspectors, and the commissioners of schools in each ward, and of the deputy superintendent of schools, from time to time and as frequently as need be, to examine and ascertain, and report to the said board of education whether any religious sectarian doctrine or

[217] Seward, *Works,* II, 309.

tenet shall have been taught, inculcated or practiced in their respective wards.—67th *Session,* Ch. 150, Sec. 14, Act April 11, 1842.[218]

The measure, approved in this form by both Houses, was signed by the Governor and became law, April 9, 1842.[219]

Thus the Maclay Bill was a pyrrhic victory for Bishop Hughes. It broke the power of the Public School Society and relieved him and his people of their anxiety about the type of religious instruction carried on in the Society's schools. The law, however, dashed the Bishop's hopes of getting state help for the parochial schools he was building to give Catholic children the education he felt they must have. Bishop Hughes' motivation seems clearly to have been a conscientious belief that he must get the Catholic children away from the type of religious instruction they were receiving from the Public School Society. Of their claims to teach religion without sectarianism he had said, "But if you exclude all sects, you exclude Christianity. Take away the distinctive dogmas of the Catholics, the Baptists, the Methodists, the Presbyterians, and so on, and you have nothing left but deism." [220] Compromise would not do. It had to be a complete change. If he could get public funds, to which he believed he had a right, so much the better. But in any case, he must get for Catholic children a Catholic education. Without intending it, Bishop Hughes by his campaign, opened the way for elimination of religious instruction of any sort in New York's Public Schools. It should be remembered that this, too, was based on an opposition to sectarianism.

The motivation of the Protestant leaders in the New York controversy seems to have been tinged with more than a little fear of the rising importance of the Catholic Church. It is clear that in the early years of the century New York Protestants sought and welcomed state aid, that they might educate their children in the tenets of their faith, as did their fellow citizens of the Catholic

---

[218] Confrey, *op cit.,* p. 93. Confrey notes (*ibid.*) that the wording of the law was changed in 1844 to "But no school shall be entitled to a portion of the school moneys in which the religious sectarian doctrine or tenet of any particular Christian, or other religious sect shall be taught, inculcated or practiced." (67th *Session,* Chap. 320, Sec. 12, Act May 7, 1844.)

[219] Connors, *op. cit.,* p. 42.

[220] Hassard, *op. cit.,* p. 226.

persuasion. In those days, as Van Kleeck puts it, "there seemed to be implicit acceptance of the principle that the parent was primarily responsible for the education of children." [221] Van Kleeck thinks that Protestants, however, changed their mind on this

> . . . when they saw which sect was inevitably headed toward supremacy in that field of schooling. Some of the Protestants preferred their own parochial schools to public schools; others were willing to support public schools, provided there was in them a degree of religious teaching of a non-sectarian nature. Both groups were quick to seize upon the refuge of public education, entirely non-sectarian, when they saw that, through very numbers, the Catholics could outdo them in the parochial field. In a word, the Protestants disliked secularism, but they disliked the Pope more. . . .[222]

In its broad outlines, the New York controversy appears a conformable link in the chain of overall American educational history. None of the parties involved was found denying the value and importance of a religious education. Sectarian teaching in the public schools, including the "sectarianism" of infidelity, was condemned all down the line, and both sides appealed to the principles of religious freedom to back up their stand. The various leaders groped for a solution to the problem, as had been done earlier in Massachusetts. The difference in New York was that Bishop Hughes and the members of his church were not satisfied, as Horace Mann and his opponents seem to have been, that the method of "to each his own" was utterly beyond consideration. To implement the plan of separate education, to which his conscience impelled him, Hughes tried to obtain a share of public funds and failed. In New York, as in Virginia and New Hampshire, the legal tradition against sectarianism in education started by Massachusetts, was spreading. The laws looked to freedom of conscience. Men strove to conserve what they held dear. The result, unforeseen, and, apparently unwanted, was a further and further decline of the amount of religious training given the American children who go to public schools.

[221] Van Kleek, *op. cit.*, p. 162.
[222] *Ibid.*, pp. 162–63. Cf. also Ray Allen Billington, *The Protestant Crusade, 1800–1860* (New York: The Macmillan Co., 1938), pp. 154–56.

CHAPTER VII

Attempts at Solving the Problem

IN THIS FINAL PART of the study attention will be given to the solution or solutions which were arrived at by the groups discussed in the preceding chapter. In the case of Massachusetts, it has been seen, the ideals of Horace Mann were adopted. Instruction in the doctrines of the older Protestant groups disappeared, but the conviction that "religion belonged" did not. In Mann's eyes, ethics, natural theology and Bible reading kept the schools "religious." Now the question is asked—How did it work out in the other original states? [1]

An effort will be made to tell the story as it developed up to the Civil War. This seems to be more than an arbitrary date. The nation then entered its most serious struggle for survival. After the war, reconstruction and adjustment opened new eras in American life. It will be valuable to know to what extent reli-

---

[1] It is *surmised* that the influence of Horace Mann outside Massachusetts was considerable in the area of religious education in public schools. His reports were widely circulated. The respect he commanded is shown by his presiding over the education convention mentioned in Chap. vi (*supra,* p. 235). Knight's *Documentary History of Education in the South,* Volume V, devotes a chapter to the "Evidence of Interest in the South in the Work of Joseph Lancaster, Horace Mann and Henry Barnard, 1818–1859" (pp. 317–81). At p. 373 there is a letter dated in 1856 to Mann from a Nereus Mendenhall asking how to present to children "our relations to the Good Spirit and the future life." But no answer from Mann is reproduced. But this study uncovered no evidence that the ideals of "the father of the public school system" *directly* influenced religious policies in the other states which had been colonies.

gious teaching could still be said to have a part in the public school program at the time of the great conflict.

The Protestant Solution

Historically speaking, the Protestants of America could view the common school as something of their own creation. In colonial times the great majority of schools were their religious foundations. In the early national period this pattern continued and the local unit, the district, as an entity distinct from an unestablished church, took over in the field of elementary education until approximately the first quarter of the nineteenth century had passed. Then, when the movement for centralization of authority commenced, the control of the common school began to pass away from the district authorities. This meant a further decrease in the control and the influence of the Protestant church groups. It seems that Protestant leaders did not react unfavorably to this until they began to see doctrinal religion disappearing from the classroom. As has been seen, several violent reactions occurred in Massachusetts, but in the long run opposition proved ineffective. By the end of Horace Mann's Secretaryship, the common schools of the Bay State could hardly be called Protestant schools, in the sense that they taught Protestant doctrine. Yet the Protestants of Massachusetts seemed satisfied with them.

But was this Protestant complacency characteristic of all the thirteen original states? Writings like those of Frederick Packard and the Rev. Charles Hodge would indicate a negative answer. These men wanted the common school to remain not only Christian but Protestant Christian. Some of them, especially Dr. Hodge, became so alarmed at the prospect of the diminishing religious influence of the common school that they incited movements to found separate systems of Protestant parochial schools.[2]

[2] Dr. Charles Hodge, who was quoted extensively *supra*, pp. 191–96, was a leading spirit in the "Old School" Presbyterian movement. Hodge turned to the parochial school idea because he saw religious doom in the curriculum of the common school of his day. One of Hodge's most bitter opponents within the Presbyterian ranks was the Rev. R. J. Breckenridge. Cf., e.g., his article, "Denominational Education," *Southern Presbyterian Review*, III (1849), 1–19.

This American Protestant activity in establishing elementary schools is described in Curran's *The Churches and the Schools*.[3] Limiting ourselves to the years before the Civil War, we summarize the author's findings as follows:

The Episcopalians, members of the Reformed Churches, Quakers, Presbyterians and Lutherans all made efforts to have parochial elementary schools at one time or another in the first half of the nineteenth century. Most of these were located in the thirteen original states. With the exception of the Quakers (whose schools lasted until the opening of the present century, and some still survive) all of these groups had abandoned their attempts by the end of the Civil War or very shortly thereafter.

The Congregationalists, Methodists and Baptists, on the other hand, made no attempt to start their own elementary schools. In their minds, education was the function of the State rather than the Church. Such religion as was taught in the public schools could be supplemented by instruction in the church and home.

After mentioning lack of teachers, money and pupils as the immediate causes of the decline of the Protestant elementary schools, Father Curran gives what he believes are the fundamental reasons:

> These more radical causes appear to have been a lack of strong interest in parochial schools, a lack of strong leadership to create and sustain that interest, and, more fundamental still, a lack of strong faith in the teachings of their churches which would have impelled Protestants to see that faith was inculcated in their children in schools under the control of their churches.[4]

Another reason for a lack of interest in Protestant parochial schools, as Curran notes,[5] was the satisfaction with which many Protestants viewed the developing common schools. These may not have realized the extent to which the schools were being secularized, or, if they realized it, they may have felt that their Sunday schools, and home instruction, plus Bible reading in the

[3] Cf. *supra*, pp. 203–04. Cf. Chaps. ii–vii of Father Curran's Study.
[4] Curran, *op. cit.*, p. 129.
[5] *Ibid.*, p. 130.

public schools, were adequately teaching religion to their children.

Reliance upon the Bible as the sole criterion of faith is one of the most fundamental dogmas of Protestantism. Added to this is the principle of "private judgment." Many Protestants believe that the Holy Spirit will illumine the mind of the individual as to what God wishes him to understand from the passage which he is reading. No authoritative interpreter on this earth, acting as God's commissioned representative, is necessary or desirable.[6]

In the light of these two dogmas one can understand the earnest desire upon the part of Protestants that the child hear the Scriptures, and hear them directly. Many Protestants would, perhaps, feel that, if a thorough program of Bible reading could be maintained in the common schools, not only would this be enough in the way of a religious instruction program, but it would be sufficient to insure the continuance of the public schools as essentially Protestant institutions. Actually there is evidence to show that there were some Protestants who, rejecting the idea of Protestant parochial schools, pressed for Bible reading as the solution of the dilemma—keep religion in the schools, but keep sectarian indoctrination out. How ardently this concept was championed by Horace Mann has already been shown in Chapter V. It has also been noted in Chapter VI that many of the Protestant leaders who advocated religion in education made specific reference to Bible reading as the means by which such instruction could and should be given.[7] A few more examples will now be cited.

In October, 1831, a report was given to the Literary Convention at New York on the "Propriety of Studying the Bible in the Institutions of a Christian Country." [8] Here the Scriptures were extolled for their literary value, but their religious value was

[6] Cf. Winfred E. Garrison, *A Protestant Manifesto* (New York: Abingdon-Cokesbury Press, 1952), pp. 20, 70.

[7] Cf. *supra*, pp. 192, 197, 200, 221–22, 223.

[8] Wm. C. Woodbridge (Chairman), *Report of the Committee on the Propriety of Studying the Bible in the Institutions of a Christian Country, Presented to the Literary Convention at New York, October, 1831* (Boston: Allen & Ticknor; New York: Joshua Leavitt; 1832).

implied and considered non-sectarian. Included in the resolutions passed at the same meeting was the phrase

> . . . that the study of its contents ought to form a part of common education.[9]

One of the great proponents of Biblical reading in common schools was the Rev. Horace Bushnell, a liberal Congregationalist of Hartford, Connecticut. In an 1840 article,[10] he decried the lack of interest in public schools on the part of the clergy. "The great point with all Christians," he concluded,

> must be to secure the bible its proper place. To this as a sacred duty all sectarian aims must be sacrificed. Nothing is more certain than that no such thing as a sectarian religion is to find a place in our schools. It must be enough to find a place for the bible as a book of principles, as containing the true standards of character and the best motives and aids to virtue. If any Christian desires more, he must teach it himself at home. To insist that the state shall teach the rival opinions of sects and risk the loss of all instruction for that, would be folly and wickedness together.[11]

Writing in the *American Journal of Education* for March, 1856, under the title "Moral Education," the Rev. Charles Brooks [12] of Medford, Massachusetts, offered four ways by which moral instruction could be given in our country where "it is forbidden by law to teach sectarian dogmas in public schools; but not forbidden to teach morals." Of the four ways in which morals can be taught, ("By the parents, by teachers, by books and by discussions") Brooks included Scripture reading and prayer under the section on teachers. The Scriptures should be read each morning, "and no school should ever be opened without reading them."

[9] *Ibid.*, p. 2.
[10] Rev. Horace Bushnell, "Christianity and Common Schools," *Common School Journal of Connecticut,* ɪɪ (January 15, 1840), 102.
[11] *Ibid.*
[12] Rev. Charles Brooks, "Moral Education," *American Journal of Education,* ɪ (March, 1856), 336–44. Other articles in the *American Journal of Education* which have a similar theme include: Z. Richards, "Discipline—Moral and Mental," ɪ (Aug., 1855), 107–19; Rt. Rev. George Burgess, "Thoughts on Religion and Public Schools," ɪɪ (Dec., 1856), 562–67; and Gideon F. Thayer, "Letters to a Young Teacher—Moral Education," ɪɪɪ (March, 1857), 71–80.

When the teacher leads their devotions (and this service should always follow the reading of God's holy word) continued the author,

> he will take great pains to pray like a child, and not like a man; and in all religious services he will be specially moved by brevity and humiliation, by earnestness and simplicity to touch the deepest fountain of feeling in his pupils. By this reading of the Scriptures and offering of prayer he will teach them that they should begin every thing with God; that they should never plan what they dare not ask him to aid, and never do what they may not ask him to approve.[13]

When he came to the subject of books, the Rev. Mr. Brooks had this to say: "The Bible should occupy the first place in the schools. Whether it should or should not be introduced is a question I would not consent to entertain; for, if God's own word is not to be read by his children, I know of no book that should be." [14]

In the second of the undated pamphlets of the Rev. R. S. Rust noted above,[15] we find mention of four "agencies" by which religion could be taught in public schools: the Christian teacher, the Bible, prayer and vocal music. The Bible content would include material "which all denominations recognize . . . the existence of God, the ten commandments, the golden rule, reverence for God and his law, salvation through the mediation of Christ, the love of truth, justice and mercy, and purity in thought, word and act." [16]

Thus the Protestants who did not wish to have their own parochial schools seem to have decided to base their hopes of religion in the public schools mainly on Bible reading, and to a lesser extent, on Protestant prayers. The confidence they felt was based on the feeling that Bible reading was a fundamental form of Protestant indoctrination which would avoid conflicts and the charge of sectarianism among Protestant groups. Bible reading also served as a historical link with the earlier days when the

---

13 *Ibid.*, p. 339.
14 *Ibid.*, p. 340.
15 Cf. *supra*, p. 202, footnote 43.
16 Rust, *op. cit.*, p. 2.

common schools were actually under the control of local Protestant bodies.

The Catholic Solution

The years between 1825 and 1860 saw a tremendous expansion of the Catholic Church in the United States. Most of the increase of population was due to immigration, especially from Ireland and Germany. Along with the immigrants came priests, brothers and sisters from the home countries. The great problem of the Bishops was to conserve the faith among these hundreds of thousands of people, as they settled themselves to a life in the New World.

Added to the intrinsic difficulties of alien customs, and (in the case of such groups as the Germans) of a foreign language barrier, the immigrants and their leaders faced a hostile Protestant population already established in America. Waves of bigotry poured upon the heads of the new arrivals. From time to time feelings burst into open rioting, as was the case in the burning of the Ursuline Convent in Charlestown, Massachusetts in 1834; the destruction of Catholic church buildings in Philadelphia in 1844; and the Know-Nothing and similar Nativist phenomena of the same period.[17]

When the student of American educational history turns to the feelings and activities of the Catholic Bishops in the first half of the nineteenth century, he must keep in mind the ideas set forth in the preceding paragraphs. The Catholic Church had a special task to perform. She had to hold the faith in her people, and hold the line against bigotry until the older American group got over their resentment and fears, and allowed the new American citizens to take the place in the nation's life to which they were entitled by the laws of the land.

When the Bishops turned to the problem of schooling, they based their thinking on the traditional position of their Church

[17] Cf. Billington, *op. cit.*

that the primary right and duty of education lies with the parents.[18] Along with this the Bishops reminded their people of the Church's divine commission to teach religious truth.[19] In discharging his duty to educate his children, the Catholic parent was told that he must seek the guidance of the Church in matters of faith and morals and even in secular branches of learning, insofar as their inculcation might redound to the interest or harm of religion and his children's spiritual life.

In the given situation of Catholics in America in the first half of the nineteenth century, then, one finds the Bishops striving for a solution of the education question in the specific framework of the times. This material was reviewed in the previous chapter.[20] First, they counted upon religious instruction in the home and in the Church. While they always held to the theory that an education completely under Church auspices is best, and fostered it where they could with the building of Church schools, they did not condemn the public school as such. Some hope seems to have been entertained, at least by Bishop Carroll in the last years of the eighteenth century, that an agreeable plan might be worked out for schools of a non-denominational type which could be supported by all citizens and which Catholic children could attend.

As time went on, however, the Bishops grew uneasy about the education situation as it was working out in practice. The textbooks used in the common schools and which, presumably, were

---

[18] Cf. *supra, passim,* pp. 204 ff .

[19] "The Saviour of the world commissioned his apostles to teach 'all nations' of the earth, during 'all days, even to the consummation of the world' promising that he would 'always be with them'; (Matt. 27:19, 20) . . . they were thereby constituted a tribunal competent and commissioned to testify the revelation of God to the whole human race, to the consummation of the world (Matt. 16:18, 19; Matt. 28, 19; Mark 16:15; Luke 24:46–49; John 14:16, 17, 26; John 16:13; Acts 1:8). This tribunal was extended and perpetuated in consequence of the authorized association to their body by the Apostles, of others whom they found duly qualified (Acts 1:21, 22, 25, 26; II Tim. 2:2; Titus 1:5), whom they fitted by ordination to perform the duty (Acts 6:6; Acts 13:2–4; Acts 14:22; I Tim. 4:14; II Tim. 1:6), and to whom they gave the necessary commission by sending them into the field when thus prepared and commissioned (Luke 10:1; John 20:21–23; Acts 13:2–4; Rom. 10:14, 15, 17), etc." "The Pastoral Letter of 1840," Guilday, *Pastorals,* pp. 126–27.

[20] Cf. *supra,* pp. 204 ff.

the only ones available for their own schools, contained slurs and inaccurate statements on Catholic beliefs, practices and history. Attempts were consequently made to put out texts measuring up to Catholic standards of accuracy and adequacy. Moreover, Catholic leaders found themselves growing more and more dissatisfied with the curriculum of the common school itself. In these schools, as they actually operated, Catholic children were reading the Protestant version of the Scriptures, participating in the prayers and hymns of other denominations, studying the objectionable textbooks, and, in the eyes of some, being proselytized into heresy by teachers or others connected with the schools. Fearing, then, for the future of the Catholic Church in America and for the faith of its children which it was their official duty to protect, the Bishops announced in the Council of 1829, and repeated with growing emphasis in the years which followed, their decision to build an elementary school system of their own, and called upon priests and people to support the venturous project.[21]

Meanwhile, the Church leaders were busy providing means to instruct Catholic children in their religion. In the first half of the nineteenth century a number of catechisms, or summaries of the Church's teachings prepared for young minds, were put into print. At the First Plenary Council (1852) a committee was assigned to study the feasibility of preparing an official catechism for all the dioceses of the United States. The Rev. Henry B. Coskery, a Baltimore priest, wrote the report which recalled that as early as 1829 the Bishops of the First Provincial Council had called for such a project in its thirty-third decree.[22] "We would farther [*sic*] respectfully suggest," the report concluded,

[21] The recommendations and pleas of the Councils up to 1852 were repeated in the Second Plenary Council of Baltimore (1866) and finally made church law in the Third Plenary Council of Baltimore in 1884. The Pastoral Letter from the Third Plenary Council stated: "We must multiply them [the parochial schools] till every Catholic child in the land shall have within its reach the means of education. There are still thousands of Catholic children in the United States deprived of the benefit of a Catholic school. Pastors and parents should not rest till this defect be remedied. No parish is complete till it has the schools adequate to the needs of its children, and the pastor and people of such a parish should feel that they have not accomplished their entire duty until the want is supplied." (Guilday, *Pastorals*, pp. 246–47.)

[22] For this decree, cf. *Provincial Councils*, p. 83.

that the extensively & favorably known catechism of the Venerable Archbishop Carroll, after having received some few merely verbal & unimportant emendations, be submitted to the judgement of the Holy See, & that, when approved, a committee be appointed to superintend its publication for general use in this country.[23]

Action on this plan, urged again by the Second Plenary Council (1866) came to fruition only after the Third Plenary Council, and in 1885 there appeared *A Catechism of Christian Doctrine Prepared and Enjoined by Order of the Third Plenary Council of Baltimore.*[24]

The teaching of Christian doctrine was carried on during these years in Sunday School classes for Catholic children in the public schools, and, of course, in the parochial schools themselves. It is interesting to note that the Bishops assigned as a question to be debated in the First Plenary Council whether such instruction should be left entirely in the hands of lay teachers or even of Sisters and Brothers. The answer of the Committee, again written by Father Coskery, was a decided "no." While it was stressed that the writer did not wish to deprecate but rather to encourage the "laudable labors of those zealous persons," he concluded that

the committee are of the opinion that children thus instructed . . . should be frequently examined & taught by the Pastor himself or his assistant—so that they may be certain that this most important of duties is discharged with all possible fidelity, & that the children are *accurately* & *thoroughly* instructed in the religion.[25]

As the Bishops struggled to build up their parochial schools difficulties were encountered from existing or proposed common school systems. The problems of Bishop Hughes in New York City have been examined in the previous chapter. Bishop Francis P. Kenrick of Philadelphia received a letter dated August 8, 1840 from his fellow-Bishop, Benedict Joseph Flaget of Bardstown, Kentucky. Flaget sought Kenrick's advice on a proposal which

[23] AAB, 32B-E-6.
[24] Cf. *The Catholic Encyclopedia*, V, 81.
[25] AAB, 22B-E-2. For the decree (the 12th) by which the Council endorsed this report, cf. *supra*, p. 219, footnote 96.

had been made by the Rev. B. B. Smith, an Episcopalian Bishop and Superintendent of public schools in Kentucky. A copy of the Superintendent's letter was included by Flaget.[26] It contains some interesting proposals:

> My first object is to give assurances on the part of the Board of Education of the state, of their disposition to respect the private religious opinions of all classes of Citizens, and to extend to them the benefits of the public funds, & of the benign operation of the proposed system. Whenever, in any school District the majority of voters are Roman Catholic, the Law leaves all the details in their hands. In mixed Schools, the Board, if desired, will take pleasure in giving instructions that, in the selection of Teachers, regard shall be had as far as practicable, to the known wishes of the Roman Catholics, & that every species of sectarian aggression be strictly prohibited. Arrangements, no doubt, could be made, for separating the children into different classes, if desired; for excusing Roman Catholic children from Protestant prayers; for providing their own translation of the Holy Scriptures for their use, or for excusing them from employing them as a School Book. In case no such understanding should satisfy the Roman Catholic community, & they should altogether decline any participation in the benefits of the proposed System, as one of the Board of Education, I shall be prompt to move the Legislature to relieve our Roman Catholic Fellow Citizens, from the burden of the neighborhood tax, from the advantages of which they may feel themselves excluded; on condition that some security be given for the education of every child of Roman Catholic parents, between the ages 7 & 17 years:—it seeming to me reasonable that the state should insist, that no portion of its population should grow up in ignorance.[27]

Bishop Flaget seems not to have been overimpressed or particularly hopeful about the proposals of the Superintendent. He stated to Kenrick that he was desirous of helping the country

---

[26] AAB, 32A-C-6, Flaget to Kenrick (no place), Aug. 8, 1840.

[27] Bishop Smith's letter to Flaget was accompanied by a covering letter to Father Martin J. Spalding of the diocese of Bardstown (later Archbishop of Baltimore), a copy of which is also included in the letter to Kenrick. In the Spalding letter Bishop Smith is more crisp in his observations about the harm resulting from the lack of education among Catholic rural children, the possibility of the Legislature turning down his request for Catholic tax-exemption, the possibility of a charge that the Catholics were no friends of universal education, etc.

children, but only if he could choose the teachers. Furthermore, he did not want them in schools with children of other faiths or to have them taught by Protestant teachers.[28]

In 1861, Bishop William H. Elder of Natchez wrote to Archbishop Kenrick, then heading the See of Baltimore, to tell of his problem of trying to keep a parish school in operation in the face of competition with the local public institution. "Children prefer the public school," he wrote, "because they have more companions, & they regard it as fashionable. Parents prefer it because they pay taxes for it." [29] So great was Elder's discouragement that he thought of closing his school, but sought the Archbishop's advice on the matter.

So the wearing, discouraging task was continued. No doubt, here and there parochial schools did limp behind the public ones, while in other places they probably excelled. The effort was not allowed to die. The Bishops had decided the parochial school was the answer to their problems, and they continued to build and to improve the system.

Meanwhile, of course, thousands of Catholic children were perforce in attendance at public schools. Among the efforts made to deal with this problem notice has been taken of the campaign of Bishop John Hughes in New York. On the question of Bible reading in the public schools, Catholic leaders formulated a policy of objection to the practice on two scores: the reading without comment, and the reading to Catholic children of a version of the Scriptures which was not approved by the Catholic Church.

Reading the Holy Scriptures without comment, given especially the historical background of the common school, implied acceptance of the principle of private interpretation, even if such

---

[28] "je vous fais passer deux lettres ecrites par un Evêque Anglican B. B. Smith resident a Lexington. il parait desirer que les enfans [sic] pauvres des catholiques puissent participer aux fonds fournis par notre gouvernement pour cette bonne oeuvre. je le desire pareillement, pourvu que je puisse faire enseigner ces enfans par des maitres de mon choix. Mais si nos catholiques doivent être confondus avec tous les petits prot. tants et recevoir leur education d'un Presbiterien ou d'un Lutherien, j'aime mieux [qu'ils renoncent?] [part of letter torn] à cette proposition tout avantageuse qu'elle paraisse. . . ."

[29] AAB, 29–D–11. Elder to Kenrick, Natchez, April 12, 1861.

a dogmatic tenet was not professedly held by the teacher or other person doing the reading. Moreover, the English language edition read in the schools was almost without exception the "King James" Version, generally accepted by all Protestants speaking the English tongue, but not approved by the Catholic Church. In the Pastoral Letter of 1840, after their vindication of the Church's right to teach in the name of God, the Bishops turned to the subject of the Scriptures. In this section they gave their position on both the use of the "King James" Version of the Scriptures, and on "Private Judgement."

Catholics base their acceptance of the Holy Scriptures, they explained, upon the testimony of the Church that a given version of the Bible is a genuine and reliable translation of the original documents. Moreover, Catholics accept the guidance of the Church when interpreting the meaning of the text itself. Hence, an edition of the Bible which did not have such ecclesiastical approbation could not be accepted by Catholics as the "word of God," not because its accuracy would necessarily be questioned, but because it lacked "the requisite evidence from the proper tribunal."

Hence Catholics reject the principle of "private interpretation" on two counts, the Bishops continued: first, the principle denies the commission to teach which Christ gave to the Church, and, second, it assumes that the right to make such interpretations lies with the individual rather than with the Church.[30]

30 "You perceive then, beloved brethren, that we receive the Holy Scriptures upon the testimony of the Church, that it is by her guardianship and her authority, we are assured of their genuineness, their integrity, their purity from corruption, their inspiration, and their original and correct meaning. We therefore profess that we receive the Holy Scriptures in that sense which our holy mother, the Church, to which it belongs to judge of their true sense and meaning, has always held and now holds: neither will we ever take and interpret them except according to the unanimous sense of the fathers.

"But it is not only by additions or multilations [sic—obviously, "mutilations"], or alterations, that the original text may cease to be of value; the sacred books may be corrupted by incorrect translations, and it is therefore necessary, that a responsible and authorised member of the tribunal of the Church, should in her name, vouch for the correctness of the translation, otherwise it is considered of no authority; it may or it may not be correct, but it is not regarded as the word of God, because it does not appear sustained by the proper evidence. All books purporting to be the Holy Bible, or any por-

After this declaration of principles, the Pastoral took up the situation which the Bishops found existing in America, especially in the public schools of their day. They pointed out that the great majority of their fellow-citizens did accept as the word of God translations which lacked the *evidence* which, as they had explained, Catholics require; that these Americans admitted that the churches could err in their interpretation of the Bible's meaning; and that they subscribed to the principle of "private interpretation"—to all of which Catholics could not conscientiously agree. "It is moreover generally prevalent," they continued,

> that in public schools, some one of those versions should be read by the children as the word of God, and frequently that the teacher who is an unauthorised individual, should give his own opinions as its proper interpretation, and that the child should be habituated practically to the principle, that it is the right of each individual to use his own private judgment, and not the public testimony of the Church as the standard of interpretation; whence you will at once perceive, the total opposi-

---

tion thereof, which are published without this testimony, are not regarded by us as the word of God, not that we examine into their correctness or corruption, but upon the plain principle of the total absence of the requisite evidence from the proper tribunal and its proper officer. Thus without pronouncing upon the merits of any translation set forth by the Churches or Societies separated from our communion, we do not receive them as the word of God, precisely upon the ground of total want of the requisite evidence.

"And as it frequently happens that persons who reject the authority of the Church, undertake to expound upon their own private views and judgment the sacred volume, or what they assume to be the word of God, it is clear that whether the interpretation given by them be correct or incorrect, they who sustain or encourage them, do thereby sustain two false principles: first, that it is not criminal to despise the Church, to oppose her authority, and having rejected it, to usurp her commission; the second, that the interpretation of the sacred books, is the right of each individual, and not that of the authorised tribunal which the Saviour established to teach all nations, during all days to the consummation of the world." Guilday, *op. cit.,* pp. 131–34.

It is interesting to find that twenty-four years earlier, the Catholic authorities in London were engaged in making the same points before a Committee of Parliament charged with investigating trouble at schools in the crowded poorer districts of the English Capital. Cf. *On the Education of Roman Catholic Children and the Rejection of the Bible by Their Priests; Chiefly Extracted from the Reports of a Select Committee of the House of Commons, On The Education of the Lower Orders in the Metropolis* (London: Baldwin, Craddock & Joy, 1816).

tion of the principle on which such schools are conducted, to the unchangeable doctrines and discipline of our Church.[31]

Answering the familiar charge that the Catholic Church is opposed to her people learning the Scriptures, the Bishops gave the program they would like to see in operation. They wanted their people well acquainted with the doctrine, as well as the historical data and moral instruction, found in the Bible. To this end they urged Catholics to have a copy of the authorized version of the Scriptures in their homes, to read it and meditate upon it. Parents were instructed to acquaint their children with its contents at an early age. This the children were to learn, not by indiscriminate reading of the parts they would scarcely be able to understand, but by having pointed out to them simple and edifying parts which would make them aware of the book's rich treasures. "Moreover, we are disposed to doubt seriously," they said further,

> whether the introduction of this sacred volume as an ordinary class book into schools, is beneficial to religion. It is thereby exposed to that irreverend [sic] familiarity, which is calculated to produce more contempt than veneration; it is placed side by side with mere human productions, with the fables of mythology and the speculations of a vain philosophy; it is thus too often made the subject of a vulgar jest, it sinks to the level of task-books, and shares the aversion and the remarks which are generally bestowed upon them by children. If the authorised version be used in a school, it should be under circumstances very different from those which are usually found in the public institutions of our States, and this shows the necessity of your better exertions to establish and uphold seminaries and schools, fitted according to our own principles, and for the education of the children who are daily rising up, and numbers of whom are lost for want of such institutions.[32]

Guided, then, by principles mandatory in the Catholic content of faith, the Bishops felt they must raise their voices in protest, not against the desirability of children learning the Scriptures, but, on the principle of religious freedom, against the, to them, sectarian method by which Catholic children were learning about

[31] Guilday, *op. cit.*, pp. 132–33.
[32] *Ibid.*, pp. 133–34.

the sacred books. The charge arose against them from many sources that the Bishops were opposed to their children learning the word of God. Over a period of years which go far beyond the Civil War, the controversies raged and laws were made and unmade on the subject of Bible reading in the public school.

One of the best known of these controversies occurred in Philadelphia, starting at the end of 1842. Under the date of November 14, the Catholic Bishop of that city, Francis P. Kenrick, wrote a letter to the school board objecting to certain regulations. "Among them I am informed," stated Bishop Kenrick,

> one is that the teachers shall read and cause to be read, The Bible; by which is understood the version published by the command of King James. To this regulation we are forced to object, inasmuch as Catholic children are thus led to view as authoritative a version which is rejected by the Church. . . . we do not ask you to adopt the Catholic version for general use; but we feel warranted in claiming that our conscientious scruples to recognize or use the other [the King James], be respected. In Baltimore the Directors of the Public Schools have thought it their duty to provide Catholic children with the Catholic version. Is it too much for us to expect the same measure of justice? [33]

The answer of the School Board came in the form of two resolutions dated January 10, 1843:

> RESOLVED, that no children be required to attend or unite in the reading of the Bible in the Public Schools, whose parents are conscientiously opposed thereto:
> RESOLVED, that those children whose parents conscientiously prefer and desire any particular version of the Bible, without note or comment, be furnished with same.[34]

Father Nolan points out that the phrase "without note or comment" ruled out the Catholic Bible, since "there was at the time no Catholic Bible in English without notes. Moreover, as can be learned from the 'Memorial of the Catholic Citizens of Philadel-

[33] Hugh J. Nolan, *The Most Reverend Francis Patrick Kenrick, Third Bishop of Philadelphia, 1830–1851* (Philadelphia: American Catholic Historical Society of Philadelphia, 1948), p. 294. Cf. also, *supra*, p. 224.
[34] *Ibid.*, p. 297.

phia to the Board,' the latter never officially communicated these resolutions to the teachers." [35]

Bishop Kenrick's letter had also noted his objections to hymn singing and prayers in the opening and closing exercises, as well as to the presence of texts and library books containing material inimical to the Catholic Church. To this the Board did not make specific reply, as it seems they thought these items had been covered by the resolution of 1834, which has already been examined.[36]

As the months went by, the Catholics of the city were not satisfied and on March 21, 1844 there appeared in the pages of the local Catholic newspaper a protest to the Board signed by forty-nine prominent members of the laity.[37] Meanwhile on March 12 the Bishop had written a second letter of his own. Cognizant of a mounting public impression that Catholics wanted the Bible banned entirely from the public schools, Kenrick reiterated his basic position as to the Scriptures: "I do not object to the use of the Bible provided Catholic children be allowed to use their own version." [38]

To emphasize his point the Bishop then offered a statement to the city's press, and had it placarded as well in various parts of Philadelphia. "Catholics have not asked that the Bible be excluded from the Public Schools," it said. "They have merely desired for their children the liberty of using the Catholic version . . ." [39]

Despite these efforts on the part of both Bishop and laity, nothing was gained for the Catholic cause. On the contrary, when the series of bloody riots broke out in May of 1844 which panicked Philadelphia for days, one of the rallying cries of the Nativist mobs was "The Bible in the Public School." [40]

Nolan is emphatic in refuting what he claims has been accepted without basis by many historians—that Bishop Kenrick's protests

[35] *Ibid.*, pp. 297–98.
[36] Cf. *supra*, pp. 229–30, esp. footnote 137.
[37] Cf. Nolan, *op. cit.*, p. 299, quoting the *Catholic Herald*.
[38] *Ibid.*, p. 301.
[39] *Ibid.*
[40] *Ibid.*, p. 311. Cf. also Billington, *op. cit.*, pp. 222, 230, and Gustavus Myers, *History of Bigotry in the United States* (New York: Random House, 1943), p. 176.

on the Bible question directly caused the Philadelphia riots.[41] Certainly, the writer's documentation makes it clear that the Bishop did not intend to ban the Bible from public institutions of learning. Moreover, Nolan points out economic and political factors of the times as also underlying the animosity between the older American group in Philadelphia itself and the recent immigrants who lived in the outlying suburbs.[42] Yet the anti-Catholic bitterness of those days, so thoroughly described by Billington, Myers and others, seems to have made the Bishop's efforts the occasion, if not the direct cause, of this lamentable chapter in the nation's history.

Another incident similar to the Philadelphia riots, at least in its general outlines, occurred in the little town of Ellsworth, Maine towards the end of 1853.[43] The School Committee approved a ruling by one of the teachers that all the pupils had to read the Protestant Bible under pain of expulsion. A protest was made by the parish priest, Father John Bapst, S.J., but a majority of the Committee rejected it. According to Father Bapst's account, one of them declared:

> We are determined to protestantize the Catholic children; they shall read the Protestant Bible or be dismissed from the schools; and should we find them loafing around the wharves, we will clap them into jail.[44]

The threat of expulsion was carried out and Father Bapst opened a Catholic school for the expellees. The town's resentment was increased when a Catholic layman, Lawrence Donohue, withdrew his daughter from the public school, arranged for private instructions and sent the bill to the State of Maine.[45]

During the disorders which followed, the priest's home, the church building, and the parish school were attacked. Father

---

[41] Nolan, *op. cit.*, p. 325.

[42] *Ibid.*, pp. 304–309.

[43] Cf. Robert H. Lord, John E. Sexton, and Edward T. Harrington, *History of the Archdiocese of Boston in the Various Stages of Its Development* (3 vols.; New York: Sheed & Ward, 1944), II, 672 ff.

[44] "Father Bapst's Narrative of the Beginnings of the Crisis at Ellsworth" (*Woodstock Letters XVIII*), 133–36 (as quoted in Lord, Sexton, and Harrington, *ibid.*, p. 673).

[45] *Ibid.*, p. 674.

Bapst was assigned to another town in the interests of peace, but during a visit which he made to Ellsworth on October 14, 1854, he was seized by a mob, tarred and feathered and ridden through the town on a rail.[46]

In 1854 Lawrence Donohue, the father of the girl expelled for refusing to read the Protestant Bible, sued in the Supreme Judicial Court of Maine for the money he had expended on the private teacher. The case was put on the grounds that damage had been done to the father. This the Court refused to allow and a "nonsuit" was ordered and confirmed.[47]

The case was then brought up on the grounds that the child was "maliciously, wrongfully and unjustifiably" expelled. The plaintiff's lawyer argued among other points, that the child's religious rights had been violated.[48] But once again a "nonsuit" was ordered at the end of a twenty-three page opinion by Associate Justice John Appleton, and the decision was concurred in by Chief Justice Ether Shepley and Associate Justices Tenny and Howard.[49]

In the summary of the second action is found the following:

> . . . For refusal to read from a book thus prescribed, [by the superintending Committee] the Committee may, if they see fit, expel such disobedient scholar.
>
> No scholar can escape or evade such requirement when made by the Committee, under the plea that his *conscience* will not allow the reading of such a book.
>
> Nor can the ordinance be nullified, because the church of which the scholar is a member, hold, and have so instructed its members, that it is a *sin* to read the book prescribed.
>
> A law is not unconstitutional, because it may prohibit what one may *conscientiously* think right, or require what he may *conscientiously* think wrong.

[46] *Ibid.*, pp. 676–78. Indications of other controversies are found in the Baltimore Archdiocesan Archives in letters to Archbishop Kenrick from Bishop Michael O'Connor of Pittsburgh, March 14, 1853 (AAB, 30-W-20) and from Bishop Martin J. Spalding of Louisville and himself successor to Kenrick in Baltimore, July 18, 1853 (AAB, 32A-N-7) and April 1, 1854 (AAB, 32A-N-15).

[47] "Donohue vs. Richards," *Maine Reports*, xxxviii, 379 (Hallowell, Maine: Masters, Smith & Co., 1856).

[48] *Ibid.*, p. 390.

[49] *Ibid.*, p. 413.

A requirement by the superintending school committee, that the *Protestant version* of the Bible shall be read in the public schools of their town, by the scholars who are able to read, is in violation of no constitutional provision, and is binding upon all the members of the schools, although composed of divers *religious sects*.[50]

Another sample of Protestant reaction to the Catholic position on both parochial schools and Bible reading in public schools occurred in 1853. The Rev. Horace Bushnell, the Congregationalist clergyman whose ideas of the importance of the Bible have already been given, preached a sermon in the North Church, Hartford, Conn., on March 25.[51] The speaker reminded his listeners that originally America had been a Protestant country with Protestant schools. In order to give equal rights to all Christian sects, all formal church connections with the state were dissolved and even the common school ceased to be a Protestant institution. However, America decided to keep her common schools at all cost. As to their nature, Bushnell declared they are to be, first, available for all classes and denominations; second, they are to be Christian schools, as he explained:

Common schools, then, are to be Christian schools—how Christian? In the same sense, I answer, that Catholics and Protestants are Christians, in the same sense that our government is Christian, in the same that Christendom is Christian, that is, in the recognition of God and Christ and providence and the Bible. I fully agree with our Catholic friends regarding what they say in deprecation of a godless system of education. . . . The chances are far too great that knowledge, without principle, will turn out to be only the equipment of knaves and felons.[52]

Later in the sermon Bushnell admitted the probability of Protestant intolerance in some cases, but said he felt that in others it was the Catholics who had been unfair. As an example of the former, he cited instances of the retaining of the Protestant Bible in

[50] *Ibid.*, pp. 379–80.

[51] Rev. Horace Bushnell, *Common Schools; A Discourse on the Modifications Demanded by the Roman Catholics* (*Delivered in the North Church, Hartford, on the Day of the Late Fast, March 25, 1853*) (Hartford: Case, Tiffany & Company, 1853).

[52] *Ibid.*, pp. 13–14.

the schools. But he considered the action of Archbishop Hughes in the matter of the New York textbooks an instance of greater intolerance. After the Bible and these textbooks were eliminated from the schools, Bushnell declared,

> the priests now change their note and begin to complain that the schools are "godless" or "atheistical"—just as they have required them to be. In facts like these, fortified by the fact that some of the priests are even denying, in public lectures, the right of the state to educate children at all, we seem to discover an absolute determination that the children shall be withdrawn, at whatever cost, and that no terms of accommodation shall be satisfactory.[53]

The speaker, nevertheless, suggested four things which might be done to satisfy both sides:

1. Make the use of the Bible in the Protestant or Douay version optional.
2. Compile a book of Scripture reading lessons, by agreement from both versions.
3. Provide for religious instruction, at given hours, or on a given day, by the clergy, or by qualified teachers such as the parents may choose.
4. Prepare a book of Christian morality distinct from a doctrine of religion or a faith, which shall be taught indiscriminately to all the scholars.[54]

These conciliatory suggestions were a far cry from the speech of Henry F. Durant, in the "Eliot School Case" in Boston in 1859.[55] A Catholic pupil of the Eliot (public) School, Thomas Wall, had been whipped by his teacher for refusing to recite the Lord's Prayer and the Ten Commandments and for allegedly causing a disturbance during the daily Bible reading session. Against this corporal punishment, suit was brought in Court. The teacher was defended by Durant. Basing his argument on the statute of Massachusetts which enjoins the teaching of "piety" in the state schools, Durant maintained: "There is but one book

---

[53] *Ibid.*, pp. 15–16.
[54] *Ibid.*, p. 16.
[55] Henry F. Durant, *Defense of the Use of the Bible in the Public Schools, Argument of Henry F. Durant, Esq., in the Eliot School Case* (Boston: Ticknor & Fields, 1859).

from which we dare teach piety, and that book is God's Holy Bible." [56]

On the question of which English translation was to be used, Durant pleaded the cause of the King James version in the following words:

> May it please your Honor, I ask now for a single candid objection to the use of King James's Bible—not the Protestant Bible, but the Christian Bible—the Saxon Bible, which we love. Are the particular portions of it which are used in the schools objectionable? Our children are to learn piety from it, not sectarianism, or creeds; but pure religion, undefiled before God. . . . Was it from sectarian views that the Lord's Prayer and the Ten Commandments were selected as fit lessons of these cardinal virtues? What sect, Catholic or Protestant, has received the monopoly of these portions of God's Word? What priest or preacher can call them his own? Are they indeed offensive to the tender consciences of children? Is it indeed dangerous that they should hear or repeat them? . . . Does bishop or priest dare to say that it would be dangerous to repeat to the children those sacred portions of the Bible? [57]

As to the Catholic objection that a translation not authorized by the Church cannot be held by Catholics to be the word of God, Durant made a flat denial:

> I repel altogether the specious pretence that our Bible is not *the* Bible, because the translation differs in some particulars from the Douay Bible. Every translation from the original Hebrew and Greek must of necessity vary—must of necessity be more or less perfect, according to the accuracy and perfection of the language into which it is translated, and the learning and skill of the translator. The Holy Scriptures have been translated into over two hundred different languages; but they are always the Bible. Not the Bible of the Catholic or the Calvinist—not the Bible of the Methodist or the Episcopalian—but the Christian Bible.[58]

"Banish the vain delusion forever," Durant concluded,

> that our Saxon Bible can be taken away; neither foreign tyrants or foreign priests will ever have that power. Until America

[56] *Ibid.*, p. 23.
[57] *Ibid.*, p. 26.
[58] *Ibid.*, p. 31.

ceases to be a republic,—until the warnings of Washington and the wisdom of Webster are forgotten,—until the sacred traditions of the past have perished,—until the memories of the dead have passed away like a dream,—until religion and freedom are banished from the land, it will remain as the rule and guide of our faith, the Great Charter of our liberties.[59]

Here was an instance where the defense lawyer would give no quarter to the objections of the Catholics about the King James version being read to their children. The case was made out to be that the intent of the Catholics was to have the Bible as such banned from the schools. Without presuming to judge the merits and demerits of the Eliot case itself, it can be concluded that such attempts to force the King James version could only have stirred up increased opposition in the minds of both priests and people.[60]

As Bishop Kenrick had done earlier in Philadelphia, Bishop John B. Fitzpatrick of Boston tried to bring about peace in the Eliot case by giving to the School Committee a calm and reasoned statement of the Catholic position. He listed his objections under three points: "The enforced use of the Protestant version of the Bible; The enforced learning and reciting of the Ten Commandments in their Protestant form; The enforced union in chanting the Lord's Prayer and other religious chants." [61] The Bishop's statement said, in part:

> 1. Catholics cannot, under any circumstances, acknowledge, receive and use, as a complete collection and faithful version of the inspired books which compose the written word of God, the English Protestant translation of the Bible. Still less can they so acknowledge, accept or use it, when its enforcement as such is coupled expressly with the rejection of that version which their own Church approves and adopts as being correct and authentic. And yet this is required of them by law. . . .

[59] *Ibid.*, p. 43.

[60] An undated pamphlet giving the report of a Committee to the Board of Education in New York City defends Bible reading on the basis that Christianity is the religion of New York State. It was after the 1842 sectarian law, because this is referred to in the document. G. Clark, Chairman, *The Bible in Schools, Report to the Board of Education of the City of New York.* Cf. also Connors, *op. cit.,* Chap. III, pp. 55–86, for a description of Bible-reading controversies in New York State.

[61] Cf. Lord *et al., op. cit.,* II, 597 (quoting *The Boston Pilot,* March 26, 1859).

II. The acceptance and recital of the Decalogue, under the form and words in which Protestants clothe it, is offensive to the conscience and belief of Catholics; inasmuch as that form and those words are viewed by them, and have not infrequently been used by their adversaries, as a means of attack upon certain tenets and practices, which, under the teachings of the Church, they hold as true and sacred.

III. The chanting of the Lord's Prayer, of psalms, of hymns, addressed to God, performed by many persons in unison, being neither a scholastic exercise, nor a recreation, can only be regarded as an act of public worship. Indeed it is professedly intended as such in the regulations which govern our public schools. . . . Protestants, however diverse may be their religious opinions . . . find no difficulty to offer in brotherhood a blended and apparently harmonious worship, and in so doing they give and receive mutual satisfaction, mutual edification. The Catholic cannot act in this manner. He cannot present himself before the Divine presence in what would be for him a merely simulated union of prayer and adoration. His Church . . . considers indifference in matters of religion . . . as a great evil which promiscuous worship would tend to spread more widely and increase. . . .[62]

Bishop Fitzpatrick concluded his statement by denying that Catholics had any design "to eliminate and practically annihilate the Bible." "This has never been true," he said, "and yet this has always been believed, and a rallying cry, 'To the rescue of the Bible' has resounded on every side." [63]

Decisions of the State

The civil authority in the states under consideration made no law against the opening of parochial schools. On the subject of Bible reading in the public schools, only New York and Massachusetts among the thirteen original states, passed any legislation before the Civil War.[64]

The 1844 law in New York stated that the reading of the Bible

[62] *Ibid.*, pp. 597–98.
[63] *Ibid.*, p. 599.
[64] Cf. *supra*, p. 242.

was not prohibited. "But nothing herein contained," says the text of the law,

> shall authorize the board of education to exclude the Holy Scriptures without note or comment, or any selections therefrom, from any of the schools provided for by this act; but it shall not be competent for said board of education to decide what version, if any, of the Holy Scriptures without note or comment, shall be used in any of the said schools; provided, that nothing herein contained shall be so construed as to violate the rights of conscience as secured by the constitution of this state and the U. S. *Laws of the 67th Session,* Ch. 320, Sec. 12, Act May 7, 1844 (regarding New York City).[65]

Six years later, a New York statute extending the refusal of public funds for religious schools in Brooklyn added the words—"this section shall not be deemed to prohibit the use of Holy Scripture without note or comment." *Laws of 73rd Session,* Ch. 143, Sec. 19, Act April 4, 1850.[66]

Massachusetts passed an Act *requiring* daily Bible reading in 1855, adding it to the 1827 textbook law:

> The school committee shall require the daily reading of some portion of the Bible in the common English version; but shall never direct any school books calculated to favor the tenets of any particular sect of Christians to be purchased or used in any of the town schools. *Acts, 1855,* Ch. 410.[67]

During the first half of the nineteenth century two currents of thought, in themselves not necessarily opposed to religion, were making great headway in the United States. Both had important consequences for education. The first was a conviction that a democracy could thrive only on an educated citizenry, and the sec-

---

[65] Confrey, *op. cit.,* pp. 95–96.

[66] *Ibid.,* p. 96.

[67] *Ibid.,* p. 76. In 1862 the law was expanded to read: "The school committee shall require the daily reading of some portion of the Bible, without written note or oral comment, in the public schools; but they shall require no scholar to read from any particular version, whose parent or guardian shall declare that he has conscientious scruples against allowing him to read therefrom, nor shall they ever permit any school books, calculated to favor the tenets of any particular sect of Christians, to be purchased or read in any of the public schools." *Gen. Laws 1862,* Chap. 57, Act March 6, 1862. (Confrey, *ibid.*)

ond that, with an expanding economy, the American democracy must teach its children more and more about how to make a comfortable living. In themselves, these ideas were not anti-religious. But they could and to a certain extent did take men's minds off the things of the spirit and fasten them on things material. The result of the rise in interest in education for citizenship and material progress tended to crowd the spiritual and lessen the importance of religion.[68]

As has been noted,[69] the move to centralize authority for public education in a single state office was a phenomenon which occurred at about the same time as the decline in religious instruction in the common schools. The impression gathered in this study is that centralization was more the occasion than the cause of the religious decline. In the first half of the eighteenth century the power over schools was taken out of local hands (town, districts, etc.), and thus many people who might have insisted that doctrinal instruction remain in the curriculum lost their power, certainly in policy-making, in matters educational. Yet the state superintendents, secretaries of education and other central leaders did not set out to eliminate religion as such from the schools. They determined to eliminate sectarianism and keep religion. The resulting decline in all religious instruction was largely an unforeseen and unintended outcome, which, it seems, probably might not have happened if control had remained local, and did not happen as a result of a formal campaign of extermination by the central authorities.

The Results for Religious Instruction

Protestants, Catholics and lay leaders having started to work on their various solutions, what became of religious instruction in the public schools during the second quarter of the nineteenth cen-

[68] On the state and education, cf. D. Bethume Duffield, "Education a State Duty," *American Journal of Education,* III (March, 1857), 81–100, and Lyman Draper, "The State and Education," *American Journal of Education,* XI (June, 1862), 323–29.

[69] *Supra,* pp. 102, 120–21.

tury? One of the most significant indications of the trends should be the school readers. It has been decided that they formed perhaps the most effective means of inculcating religion, after the catechetical and Biblical texts.[70] What happened to the contents of the readers, when anti-sectarian laws were enacted in New York, Massachusetts, New Hampshire and Virginia?

Sherman Smith's study on Massachusetts, using the *Abstract of School Returns* for 1835, lists the following readers in order of their popularity: Bible and Testament, *National Reader,* Young's *Reader,* Pierpont's Reading Books, *Improved Reader, Intelligent Reader, Child's Guide, Analytical Reader,* Murray's *English Reader,* and *Franklin Primer.*[71] After a discussion of their contents and those of a few other volumes which appear to have been secondary school material, Smith concludes:

> We note, then, in the textbooks produced after the sectarian book law, nothing that could be termed sectarian in character, at least between Protestant sects. There was a diminishing amount of space devoted to selections of Bible quotations and Bible stories; occasionally we find selections on Creation, or others of a broad religious character; and sometimes a hymn or sermon was inserted. Morality and ethics had come by 1837 to replace practically all the definitely religious content in the textbooks, and what religion remained was given incidentally or as literature. After this there was no tendency to restore the religious element.[72]

In the Nietz collection, several books were found which have publication dates after 1827. Some of their contents will now be examined to see if the pattern described by Smith held true in their case.

In 1828 appeared *Boston Reading Lessons for Primary Schools.*[73] In its Table of Contents were such titles as:

---

[70] Cf. *supra,* p. 78. Another point to be remembered is that some of the school books in the Nietz Collection seem to have been used over a considerable length of time. Cf. *supra,* pp. 79–80.

[71] Smith, *Relation of the State to Religious Education in Massachusetts,* p. 104.

[72] *Ibid.,* p. 106.

[73] (Anon.) *Boston Reading Lessons for Primary Schools* (Boston: Richardson & Lord, 1828).

Moral Lessons; Heaven; Bible Lessons; Solomon's Choice; The Goodness of God; God is Everywhere; Agar's Prayer; The Lord's Prayer; Trust in God; Christ's Love of Children; An Evening Hymn; A Child's Prayer in Sickness; Time & Eternity; Who Made the Sun, Moon and Stars; Praise for Creation and Providence.

A sample of "Moral Lessons" seems to contain more than mere natural theology:

> Thy body shall return to the dust from whence it came, but thy soul to God who gave it; and, if thou act good, thou shalt be happy evermore.
>
> Who is he that cometh to save from sin and from eternal death?
>
> He descended on a fiery cloud; the sound of a trumpet goeth before him; thousands of angels are on his right hand.
>
> It is Jesus the Son of God, the Savior of man, the friend of the good.
>
> He cometh in the glory of his Father. He hath received power from on high.
>
> Mourn not, therefore, child of immortality; for the spoiler, the cruel spoiler, that laid waste the works of God, is subdued; Jesus hath conquered death; child of immortality, mourn no longer.[74]

Rev. F. W. P. Greenwood and G. B. Emerson put out *The Classical Reader* in 1830.[75] Its table of contents lists many topics like those mentioned in the *Boston Reading Lessons*. In one of them, "Early Piety," the following will serve as a sample:

[74] *Ibid.*, p. 81. Also appearing in 1828 was Lindley Murray's *Introduction to the English Reader* (Philadelphia: S. Probasco, 1828). Selections included "Heaven," "The Character of Christ," "Excellence of the Bible," "The Divine Being Knows and Sees Everything." (An autograph on the Nietz copy of this book reads: "Miss Catherine G. Bickel, February the 12th, 1840.") In the same year appeared (Anon.) *The Fourth Class Book: Containing Lessons in Reading for the Younger Classes in Schools* (Brookfield: E. & G. Merriam, 1828). A section goes: "Come, let us praise God, for he is exceedingly great; let us bless God, for he is very good. He made all things; the sun to rule the day, the moon to shine by night. . . . Let him call me, and I will come unto him; let him command and I will obey him. When I am older, I will praise him better; and I will never forget God, so long as my life remaineth in me." Pp. 5–6.

[75] F. W. P. Greenwood and G. B. Emerson, *The Classical Reader* (Boston: Lincoln and Edwards and Carter and Hendee, 1830).

. . . Such is the invitation which religion makes to the young. And never, in the long annals, of time, was there one human being, who at the close of life, did not rejoice if he had listened to it, and lament with bitter tears, if he had rejected it. Let us inquiry [sic]; what is here meant by giving the heart to religion. . . .[76]

In the list given by Sherman Smith, John Pierpont's *National Reader* is listed as "Most (popular)." [77] In an edition put out in 1831,[78] many of the familiar titles are listed: Portrait of a Patriarch, selected from Job; Religious Contemplations of the Works of God; Obedience to the Commands of God Rewarded; Promises of Religion to the Young; Religion the Basis of Society; Religion the Best Preparation for Duty in Life; Religious Education Necessary; God's First Temples. A section from "Religious Education Necessary" reads:

. . . Let, then, religion be the primary object in the education of the young. Let it mingle, naturally, easily, and gracefully, in all their pursuits and acquirements. Let it be rendered intelligible, attractive, and practical. Let it win their affections, command their reverence, and ensure their obedience. Children, of any class whatever, may be taught in a great compass of liberality and knowledge, not only without apprehension, but with assiduity and encouragement; but, let them, above all things, be taught of the Lord.[79]

A tendency to play down sectarian beliefs is shown in a quotation from Lyman Cobb's *Juvenile Reader, No. 3*, also published in 1831.[80] The section has the title "Religion."

1. Religion is the daughter of Heaven, parent of our virtues, and source of all true felicity; she alone gives peace and contentment, divests the heart of anxious cares, bursts on the mind a flood of joy, and sheds unmingled and perpetual sunshine in the pious breast. By her the spirits of darkness are banished

[76] *Ibid.*, p. 10.

[77] Smith, *op. cit.*, p. 104.

[78] *National Reader* (Boston: Richardson, Lord & Holbrook & Hilliard Gray, Little & Wilkens, 1831).

[79] *Ibid.*, p. 185.

[80] Lyman Cobb, *Juvenile Reader, No. 3, Containing Interesting Historical, Moral and Instructive Reading Lessons* (Baltimore: Joseph Jennett, 1831).

from the earth, and angelick [sic] ministers of grace thicken unseen the regions of mortality. . . .

3. Would you wish, amidst the great variety of religious systems in vogue, to make a right distinction and prefer the best? Recollect the character of Christ; keep a steady eye on that universal and permanent good will to men, in which he lived, by which he suffered, and for which he died. . . .

5. Go search the religion He has left, to the bottom; not in those artificial theories, which have done it the most essential injury; or in their manner who assume His name, but overlook His example, and who are for ever talking about the merits of His death, at the expense of those virtues which adorn His life. . . .

9. Christianity, however, is not less precious to the honest, because knaves and fools have abused her; and let bigots and skepticks [sic] say what they please, she softens and enlarges the heart, warms and impregnates the mind of man, as certainly, and essentially, as the sun does the earth.[81]

The *American Primary Class Book* appeared in a second edition in 1832.[82] Lesson VIII is entitled "The Bible."

1. This is a precious book indeed!
   Happy the child who loves to read!
   'Tis God's own word, which he has given
   To show our souls the way to heaven!

2. It tells us how the world was made,
   And how good men the Lord obey'd;
   There his commandments are written too,
   To teach us what we ought to do. . . .

5. Be thankful children, that you may
   Read this good bible every day;
   'Tis God's own word, which he has given
   To show our souls the way to heaven.[83]

1833 saw the appearance of the Rev. John S. C. Abbot's *The Child at Home, or The Principles of Filial Duty*.[84] This was the book submitted to Horace Mann by Frederick A. Packard as a

[81] *Ibid.*, pp. 114–16 (*passim*).

[82] Anon., *The American Primary Class Book* (second edition; Providence: A. S. Beckwith & Hutchens and Shepard, 1832).

[83] *Ibid.*, p. 28.

[84] Rev. John S. C. Abbot, *The Child at Home, or The Principles of Filial Duty* (New York: American Tract Society, 1833).

sample of what might be found in the Tract Society's Library. Mann's reaction to what he considered its sectarian doctrines has been studied in Chapter V. The following are some of the titles:

Chap. I—Responsibility; The Police Court. The Widow and her Daughter . . . Consequence of Disobedience. A Mother's Grave. The sick child.

Chap. II—Deception, George Washington and his hatchet . . . The dying child . . . Various ways of deceiving. Thoughts on death. Disclosures of the judgement day.

Chap. V—Religious Truth—Human Character . . . Love of God . . . The sufferings of the Savior. The Holy Spirit.

Chap. VI—Piety. The pious boy . . . How children may do good . . . The Christian child in heaven. Uncertainty of life.

A revised edition of Eliza Robbins' *American Popular Lessons* came out in 1839.[85] Its Table of Contents lists several "general religious" titles. A few lines from "Punishment of Sin," however, suggest doctrinal content, as well as does another poem entitled "The Son of God."

Punishment of Sin

1. If I do wrong, my troubled breast
Shall vainly seek the bed of rest;
Peace will from my pillow fly,
Sleep will shun my weary eye. . . .

5. When the arm of death destroys
All my false and fatal joys
In that hour of deep despair,
God will not regard my prayer.

6. I shall see the blest afar
Radiant as the morning star
While with aching steps I go,
To the darker realms of wo.[86]

---

[85] Eliza Robbins, *American Popular Lessons Chiefly Selected from the writings of Mrs. Brabauld, Miss Edgeworth and other approved Writers* (New York: R. Lockwood, 1839).

[86] *Ibid.*, pp. 140–41.

The Son of God

1. The Son of God who came from heaven
   The erring world to save
   Who says "repent and be forgiven
   And live beyond the grave."

2. By actions holy and serene
   He won his Father's love
   And though superior far to men
   Was harmless as the dove. . . .

6. They nailed him to the cross, and there
   Deep insult on him threw,
   And yet "Forgive them" was his prayer
   "They know not what they do. . . ." [87]

In 1840 Charles Sanders' "First and Second Books" of *The School Reader* were published.[88] A smaller number of titles listing religious subjects was found in the Table of Contents than in previous books examined. From one of the titles in the *First Book*, "The Funeral of a Little Boy," we quote the following:

. . . Son—Mother, where is his soul?

Mother—My son, I think his soul is in heaven.

Son—Oh, Mother, tell me about heaven, then I shall not be afraid to die.

Mother—My child, every one that loves Christ goes to heaven. There is nothing bad in heaven. No one does anything bad there. No one is sick there. No one is sorry in heaven. God is there; Jesus is there, all good people are there.

Son—Oh, Mother, how shall I get to heaven?

Mother—Believe in Christ, love God, and do that which is good, and then you need not be afraid to die. All who truly love and obey God, will go to heaven.[89]

In the 1840's the famous readers of William H. McGuffey began to appear on the American scene. Of them Warren says, "As the

[87] *Ibid.*, p. 143.

[88] Charles Sanders, *The School Reader* (*First Book* and *Second Book*; New York: Mark H. Newman, 1840).

[89] Sanders, *First Book*, p. 91. Eight other readers in the 1830 decade were examined and all contained practically the same type of religious material. These authors were "The Compiler" (pseud.), Samuel Putnam (2 vols.), Lindley Murray, Joshua Leavitt, John Pierpont (*First Class Book*), S. G. Goodrich, and (anonymous author) *The Reader's Manual*.

McGuffey Readers entered the field and assumed prominence, they effected a retardation of the process of elimination of the religious and moral elements from the school readers of the United States. This was due partly to their authorship, but largely due to their western origin and reading public." [90] Though the McGuffey books were used in the original thirteen states, they were mostly a mid-Western phenomenon. Therefore we shall here give them only this brief mention.

The Third Class Reader of B. D. Emerson came out in 1845.[91] The only titles suggesting religion in the entire Vol. III were the last two: "The Creator" and "The Child's Prayer." The "Prayer" mentions the redemption of humanity by Christ's death, but is otherwise very general in character. The steady decline of religious content is marked clearly by this reading book.

Three readers were examined from the 1850 decade. They were: Osgood's *Progressive First Reader,* Parker and Watson's *The National Second Reader* and (Anon.) *The Progressive Pictorial Primer.*[92] Only one religious passage was found in the Osgood work. It is a discourse between two children about God's control of the universe and man's duty to love God and be good.[93] The Parker and Watson book has three religious titles: "Faith in God," "Calling His Sheep by Name" and "King Edward and His Bible." *The Progressive Pictorial Primer* includes a bit of religion in the last two selections in the book:

(1) The word of God has been read and a hymn read, too. Now all join in the song of praise.

"There is no place like home" where we kneel to give thanks for life and health and all our joys.

[90] Harold C. Warren, *Changing Conceptions in the Religious Elements in Early American School Readers,* p. 63.

[91] D. B. Emerson, *The Third Class Reader Designed for the Use of Younger Classes in the Schools of the United States,* III (Bradford, Vermont: Asa Law, 1845).

[92] Lucius Osgood, *Progressive First Reader* (Pittsburgh: A. H. English Company, 1855); Richard S. Parker & J. Madison Watson, *The National Second Reader* (New York: A. S. Bower & Company, 1857); and Anon., "An Eminent Practical Teacher," *The Progressive Pictorial Primer* (Boston: Oliver Ellsworth, 1857).

[93] Osgood, *op. cit.,* pp. 91–92.

There is no hour so sweet as when we pray with those we love. We feel that "God is love."

(2) The Lord's Prayer [King James Version].[94]

As this review of readers, extending from 1828 to 1857, shows, the trend found by Sherman Smith in Massachusetts was duplicated elsewhere. As the years passed by, even the content itself of the diminishing number of selections that might be called religious became more and more general and even vague. Beyond the Bible reading which has been noted, there was little in the textbook content by the time of the Civil War to give the public school child an understanding of natural theology, and even less of Christianity itself.

In an attempt to gauge the state of religious instruction at the end of the period studied, the outbreak of the Civil War, a close examination was made of state superintendents' reports for the year 1861. Of the thirteen original states, Delaware, Georgia, Maryland, South Carolina and Virginia had not published such reports up to that time.[95] In the remainder of the reports, accounts were studied on the level of the superintendent himself and on the county and town levels, if given. A study of the reports from towns and cities, as printed in individual volumes, was not attempted because of the magnitude of such a task.

Within the limits so described, nothing pertinent to religion was found in the report from the state of New York.[96] No county reports were included in this volume.

Religious instruction, sometimes listed under the head of "Morals" or a like title, was mentioned in the 1861 reports from Connecticut, Massachusetts, New Hampshire, Rhode Island, New Jersey, North Carolina and Pennsylvania.[97] It is significant to note

[94] *The Progressive Pictorial Primer*, pp. 63–64. These selections are accompanied by pictures of a family at prayer.

[95] The initial reports in these states were: Delaware, 1877; Georgia, 1871; Maryland, 1866; South Carolina, 1866; and Virginia, 1871.

[96] *Eighth Annual Report of the Superintendent of Public Instruction of the State of New York (Transmitted to the Legislature January 8, 1862)* (Albany: C. Van Beuthhuysen, 1862).

[97] In the 1861 Report from the District of Columbia the only religious reference was the placing of the "Holy Bible" at the head of the list of books for primary schools. Cf. *Seventeenth Annual Report of the Trustees of Public Schools of the City of Washington* (1861) (no place, publisher, or date), p. 41.

that in none of these reports was there any denial of the value of religious education as such. In one of them there was an emphatic statement that sectarian instruction is not a proper activity for the public school. This last occurred in an unsigned section called the "History of Pennsylvania Common Schools," [98] and reads as follows:

> In this system there is no place, because in our government there is no power, for denominational religious instruction of any kind, by public authority. But it must not hence be concluded that the patriots and good men who throughout the course of our history framed its parts, intended to exclude the religious element from the idea of a sufficient training for the youth of the land. The very reverse is the truth. They perceived that, while this kind of instruction was excluded from, it was not necessary to, the proper functions of the day or common school;—that indispensable duty devolving during the child's attendance in the day school upon the parental and clerical teaching of the home. [99]

In the reports of the other states there was an occasional tribute to the importance of religion and religious instruction. Thus, in the Massachusetts Report, the Amesbury officials declared, when treating the subject of discipline:

> . . . The scholar should be led to feel that he has disobeyed a higher than human authority—that both teacher and pupil are under the inspection of their Maker, and accountable to Him for their acts . . . [they] should regulate their actions by the will of God. [100]

[98] *Report of the Superintendent of Common Schools of Pennsylvania for the Year Ending June 3, 1861* (Harrisburg: A. Boyd Hamilton, 1862).

[99] *Ibid.*, p. 23.

[100] *Twenty-fifth Annual Report of the Board of Education* (Boston: William White, 1862), "School Committees' Reports," p. 14. In the 1859 report from Massachusetts, George S. Boutwell, the Secretary, suggested that the following be told to parents who feared to send their children to public school on account of religious scruples: ". . . It is no part of the purpose of the school system to undermine one faith or to build up another; that the schools are educational and not religious institutions; but that the school in every Christian Commonwealth must recognize the authority of the Bible, the mission of the Redeemer, and the government of the Supreme Being." *Twenty-third Annual Report of the Board* (Boston: William White, 1860), "Secretary's Report," p. 59.

From the Bridgewater (Massachusetts) Report:

We assume, what all will admit, that our public schools, associated as they are with the teachings of the Sacred Scriptures, in the duties of "piety, religion and morality", are indispensable to the good order and prosperity of States and Nations.[101]

So, too, the opinion of Horatio Merrill, Superintendent for Merrimack County, New Hampshire:

. . . Our common schools, together with the institutions of the gospel of Christ, lie at the very foundation of our national character and prosperity. . . . Religion . . . reaches its highest manifestation, and contributes most largely to the welfare of society, when joined with the best education of the people.[102]

In Rhode Island, the Commissioner, H. Rousmaniere, observed in his 1861 Report that it was characteristic of an educated mind that it will be "loyal to God, to the state and to the whole country."[103] Similar statements were found from town officials in Princeton and Westfield in New Jersey.[104]

C. H. Wiley, Superintendent for North Carolina, made no report for the year 1861, because, as he explained to Governor Vance a year later, a change in the fiscal year and other problems made a report impossible.[105] In his 1860 Report, Wiley's only religious reference had been to remind the state officials:

that none who deny the Being of God, or the divine authority of the Old or New Testament, are allowed to hold any civil trust under the Constitution of our State, and in this connection I may add that all who had been resistant to the powers that be, resist the ordinance of God; and that if you will keep these plain tests in view, you cannot be accused of attempting to exercise any unjust authority over the rights of conscience.[106]

[101] *Twenty-fifth Annual Report,* "School Committees' Reports," p. 207.

[102] *Fifteenth Annual Report of the Common Schools of New Hampshire* (Concord: Henry McFarland, 1861).

[103] *Seventeenth Annual Report on Public Schools in Rhode Island* (Providence: Cooke & Danielson, 1862), p. 16.

[104] *Annual Report of the Superintendent of Public Schools of the State of New Jersey* (Jersey City: John H. Lyon, 1862), p. 124.

[105] *Report of the Superintendent of Schools for North Carolina for the year 1862* (Raleigh: W. W. Holden, 1862), p. 3.

[106] *Report of the Superintendent of Common Schools of North Carolina, for the year 1860* (Document No. 10, Session of the Legislature, 1860–61) (no place: John Spelman, Printer to the State, no date).

In the 1862 Report, Wiley included some documents from the year 1861. Among them is a letter he had sent in May, 1861, to the committees who examined and appointed teachers. Wiley wrote, in part:

> Nearly two hundred thousand immortal souls are receiving their first instructions in the Common Schools of North Carolina, and the character of all who teach in these schools is, under Providence, to a great extent dependent on you. . . .
> We advocate universal education as a means of vastly economizing and expanding the agencies for spreading the Gospel, and there is no temporal difficulty that can justify a voluntary suspension or relaxation of energies with such purposes and to such results.[107]

Side by side with the above declarations, however, were others which indicated a serious worry on the part of some educators that the public schools were deficient in their lack of an effective religious element in the curriculum. From Methuen, Massachusetts, came the statement: "We fear that of late years the efforts of education have been devoted too exclusively to the development of the intellect, to the neglect of the moral and physical." [108] The same note was sounded from Melrose, Massachusetts:

> If there exists any important error in the education of the present day, it seems to be found in a lack of systematic, moral and Christian training. . . . This department, as it respects the masses, is, by common consent, entrusted to the teaching of the pulpit. Sectarian jealousy should not exclude from the schoolroom the discussion of those topics, the principles of which enter into the creed of all Christian communities. It is believed that compendious treatises of the above named subjects might be prepared and introduced into our schools with great benefit.[109]

Three more statements in this same vein were found in the New Hampshire Report. J. W. Patterson, the State Superintendent, lamented the emphasis on intellectual culture to the exclusion of

---

[107] *1862 North Carolina Report*, pp. 32, 38.
[108] *Twenty-fifth Annual Report of the Board of Education*, "School Committees' Reports," p. 39.
[109] *Ibid.*, p. 81.

moral training.[110] A man who seems to have been the same J. W. Patterson, writing as Commissioner from Grafton County, stated:

> . . . The primary elements and universal truths of Christianity may be so inculcated as to determine the principles, and mold the habits of thought and feeling, without meddling with sectarian dogmas and the vexed questions of theology . . .
>
> In view of the thousands growing to the estate of manhood, with no religion and no proper home influences to prepare them to discharge the manifold important trusts of society . . . who will say that our schools have not hitherto been delinquent in a most important branch of their work? [111]

The Commissioner from Hillsborough County, Harry Brickett, wrote:

> The great want in our schools is moral and religious training —not in any sectarian sense—but a real and thorough training in those duties which pertain to a Christian citizen. We must, if we would succeed, give the Bible a prominent place among the textbooks in our schools, and allow it to remain clothed with the sanctions of Divine Authority. In our fear of sectarianism we are in danger of pushing all religious, and even moral culture, out of our schools, thus leaving the children, so far as the school is concerned, without any fixed principles to guide them, like a ship under full sail, it may be, but without chart or rudder by which to steer. One great want in our New England mind, is reverence for sacred things, and recognition of God in public and private. Our schools need in them, to secure the greatest good they can accomplish, a larger infusion of the religious element.[112]

In the town reports from Rhode Island, laments are also recorded about the bad moral conditions found in some of the public schools.[113]

What indication did these reports give of actual religious teaching in the schools of 1861? One reference was found in the Connecticut Report and a highly detailed and significant one came from Pennsylvania. The official who wrote from the Haddam

[110] *1861 New Hampshire Report,* p. 17.
[111] *Ibid.,* p. 84.
[112] *Ibid.,* pp. 65–66.
[113] 1861 *Rhode Island Report,* pp. 12–14.

school district in Connecticut started off with an amusingly vague statement, but then gave important details:

> With respect to the moral influence as exerted in our schools I am happy to say that there is more or less attention paid to it. The Bible is read in all the schools, and in several of them the teacher has opened the exercises of the day with prayer, and closed them with singing. In some of the schools pupils unite with the teacher in repeating the Lord's Prayer, and in some they rehearse, at proper times, the ten commandments, and in some a verse from the Bible is expected to be learned and daily repeated by each scholar,—and it is to be presumed that teachers avail themselves of varied fit occasions for enforcing the duties of morality and religion.[114]

In the case of Pennsylvania, it seems that the county superintendents were asked to fill out a detailed questionnaire regarding many phases of their school's condition. Among the questions asked under the heading of "Moral Instruction" appear to have been the following three: Is the Bible read regularly or at all in your schools? Is moral instruction given by means of a textbook? Is moral instruction given orally or in any other way?

Of the sixty-four county reports quoted, forty answered the moral instruction category. The rest made no reference of any sort to it. In the answers of the forty officials who complied, no uniformity of presentation was followed. Hence it is impossible to estimate with statistical accuracy the composite picture. The following table, however, is an attempt to condense the replies:[115]

Replying county	I Is the Bible read?	II Moral instruction by textbook?	III Moral instruction orally or otherwise?
Cambria	King James Version ⅓ of schools	Catholic Catechism ⅓ of schools	Remaining ⅓ of schools
Chester	No profanity in 171 schools	Some profanity in 145	Much profanity in 10

[114] *Sixteenth Report of the Superintendent of Common Schools to the General Assembly* (New Haven: Carrington & Hotchkiss, 1861), p. 70.
[115] Cf. *1861 Pennsylvania Report*, pp. 45–152.

Replying county	I Is the Bible read?	II Moral instruction by textbook?	III Moral instruction orally or otherwise?
Clarion	141—regularly	None	6 (nothing in 95 schools)
Clearfield	¾ get MI either by Bible; with a text; or without a text.		
Clinton	71—daily 12—occasionally 21—never	————————	————————
Cumberland ..	124—regularly	15—using Bible 1—using Catechism	140—orally and perceptively
Dauphin	145—regularly 54—never	————————	————————
Delaware	Read in about ½	————————	————————
Erie	Read in about ⅛	None	In a few, only to prohibit grosser forms of immorality such as profanity, falsehood and intemperance
Fulton	20—as reading book 5—as moral textbook	10	30
Greene	12—regularly Others—occasionally	————————	In many, but in sporadic manner
Huntingdon ...	92—regularly 10—also with prayer	————————	10
Juniata	Majority—regularly	————————	All but 4
Lancaster	332—regularly	3	347
Lawrence	All—regularly	————————	————————
Lebanon	All except 10—regularly	None	Practically all
Lehigh	182—regularly and with prayer	Either orally or by textbook—153	
Lycoming	102	9	All
McKean.......	Probably ½—regularly	————————	None

Replying county	I Is the Bible read?	II Moral instruction by textbook?	III Moral instruction orally or otherwise?
Mercer	200 (out of 240)—regularly	None	240 (all)
Mifflin	80—regularly	3	37
Monroe	100	48	50
Montgomery ..	Most	None	Most
Montour	Read in nearly all	————————	————————
Northampton ..	151—regularly	Some	A few
Northumberland	43—regularly	None	12
Perry	90—regularly	None	In a number, with good effect
Pike	19—regularly	————————	————————
Potter	60 plus—regularly	————————	4
Schuylkill	131—regularly	None	None
Snyder	All but 6—regularly	None	All
Somerset	"Will urge them to do better"		
Sullivan	Scripture read—20 Prayer—4 Singing—10	————————	25
Susquehanna ..	Small number	6 or 8	————————
Tioga	About 70—regularly	None	A few
Union	All schools	A few	————————
Warren	23	None	Some with reading lessons
Wayne	198 by teachers—regularly 66 by teachers—irregularly	None	Nearly all
Wyoming	No figures, but corporal punishment used by all but 4 teachers. Thus practical teachings not neglected.		
York	208—regularly	86	31

It is clear that there was a considerable amount of Bible reading, but it was by no means a uniform custom. Very little teaching of morals was done by textbook. Where the practice occurred, there are indications that books on ethics rather than religion were used. For instance, Emma Willard's *Morals for the Young* is mentioned in the Lebanon County Report,[116] and Cowdrey's *Elementary Moral Lessons* is cited in those from Sullivan County,[117] and Union County.[118] In Fulton County, however, the Bible was used as a moral textbook in five schools,[119] and, as the table indicates, a Catholic Catechism was so used in one third of the schools of Cambria County.[120]

In answering the questionnaire, thirteen of the forty superintendents added comments. Some mentioned with regret the lack of adequate instruction in the moral field.[121] Others commented favorably on sporadic examples of such instruction found.[122] Still

[116] *Ibid.*, p. 98.

[117] *Ibid.*, p. 132.

[118] *Ibid.*, p. 140.

[119] *Ibid.*, p. 81.

[120] James M. Swank, the Cambria Superintendent, observed with reference to the King James Bible and the Catechism: "It is proper to mention that no instance has been reported to me of an attempt having been made to *compel* a Catholic pupil to read the Protestant Bible or a Protestant pupil to study the Catholic Catechism." (*1861 Pennsylvania Report*, p. 52.)

[121] *Clarion* (referring to the fact that in ninety-five of his schools there was no moral instruction): "This last class of schools is fearfully large. The result of the investigation of this subject astounded me. . . ." (p. 61). *Clearfield:* "I must, however, in truth but with pain say that in many schools no such instruction is given in any way whatsoever. . . ." (p. 63). *Clinton:* "I regret exceedingly that in twenty-one schools of this county the word of God was not read to the children." (p. 64). *Delaware:* "Moral instruction receives far too little attention." (p. 73). *Huntingdon:* "That the moral education of any of the youth and the elementary and religious training which should enter into . . . all systems of education should be neglected in the schools of our country, is much to be regretted. . . ." (p. 84). *Tioga:* "This branch of education seems to be neglected." (p. 137).

[122] *Fulton:* "Where [the Bible was] used to inculcate morally, better order, attention and progress were clearly observable." (p. 81). *Greene:* "Many teachers were very constant and efficient in imparting moral instruction, though few . . . at regular and stated periods." (p. 82). *Lancaster:* "[Teaching rightness and wrongness of actions] . . . has a tendency to awaken conscience. . . ." (p. 92). *Lycoming:* "All our teachers profess to give moral instruction perceptively, but to what extent, or how usefully, I am unprepared to say." (p. 105). *Mifflin:* "Nearly all the teachers talk to their scholars, and mean well by it, but it would hardly be proper to report such efforts under this [morals] head." (p. 110).

others indicated they had urged teachers to do more along this line.[123]

Further light is shed on the status of religious instruction in schools of some of the eastern cities by a document published in 1871. Henry Barnard, by that time U. S. Commissioner of Education, made a report on the condition of schools in the District of Columbia.[124] In it he compared Washington schools with those in other sections, thus furnishing significant data about many places. The information is in many instances dated from the previous decade, thus making it pertinent to the present study.

The following are the only items to be gleaned from the report which touch either directly or indirectly on religion:

Holidays: (Philadelphia, 1867) Good Friday, National and State Fast and Thanksgiving Days.

(Rochester) Thanksgiving, Christmas, New Year's and the days between public Fasts.

(Washington) Good Friday, Easter Monday and Thanksgiving Day.[125]

Courses in "Manners and Morals:" (Regulations drawn up in New York City, December 18, 1867):

Sixth Grade [the lowest grade]—"Instruction to be given in manners and morals, and illustrated by means of incidents of school and home."

Fifth Grade—"Instructions of the same character as for the sixth grade."

Fourth Grade—"Instruction for cultivating love to [*sic*] parents, kindness, obedience, neatness, truthfulness, and politeness, to be illustrated by examples, incidents, anecdotes, etc."

Third Grade—"Continue the instructions of the Fourth Grade."

---

[123] *Dauphin:* "I have always urged the reading of the Scriptures . . . but have as strongly objected to the use of the Bible . . . as a textbook for reading." (p. 71). *Somerset:* "We all believe the Bible, and shall urge this duty upon all that shall be thought capable of attending to it in a becoming manner." (p. 131). *Wayne:* "The attention of the teachers has been particularly called to this important duty [moral instruction]." (p. 146).

[124] Henry Barnard, *Special Report of the Commissioner of Education on the Condition and Improvement of Public Schools in the District of Columbia* (Washington, D. C.: Government Printing Office, 1871).

[125] *Ibid.,* p. 444.

Second Grade—"Improve opportunities in the daily exercises of the school, by conversations upon the subject of the reading lessons and all appropriate incidents, to inculcate respectfulness, obedience to parents, honesty and truthfulness."

First Grade—"Instruction by means of school incidents and anecdotes, so conducted as to aid in the discipline of the school." [126]

Religious Exercises: (Newark, N. J., 1864) "Whenever religious services take place in the school the Lord's prayer is recommended as a part thereof." [127]

(Brooklyn, N. Y., 1867) "A portion of the Scriptures shall be read by one of the teachers without note or comment."

(Newark, N. J., 1864) "Reading of the Scriptures without comment, and, at the discretion of the teacher, the invocation of the divine blessing and singing, the exercises not to exceed fifteen minutes." [128]

Language: (Troy, N. Y., 1866) "No pupil shall remain in school who is guilty of the habitual use of profane or obscene language." [129]

Our study of the fate of religious instruction in the twelve original states besides Massachusetts has shown two things: First, the social tradition that religion belonged in public education remained strong and unchallenged until the 1840's. In this decade it met sporadic negations on the part of secular-minded people, negations which became more frequent after 1850. Secondly, the conviction that sectarian indoctrination has no place in the schools of the state was meanwhile strongly supported from all sides. Among the types of sectarianism condemned, the "sectarianism of infidelity" also came in for censure, especially from the Catholic leaders in New York.

A sense of violation of the principles of freedom of religion and of the right of the parent to determine the child's education seems to have lain at the bottom of the strong opposition to sectarian

---

[126] *Ibid.*, pp. 511–14 (*passim*). The report states that the Philadelphia schools also had courses on "Manners and Morals" in the primary and secondary grades in 1871 (pp. 544–45).

[127] *Ibid.*, p. 446.

[128] *Ibid.*, p. 449.

[129] *Ibid.*

indoctrination. As has already been noted in the case of Massachusetts, it seems always to have been implied that any indoctrination would be given to all children indiscriminately. In two or three instances only, reference was made by writers to the Federal Constitution, with one specific reference to the language of the First Amendment. Compared to the large number of references cited from so many people with so varied a background, these allusions to the Constitution are practically lost. Even in themselves, these references were tied in with opposition to sectarianism, with the notion of the free exercise of religion, rather than with any idea that religion "did not belong."

As they faced up to the dilemma created by the "religion in—sectarianism out" conviction, the three groups examined came up with varying plans as a result of their groping. Protestant leaders were divided on the method of inculcating the religion they insisted must be in education. Some tried parochial schools, and these failed after a few years of tenuous existence. Others placed their hopes in Bible reading and the influence of Protestant public school teachers.

Catholics first tried to concentrate on religious training at home. Later they decided that this, at its best, would not offset the Protestant flavor and the growing secularism of the public schools. Consequently, they set themselves to building parochial schools and urging their people to lend their support and send their children. Since many Catholics still went to public schools, determined opposition to the requirement that Catholic children listen to Bible reading and praying of a Protestant variety was manifested in many places.

As a result, by the outbreak of the Civil War, religion in the public schools had practically disappeared. By this is *not* meant that the schools had become "godless" in the sense that all reference to the existence of a Supreme Being and our duties towards Him had been *suppressed*. Prayers and Bible reading still remained as an official part of the curriculum. Doubtless, some moral instruction continued to be given, and, in some instances, at least, given with reference to the Bible. But doctrinal instruction according to the teachings of Christian groups was clearly reduced to the vanishing point, unless one wishes to call the daily reading of a few Bible verses, without comment, "doctrinal instruction."

The prohibition of doctrinal instruction is indicated by the laws against sectarian instruction and textbooks, and by the evidence from the readers and the school reports. It is further indicated by the anxieties expressed by educators and by their declarations that they were trying to *put religion and morals into the schools.* To them, it simply wasn't there.

It may be argued that some Protestants believed that doctrine was still taught inasmuch as the Bible was read and children could learn from this, using the principle of private interpretation. How much *information* or *instruction* this gave to children of elementary school age seems highly debatable. Bushnell, indeed, thought it was "enough to find a place for the bible as a book of principles" but that "if any Christian desires more, he must teach it himself at home." [130] This seems to imply that what was done in the schools was "not enough" to be considered in itself as adequate religious instruction. In this sense, it is here maintained that the teaching of religion had vanished.

The task of the teacher of religion, moreover, is not merely to inform but to "form." Inculcating knowledge is a part, but only a part, of the process. Attitudes must be formed. Habits must be developed. The child is to be convinced that a stand must be taken, a program of living started as a result of his convictions. It is difficult to see how such a concept of religious training can be predicated of the school system in 1861. In *this further* sense it is maintained that the teaching of religion had vanished.

A similar conclusion seems to have been drawn just four years later when, in 1865, the Rev. James Fraser, an English clergyman, observed American public schools. His words have been preserved in the report of Henry Barnard as U. S. Commissioner of Education.[131] What Fraser *saw* was the culmination of the processes of the previous four decades. What he *concluded* is not without significance:

> The tone of an American school—that "nescio quid" so hard
> to be described, but so easily recognized by the experienced

130 Cf. *supra*, p. 260.
131 Barnard, *op. cit.* (1871).

eye, so soon felt by the quick perceptions of the heart—if not unsatisfactory, is yet incomplete. It is true that the work of the day commences with the reading of the Word of God, generally followed by prayer. It is true that decorous if not reverent attention is paid during both those exercises; but the decorum struck me as rather a result or a part of discipline than as a result of spiritual impressions; there was no "face as it had been the face of an angel"; no appearance of kindled hearts. The intellectual tone of the schools is high; the moral tone, though perhaps a little too self-conscious, is not unhealthy; but another tone, which can only be vaguely described in words but of which one feels oneself in the presence when it is really there, and which, for want of a better name, I must call the "religious" tone, one misses, and misses with regret. . . .[132]

Towards the end of the period studied, out-and-out secularism appeared in declarations that religion had no place in public education. This was supplemented by the ever-increasing stress on public schools as vehicles of both civic and sheerly materialistic education. In the face of the new wave, Protestant leaders, avidly anti-sectarian, settled for very little compared to what the common school had been in earlier years. Catholic leaders, also

[132] *Ibid.*, p. 577. Later in the same writing Fraser emphasized the total lack of doctrinal religion in the American school, but hesitated to call the system "irreligious" or "non-religious" and felt it might at least lay a foundation for true religious instruction elsewhere: "It might be thought also that amid the wildness of religious fancy and the strangeness of theological opinions, which prevail in America to an extent far beyond anything within an Englishman's experience, the blessings of a fixed creed would more easily be recognized and more strongly felt than where traditional beliefs still largely influence public thought, and men are less tossed about by winds of doctrine. It is unnecessary to say, however, that no attempt to lay the foundations of such a creed, or in any way to presume that such a creed even exists, is made in the common schools.

"I do not like to call the American system of education, or hear it called, *irreligious.* It is perhaps even going too far to say that it is *non-religious,* or purely secular. . . . But if, as I believe, the cultivation of any one of God's good gifts and the attempt to develop any one right principle or worthy habit, are, so far as they go, steps in the direction, not only of morality but of piety, materials with which both the moralist and the divine, the parent and the Sunday school teacher, may hope to build the structure of a 'perfect man' which they desire, then it is manifestly ungenerous to turn round upon the system which does this, which supplies these materials of the building, and is prohibited by circumstances over which it has no control and to which it is forced to adapt itself from doing more, and stigmatize it with the brand of godlessness." P. 580.

highly anti-sectarian, left religion in the public school to itself and bent every effort to make successful the parochial school system.

If the secularization of the elementary public schools *in the sense explained above* was well-nigh complete in the thirteen original states by the outbreak of the Civil War, then the *fait accompli* was more a negative result of the failure of religious-minded Americans to solve their great dilemma than it was a positive result of avowed secularist activity on the part of men whose voices were heard only at the eleventh hour of the period studied.

CHAPTER VIII

Conclusions

GIVEN THE CURRENT INTEREST in the problem of im-parting religious instruction in the public school, this study set out to determine the extent to which Christian doctrinal religion was once taught in the American elementary school and the cause or causes of the decline in such instruction.

Given the decisions of the Supreme Court of the United States, particularly the McCollum decision, that certain current efforts to teach religion in public schools were unconstitutional and others constitutional because of the force of the First Amendment (made applicable to the States by the Fourteenth) in regulating the relations of Church and State in America, the hypothesis was formed that doctrinal religious instruction was abandoned for a reason or reasons other than because those responsible for educational policy believed that the First Amendment ruled out such cooperation between Church and State.

Findings

THE STORY

1. Christian doctrinal religious instruction was a basic and integral part of the elementary school curriculum during the colonial period of American history. This was an inheritance

from the Old World tradition. Religion, the colonists believed, belonged in life, and, accordingly, it belonged in education which was a preparation for life both here and hereafter.

2. During the decade and a half (1776–1791) following the start of the Revolution, the former colonists legislated to continue to recognize the importance of religion in life, but in the interests of religious liberty they also legislated that the newly-formed federal government itself should not establish a national church nor inhibit the free exercise of the rights of conscience.

3. In this same early national period starting with 1776 and continuing until 1827, the former-colony states, in whose hands was left the control of education, legislated to keep religion prominent in public life, and in several instances, to encourage its development in private life, by protecting religious institutions and by directing the continuance of religious instruction of the young. In accordance with this spirit doctrinal religious instruction continued in the existing elementary schools of the original states, although to a somewhat diminished degree, and was provided for in the plans drawn up for many new elementary institutions.

4. An 1827 Massachusetts law forbidding the use of textbooks calculated to favor the doctrines of individual sects marked a substantial change of policy on the part of an individual state in the religious instruction program of its elementary schools.

5. Under the leadership of Horace Mann, Massachusetts vigorously applied the 1827 anti-sectarian textbook law, extending the letter of the law to prohibit teaching by any method the sectarian tenets of any religious group. Mann's policy, avowedly a program to keep religion in but to keep sectarianism out, met bitter and prolonged opposition, but eventually triumphed and became the accepted Massachusetts practice. The resulting phenomenon in the elementary school curriculum was a program which urged the imparting of ethical instruction and such "basic Christianity" as might be gleaned from the reading of the Bible to the pupils, a program which was not unlike the sectarian position of Horace Mann as a member of the Unitarian Church, and seems to have been an epitome of the Secretary's own religious creed.

6. The Massachusetts plan to eliminate sectarianism in the elementary school gradually spread to the other twelve states which had been colonies, and to the District of Columbia. In some of these states laws forbidding sectarian textbooks and/or sectarian teachings were passed.

7. By the outbreak of the Civil War (1861), the elementary public schools of these thirteen states and the District of Columbia had abandoned almost entirely the inculcation of Christian doctrinal teachings. They continued to give some moral instruction and, in many elementary schools, continued to read the Bible to the students or have it read by them, as a part of the opening exercises of each day.

8. Church groups did not acquiesce completely, nor did they give up the effort to have their children taught the doctrines of their faiths as a part of the daily curriculum. Several Protestant Churches made ineffectual attempts to create lasting schools of their own. Catholics tried here and there to have the use of the Douay Version allowed for their children. The main answer of the Catholic Bishops, however, was a decision to expand their parochial school system and make it stick. Bishop Hughes' effort to get public financial support failed, but he and his fellow-Bishops stayed at the task, and at the outbreak of the Civil War were witnessing the gradual unfolding of the Catholic school system as a lasting phenomenon in American life.

THE SPIRIT OF '76–'61 CONCERNING RELIGION
(A SOCIAL TRADITION)

There existed among the religious leaders, educators and statesmen whose writings have been examined in this study, a tradition, unbroken in any major way from 1776 to the decade starting with 1850, that religion belonged in public life and hence instruction in religion belonged in public education. In two or three instances in the 1840 decade and more frequently after 1850, writings were published in which it was maintained that, although it was important that religion be taught to the young, such instruction had no place in the American public school.

THE EXISTENCE OF INSTRUCTION IN DOCTRINAL TENETS
IN ELEMENTARY SCHOOLS

Throughout the colonial period and in the first fifty years following the American Revolution, that is, until at least the end of the first quarter of the nineteenth century, the doctrinal tenets of many Protestant Christian groups were taught in schools which received their financial support and direction from the newly formed states which had been the thirteen original colonies.

THE FATE OF DOCTRINAL INSTRUCTION
IN THE ELEMENTARY SCHOOLS

Doctrinal instruction formed a considerable part of the curriculum from 1776 until at least 1825, although even during this period it seems to have been gradually diminished. During the period from 1825 to 1861 such doctrinal instruction decreased more and more, so that by the outbreak of the Civil War the evidence found indicates that it had practically vanished.

It is not here maintained that the public schools of 1861 were "completely secularized" or "godless" in the sense that every vestige of religion was gone and every mention of it was forbidden. But a child in the school of 1861 knew nothing of the doctrinal instruction and little or nothing of the religious formation which were part and parcel of his grandfather's and, to a great degree, his father's curriculum.

THE FORMATION OF A LEGAL TRADITION

As an inheritance from the philosophy of the First Amendment's freedom of religion clause, several states among the original thirteen, starting with Massachusetts in 1827, had enacted by 1861 laws against the use of sectarian textbooks and the teaching of sectarian tenets in the public schools. This began a legal tradition of separation of public education from sectarian indoctrination which looked toward the rights of conscience but did not express hostility or indifference toward religion as such.

WHAT DID NOT CAUSE THE DECLINE
IN DOCTRINAL INSTRUCTION

1. A concept that the First Amendment to the Constitution, by making unconstitutional such cooperation between Church and State as would enable the thirteen original states to foster the teaching of religion in the elementary public schools, did not cause the decline of doctrinal instruction therein during the period covered by this study.

2. Secularism, the concept that religion did not have a proper place in public life and consequently in public education did not cause the decline of the teaching of doctrinal religion in the elementary public schools, at least before 1850.

3. The rising interest in secular subjects such as civics, history, preparation to earn a living and the like contributed somewhat to the decline. Interest in these subjects seems to have crowded religion out of the central and basic spot it had occupied in the colonial period, but does not seem to have opposed the teaching of doctrinal religion as such.

4. The passing of authority over elementary education from purely religious groups and theocratic-state groups to state control during the period studied did not cause the decline in the teaching of doctrinal religion in the sense that the states set out to destroy the teaching of doctrinal religion as such. The evidence examined seems to indicate that such change of control was the occasion rather than the cause of the decline.

WHAT DID CAUSE THE DECLINE

The thesis formulated at the conclusion of this study is that during the period from the Revolution to the Civil War Christian doctrinal instruction declined in the elementary public schools of the thirteen original states (and the District of Columbia) because religious and educational leaders gradually formed a conviction that, whereas religion itself belonged in public life and public education, the inculcation of sectarian doctrines in public schools constituted a violation of the rights of conscience and the democratic concept of the free exercise of religion. In the expression and implementation of this conviction, sectarian jealousies and fears played a considerable part.

This conviction seems not to have reflected a feeling that the First Amendment ordained an absolute separation of Church and State or that its framers intended to drive a wedge between religion and society. The conviction does seem to have reflected the philosophy of the freedom (second) clause of the Amendment. It is the deduction of this study that a reflection of this philosophy of the freedom clause is the only extent to which the First Amendment may be said to have been involved in the decline of doctrinal religious instruction in the area and time span examined.

In holding two convictions, namely that religion belonged in public education and that instruction in sectarian doctrines could not remain in the curriculum, the people whose writings have been examined created for themselves a dilemma, in the attempt to resolve which they eliminated both religion and sectarianism. Such seems not to have been their intent, but such was the result of their actions. The struggle over sectarianism, then, and not hostility or indifference to religion as such mainly caused the decline of religious teaching.

In the light of its thesis, this study, then, must take issue with those historians of education who speak as does Dr. Brubacher: "The educational counterpart of the political divorce of church and state was the exclusion of religion from the public school curriculum." [1] As we interpret this statement, it means that there was an absolute Church-State separation, a "divorce," and it was followed by a "divorce" or a purposeful expulsion of religious teaching, as such, from the public school. It has been the deduction of this study that there was no intentional expulsion of religious teaching as such from the public schools, at least in the area and time-span examined.

By the same token, issue must be taken with certain statements

[1] Cf. *supra,* p. 10.

made by Mr. Justice Felix Frankfurter in the short history of religion in American education which he included in his concurring opinion in the McCollum Case.[2] "The evolution of colonial education, largely in the service of religion, into the public school system of today," the Justice declared,

> is the story of changing conceptions regarding the American democratic society, of the functions of State-maintained education in such a society, and of the role therein of the free exercise of religion by the people. The modern public school derived from a philosophy of freedom reflected in the First Amendment. . . .[3]

With these statements the present study would not differ. Mr. Frankfurter then proceeded to review certain events in colonial and early national history, including Madison's "Remonstrance" and controversies in New York and Massachusetts. "The upshot of these controversies often long and fierce," he then stated,

> is fairly summarized that long before the Fourteenth Amendment subjected the states to new limitations, the prohibition of furtherance by the states of religious instruction became the guiding principle, in law and feeling of the American people. Separation in the field of education, then, was not imposed upon unwilling States by force of superior law. . . . Jealous watchfulness against fusion of secular and religious activities by Government itself, through any of its instruments but especially through its educational agencies, was the democratic response of the American community to the particular needs of a young and growing nation, unique in the composition of its people.[4]

The present study has found that there *was* fusion of secular and religious activities, "especially in the Government's educational agencies." Such cooperation aimed to achieve the will of the people in carrying out their social tradition that religion "belonged."

It seems that the Justice's position is not saved by the succeed-

[2] 333 U.S. 203.
[3] *Ibid.*, p. 214.
[4] *Ibid.*, pp. 215–16.

ing paragraphs in which he declared that "the establishment of this principle of separation in the field of education was not due to any decline in the religious beliefs of the people." [5] "The Secular public school" he continued,

> did not imply indifference to the basic role of religion in the life of the people, nor reject religious education as a means of fostering it. The claims of religion were not minimized by refusing to make the public schools agencies for their assertion. . . .[6]

The answer of the present study to the above is a simple denial of the implication. There was no refusal to make the public schools agencies for the assertion of the claims of religion, at least from 1776 to almost 1850. On the contrary, there were continued and unremitting attempts to assert the claims of religion through the period we have studied, and when the attempts had foundered on the rocks of the sectarian problem, the 1861 reports contained several laments and expressions of fear at what would result from the demise of religious instruction in the public schools. The vast majority of the Americans whose writings have been examined wanted freedom *of* religion but not freedom *from* religion. This view is supported by a modern writer, Will Herberg:

> . . . in the period of the emergence of the public school system, 'non-sectarian' meant something very different from what it has come to mean today. In those days, 'non-sectarian' did not mean non-religious; very much the reverse, it meant Christian and Protestant, but dissociated from the sectarianism of the multiplying Protestant denominations. It was taken for granted that religion, in a generalized Protestant sense was the foundation of education; that much is evident from the discussions of the time and from reports of Horace Mann and other protagonists of public education in this country.[7]

[5] *Ibid.*, p. 216. Justice Frankfurter cited by way of example: "Horace Mann was a devout Christian:" (*Ibid.*) It has been seen in Chap. V that this would need qualification.

[6] *Ibid.*

[7] Will Herberg, "Religious Communities in Present Day America," *The Review of Politics,* April, 1954, p. 157. (Reprinted by Notre Dame Press, Notre Dame, Indiana.)

The Need of Our Times

There is a space of almost a century between 1861 and our times. Minus the evidence from this period on what happened to the social tradition that "religion belongs" and the legal tradition that religious liberty must be guaranteed, what can be recommended at the end of this study?

Since each tradition has an honorable history reaching far into the American past, each has a claim upon our attention today. Neither should be ignored. Both are roots of the American democracy and must be guarded for the sake of the common weal. One cannot preserve the fruits of democracy by destroying its roots.

The two traditions must be kept intact and must also be balanced. In the field of public education the legal tradition was once allowed seriously to cripple, if not practically to destroy, the social one. The solution attempted by Horace Mann was not adequate to the problem. A restoration of the tradition that "religion belongs" is one of the tasks of educators devoted to the "American way of life." As religion comes back into public education, care must be taken that its operation does not violate the rights of conscience. Nor must an over-emphasis on these rights be allowed to strike down religious instruction again.

Parents, educators, religious leaders and statesmen who are working at the problem have come up with the "factual study of religion" and with programs of "released time." They are rungs on a ladder. Though the challenge is great and the responsibility most serious, those who will achieve for education an adequate and workable balance between the two traditions will merit the gratitude and esteem of Americans now living and those yet to be born.

Bibliography

Manuscripts

Burnside, Samuel M. "Address at the Opening of Larger Quarters for the Female School in Worcester." Burnside Papers, American Antiquarian Society, Worcester, Mass., undated.

Everett, Edward. Letter to E. A. Newton, Esq.; Boston, July 13, 1838. Letter to the Bishop of London; Boston, May 11, 1840. Letter to Amos Lawrence, Esq.; Cambridge, Mass., June 6, 1846. Letter to Rev. Dr. Totten; Cambridge, Mass., Feb. 12, 1847. (Edward) Everett Papers, Massachusetts Historical Society, Boston. Vols. 68, 79, 80.

Mann, Horace. Correspondence with Fred. A. Packard. Horace Mann Papers, Massachusetts Historical Society, Boston.

————. Diary, May 4, 1837–April 30, 1843. Horace Mann Papers, Massachusetts Historical Society, Boston.

————. Letters: Horace Mann to Lydia B. Mann, Boston, Oct. 30, 1836; George Combe to Horace Mann, New Haven, Conn., March 5, 1840. Horace Mann Papers, Massachusetts Historical Society, Boston.

————. "The Union of Church and State." Address delivered at Brown University, Providence, R. I., on June 13, 1817. Horace Mann Papers, Massachusetts Historical Society, Boston.

Massachusetts. H.R. 29. Acts of 1826, Chap. 143. Archives, Boston State House.

Massachusetts General Court. House Journal, Vol. 10 (May, 1789–March, 1790). Archives, Boston State House.

————. Senate Journal, Vol. 10 (May, 1789–March, 1790); Vol. 47 (May, 1826–March, 1827). Archives, Boston State House.

Purcell, Richard J. "Research on Church-State Relations in Revolutionary and Early National Period." Archives of The Catholic University of America, Washington, D. C.

Whitfield, Eccleston and Kenrick. Papers, Correspondence and Other Documents of the Archbishops of Baltimore. Archives of the Archdiocese of Baltimore, Chancery Office, the Cathedral of the Assumption, Baltimore, Maryland.

Pamphlets

Address of the Roman Catholics to Their Fellow Citizens of the City and State of New York. New York: Hugh Cassidy, 1840.

The American Annual Register, or Historical Memoirs of the United States for the Year 1796. Philadelphia: Bioren & Madden, 1797.

Aydelot, B. P. *Report on the Study of the Bible in Common Schools.* Cincinnati: N. S. Johnson, 1837.

Benedict, Erastus C. *Religion in Public Schools, a Paper Read before the American Association for the Advancement of Education at Their Third Session, Pittsburgh, Pa., August, 1853.* Newark, N. J.: A. S. Holbrook, 1854.

————. *Remarks of Erastus C. Benedict, Esq., on His Re-election as President of the Board of Education, at Its Organization, January 14, 1852.* No place, publisher, or date given.

Brown, A. B., and Maclean, John. *Letters on the True Relations of Church and State to Schools and Colleges.* Princeton: John T. Robinson, 1853.

Burnap, G. W. *Church and State, a Discourse.* Baltimore: John D. Toy, 1844.

Burnside, Samuel M. *Memoir of Isaiah Thomas, LL.D., Founder and First President of the American Antiquarian Society.* In *Archaeologica Americana, Transactions and Collections of the American Antiquarian Society,* Vol. ii. Cambridge, Mass.: University Press, 1836.

————. *On the Classification of Schools.* In *The Introductory Course and the Lectures Delivered before the American Institute of Instruction in Boston, August, 1833.* Boston: Carter, Hendee & Co., 1834.

————. *Oration Delivered at Worcester on the Thirtieth of April,*

A.D. *1813, before the Washington Benevolent Society of the County of Worcester in Commemoration of the First Inauguration of General Washington as President of the United States.* Worcester, Mass.: Isaac Sturtevant, 1813.

———. *Oration Delivered before the Officers and Members of the Merrimack Lodge, Haverhill, on the Festival of St. John the Evangelist, Dec. 27, 1806.* Haverhill, Mass.: Francis Gould, 1807.

Bushnell, Horace. *Common Schools, a Discourse on the Modifications Demanded by the Roman Catholics (Delivered in the North Church, Hartford, on the Day of the Late Fast, March 25, 1853).* Hartford: Case, Tiffany, & Co., 1853.

Carter, James Gordon. *The Schools of Massachusetts in 1824.* (From *Essays on Popular Education.*) Old South Leaflets, No. 135, vi, 201–24. Boston: Old South Meeting House, no date.

———. *Speech of Mr. Carter of Lancaster Delivered in the House of Representatives of Massachusetts (Feb. 2, 1837).* Boston: Light & Stearns, 1837.

Clark, G. *The Bible in Schools, Report to the Board of Education of the City of New York.* No place, publisher, or date given.

The Common School Controversy: Consisting of Three Letters of the Secretary of the Board of Education of the State of Massachusetts. In Reply to Charges Preferred against the Board by the Editor of The Christian Witness and by Edward A. Newton, Esq. of Pittsfield, Once a Member of the Board, to Which Are Added Extracts from the Daily Press, in Regard to the Controversy. Boston: J. N. Bradley & Co., 1844.

Durant, Henry F. *Defence of the Use of the Bible in the Public Schools. Argument of Henry F. Durant, Esq. in the Eliot School Case.* Boston: Ticknor & Fields, 1859.

Dwight, Timothy. *Boston at the Beginning of the 19th Century.* (From *Travels in New England.*) Old South Leaflets, No. 136, vi, 225–48. Boston: Old South Meeting House, no date.

Evidence on the Religious Working of the Common Schools in the State of Massachusetts, with a Preface by the Hon. Edward Twistleton, Late Chief Commissioner of Poor Laws in Ireland. London: James Ridgway, 1854.

Kerfoot, John B. *Three Addresses Delivered at the Commencement of the College of St. James, Washington County, Md.* Fountain Rock, Md., 1848.

Kerney, Martin J. *Public Education, or the School Question Examined.* Baltimore, 1852.

Key, Francis Scott. *A Discourse on Education, Feb. 22, 1827.* (Published at request of Faculty and Alumni of St. John's College, Annapolis, Md.)

M'Cullogh, John. *A Concise History of the United States from the Discovery of America till 1795 (With a Correct Map of the United States).* (2d ed.) Philadelphia: By the author, 1797.

Mann, Horace. *Answer to the "Rejoinder" of Twenty-Nine Boston Schoolmasters, Part of the "Thirty-One" Who Published "Remarks" on the Seventh Annual Report of the Secretary of the Massachusetts Board of Education.* Boston: W. B. Fowle & N. Capen, 1845.

————. *Reply to the Remarks of Thirty-one Boston Schoolmasters on the Seventh Annual Report of the Hon. Horace Mann, Secretary of the Massachusetts Board of Education.* Boston: W. B. Fowle & N. Capen, 1844.

————. *Sequel to the So-called Correspondence between Rev. M. H. Smith and Horace Mann. Surreptitiously Published by Mr. Smith; Containing a Letter from Mr. Mann, Suppressed by Mr. Smith, with the Reply Therein Promised.* Boston: W. B. Fowle, 1847.

Mayer, Brantz. *Address at the Third Annual Commencement of the Central High School of Baltimore, August 1, 1853.* Baltimore: James Lucas, 1853.

Monmonier, John F. *Address Delivered at the Laying of the Cornerstone of the Eastern Female High School, Sept. 21, 1851.* Baltimore: James Lucas, 1851.

Monmonier, John F., M'Jilton, J. N., and Abbett, Thomas M. *Report of the Delegation Appointed by the Commissioners of the Public Schools of Baltimore to Represent the Board in the National Convention of the Friends of Common School Instruction, Philadelphia, Oct. 17–19, 1849.* Baltimore: The Publication Rooms, 1849.

On the Education of Roman Catholic Children and the Rejection of the Bible by Their Priests. Chiefly Extracted from the Reports of a Select Committee of the House of Commons, On the Education of the Lower Orders in the Metropolis. (2d ed.) London: Baldwin, Craddock & Joy, 1816.

Packard, Frederick A. (?) *The Question, Will the Christian Religion Be Recognized as the Basis of the System of Public Instruction in Massachusetts? Discussed in Four Letters to the Rev. Dr. Humphrey, President of Amherst College.* Boston: Whipple and Damrell, 1839.

————. "Religious Instruction in Common Schools." *Princeton Review,* July, 1841. Princeton: John Bogart, 1841.

Park, R. *Religious Education.* In *Lectures Delivered before the Ameri-*

can Institute of Instruction in Boston, August, 1835. Boston: Charles J. Hendee, 1836.

Peabody, Andrew P. *The Bible in the Public School.* No place, publisher, or date given.

———. "Memoir of Hon. Emory Washburn." In *Proceedings of the Massachusetts Historical Society, 1879–1880,* Vol. xvii.

Perkins, James H. *Christian Civilization, an Address Delivered before the Athenian Society of the University of Ohio at Athens, Sept. 16, 1840.* Cincinnati: A. Pugh, 1840.

"Publicola" *(pseud.). Reply to Mr. M. J. Kerney's Letter on the Public School Question, Oct. 1, 1852.* No place, publisher, or date given.

Rantoul, Robert. *Remarks on Education by Mr. Rantoul of Gloucester.* ("First published in the *North American Review.*") No place, publisher, or date given.

Rejoinder to the "Reply" of the Hon. Horace Mann, Secretary of the Massachusetts Board of Education, to the "Remarks" of the Association of Boston Masters, upon His Seventh Annual Report. Boston: C. C. Little & J. Brown, 1845.

Remarks on the Seventh Annual Report of the Hon. Horace Mann, Secretary of the Massachusetts Board of Education. Prepared by a Committee of the "Association of Masters of Boston Public Schools" and Published by That Body. Boston: C. C. Little and J. Brown, 1844.

Rust, R. S. *The Method of Introducing Religion into the Common Schools.* (Tract No. 480.) New York: Tract Society, no date.

———. *Religion in Common Schools.* (Tract No. 479.) New York: Tract Society, no date.

Smith, Matthew Hale. *The Bible, the Rod, and Religion in Common Schools.* Boston: Redding and Co., 1847.

———. *Reply to the Sequel of Hon. Horace Mann, Being a Supplement to The Bible, the Rod and Religion in Common Schools.* Boston: J. M. Whittemore, 1847.

Spalding, Martin J. *An Address to the Impartial Public on the Spirit of the Times.* Louisville, Ky.: Webb & Levering, 1854.

Stowe, Calvin E. *The Religious Element in Education, An Address Delivered before the American Institute of Instruction, Portland, Me., Aug. 30, 1844.* Boston: William D. Ticknor, 1844.

Streeter, S. F. *The Teacher's College, An Address Delivered before the Maryland Institute of Education, September 24, 1852.* Baltimore: John Murphy Co., no date.

Tyler, Edward R. (ed.). *The Proposed Substitution of Sectarian for*

Public Free Schools; Being Copious Extracts from an Article First Published in the New Englander: a Religious Quarterly, Printed at the College Press, New Haven, and Reprinted in the Common School Journal of Massachusetts, May 1, 1848.

Washburn, Emory. *An Address at the Dedication of the Massachusetts State Reform School in Westborough, Mass., Dec. 7, 1848.* (Boston Athenaeum, *Tracts*, Series B, 1587, pp. 17–18.) Boston: Dutton & Wentworth, 1849.

————. *A Lecture Read before the Worcester Lyceum, March 30, 1831.* (Boston Athenaeum, *Miscellaneous Tracts*, Series B, 2089, Vol. 31.) Worcester: Dorr & Howland, 1831.

————. "The Political Influence of Schoolmasters," from *Lectures Delivered before the American Institute of Instruction in Boston* (Aug., 1835). Boston: Charles J. Hendee, 1836.

Winchester, H. *A Lecture on Popular Education Delivered in the Hall of the House of Delegates, Annapolis, Md., March 2, 1853.* Frederick, Md.: Schley and Haller, 1853.

Woodbridge, Wm. C. *Report of the Committee on the Propriety of Studying the Bible in the Institutions of a Christian Country, Presented to the Literary Convention at New York, October, 1831.* Boston: Allen and Ticknor, 1832.

Newspapers

Columbian Centinel. March 2, 1827; March 21, 1827; April 4, 1827.

New England Palladium and Commercial Advertiser. March 23, 1827; March 30, 1827.

The Scholar's Penny Gazette (Boston). Vol. i, 1848.

Textbooks

Abbot, John S. C. *The Child at Home, or The Principles of Filial Duty.* New York: American Tract Society, 1833.

Adams, Daniel. *The Understanding Reader: or Knowledge before Oratory.* Brookfield: E. Merriam & Co., 1804.

The American Primary Classbook, or Lessons in Reading for Younger Classes of Children in School and Families. (2d ed.) Providence: A. S. Beckwith & Hutchens and Shepard, 1832.

Bentley's Blue Pictorial Primer. New York: Geo. P. Cooledge & Bro., no date.

Bingham, Caleb. *The American Preceptor Improved; Being a New Selection of Lessons for Reading and Speaking Designed for the Use of Schools.* (64th [4th improved] ed.) Boston: U. Bingham & Co., 1821.

Boston Reading Lessons for Primary Schools. Boston: Richardson & Lord, 1828.

The Child's Christian Primer. New York: T. W. Strong, no date.

Cobb, Lyman. *Juvenile Reader, No. 3, Containing Interesting, Historical, Moral, and Instructive Reading Lessons.* Baltimore: Joseph Jewitt, 1831.

Collier, William. *The Evangelical Instructor: Designed for the Use of Schools and Families.* Boston: Richardson & Lord, 1821.

"The Compiler." *Introduction to the Academical Reader.* Baltimore, 1830.

Emerson, B. D. *The Third Class Reader, Designed for the Use of the Younger Classes in the Schools of the United States,* Vol. III. Bradford, Vt.: Asa Law, 1845.

Emerson, Joseph. *The Evangelical Primer, Containing a Minor Doctrinal Catechism, and a Minor Historical Catechism; to Which is Added the Westminster Assembly's Shorter Catechism; with Short Explanatory Notes and Copious Scripture Proofs and Illustrations; for the Use of Families and Schools.* (10th ed.) Boston: Samuel T. Armstrong, 1819.

"An Eminent Practical Teacher." *The Progressive Pictorial Primer.* Boston: Oliver Ellsworth, 1857.

The Fourth Annual Classbook: Containing Lessons in Reading for the Younger Classes in Schools. (2d ed.) Brookfield: L. & G. Merriam, 1828.

Fraser, Donald. *The Columbian Monitor: Being a Pleasant and Easy Guide to Useful Knowledge. Containing 1. A Variety of Entertaining and Moral Dialogues, 2. Religious Dialogues, etc., etc.* New York: London & Brower, 1794.

Goodrich, Jeremiah. *Murray's English Reader.* Philadelphia: Jos. B. Smith & Co., 1822.

———. *Murray's English Reader.* Philadelphia: Brown & Peters, 1929 (i.e., 1829).

Goodrich, S. G. *Third Reader.* Cambridge, Mass.: Folsom, Wells and Thurston, 1839.

Greenwood, F. W. P., and Emerson, G. B. *The Classical Reader.* Boston: Lincoln & Edmonds and Carter & Hendee, 1830.

Johnson, Samuel. *A Short Catechism for Young Children.* New York: Holt, 1765.

Leavitt, Joshua. *Easy Lessons in Reading for the Use of the Younger Class in Common Schools.* Keene, N. H.: J. & J. W. Prentiss, 1834.

Lyman, Asa. *The American Reader . . . Particularly for the Use of Schools.* Portland, Me.: A. Lyman & Co., 1811.

McGuffey, William H. *McGuffey's Newly Revised Eclectic Fourth Reader.* New York: Clark, Austin & Smith, 1848.

————. *McGuffey's Newly Revised Eclectic Primer.* Cincinnati: Wilson, Hinkle & Co., 1849.

————. *McGuffey's Rhetorical Guide, or Fifth Reader of the Eclectic Series.* Cincinnati: Winthrop B. Smith Co., 1844.

Moore, Hamilton. *The Young Gentleman and Lady's Monitor and English Teacher's Assistant.* (9th ed.) Hudson: Ashbell Stoddard, 1795.

Murray, Lindley. *The English Reader: or Pieces in Poetry and Verse . . . to Inculcate the Most Important Principles of Piety and Virtue.* Baltimore: Armstrong and Plaskett, 1799.

————. *The English Reader, or, Pieces in Prose and Verse, Selected from the Best Writers. Designed to Assist Young Persons to Read with Propriety and Effect; to Improve Their Language and Sentiments, and to Inculcate Some of the Most Important Principles of Piety and Virtue.* Utica: William Williams, 1823.

————. *Introduction to the English Reader.* Philadelphia: S. Probasco, 1828.

————. *Sequel to the English Reader.* (3d ed., with alterations and additions.) Philadelphia: Alexander and Phillips, 1807.

The New Catechism, Wherein the Principles of the Christian Religion Are Briefly Set Forth in a Plain, National and Scriptural Manner and Adapted to the Capacities of Young Persons, Chiefly Collected from the Catechisms of Dr. Watts, Dr. Mann, and the General Assembly. London-Derry: G. Douglas, 1788.

The New England Primer: Containing the Assembly's Catechism, The Account of the Burning of John Rogers; a Dialogue between Christ, a Youth, and the Devil; and Various Other Useful and Instructive Matter. Adorned with Cuts. With a Historical Introduction by Rev. H. Humphrey, D.D., President of Amberhurst [Amherst] College. Worcester, Mass.: S. A. Howland, no date. Providence, R.I.: C. Shepard, 1835. Concord, N. H.: Roby, Kimball, and Merrill, 1841.

Osgood, Lucius. *Progressive First Reader.* Pittsburgh: A. H. English Co., 1855.

Parker, Richard Greene, and Watson, J. Madison. *The National Second Reader.* New York: A. S. Barnes & Co., 1857.

Pierpont, John. *The American First Class Book.* (26th ed.) New York: George F. Coolege, 1835.

———. *The National Reader.* Boston: Richardson, Lord, and Holbrook & Hilliard, Gray, Little & Wilkins, 1831.

———. *The Young Reader.* New York: George F. Coolege, 1835.

Putnam, Samuel. *The Analytical Reader.* Dover, N. H.: S. C. Stevens, 1830.

———. *Sequel to the Analytical Reader.* Dover: E. French, 1832.

Reader's Manual. Ellington, Conn., 1839.

Richardson, John. *The American Class Book.* Philadelphia: Merrit, 1815.

Richardson, Joseph. *The American Reader . . . To Improve the Scholar in Reading and Spelling, While Enriching the Mind with Religious, Virtuous and Useful Knowledge.* Boston: Lincoln & Edmonds, 1810.

Robbins, Eliza. *American Popular Lessons, Chiefly Selected from the Writings of Mrs. Brabauld, Miss Edgeworth and Other Approved Writers. (Revised and Improved by the Author.) Designed Particularly for the Younger Classes of Children in Schools.* New York: R. Lockwood, 1839.

Sanders, Charles W. *The School Reader, First Book.* New York: N. H. Newman, 1840.

———. *The School Reader, Second Book.* New York: N. H. Newman, 1840.

Scott, William. *Lessons in Education.* Philadelphia: John Bioren, 1814.

———. *Lessons in Education.* Concord, N. H.: Hill & Moore, 1820.

Staniford, Daniel. *Art of Reading.* (10th ed.) Boston: West & Richardson, 1814.

Strong, T. *The Common Reader (For Scholars of the First & Second Classes).* Greenfield, Mass.: Denis & Phelps, 1818.

Webster, Noah. *An American Selection of Lessons in Reading and Speaking.* (New ed.) Boston: Isaiah Thomas and Ebenezer T. Andrews, 1807.

Worcester, Samuel. *A Primer of the English Language for the Use of Families and Schools.* Boston: Hilliard, Gray & Co., 1826.

School Reports

Annual Report of the Superintendent of the Public Schools of the State of New Jersey. Jersey City, N. J.: John H. Lyon, 1862.

Barnard, Henry. *Fifth Annual Report of the Superintendent of Common Schools of Connecticut to the General Assembly, May Session, 1850.* New Haven: Osborn & Baldwin, 1850.

————. *Special Report of the Commissioner of Education.* Washington, D. C.: U.S. Government Printing Office, 1871.

Board of School Commissioners of Baltimore City. *Annual Reports,* 1829–1844.

District of Columbia. *Reports of Board of Trustees of Public Schools.* Washington, D. C., 1844–1861.

Eighth Annual Report of the Superintendent of Public Instruction of the State of New York. (Transmitted to the Legislature January 8, 1862.) Albany: C. Van Beuthhuysen, 1862.

Fifteenth Annual Report of the Common Schools of New Hampshire. Concord, N. H.: Henry McFarland, 1861.

M'Jilton, John N. *Regulations and Course of Instruction.* Baltimore: James Lucas, 1846.

Mann, Horace. *Annual Reports of the Board of Education, together with the Annual Reports of the Secretary of the Board (1837–1848).* Boston: Dutton & Wentworth, 1838–1849. (Facsimile edition by the Horace Mann League, commencing June, 1947.)

Monmonier, John F., M'Jilton, J. N., and Abbett, Thomas M. *Report of the Delegation Appointed by the Commissioners of the Public Schools of Baltimore to Represent the Board in the National Convention of the Friends of Common School Instruction.* Baltimore: The Publication Rooms, 1849.

Report of the Superintendent of Common Schools of Pennsylvania for the Year Ending June 3, 1861. Harrisburg: A. Boyd Hamilton, 1862.

Report of the Superintendent of Schools for North Carolina for the Year 1862. (Document No. 10, Session of the Legislature, 1860–61.) No place: John Spelman, Printer to the State, no date.

Seventeenth Annual Report on Public Schools in Rhode Island. Providence: Cooke & Danielson, 1862.

Sixteenth Annual Report of the Superintendent of Common Schools of Connecticut to the General Assembly. New Haven: Carrington and Hotchkiss, 1861.

Twenty-fifth Annual Report of the Massachusetts Board of Education.
Boston: William White, 1862.
Twenty-third Annual Report of the Massachusetts Board of Education.
Boston: William White, 1860.
Van Bokkelen, L. *First Annual Report of the State (Md.) Superintend-
ent of Public Instruction.* (Year ending June 30, 1866.) Annapolis:
Henry A. Lucas, 1867.

Legislative Documents

"An Act for Establishing Religious Freedom, Passed December 16,
1785." In *Revised Code of the Laws of Virginia*, I, Chap. 31, 77–78.
Richmond: Thomas Ritchie, 1819.
"An Act Further to Provide for the Instruction of Youth." In *Laws of
Massachusetts, 1825–1828*, Vol. X, Chap. 170. Boston: Dutton and
Wentworth, 1828.
"An Act to Provide for the Instruction of Youth, and for the Promo-
tion of Good Education." In *Laws of Massachusetts, 1788–1789*,
Chap. 19, pp. 416–21.
"Address of Gov. Levi Lincoln to the Session of the General Court,
June 6, 1827." In *Resolves of the General Court of the Common-
wealth of Massachusetts*, May–June, 1827, pp. 580–81. Boston:
Dutton and Wentworth, 1827.
Board of Assistant Aldermen, New York City. *Report of the Committee
on Arts and Sciences and Schools of the Board of Assistants on the
Subject of Appropriating a Portion of the School Money to Religious
Societies for the Support of Schools.* (Document 80.) New York:
1840.
"Donohue vs. Richards." In *Maine Reports*, xxxviii, 376–413. Hallo-
well, Maine: Masters, Smith & Co., 1856.
Elliot, Jonathan. *The Debates in the Several State Conventions on
the Adoption of the Federal Constitution as Recommended by the
General Convention at Philadelphia in 1787, together with the
Journal of the Federal Convention, etc.* 5 vols. (2d ed., 1836, with
considerable addition.) Philadelphia: J. B. Lippincott & Co., 1881.
Farley, Joseph. "Report of Committee on Education to House of Repre-
sentatives, Jan. 29, 1827." In *Massachusetts Legislative Documents,
Senate & House, 1826 & 1827* (1st and 2d Sessions), H.R. 29, Com-
monwealth of Massachusetts, pp. 8–9.
Gates, Joseph (ed.). *The Debates and Proceedings in the Congress of*

the United States, Vol. I. Washington, D. C.: Gates & Seaton, 1834.

"H.R. 29—Commonwealth of Massachusetts—Report of Committee on Education to House of Representatives—Jan. 29, 1827." In *Massachusetts Legislative Documents, Senate & House, 1826 & 1827.*

Journal of the First Session of the Senate of the United States of America. New York: Thomas Greenleaf, 1789.

The Laws and Liberties of Massachusetts. Cambridge: Harvard University Press, 1929.

Laws & Resolves of Massachusetts, 1800–1801.

Laws of Massachusetts. March 31, 1834, Chap. 169.

Laws of Massachusetts, 1837. Boston: Dutton and Wentworth, 1837.

Massachusetts General Court. *House Journal,* Vol. 47 (May, 1826–March, 1827).

"Message of Governor Levi Lincoln to the Session of the General Court of the Commonwealth of Massachusetts, Jan. 3, 1827." In *Massachusetts Resolves, 1824–1828,* 17, 443–44.

New York Laws. Thirty-fifth Session (1812). (Title-page missing.)

New York Laws. Thirty-sixth Session (1813). Albany: Webster and Skinner, 1815.

Report Read at a Legal Meeting of the Inhabitants of the Town of Boston, Held at Faneuil Hall on Monday, 31st of May, A.D. 1819. No place, publisher, or date given.

Resolves of the General Court of the Commonwealth of Massachusetts, May–June, 1827. Boston: Dutton & Wentworth, 1827.

Resolves of the General Court of the Commonwealth of Massachusetts, January–April, 1837. Boston: Dutton & Wentworth, 1837.

Revised Statutes of the Commonwealth of Massachusetts, 1835. Boston: Dutton and Wentworth, 1836.

Thorpe, Francis N. *The Federal and State Constitutions, Colonial Charters, and Other Organic Laws of the States, Territories and Colonies Now or Heretofore Forming the United States of America.* 7 vols. Washington, D. C.: U.S. Government Printing Office, 1909.

Theses

MASTERS' THESES

Buckner, Sister Mary Leonita. "The History of Catholic Elementary Education in the City of Baltimore." Unpublished Master's thesis. Washington, D. C.: The Catholic University of America, 1948.

Dunn, William Kailer. "James A. Leuba's Theory of Religion." Unpublished Master's thesis. Washington, D. C.: The Catholic University of America, 1935.

Eismann, Nathaniel J. "Ratification of the Federal Constitution by the State of New Hampshire." Unpublished Master's thesis. New York: Columbia University, 1938.

DOCTORS' THESES

Brown, Samuel W. *The Secularization of American Education, As Shown by State Legislation, State Constitutional Provisions and State Supreme Court Decisions.* (Teachers College, Columbia University Contributions to Education, No. 49.) New York: Teachers College, Columbia University, 1912.

Confrey, Burton. *Secularism in American Education: Its History.* (Educational Research Monographs, Thos. G. Foran, ed.) Washington, D. C.: The Catholic Education Press, 1931.

Connors, Edw. M. *Church-State Relationships in Education in the State of New York.* Washington, D. C.: The Catholic University of America Press, 1951.

Cremin, Lawrence A. *The American Common School, an Historic Conception.* New York: Teachers College, Columbia University, 1951.

Dawson, John H. "A Survey of the Religious Content of American World History Textbooks Written Prior to 1900." Unpublished Ph.D. thesis. Pittsburgh: University of Pittsburgh, 1954.

Dunn, Wm. Kailer. *The Decline of the Teaching of Religion in the American Public Elementary School in the States Originally the Thirteen Colonies, 1776–1861.* The Johns Hopkins University, 1956.

Fell, Sister Marie Leonore. *The Foundations of Nativism in American Textbooks, 1783–1860.* Washington, D. C.: The Catholic University of America, 1941.

Gabel, Richard J. *Public Funds for Church and Private Schools.* Washington, D. C.: The Catholic University of America, 1937.

Hall, Arthur Jackson. *Religious Education in the Public Schools of the State and City of New York.* Chicago: The University of Chicago Press, 1914.

Hansen, Allen Oscar. *Liberalism and American Education.* Faculty of Philosophy, Columbia University. New York: The Macmillan Co., 1926.

Hunter, Margaret A. *Education in Pennsylvania Promoted by the Presbyterian Church, 1726–1837.* Philadelphia: Temple University, 1937.

Kinney, Charles B. *Church and State, the Struggle for Separation in New Hampshire, 1635–1900.* New York: Teachers College, Columbia University, Bureau of Publications, 1955.

McCormick, Leo J. *Church-State Relationships in Education in Maryland.* Washington, D. C.: The Catholic University of America Press, 1942.

Maddoc, William Arthur. *The Free School Idea in Virginia before the Civil War, Phase of Political and Social Evolution.* New York: Teachers College, Columbia University, 1918.

Mahoney, Charles J. *The Relation of the State to Religious Education in Early New York, 1633–1825.* Washington, D. C.: The Catholic University of America Press, 1941.

Mason, Sister Mary Paul. *Church-State Relationships in Education in Connecticut, 1633–1953.* Washington, D. C.: The Catholic University of America Press, 1953.

Matzen, John M. *State Constitutional Provisions for Education.* New York: Teachers College, Columbia University, 1931.

O'Connell, Geoffrey. *Naturalism in American Education.* Washington, D. C.: The Catholic University of America Press, 1936.

Reynolds, Clarence. *The Basis of Cooperation in Religious Education between Religion and the Public Schools.* Stanford, Cal.: Leland Stanford University, 1945.

Robinson, R. R. *Two Centuries of Change in the Content of School Readers.* Nashville, Tenn.: George Peabody College for Teachers, 1930.

Rosenkranz, Samuel. *Religious Education for One World.* St. Louis, Mo.: Washington University, 1950.

Schultz, Joseph R. *A History of the Protestant Day Schools in the United States.* Fort Worth, Texas: Southwestern Baptist Theological Seminary, 1954.

Sherrill, Lewis Joseph. "Parochial Schools in the Old School Presbyterian Church, 1846–1879." Unpublished Ph.D. thesis. New Haven: Yale University, 1929.

Smith, Sherman M. *The Relation of the State to Religious Education in Massachusetts.* Syracuse, N. Y.: Syracuse University Book Store, 1926.

Thursfield, Richard Emmons. *Henry Barnard's American Journal of Education.* Baltimore: The Johns Hopkins Press, 1945.

Van Kleeck, Edwin R. "The Development of Free Common Schools in New York State—The Campaign to Eliminate the Rate Schools and to Divert Public Funds from Sectarian Schools." Unpublished Ph.D. thesis. New Haven: Yale University, 1937.

Warren, Harold C. "Changing Conceptions in the Religious Elements in Early American School Readers." Unpublished Ph.D. thesis. Pittsburgh: University of Pittsburgh, 1951.

Wilson, Earl Kenneth. "Historical Survey of the Religious Content of American Geography Textbooks, 1784–1895." Unpublished Ph.D. thesis. Pittsburgh: University of Pittsburgh, 1951.

Woody, Thomas. *Early Quaker Education in Pennsylvania.* New York: Teachers College, Columbia University, 1920.

Supreme Court Cases and Related Material

Everson v. Board of Education. 330 U.S. 1.

Franklin, John L., *et al. Appellees' Brief—Vashti McCollum vs. Board of Education of School District No. 71, Champagne County, Illinois.* In the Supreme Court of the U.S., Oct. term, A.D. 1947. Chicago: Barnard & Miller, 1947.

McCollum v. Board of Education. 333 U.S. 205–256.

Zorach v. Clauson. 343 U.S. 306–325.

Articles in Periodicals

NINETEENTH CENTURY

Barnard, Henry. "Schools As They Were Sixty Years Ago," *American Journal of Education,* xiii (1863), 123–44.

Breckenridge, R. J. "Denominational Education," *Southern Presbyterian Review,* iii (1849), 1–17.

Brooks, Charles. "Moral Education," *American Journal of Education,* i (March, 1856), 336–44.

Brownson, Orestes. "Paganism in Education," *Brownson's Quarterly Review,* vi (new series, April, 1852), 227–47.

Burgess, George. "Thoughts on Religion and Public Schools," *American Journal of Education,* ii (Dec., 1856), 562–67.

Bushnell, Horace. "Christianity and Common Schools," *Common School Journal of Connecticut,* II (Jan., 15, 1840), 102.

"Common School Education in Virginia," *Common School Journal of the State of Pennsylvania,* I, No. 8, 225–32.

"The Daily Use of the Bible in Schools," *The Connecticut Common School Journal,* I (Sept., 1838), 14.

Dodge, Allen W., *et al.* "Majority Report, Education Committee: An Act to Abolish the Board of Education," *Common School Journal,* II (Aug. 1, 1840), 225–34.

Duffield, D. Bethune. "Education a State Duty," *American Journal of Education,* III (March, 1857), 81–100.

"Editorial: Suggestions to Parents," *American Journal of Education of 1827,* II (Sept., 1827), 542.

"Editorial Comment on Travels on the Continent of Europe," *The Connecticut Common School Journal,* I (Sept., 1838), 13.

"Frederick Adolphus Packard," *Princeton Review, Index Vol.* (1825–1868), pp. 265–71.

Greenwood. "Moral Education," *The Christian Examiner,* x (March, 1831), 1–14.

Hodge, Charles. "Covenant Education," *Princeton Review,* XXXIII (April, 1861), 238–61.

———. "The Education Question," *Princeton Review,* XXVI (1854), 504–44.

———. "The General Assembly," *Princeton Review,* XVIII (July, 1846), 433–41.

———. "Introductory Lecture Delivered in the Theological Seminary, Princeton, New Jersey, Nov. 7, 1828," *Biblical Repertory and Princeton Review,* I (new series, 1829), 73–98.

———. "Parochial Schools," *Princeton Review,* XVIII (1846), 433–41.

———. "A Review of Sprague's Lectures to Young People," *Princeton Review,* III (new series, 1831), 295–306.

Mann, Horace. "Moral and Religious Education," *The Common School Journal,* I (Nov., 1838), 3–15.

"Moral and Religious Instruction in Public Schools, Report of a Discussion before the American Association for the Advancement of Education," *American Journal of Education,* II (July, 1856), 153–72.

Packard, Frederick A. "Religious Instruction in Common Schools," *Biblical Repertory and Princeton Review,* XIII, 315–68.

———. "Review of *The Life of Horace Mann,* by Mary P. Mann," *Biblical Repertory and Princeton Review,* XXXVIII (1866), 74–94.

"Reviews," *American Journal of Education for the Year 1826*, I (1826), 45.

Richards, Z. "Discipline, Moral and Mental," *American Journal of Education*, I (Aug., 1855), 107–19.

"Secular Education," *The Westminster and Quarterly Foreign Review*, II (new series, July–Oct., 1852), 1–32.

Seeyle, J. H. "The Bible in Schools," *Bibliotheca Sacra and American Biblical Repository*, XIII (Oct., 1856), 725–41.

Thayer, Gideon F. "Letters to a Young Teacher—Moral Education," *American Journal of Education*, III (March, 1857), 71–80.

Yates, John L. "The Power of Education," *The Baltimore Literary Monument* (J. N. M'Jilton, ed.), I (1839), 36–40.

TWENTIETH CENTURY

Brown, Francis J. "Studies of Religion in Public Education," *Phi Delta Kappan*, XXXVI (April, 1955), 252–56.

Bush, Merrill E. "The Common Denominator in Religious Values," *Educational Leadership*, XI (Jan., 1954), 228–29, 232.

Coe, George A. "Shall the State Teach Religion?" *School and Society*, XV (1922), 129–33.

Demaree, Paul H. "By-Products of the Attacks on the Public Schools," *California Journal of Secondary Education*, XXIX (Jan., 1954), 51–52.

Fahs, Sophia L. "Religion in the Public Schools," *Religion and the Child*, July, 1944, pp. 25–31. Washington, D. C., Association for Childhood Education.

Herberg, Will. "Religious Communities in Present Day America," *The Review of Politics*, XVI (April, 1954), 155–74.

Hunt, R. L. "Religion in Public Education," *Phi Delta Kappan*, XXXVI (April, 1955), 243–44, 256.

"Limiting State Action by the 14th Amendment: Consequences of Abandoning the Theory of First Amendment Incorporation," *Harvard Law Review*, LXVII (1954), 1016–30.

Lucks, Henry A. "Integrating Religious Instruction and Public School Studies," *Catholic Educational Review*, LII (Jan., 1954), 26–35.

McAlpin, William B. "Presbyterians and the Relation of Church and State," *Journal of the Presbyterian Historical Society*, XXXII (Sept., 1954), 187–202.

Murray, John Courtney. "Contemporary Orientations of Catholic

Thought on Church and State in the Light of History," *Theological Studies*, x (June, 1949), 177–234.

————. "Current Theology on Religious Freedom," *Theological Studies*, x (Sept. 1949), 409–432.

————. "The Problem of Pluralism in America," *Thought*, XXIX (Summer, 1954), 165–208.

Nietz, John A. "Some Findings from Analyses of Old Textbooks," *History of Education Journal*, III (Spring, 1952), 79–87.

Punke, Harold. "Religious Issues in American Public Education," *Law and Contemporary Problems*, XX (Winter, 1955), 38–168.

Read, Gerald. "Concerns for Religion and Education," *Phi Delta Kappan*, XXXVI (April, 1955), 267–68.

"Religion and the State," *Law and Contemporary Problems*, LIV (1949), 1–159.

"The State and Sectarian Education," *National Education Association Research Bulletin*, XXIV (Feb. 1946).

"The Testimony of a Devout President," *Life*, XXXIX, No. 26, XL, No. 1. Dec. 26, 1955, p. 12.

Van Loon, Thomas. "Breaking Down a Big Question," *Phi Delta Kappan*, XXXVI (April, 1955), 261–62.

Books

NINETEENTH CENTURY

Ackermann, R. *The History of St. Paul's School*. London: Hans, Kane & Vincent, 1816.

Bourne, W. O. *History of the Public School Society of the City of New York*. New York: William Wood & Co., 1870.

Browne, Wm. Hand (ed.). *Archives of Maryland. Proceedings and Acts of the General Assembly of Maryland, Jan. 1637/8 in September, 1664*. Baltimore: Maryland Historical Society, 1833.

Burton, Warren. *The District School As It Was*. (First pub. in 1833; ed. and repub. by Clifton Johnson.) Boston: Lee and Shepard, 1897.

Concilia Provincialia Baltimori Habita, (1829–1849). Baltimore: John Murphy Co., 1851.

Concilium Plenarium Totius Americae Septentrionalis Foederatae Baltimori Habitum Anno 1852. Baltimore: John Murphy Co., 1853.

Dillway, C. K. *A History of the Grammar School in Roxburie.* Roxbury, Mass., 1860.

Emerson, George B. *Reminiscences of an Old Teacher.* Boston: Alfred Mudge & Son, 1878.

Furnivall, Frederick. *Education in Early England.* London: N. Trubner & Co., 1867.

Hassard, John R. G. *Life of Most Reverend John Hughes, D.D., First Archbishop of New York, With Extracts from His Private Correspondence.* New York: D. Appleton and Company, 1866.

Henry, W. W. *Patrick Henry.* 2 vols. New York: Charles Scribner's Sons, 1891.

Leach, Arthur F. *English Schools at the Reformation.* Westminster, Eng.: A. Constable & Co., 1896.

Lee, Richard H. *Memoir of the Life of Richard Henry Lee and His Correspondence.* 2 vols. Philadelphia: Carey & Lea, 1825.

Mann, Horace. *Lectures and Annual Reports,* Vol. II of *The Life and Works of Horace Mann* (5 vols.). Boston: Walker, Fuller & Co., 1865–68.

Mann, Mary P. *The Life of Horace Mann, by His Wife,* from *The Life and Works of Horace Mann* (5 vols.). Boston: Walker, Fuller & Co., 1865–68.

Miolay, John G., and Hay, John (eds.). *Abraham Lincoln, Complete Works.* 2 vols. New York: The Century Co., 1894.

Pearson, E., and Holmes, A. *Address of the Directors of the Massachusetts Society for Promoting Christian Knowledge* (Andover, Mass., March 10, 1818). Andover: Flagg & Gould, 1818.

Pratt, Daniel J. *Annals of Public Education in the State of New York.* Albany: The Argus Co., 1872.

Randall, Henry S. *The Life of Thomas Jefferson.* 2 vols. New York: Derby and Jackson, 1858.

Rashdall, Hastings. *The Universities of Europe in the Middle Ages.* Oxford: The Clarendon Press, 1895.

Schaff, Philip. *Church and State in the United States.* New York: Charles Scribner's Sons, 1888.

Seward, William H. *The Works of William H. Seward,* ed. by George L. Baker. New York: Redfield, 1853.

Shea, John Gilmary. *The History of the Catholic Church in the United States.* 4 vols. New York: 1886, 1888, 1890, 1892.

Smith, William. *The Popular Works of Johann Gottlieb Fichte.* London, 1849.

Sprague, William B. *Lectures to Young People.* New York: John P. Haven, 1831.

Story, Joseph. *Commentaries on the Constitution of the United States.* 3 vols. Boston: Hilliard, Gray & Co., 1833.

————. *Commentaries on the Constitution of the United States.* 2 vols. 2d cd. Boston: Charles C. Little and James Browne, 1851.

Tocqueville, Alexis de. *The Republic of the United States of America, and Its Political Institutions, Reviewed and Examined.* (Translation of *De La Democratie en Amerique.*) New York: Edward Walker, 1849.

TWENTIETH CENTURY

Andrews, Charles M. *The Colonial Period in American History.* New Haven: Yale University Press, 1934.

Andrews, Matthew P. *Tercentenary History of Maryland.* Baltimore: S. J. Clarke Pub. Co., 1925.

Association for Childhood Education. *Religion and the Child.* Washington, D. C.: The Association, 1944.

Atkins, Gaius G., and Fogley, Frederick L. *History of American Congregationalism.* Boston: The Pilgrim Press, 1942.

Beck, Walter H. *Lutheran Elementary Schools in the United States.* St. Louis, Mo.: Concordia Pub. House, 1939.

Bestor, Arthur E. "Horace Mann, Elizabeth P. Peabody and Orestes A. Brownson, an Unpublished Letter with Commentary." Reprinted from *Proceedings of the Middle States Association of History and Social Science Teachers, 1940–1941,* pp. 47–53. New York: Teachers College, Columbia University, 1941.

Billington, Ray Allen. *The Protestant Crusade, 1800–1860.* New York: The Macmillan Co., 1938.

Blanshard, Paul. *American Freedom & Catholic Power.* Boston: Beacon Press, 1958.

Blau, Joseph L. *Cornerstones of Religious Freedom in America.* Boston: Beacon Press, 1949.

Bower, William Clayton. *Church and State in Education.* Chicago: University of Chicago Press, 1944.

Bradford, William. *History of Plymouth Plantation, 1620–1647,* ed. by Samuel E. Morison. New York: Alfred A. Knopf, 1952.

Brady, Joseph H. *Confusion Twice Confounded.* South Orange, N. J.: Seton Hall University, 1954.

Brinsley, John. *A Consolation for Our Grammar Schools,* ed. by Thomas Clark Pollock. New York: Scholars Facsimiles & Reprints, 1943.

Brown, J. Howard. *Elizabethan School Days.* Oxford: B. Blackwell, 1933.

Brubacher, John S. *A History of the Problems of Education.* New York: McGraw-Hill, 1947.

––––––. *The Public Schools and Spiritual Values.* New York: Macmillan Co., 1944.

Brumbaugh, Martin G. *The Life and Works of Christopher Dock.* Philadelphia: J. B. Lippincott Co., 1908.

Burnett, Edmund Cody. *The Continental Congress.* New York: The Macmillan Co., 1941.

Burns, J. A., and Kohlbrenner, Bernard J. *A History of Catholic Education in the United States.* New York: Benziger Bros., 1937.

Butts, R. Freeman. *The American Tradition in Religion and Education.* Boston: Beacon Press, 1950.

––––––. *A Cultural History of Education.* New York: McGraw-Hill Book Co., 1947.

––––––, and Cremin, Lawrence A. *A History of Education in American Culture.* New York: H. Holt & Co., 1953.

Catholic Encyclopaedia, Vol. XIII. New York, 1912.

Committee on Religion and Education. *The Function of the Public Schools in Dealing with Religion.* Washington, D. C.: American Council on Education, 1953.

Cousins, Norman. *In God We Trust.* New York: Harper & Bros., 1958.

Cubberly, Elwood P. *The History of Education.* Boston: Houghton Mifflin Co., 1920.

––––––. *Public Education in the United States, a Study and Interpretation of American Educational History.* (Rev. and enl. ed.) Boston: Houghton Mifflin Co., 1934.

––––––. *Readings in Public Education in the United States.* Boston: Houghton Mifflin Co., 1934.

Culver, Raymond B. *Horace Mann and Religion in the Massachusetts Public Schools.* New Haven: Yale University Press, 1929.

Curran, F. X. *The Churches and the Schools.* Chicago: Loyola University Press, 1954.

––––––. *Major Trends in American Church History.* New York: America Press, 1946.

Curti, Merle. *The Social Ideas of American Educators.* New York: Charles Scribner's Sons, 1935.

Dawson, Christopher. *Religion and the Modern State.* New York: Sheed and Ward, 1935.

Educational Policies Commission. *Moral and Spiritual Values in the Public Schools.* Washington, D. C.: National Education Association of the United States and the American Association of School Administrators, 1951.

Ehlers, Henry (ed.). *Crucial Issues in Education, an Anthology.* New York: H. Holt & Co., 1955.

Ellis, John Tracy. *American Catholicism.* Chicago: Chicago University Press, 1956.

———. *Documents of American Catholic History.* Milwaukee: The Bruce Pub. Co., 1956.

———. *The Life of James Cardinal Gibbons, Archbishop of Baltimore.* 2 vols. Milwaukee: The Bruce Pub. Co., 1952.

Fitzpatrick, Edward A. *St. Ignatius and the Ratio Studiorum.* New York: McGraw-Hill Book Co., 1933.

Garrison, Winfred E. *A Protestant Manifesto.* New York: Abingdon-Cokesbury Press, 1952.

Gobbel, Luther L. *Church-State Relationships in Education in North Carolina since 1776.* Durham, N. C.: Duke University Press, 1938.

Greene, Evarts B. *Church and State.* Indianapolis: National Foundation Press, 1947.

———. *Religion and the State, the Making and Testing of an American Tradition.* New York: New York University Press, 1941.

Guilday, Peter. *A History of the Councils of Baltimore.* New York: The Macmillan Co., 1932.

———. *The Life and Times of John Carroll, Archbishop of Baltimore, 1735–1815.* New York: The Encyclopaedia Press, 1922.

———. *The Life and Times of John England, First Bishop of Charleston, 1786–1842.* 2 vols. New York: The America Press, 1927.

——— (ed.). *The National Pastorals of the American Hierarchy, 1792–1919.* (First pub., 1923; reprint, 1954.) Westminster, Md.: The Newman Press, 1954.

Hans, Nicholas A. *New Trends in Education in the Eighteenth Century.* London, 1951.

Henry, Virgil. *The Place of Religion in Public Schools.* New York: Harper & Bros., 1950.

Herberg, Will. *Protestant–Catholic–Jew.* Garden City, N. Y.: Doubleday & Co., 1955.

Hinsdale, Burke A. *Horace Mann and the Common School Revival.* New York: Charles Scribner's Sons, 1937.

Ives, J. Moss. *The Ark and the Dove, the Beginning of Civil and Religious Liberties in America.* New York: Longmans, Green & Co., 1936.

Johnson, Alvin W. and Yost, Frank H. *Separation of Church and State in the United States.* Minneapolis: University of Minnesota Press, 1948.

Johnson, Clifton. *Old Time Schools and School Books.* New York: Macmillan Co., 1904.

Johnson, F. Ernest (ed.). *American Education and Religion, the Problem of Religion in the Schools.* (Religion and Civilization Series.) New York: Pub. by the Institute for Religious and Social Studies, Distributed by Harper & Bros., 1952.

———. *The Social Gospel Re-examined.* New York: Harper & Bros., 1940.

Kane, John J. *Catholic-Protestant Conflicts in America.* Chicago: Henry Regnery Co., 1955.

Kane, W. *An Essay toward a History of Education Considered Chiefly in its Development in the Western World.* Chicago: Loyola University Press, 1938.

Keller, James. *All God's Children, What Your Schools Can Do For Them.* Garden City, N. Y.: Hanover House, 1953.

Kimball, Marie G. *Jefferson.* New York: Coward-McCann, 1947.

Knight, Edgar W. *A Documentary History of Education in the South Before 1860.* 5 vols. Chapel Hill, N. C.: The University of North Carolina Press, 1949.

———. *Education in the United States.* (3d rev. ed.) Boston: Ginn and Co., 1951.

———. *Readings in Educational Administration.* New York: H. Holt, 1953.

———, and Hall, Clifton L. *Readings in American Educational History.* New York: Appleton-Century-Crofts, 1951.

Livingood, F. G. "Eighteenth Century Reformed Schools." *Proceedings of the Pennsylvania German Society,* Vol. xxxviii. Morristown, Pa.: Pub. by the Society, 1930.

Lord, Robert H., Sexton, John E., and Harrington, Edward T. *History of the Archdiocese of Boston, In the Various Stages of Its Development.* 3 vols. New York: Sheed & Ward, 1944.

McCollum, Vashti Cromwell. *One Woman's Fight.* Garden City, N. Y.: Doubleday & Co., 1951.

Mangun, Vernon Lamar. *The American Normal School, Its Rise and Development in Massachusetts.* Baltimore: Warwick & York, 1928.

Mann, Horace. *Go Forth and Teach, an Oration Delivered before the Authorities of the City of Boston, July 4, 1842.* (Centennial edition.) Washington: National Education Association, 1937.

Martin, George H. *The Evolution of the Massachusetts School System.* New York: Appleton & Co., 1925.

Maurer, Charles L. "Early Lutheran Education in Pennsylvania," *Proceedings of the Pennsylvania German Society*, XL, Part II, 1–285. Morristown, Pa.: Pub. by the Society, 1932.

Maynard, Theodore. *Orestes Brownson, Yankee, Radical, Catholic.* New York: The Macmillan Co., 1943.

———. *The Story of American Catholicism.* New York: The Macmillan Co., 1941.

Mead, Frank. *Handbook of Denominations in the United States.* New York: Abingdon-Cokesbury Press, 1951.

Melville, Annabelle M. *John Carroll of Baltimore.* New York: Charles Scribner's Sons, 1955.

Meriwether, Colyer. *Our Colonial Curriculum.* Washington: Capitol Pub. Co., 1907.

Meyer, Jacob C. *Church and State in Massachusetts, from 1740 to 1833.* Cleveland: Western Reserve University Press, 1931.

Miller, Perry. *The New England Mind, The Seventeenth Century.* Vol. I—New York: The Macmillan Co., 1939. Vol. II—Cambridge, Mass: Harvard University Press, 1953.

Moehlmann, Conrad Henry. *School and Church, the American Way.* New York: Harper & Bros., 1944.

———. *The Wall of Separation between Church and State.* Boston: Beacon Press, 1951.

Morgan, Joy Elmer. *Horace Mann, His Ideas and Ideals.* Washington: National Home Library Foundation, 1936.

Muzzey, David Saville. *History of the American People.* Boston: Ginn & Co., 1927.

Myers, Gustavus. *History of Bigotry in the United States.* New York: Random House, 1943.

Nolan, Hugh J. *The Most Reverend Francis Patrick Kenrick, Third Bishop of Philadelphia.* Philadelphia: American Catholic Historical Society of Philadelphia, 1948.

Padover, Saul K. (ed.) *The Complete Jefferson.* New York: Duell, 1943.

——— (ed.). *The Complete Madison, His Basic Writings.* New York: Harper & Bros., 1953.

Parsons, Wilfrid. *The First Freedom.* New York: Declan X. McMullen, 1948.

Pfeffer, Leo. *Church, State and Freedom.* Boston: Beacon Press, 1953.

Phelan, M. *New Handbook of All Denominations.* Nashville, Tenn.: Cokesbury Press, 1937.

Pius XI, Pope. "The Christian Education of Youth." In *Four Great Encyclicals,* pp. 36–72. New York: Paulist Press, 1931.

Rian, Edwin H. *Christianity and American Education.* San Antonio, Texas: The Naylor Co., 1949.

Rossiter, Clinton. *Seedtime of the Republic.* New York: Harcourt, Brace & Co., 1953.

Russell, William T. *Maryland, the Land of Sanctuary, An Ideal of Religious Tolerance in Maryland from the First Settlement until the American Revolution.* Baltimore: J. H. Furst Co., 1907.

Schlaerth, William J. (ed.). *Alexis de Tocqueville's Democracy in America—A Symposium.* (Burke Society Series, No. 1.) New York: Fordham University Press, 1945.

Sherrill, Lewis J. *Presbyterian Parochial Schools, 1846–1870.* New Haven: Yale University Press, 1932.

Smith, H. Shelton. *Changing Conceptions of Original Sin.* New York: Charles Scribner's Sons, 1955.

Smith, John Talbot. *The Catholic Church in New York.* 2 vols. New York: Hall and Locke Co., 1905.

Spurlock, Clark. *Education and the Supreme Court.* Urbana, Illinois: University of Illinois Press, 1955.

Stokes, Anson Phelps. *Church and State in the United States.* New York: Harper & Bros., 1950.

Sweet, William Warren. *American Culture and Religion (Six Essays).* Dallas, Texas: Southern Methodist University Press, 1951.

———. *Religion in Colonial America.* New York: Charles Scribner's Sons, 1942.

Tavard, George H. *The Catholic Approach to Protestantism.* New York: Harper & Bros., 1955.

Tharp, Louise Hall. *Until Victory—Horace Mann and Mary Peabody.* Boston: Little, Brown & Co., 1953.

Thayer, Vivian T. *The Attack upon the American Secular School.* Boston: Beacon Press, 1951.

Thorning, Joseph F. *Religious Liberty in Transition, a Study of the Removal of Constitutional Limitations on Religious Liberty as Part of the Social Progress in the Transition Period.* New York: Benziger Bros., 1931.

Vincent, William A. L. *The State and School Education, 1640–1660, in England and Wales.* London: Society for the Propagation of Christian Knowledge, 1950.

Woody, Thomas. *Quaker Education in the Colony and State of New Jersey.* Philadelphia: Pub. by the author, 1923.

Wright, Arthur D. and Gardner, George E. *Hall's Lectures on Schoolkeeping.* Hanover, N. H.: Dartmouth Press, 1929.

Wright, Louis B. *Culture on the Moving Frontier.* Bloomington: Indiana University Press, 1955.

———. *The First Gentlemen of Virginia.* San Marino, California: Henry E. Huntington Library and Museum, 1940.

Wyman, Dorothy S. *Cardinal O'Connell of Boston, a Biography of William Henry O'Connell.* New York: Farrar, Straus & Young, 1955.

Zollmann, Carl. *American Civil and Church Law.* New York: Columbia University, 1917.

Index